A THERAPIST AND A CLIENT DISCOVER THE CHILD WITHIN... THE CHILD THAT LIVES WITH THE PAIN OF THE PAST.

"How old were you at the time?"

"Nine. I couldn't believe what I'd seen. When I asked the half sister later, she said she loved him, he was her father and she loved him. She was seven years old."

Stanley had what he thought of as a brilliant idea. The soft face and the very young voice told him it was brilliant. "And how old are you, right now?" he asked.

"Twelve. I'm twelve years old."

The voice had faded to almost nothing and Stanley had to lean over to catch the words.

"That's when I knew I had to be crazy. His own daughter loved him, people said it was wrong not to love your parents. Yet I hated the stepfather with a passion . . ."

When Rabbit Howls

The Troops for
TRUDDI CHASE

Introduction and Epilogue by Robert A. Phillips, Jr., Ph.D.

JOVE BOOKS, NEW YORK

This Jove Book contains the complete
text of the original hardcover edition.
It has been completely reset in a typeface
designed for easy reading and was printed
from new film.

WHEN RABBIT HOWLS

A Jove Book / published by arrangement with
E. P. Dutton, a division of NAL Penguin Inc.

PRINTING HISTORY
E. P. Dutton edition published 1987
Published simultaneously in Canada by Fitzhenry and Whiteside,
Limited, Toronto
Jove edition / April 1990

ISBN: 0-515-10329-2

Jove Books are published by The Berkley Publishing Group,
200 Madison Avenue, New York, New York 10016.
The name "JOVE" and the "J" logo
are trademarks belonging to Jove Publications, Inc.

PRINTED IN THE UNITED STATES OF AMERICA

30 29 28 27 26 25 24 23 22 21

This book is dedicated to Robert A. Phillips, Jr., Ph.D., for enduring "Stanley" and making the battleground safe; Lois B. Valladares, M.S., for exposing the location of the other bomb; Joan Uri of A Woman's Place, for the sense of urgency; our agent Rebecca McCormick and Mr. McCormick, for giving the Irishman his due; Leezie Dameron, Dennis V. Kosineski and Boo, Suzanne Turner McBride, Dottie Reich, Alice Randall, Ernie Fears, Sandra R. Gregg, Karen Chenoweth, and Pat Martin, for the light in the window; Sergeant York and the women and men of the Montgomery County Police Youth Division; to "Mr." Stone, who will remember and do; Mike and Ken and the entire Men's Group—and Terry and Apple Blossoms for their guts and a beautiful reflection; to Mervie, Arthur, and the grandfather in fond memory—most especially to our daughter, Kari Kathleen Cupcake with love beyond time—and to our Daniel Davis for whom the eight horses ride.

Introduction

This volume is a direct window into the experience we call multiple personalities. Not the report of a professional journalist or even an interpretive study by a psychotherapist, it is instead an autobiography constructed by the various personalities themselves. In these pages we see through the eyes of Truddi Chase, who was sexually abused by her stepfather from the age of two until the age of sixteen and who manifests at least ninety personalities—personalities that developed to enable her to cope, for more than forty years, with the emotional and physical trauma of that abuse. We are able to see the developing awareness of her reality as it unfolded in psychotherapy and in the writing of this manuscript.

A number of books have been written by survivors of child sexual abuse, and a few about multiple personalities; the most notable are *The Three Faces of Eve*, *Sybil*, and *The Minds of Billy Milligan*. *The Three Faces of Eve* was written by the therapists involved in the process of psychotherapy. *Sybil* was written by a professional writer who attempted to re-create a total early life experience and a lengthy period of psychotherapy. *The Minds of Billy Milligan* is the result of interviews done by a professional writer. *When Rabbit Howls* is the only book I am aware of that has been written by a victim of child sexual abuse who developed multiple personalities. What makes this book especially fascinating is that while it initially appears to be written about and by Truddi Chase, it is in actuality the story and creation of the many persons who cluster within her.

You will *not* find here the story of one clearly identifiable person in one body. In fact, according to our most current information, Truddi Chase—the "first-born"—has not been present since she was two years old. She lived in a small recess, "asleep," and her place was taken by a succession of persons. This in itself creates a dilemma: how to refer to the person or persons whom we meet in these pages? At the least, we expect to read about one unified person who presents herself to the world most of the time, but who "fades out" for brief periods when others take over. Yet here we have many persons speaking and writing the story (the original manuscript shows distinctively different handwritings), and gradually we learn that the woman whom we see much of the time is in truth a façade who initially knew nothing about the others. I shall deal with this dilemma in this introduction by simply using the name "Truddi Chase." However, the reader should remember that the original Truddi Chase "sleeps" and that I use the name to refer to the cluster of personalities who present themselves through her body.

The persons who speak and write refer to themselves collectively as "the Troops." It is they who created the book as part of the sorting-out process that we call psychotherapy, and the book has been a critical element in the therapeutic process. Since it was written in the midst of the discovery through psychotherapy it is also a unique means of examining the process of psychotherapy itself through the eyes of the persons experiencing it. The book then is an opportunity for the reader to see inside the painful experience of sexual abuse. We are able to follow Truddi from the beginning of her psychotherapy, when she was unable to recall any of her experiences, through her realization of what had happened to her and of the way she developed multiple personalities as a creative means of coping with that experience. The book explores how she, and I as her therapist, became aware of the presence of multiple personalities.

For many this book will seem both unbelievable and frightening. It challenges much of what is commonly believed about human personality, and is far beyond most people's experience. It may even seem to have the flavor of science fiction. Certainly Truddi (and the Troop members themselves) had to overcome her own initial disbelief concerning her condition. Yet it is a true account of processes that researchers are only beginning to describe and report in depth.

Among professionals there has been a great deal of controversy over the years as to whether the condition of multiple personalities actually exists. Cases have been reported since the seventeenth century and a significant number of examples have been discussed and noted over the past one hundred years. There is now a growing body of empirical data demonstrating the validity of the existence of multiple personalities. In fact, in the American Psychiatric Association's *Diagnostic and Statistical Manual of Mental Disorders* (1980), which describes the established clinical categories recognized by mental health professionals, the condition of multiple personalities has been listed as a clinical and diagnostic category. The definition reads:

> The essential feature is the existence within the individual of two or more distinct personalities, each of which is dominant at a particular time. Each personality is a fully integrated and complex unit with unique memories, behavior patterns, and social relationships that determine the nature of the individual's acts when that personality is dominant. Transition from one personality to another is sudden and often associated with psychosocial stress. . . . Usually the original personality has no knowledge or awareness of the existence of any of the other personalities (subpersonalities). (p. 257)

The entry goes on to discuss the individual's time loss, amnesia, and internal conversations, and notes differences among the personalities found by psychological and physiological testing.

The work of Frank Putnam, M.D., a psychiatrist who has been conducting basic research on multiple personalities at the National Institutes of Mental Health in Bethesda, Maryland, and Washington, D.C., and Richard Kluft, M.D., a Philadelphia psychiatrist who has worked with over two hundred cases of multiple personalities, provides empirically tested and clinically described data that establish the validity of the diagnosis of multiple personality and differentiates it from other diagnostic categories with which it has been confused. Dr. Putnam has discovered that there are significant differences in brain wave patterns, voice tone and inflection, eye responses to stimuli, and other responses to both physical and psychological stimuli among the personalities, even though they are found in the same body. My own clinical observation has noted differences in handwriting, syntax, voice, accent, facial appearance, and body stance.

Multiple personalities are quite different from those people who have been diagnosed as schizophrenic or manic-depressive. Multiple personality, for example, does not respond to chemotherapy (the use of psychoactive drugs). The growing body of data indicates that the personalities (or "persons," as some multiples prefer to call them) are quite different and in fact are unique individuals. Voices speak, yet they are not merely internal voices but can be heard by others. Medical conditions have been observed when the body is under the control of one personality that are not present when the body is under control of another. In clients with whom I am familiar, medical conditions such as allergy-induced skin rashes, tumors, cysts, severe headaches, and even the signs of pregnancy have been noted when one personality has taken over but have disappeared when other personalities control the body.

Multiple personality is also not merely the mood swings that most of us experience. Since each personality is significantly different from the others (and Dr. Putnam has demonstrated that the differences are measurable), what we see are the reactions and actions of different people. Often in a matter of minutes a client will seem to express a range of emotions, which on closer examination may be the crying of a small child, the bewilderment of a young woman, the terror of a child, the rage of a man, and the carefree laughter of an adult woman. Professional actors have been asked to express these differences under controlled clinical conditions. The results of such tests indicate that one person cannot simulate these differences in as distinct a manner as can the multiple. As incredible as these findings may seem, they indicate that many persons can exist in one body.

Multiple personality may differ in its expression from one case to another. Sybil, Eve, and Billy Milligan all have one primary person who has existed since birth and continues to be present and act in everyday life. But the person who was originally born as Truddi, the "first-born," has not been present since the age of two. The person known as "the woman" is not truly Truddi, but a person who came into being later. As the book demonstrates, the complex structure differs in form and expression from the other cases with which the public may be familiar.

The majority of reported cases of multiple personality occur in men and women who have experienced severe and repeated sexual and physical abuse over a significant period of time. My colleague Lois Valladares and I have seen clients who were sexually abused in sadistic ways by fathers, stepfathers, mothers, stepmothers, grandparents, adolescent siblings and cousins of both sexes, live-in partners, and babysitters. Brutal beatings and emotional torment were part of the abuse. A child victim may cope with the emotionally overloading experience of severe and repeated abuse through the process of dissociation. Thus multiple personality becomes a very functional means to survive. Instead of committing suicide or becoming psychotic, Truddi Chase survived by being able to "go away in her mind," to create others to cope with the trauma; and, in effect, she became many persons housed in one body. Multiple personality, as complicated and frightening as it is to many, both among professionals and the general public, is the response of a creative mind seeking to escape the saturation of childhood terror and pain.

It is time for us all to realize that child sexual abuse is not an isolated problem affecting only a small number of people. Both the community of professionals and the general public are painfully becoming aware that child sexual abuse occurs among all socioeconomic sectors of our society. Conservative estimates suggest that at least 20 percent of all persons have experienced sexual abuse at the hands of an older caretaking person. That translates into millions of people, men and women, boys and girls, who have experienced or are experiencing inappropriate sexual touching, fondling, and/or intercourse. This estimate of sexual abuse is staggering, especially since a small percentage of abuse is actually reported.

The results of the national tragedy of child sexual abuse, virtually ignored until recently, are seen in the millions of scarred lives of those adults who were sexually abused as children. The impact on human lives can be seen in the offices of mental health professionals. In my clinical practice alone, which includes a cross section of our society, I have been amazed at the number of people who have come to me to reveal that they had been sexually abused as children. Many of these have been students from university classes I have taught on the topic. The students often tell me that I am the first person to whom they have revealed their experience of abuse. Many of their abusers are professional men and businessmen, and their families on the surface appear to be no different from nonabusing families. And these people—students, professional men and women, men who have molested their own children, people who come experiencing personal and relationship problems, people who often appear to be coping well—tell me of their fears and anxieties, their inability to trust, their difficulties in marriages or intimate relationships, and their severe sexual problems. They come with profound guilt, confusion, and conflict. And some come with what we know as multiple personalities.

It is important to understand that sexual abuse also includes components of both physical and emotional abuse. Some victims tend to minimize the physically abusing aspects of sexual abuse, especially when the abusing person limits his behavior to erotic touching or fondling of genitals. Yet such touching or fondling is a physical invasion and has emotionally damaging effects. There is no such thing as "harmless" abuse of a child or an adolescent. I have interviewed younger and older women and men who have experienced fondling, those who have experienced sexual intercourse, and those who have experienced more violent rape, and all bear emotional scars from their experiences. In all, trust has been betrayed and young bodies have been violated and misused. An adult has taken advantage of a young child's natural curiosity, innocence, and desire to please. In a significant number of cases such victims report nonsexual physical abuse as well, which also has significant emotional consequences. Such abuse may be accompanied by emotional abuse—abuse that may be perpetrated by not only the sexually abusing parent but also the nonoffending parent.

Truddi Chase was born about 50 years ago in Rochester, New York. We cannot be sure of the date of her birth because there are large gaps (at this time) in her memory. The amnesia characteristic of individuals with multiple personalities leaves large blank spots in personal histories. Details of family life are not remembered. In addition Truddi was so fearful that her parents might be able to trace her that she has worked diligently over the years to cover her past. Important papers have been lost, and much of the basic personal data that we take so much for granted are not available.

We have pieced together a number of facts. The parents of the "primary person" (or the "first-born child") known to us as Truddi separated when the child was two years of age, and her mother went to live with a man on a farm near a small town in the vicinity of Rochester. This man is the one whom we come to know in the book as "the stepfather," the perpetrator of the heinous acts against Truddi (and the evolving Troop members). When only two years old the first-born child, Truddi, suffered the act of penile penetration. The stepfather's abuse of Truddi (in truth, as we know it now, of various other Troop members who came to take her place) continued for fourteen years, during which time he warned her against disclosure. At the same time the mother punished the child, without admitting she was aware of the continuing sexual abuse. There were three other children born of this union, and it appears that two of them also were physically and sexually abused. When Truddi was sixteen the stepfather was forced to leave the home. Two years later Truddi herself left to begin years of work, relationships, and study, years about which we know very little. Eventually she came to the Washington, D.C., area where she worked as a commercial artist. She married and had one child, but after eight years found herself unable to cope with the marriage and was divorced. During her marriage she had tried unsuccessfully to discover a medical reason for her temper tantrums, periodic blackouts, and a feeling of continual "dizziness." Custody of her daughter was given to her husband, although Truddi has continued to maintain contact. She became a real estate agent and then a broker, and in September 1980, when she began therapy with me, she had her own firm. During and up to this time she had no awareness that she was experiencing multiple personalities. She only knew that she was afraid much of the time.

Since the time our therapy began, her area of the real estate business suffered because of the changing economy, and Truddi has worked as an artist, an illustrator, and a legal secretary. At the present time she works in that capacity for a major firm in another metropolitan area.

Truddi Chase and the Troop members suffered severe and sustained sexual abuse. The feelings and sensations associated with such experiences are beyond the developmental ability of a young child to understand and assimilate. The feelings are too intense and the experiences too bewildering, especially when the abusing parent warns against disclosure. For some children a process of dissociation begins to take place in order to cope with the overwhelming emotional overload. In Truddi's case, we think that the first-born child "died" almost immediately after being subjected to penile penetration at the age of two. It was at this point that the other selves began to evolve, selves who "took over" during that child's life all of the daily tasks of living. Overwhelmed by conflicting messages from its parents, the child simply "went away" while alternate persons developed to serve the major function of the dissociation—the protection of the child.

The alternate persons developed into a structure comparable to the walls of defense in a medieval fortress. As nonsexual physical abuse increasingly became part of the experience, there came to be the need for even more protection. Persons developed to control and to embody powerful but separate emotions. Other persons had developed to experience the trauma of the abuse. And still others developed to deal with the various stages of the life cycle. The reader may ask, What happened to Truddi, the primary person, during the periods of time when the others took over? As the Troops explain, she "slept" so that she would not have to experience the conflict and the pain.

Over much of the past ten years, my own clinical practice of psychotherapy has focused on the tragic consequences of sexual abuse as seen in the lives of both men and women. The woman whom I believed to be Truddi Chase called me, as a therapist who had experience working with sexual abuse and its aftermath, for help in dealing with the consequences of the sexual abuse suffered at the hands of her stepfather. She was also aware of nonsexual physical and emotional abuse from her mother. When I began to take a psychosocial history, usually my first step in a new therapeutic relationship, Truddi appeared to have few memories. In fact, after six years, we have yet to obtain a complete history. There were major blank periods in her life. As we began to develop the therapeutic relationship, and she began to trust me more, she told me, though hesitant and afraid, of an awareness of different "sides" of her.

During the initial therapy sessions that were videotaped at the university where I taught, there was no way for me to know that I would be treating over the next six years not merely one woman but more than ninety separate, distinct individuals, ranging from children to adults, both male and female, some of different ethnic backgrounds, and all sharing the body of one woman.

Had I been looking for multiple personality I might have recognized various clues: the major blank periods in the woman's life, her distress at any reference to "time" in general, the mention of headaches that "didn't hurt," an enormous amount of driving energy, the expressions "us" and "we," seemingly in reference to herself, and what I initially perceived to be varying sides of her personality.

At the same time during this early period of psychotherapy, in an effort to remember the details of the sexual abuse, Truddi began writing a book about her life. Yet her initial draft made no mention of sexual behavior. She had no clear memories of any sexual experiences, including the one that led to her conceiving a daughter. She could not even use words with sexual connotations, which made it very difficult to communicate about the sexual abuse. As we together explored her special world, a world haunted by vague memories of sexual abuse, I came to learn that this world was peopled by distinct alternate persons who shared the same body. As therapy progressed, and as Truddi came to be better able to trust me, she began to reveal an awareness of those other distinct persons who in a sense took over and continue to take over the person whom we know as Truddi. I was told that the persons to whom I spoke were not Truddi, and that Truddi very seldom was present or even available for contact. The "presenting" person, whom I assumed was Truddi Chase, had few memories or even an awareness of the sexual abuse. It was the others who held the keys to those memories.

The others slowly emerged and they remain. Who are they? We refer to them by name in the manuscript although most of them were afraid to be known by name and will still not admit their identities elsewhere. Rabbit, Miss Wonderful, Catherine, Elvira, Lamb Chop, Ean, Mean Joe Green, Twelve, Sister Mary Catherine, Nails, the Zombie, the Front Runner, the Interpreter, and the others are persons in their own right. They insist on their individuality. As I came to know them I began to realize that they were complex persons, and I followed their desire to be referred to as such and not as personalities. At times some were one-dimensional, but they appeared as separate from each other yet sharing. In time it became clear that each performed certain functions for Truddi.

Even after I became aware of the dissociation—what I initially called multiple facets of her personality—I was not able clearly to state that this was a woman with multiple personalities. My training had included minimal information about multiple personalities, but Truddi did not appear to be like the textbook cases. And the manifestations of the others (when one person took over from another) did not occur as did those in the popular books and movies. There were no parades of personalities who would introduce themselves. In Truddi's case, the various persons would make themselves known in a session only by a different facial expression or tone of voice, and a reference to "her" when Truddi was discussed.

After working with other persons with multiple personalities I have discovered that they differ in the ways in which they present themselves and in the basic structures of the ways in which they organize themselves. Some come forth only while the primary person is in a state of hypnosis. Some come when called by name. In Truddi's case the transitions during the initial sessions occurred with more subtle changes and often lasted only a brief time.

Truddi had undergone psychotherapy previously and had been given drugs to deal with what her doctors labeled mood swings. She had been tested for epilepsy. But such treatment had not uncovered the basic awareness of her personal difficulties. In most ways her body was in perfect health, and the drugs could not affect her changing behaviors, moods, and emotions which others saw as inconsistent. And then there were the memory lapses that could not be explained. A counselor recommended that she see a therapist with a clinical, working knowledge of incest and physical child abuse in order to resolve "a case of extreme anxiety."

When Truddi first came to see me in the fall of 1980 her real question was, Am I insane? She did not voice this directly, but the underlying question was there. As I began to know Truddi, and gradually became aware of the Troops, I found no evidence of psychosis. There was anxiety and confusion, but there was also tremendous strength and ability to cope. The Troops served their function well: they were able to handle brutal and overwhelming experiences.

It is important for the reader to realize that the book is not the product of one person. Most especially, it is not the product of the first-born child. The Troops cooperated to bring back the memories and compose the pages. It has been a way of sorting out and making sense out of a very complex series of experiences, a way for various persons to reveal themselves and to explain themselves. The book became a vehicle by which they could work together in a common, concrete effort to tell their stories and to share their awarenesses. Over time they all have had to decide whether they were willing to cooperate and then decide how to do so. The original manuscript appeared to be disjointed, and avoided reference to anything sexual. It displayed significantly different handwritings and expressed differing conflicting concerns. As new levels of awareness were reached the Troops rewrote the manuscript incorporating the new memories that surfaced. Over the period of the first three years of therapy the manuscript was rewritten a number of times, and each time new awareness of the details of the sexual abuse were incorporated. In each writing, what began as a skeletal outline became filled out until the manuscript as it is presented in this book was completed. Initially the manuscript focused only on the memories of the sexual abuse. Then the focus changed to a description of the therapeutic process and how the memories of the abuse came and the awareness of the multiple others grew. Writing this book has been an important part of the unfolding "healing" process in that it became a means of integrating awareness and spurring new awareness by opening new memories.

The therapy sessions gradually became a safe place to come out, to explore, to test, and to share. I attempted to create a nurturing environment where the Troops could gradually begin to feel trust. They had never dared to trust enough to depend on anyone but themselves. The first step in therapy was for them to trust themselves, and, as their self-esteem grew, to begin to look at the world as a less frightening place. Initially no Troop member trusted either herself or another Troop member, so I began by trusting each one. Each member of the Troop formation had to be reached on this issue. Especially for the children (of whom there are more than seven, to date), risking trust and therefore possible rejection (or even "death") was in and of itself an enormous step forward. I encouraged them to test out new people and situations, and to learn to differentiate between safety and danger.

The need to talk to someone in order to bring out into the open the secret that has been held for so long begins the critical process of trust, but the client is constantly attuned to the reaction of the therapist to the revelations. The underlying fear of a client is that she is responsible for all of the horrible things that happened to her. She fears that when her story is heard the listener will recoil with disgust. I find that most child abuse victims have been manipulated into silence with threats and negative messages about themselves and are all too ready to blame themselves rather than anyone else.

As a therapist I try to create an atmosphere in which clients feel accepted no matter what their experiences have been. The client needs to be reassured that the fact that adults have done evil things to her does not make her an evil child who deserved the abuse or brought it on herself. Initially, much of the therapy with Truddi involved listening and reassuring, supporting and affirming. It was necessary for her to learn to trust her awareness, experience, feelings, and fears as credible. She needed assurance that she was not "crazy" as she feared but that, given her experience of having lived through severe sexual and physical abuse as a child, her feelings and responses were "normal."

Sexual abuse destroys a very basic trust. It violates the child at an essential level, creating a natural defense against the perceived dangers of trusting. As a child Truddi did trust persons who were expected to be trustworthy, and gradually over time she learned that she had been betrayed. When she was sexually misused on a day-to-day basis by the stepfather whom she was taught to obey and believe, the capacity for basic trust was destroyed.

For Truddi to trust herself would be contrary to all she was taught in her family. Truddi was told daily that she was bad and that she lied. There was no escape, no one to turn to for consistent nurturing. She had a sense of complete powerlessness and aloneness, and with it a tremendous fear and confusion. What better way to cope than to "go away," to find a hiding place in the recesses of . . . where we cannot be sure. But she went somewhere safe, and someone came to take her place.

This is my dilemma as a therapist: to create the atmosphere in which Truddi would trust me enough that she would lower her defenses and let me inside the walls surrounding her. When I first met Truddi I became aware that I had to get through layers of defenses. I now realize that I had to convince whomever was in control that I would do no harm. I accepted whatever came out in our sessions and reassured Truddi that her responses were similar to those of other women who had been abused. I could open doors for her to reveal more by sharing in general terms the feelings and experiences of other women. At times she would appear greatly relieved and indicate that she had had similar feelings but had been afraid to speak of them.

When Truddi began to talk about her awareness of the others I could also confirm the reality of her experiences. My acceptance of what appeared to her as "craziness" did much to help her risk telling more. As the picture of multiple personalities developed I made strong efforts to reach out to the alternate persons to affirm their reality and to accept what they remembered as real. I did not press them to give me their names, because to them that would give me more control than they could feel comfortable with.

As I worked with Truddi I concentrated on the strengths and positive aspects of her ability to cope. I often had to challenge the negative messages that she had received as a child and had internalized. At times she spoke so vehemently of how vile, dirty, and horrible she was that it seemed that my positive affirmation could not counteract the force of the ego-destructive messages her parents had given to her. Every time she concentrated on her "bad" aspects I would point out her strengths. Eventually she began to gain some perspective on herself and to believe that she had been brainwashed by her parents in order to keep her under control.

Therapy was complicated by the fact that Truddi was in actuality not one but many victims. I was working with people of varying ages, intelligence, fears, interests, desires, needs, capabilities, and memories. Methods that worked with one Troop member did not necessarily work with the others. I had to try to convince over ninety persons that trusting themselves and others was no longer dangerous to their well-being, and that punishment would not be meted out for talking. Since they had been warned daily as children that they would be killed if they told, the fear that they were bad and would not be believed had colored every moment. For many Troop members fear remains. Some of these give evidence of their presence in the sessions only peripherally, and refuse to come forth openly. Their overriding concern was and is to escape any form of communication or closeness to any human being. I have come to understand that these particularly reticent Troop members carry the burden of the utmost rage and fear, and seldom appear in public. Instead they have "mirror-images" who handle their specific daily living chores.

One Troop member in particular felt that as soon as the decision was made to enter therapy and divulge details to a stranger, "something awful" was going to happen. As therapy progressed and the Troops became better able to trust me, the apprehensive Troop member began to reveal what was for her a new and growing awareness of the other distinct persons. Only as time went on and the Troops began sorting themselves out was I told that the persons to whom I spoke were not the primary person or the first-born child. As we delved more deeply into the relationship of one person to another and explored their memories of the abuse, they and I slowly became aware that the abuse not only "destroyed" a number of very young selves but left the primary person or first-born child in a state of "sleep" after the second year of her life. Coming to grips with that and with Troop reality as a whole was difficult both for them and for me as their therapist.

The woman whom I had met, whom I had considered Truddi, had been created and had grown up as a façade to present to the world. It was she who experienced the amnesia and therefore was free of all memory of the abuse. She lived in the shadow of a vague daily apprehension that she did not understand, but was able to present herself to the world in which she lived as a normal and proper woman. She was meant to hide from the world the results of the abuse and to enable the other Troop members to go undetected. But behind the façade were many others who at first subtly made themselves known.

I grew to understand that with the first-born safely submerged and "sleeping" from the age of two, the other Troop members began to evolve one by one and to undergo the abuse for her. The evolution of yet other selves in effect buried the first-born child deeper over the years. What is the first-born child like now? A Troop member told me how she "received" the mind of the sleeping child "core" who surfaced briefly. It was a description of what an infant mind is like: unformed, unevolved, innocent, and still for all intents and purposes "asleep." Such a revelation made me aware of how the basic person is protected by the development of the other person, and yet is kept from developing in a natural manner.

Therapy with Truddi was an exploration of various experiences that went beyond the traditional one-on-one sessions. In order for "multiples" to admit and accept that they express themselves in multiplicity, I believe they must recognize that they are not alone. Therefore, I introduced her to other students and clients who were experiencing or who had experienced multiple personalities. Such meetings provided the opportunity for excited recognition and the affirming realization that they are not the only ones who have their experiences and to discover that their experiences could be considered "normal" within the context of multiple personalities.

In an early experiment, Truddi was placed in a group for women who had been sexually abused as children but who were not multiples. This proved to be an inappropriate mode of treatment for Truddi, but it did expose her deep hatred of women. She expressed her belief that women as a group were worthy only of hatred and disdain, and that their passivity made them doormats for anyone to step on. She was overwhelmed with her outrage at the vulnerability of women. The Troops, who included women, realized that they had to do something to shape themselves up. I realized that Truddi's antipathy toward women must have its root cause in her relationship with her mother, and we began to explore that relationship in her therapy. As further memories were evoked we found that some Troop members recalled both physical and emotional abuse at the hands of her mother. That, together with the vulnerability of Truddi as a little girl, accounted for an immense amount of rage.

As more memories were called up the realization came that much of the negative reaction to sexuality and the negative feelings about herself were the result of Truddi's mother's constant criticism of her child. The message was very clear: Sex is wrong, and good girls neither engage in nor think about sexual activities; bad girls bring bad things on themselves, and therefore it must be the girl's fault. Truddi should be a good girl, but that seemed impossible; therefore, Truddi was bad. In addition, the mother criticized Truddi constantly for being unappreciative ("You owe me for the breath of life"), clumsy, and unattractive ("You may not be pretty but you can be neat"). The stepfather did all that he could to make Truddi feel responsible for the sexual activities and berated her for being dumb. These reactions to her did much to lower an already low self-image. Truddi began to believe that she was bad, ugly, and could do nothing right. The conflict about sexuality intensified because at times she was sexually aroused and had pleasurable feelings, which she interpreted as proof that she was bad. Thus the Troops stepped in, so that only a few had memories of anything sexual. When I attempted to take a sexual history, I discovered no memories—because the one to whom I was speaking was not present during any sexual activities.

Perhaps the most controversial aspect of my treatment of Truddi was when I invited her to speak about her experiences to two groups of men who had sexually abused their children and who were in therapy with me. I was attempting to confront the fathers with the damage their behavior had caused to their children, and to enable Truddi to confront the problem of sexual abuse in a concrete way.

The result was a most valuable and positive experience for both the offenders and the Troop members. The Troops learned that some of the men had been abused as children, and that even these men had reacted with an overwhelming fear of their tormentors. They saw a tall, muscular man talk about how afraid he was of his grandfather, who had abused him when he was five. The disgust of Troop members at this man and at others in the group for what they had done to their own children diminished somewhat in the face of a newfound, more human perspective.

It may be difficult for readers to follow passages in this book that describe the presence of more than one person at a time, and conversations between those persons. The Troop members "see" and "hear" each other and carry on conversations with one another that are real to them. Often these conversations take place in a manner similar to what goes on in our own minds when we are thinking but not speaking our thoughts. However, the major difference is that more than one person is communicating. When they externalize these conversations the listener becomes aware of differing voices. Perhaps the closest we can come to understanding this phenomenon is to look at what we know of altered states of consciousness. Subjects under hypnosis for example often report that they can imagine vividly scenes, images, places, and people in a way that is very real to them but is not shared by those around them. In a similar manner a conversation involving many Troop members may be going on, and yet the outside observer may be totally unaware of that very special reality that the Troop members share.

It is important to realize that for various Troop members the concept of time may be very different. The woman and each of the others have significant periods of time missing from their awareness, periods lasting from a few minutes to days. For those times when a particular self is not present, it is difficult to know how much time has passed or when specific events took place. For the absent selves, that time did not exist.

Most victims of child sexual abuse, particularly those who experience multiple personalities, strive for perfection in the face of what they perceive as their constant failings. This drive often threatens any personal relationships. The Troops could not at first see their own suspicion, mistrust, and anger at any person who came close to them. Gradually they began to understand what had been buried so deep: the cause of those feelings was a lack of self-esteem, itself the result of what the mother and step-father had taught them as children. Only with that understanding could they begin to be less hard on themselves and others.

Various Troop members have recognized that the environment of the household they grew up in very much affected their attitudes. One of them noted that the expression of sexuality had held particular terror. She informed me that had she not hewed to the mother's edicts against "wanton" behavior she would have become a very promiscuous person, most likely a prostitute. "The mother was right," she told me. "I was so bad, I was born that way." Yet another Troop member had learned, as a result of the restrictiveness of her upbringing, to despise and fear all adult authority figures. She explained to me that no person is ever free, and that "even time is not ours to deal with as we will. In the fall whether we want it or not we're given an extra hour, and in the spring it's taken away. There's always somebody, government, parents, church, telling you what to do and how to do it. No wonder people never learn to depend on themselves for anything."

There are, of course, many unanswered questions. For example, the Troops through it all have wondered about the specifics regarding the act of their creation. They continue to speculate on whether instead of the birth of each self being a conscious or unconscious response of the first-born child to the overwhelming abuse, the births might have been triggered in response to that abuse by some as-yet-unknown area of the human brain. Could there not be an area where, in ways we do not as yet understand, personality originates and is nurtured, and perhaps even to one degree or another is fixed and made immutable? They ask if perhaps their creation might be the product of a sort of intellectual reproduction system, just as normal births are part of our sexual reproduction system. During their therapy the Troops have raised and continue to raise many questions that neither I nor any other professional to date can answer with certainty.

Therapy with someone who experiences multiple personalities is a difficult process, requiring more than the usual client-therapist involvement. It also takes a greater investment of time. The therapist must be willing to become a support system, and this involves contact beyond the therapeutic hour. I believe that a therapist must also be willing to use nontraditional methods over and above the usual talking therapy. One must be able to establish trust with those clients who have perhaps the greatest reason never to trust. A therapist must be willing to explore new areas and must be open to the possibility of multiple personalities when the client desperately does not want to believe her own experience.

This then is the story of Truddi Chase and the Troops, persons who have chosen to go beyond the survival of childhood experiences of abuse in order to find a life free from debilitating fear. Therapy continues and progress is being made. We regularly consult by telephone and I have travelled to meet and to process with the Troops what is happening in their lives. Of the ninety-two selves we know as the total "whole" of the Troop Formation, seventy-four have stepped forward to date and been delineated. Another eighteen still remain in the shadows, harboring the deepest trauma and the remaining memories. As you read this story you will have the opportunity to explore a world that may seem strange, a world where many actual people express themselves through the physical body of one person. It is a world that has become quite real to me, and one that the Troop members hope others like them will recognize. It is the world of multiple personalities.

—ROBERT A. PHILLIPS, JR., PH.D.

Authors' Note

This book encapsulates, into a nine-month period, four years of our therapy with Robert A. Phillips, Jr., Ph.D., Psychotherapist. We, the Troops, have written this book as a self-imposed part of our therapy process. It is the factual documentation taken literally from our daily journals, our combined recall which we tape-recorded, and our sessions, which were videotaped. Thanks to the Recorder, a Troop member with almost "photographic" conversational recall, the book reflects those occasions when we could not take notes or tape-record: the interaction between ourselves and Dr. Phillips, his students, other incest victims, other multiples, members of the Montgomery County (Maryland) Police Youth Division, the Maryland State's Attorney's office, members of the D.C. Children's Hospital and Prince Georges County (Maryland) Hospital staffs, Protective Services workers; mothers of victims and a number of offenders themselves.

Except for our own, the names of locations and of all persons, including other victims and our daughter, have been changed. Captain Albert Johnson is a compilation of several persons, several situations. Marshall Fielding, the psychologist whom Stanley consults, is a composite picture of all that we began to realise and formulate during our therapy, of exactly what Multiple Personality Disorder (MPD), as a process, was for us.

Fortunately, Dr. Phillips did not try to force us into somewhat established multiple patterns, but allowed us to discover and reveal our own. Consequently, as we emerged individually in the manuscript pages, we were able to escape the cage in which we've always lived—the cage wherein the pseudo-tiger, pseudo-lamb is never really itself but only a mirror-image of what society wishes, demands, to see.

The various spellings (British, Middle English, Old English, Old French, etc.) originate from Ean, the Irish Troop member who says simply that they are part of his background, his heritage. He also seems to be more familiar than other Troop members with the bible. While this may be true for Ean, neither he nor any other Troop member will allow any reference to religion or relatives to be capitalised within this book, except at the beginning of a sentence.

Ean is responsible for the "Tunnel" passages, those portions of the book which appear in bold type; they portray the inner walls of our fortress. It was Ean who first refused the idea of integration, the melding of us all into one composite human being. We may never accept that option.

We've written in a semi-documentary style, because we felt that Sybil and Eve and Milligan were clinical studies that could not reflect the actuality of our experience within the Multiple Personality Disorder process. Third person singular was employed because there is no "one" author here with total memory of the abuse. Even the Troop member who stepped in and unknowingly lived Truddi's life for her from infancy could not serve as spokesperson in the first person singular—since she had less memory than any of us. Nor was she aware of her precise "job" within our ranks. Had we given up our names immediately in the manuscript and to Dr. Phillips as the sessions progressed, she would have retreated, perhaps, into an unreachable state of mind along with the cores, unable to continue the performance of her particular job. Dr. Phillips would call our individual jobs "multiplicity's coping mechanisms."

As to the matter of energy discussed in this book, Dr. Phillips says our experiences must stand on their own. While other multiples of our acquaintance have mentioned similar happenings, and while experiments are being conducted within the scientific community in this field, the subject is neither widely understood nor accepted. Dr. Phillips does say, however, that each individual human being is made up of energy—and since we are more than one, we naturally evidence more of it, especially when a number of us are coming and going at one time. Added to this is the factor of repressed rage. As the rage builds, so does the energy, much like steam in a pressure cooker.

Most incest victims and multiples never get therapy. We were fortunate to have the best available, but one thing we could not put away was the rage. Contrary to established belief that a "well" victim has kissed anger good-bye, we've learned that almost no victim can completely. Our ending, therefore, is the only thing in this book that did not really take place, except as a literary compromise among ourselves. To the children here who envisioned it, the ending is quite real, a comfort created of a rage they will always hold.

—THE TROOPS

1

Protective Services, federally funded and operating statewide, dealt with a variety of family ills—among them, child abuse. The branch agency for Cashell, Maryland, was housed on the outskirts of suburbia in a long, concrete building. As he pulled into his parking space that morning, the back windows already streamed with light. The spring wind that had buffeted his car on the highway shoved him bodily across the parking lot, whipping at his tweed jacket and tearing at his briefcase. Reflected in the glass doors as he strode through them was the blurred image of his six-foot, forty-year-old frame. His dark brown hair and Vandyke beard needed a trim.

The muted sound of a typewriter and ringing phones followed him down the maze of hallways, past the playroom where small children came to say things that most adults did not believe, and which some judge would eventually throw out of court. The sign on his door said "Robert A. Phillips, Jr., Ph.D., Psychotherapist." He eyed his desk with no surprise at the overflow. Troubled families forced into weekend familiarity seemed to explode. By Monday morning they'd landed at Protective Services in the form of police reports and phone messages.

For five and one half years, he'd worked with incest families. Based on those credentials, he'd been asked several years ago to use his expertise in male sexuality and take things one step further. He'd set up a program to act as therapist to men who sexually abused their children. Part of the overflow on his desk had to do with that program: phone calls from the abusers themselves and from irate or merely suspicious mothers, countless referrals from Children's Hospital and more from the District Attorney's office.

The familiar sound of Mrs. Greenwood's four-inch heels echoed down the hallway and paused outside his door. Mrs. Greenwood was a short woman who did everything possible to make herself taller and who still looked like a tiny gnome. There was nothing gnomelike about her skills with the public. As intake director, she often heard things that sent her into a spin. Her solution to burnout was to choose the proper co-worker and unload. Once rid of whatever she found troublesome, irritating, or appalling, Mrs. Greenwood went about her business, refreshed and ready for more.

Now she clattered into his office, black hair loose around her face, her eyes glinting.

"Remember the cheers when the child abuse hot line number went up on the Jersey Turnpike? Well, cancel the cheers. The sign came down this morning. The Jersey agency couldn't handle it. In twenty-four hours they logged seven hundred and fifty bona fide calls. Can you imagine that? You missed one." She retrieved a slip of paper from the floor where it had fallen. "This person is forty-one, a victim. A Woman's Place was her first contact, but they aren't allowed to recommend therapists. Do you know that for two months she's been referred from one agency to the other? She tried everyone, from the American Psychiatric Association to the Rape Crisis Center, asking for a therapist with a clinical, working knowledge of incest treatment. She was told that cards aren't indexed according to specialty. When somebody calls, there's no way to know which psychoanalyst or psychiatrist handles what. Finally, someone at the Rape Center gave your name as a referral from Children's Hospital."

Doctor Phillips shook his head. "The wheels grind slowly."

There was a look of exasperation on her face. "The woman told me something else I didn't know. Bet you don't, either."

"What?"

"She went to our town library, wanting to see in black and white that others had been victims, too. The shelves were bare. Not a single volume on anything to do with child abuse. The librarian told her that children come in and sweep the shelves clean, borrowing every book in sight. Then the librarian said,

2

'I guess you know why. The adults abuse them and the children keep silent. The books tell them they aren't alone.' "

"No. I didn't know that."

"There's something peculiar about her." Mrs. Greenwood hesitated.

"The librarian?"

"The woman. She can't tell time. Not by the clock, unless she strains, and as for blocks of time—I had to help her figure out how long it had been between the phone calls she made. It's difficult to explain," she said, noting his puzzled look. "But trust me. The woman has trouble with time."

He drove carefully along the dirt road, wondering why anyone wanted to live at the tail end of nowhere. Along with his duties at Protective Services, he taught a course in family living at the university. It would have been easier to interview her there, as he did most of his private clients. When scheduling became extremely tight, he interviewed wherever he could—or wherever it was convenient for the victim. After that first call for help, some victims just wanted to hide in familiar territory; either you went to them or they never made the second phone call.

He spotted the address on the mailbox, but had to look hard for the house. A-frame, snug and rustic, it sat behind fir trees at the end of a long, unpaved driveway. Midway up the drive, he parked and took his time walking, listening to the complete country silence. A tub of daffodils stood under the front window and three bees circled in endless frustration above the nodding golden blooms. When the door opened, he saw a loft above the living room and an enormous white collage on the brick entry wall. The rooms had been decorated with an eye to polishing and creative making do instead of spending. The overall effect was one of charm and warmth. Except that on looking more closely, he noticed the drawn curtains, absolute spotlessness, and a rigid alignment.

The woman introduced herself with a firm handshake and a warm smile. She waved him to the sofa and knelt on a pair of orange floor cushions. She said she hated chairs.

There was no objection when he took out his tape recorder. He accepted an offer of iced tea. She poured black coffee for herself and lit a cigarette, with little reservation in her manner. Having interviewed countless incest families, he knew the reservation was there, a gulf between them that would only be

3

bridged with caution. He kept his observations as oblique as possible, intent on giving her the measure of privacy that most incest victims seemed to need.

She was blond and slender, but big boned and moderately tall, her body well muscled, her movements fluid. Her cheekbones were high, and her eyes, which were partially obscured by bangs, had an oriental slant. Composed and in charge, she asked about his background and qualifications. He told her.

"Thank god," she said. "At least you know what you're doing, which is more than I can say for myself."

"Do I detect an accent? Where were you born?"

"Upper New York State, in a very large city. But I grew up in nearby towns, no bigger than spit. I left home right after high school and never went back. That was over twenty years ago. I don't know if the family is dead or alive and aside from missing my half brother who was a very nice person, I don't care. That upsets a lot of people to whom the idea of 'family' is sacred."

"Depends on the family, doesn't it?"

"Thank you." Her gaze was direct as she spoke. Then the ferns hanging from the loft above started to swing in the morning breeze. Immediately she jumped. A bowl filled with white daisies tilted and water ran onto the glass coffee table. With a handful of paper napkins, he helped her mop up. She apologised and rearranged herself on the cushions. He had never seen a woman who could kneel that way, in a tailored business suit with a narrow skirt, and not show an inch of leg.

"Shadows," she said. "A waiter coming up behind me too quietly in a restaurant—lately, I scream. I don't know why. People, my agents, my buyers, it makes them uneasy. If it gets much worse, they'll think I can't cope and I can, you know."

She told him what she wanted: therapy with fast results so that she could get on with her business and personal life. She expressed anger over her situation in a no-nonsense, businesslike fashion.

"I've been told that treatment for incest victims hasn't improved very much over what I got eight years ago. My marriage was in jeopardy then, mostly because of me, and I spent six weeks or six months—I can't remember which—with a highly touted psychoanalyst and stopped. Now it's erupted again and I'm scared. The counselor said I'd better make a careful choice of therapist this time."

She passed him several pages of yellow legal paper that showed

4

erasures, one after the other. The final, inked version came out of her pocket, in hands that shook.

"It's yours," she said. "When I was born, how old I was when I left the farm where I grew up, when I got married, when my daughter Page was born. She's fourteen now, and lives with her father. These dates, I have trouble with dates, I told your Mrs. Greenwood the same thing. Every calculation on those pages was an effort. Wait. That's a lie. My mother said I lied a lot. When I was making those calculations, some of them just popped into my head. From somewhere. If they're wrong—" Her hands were shaking harder.

"Please don't worry. Dates aren't important."

"You don't want me to be precise? Shouldn't I go back and differentiate between what I calculated and what popped into my head? I will, if you want me to."

He wanted her to relax.

"My mother thought precision in general was very important." She held up the index finger of her left hand and pointed to a black mark just under the skin's surface. "During math homework one night, she jabbed me with a lead pencil."

"How did you feel about that?"

"Nothing. I felt nothing."

He wrote it on his clipboard: "Distanced. Removed." All victims, to one degree or another, distanced themselves from their feelings.

"Maybe," she said, "we'd better clarify one thing right now. If there's . . . fondling, I guess you call it, from your stepfather, is that incest?"

"In my book, yes. A stepfather is a close, adult authority figure; somebody you should be able to trust."

The woman on the orange floor cushions, cigarette burning unnoticed between her fingers, hugged herself and bent from the waist until her forehead touched the floor.

"So many people," she said, "saying so many things. Nobody agrees on anything. How do you know when you're right or wrong, if you hurt or if you don't? People say that it's only incest if it's your own father, your own flesh and blood—"

"For one thing," he said, "there is no harmless sexual trespass against a child, no matter what it's called. And I'm not concerned with 'people.' This is about you."

He saw the first tears.

5

"Maybe it wasn't incest in the beginning. My mother lived with him for a long time before they got married."

"Sorry," he said, because it was obvious that reinforcement was needed, "it's still incest. He was an authority figure. Your mother's acceptance of him created that authority, even if they never married."

He'd given it to her: permission to call the abuse by name. He watched her stubbing out the cigarette. She gave no sign that the visible burn on her fingers had caused pain.

"The psychoanalyst eight years ago, he never said exactly what it was that we were discussing. And I had trouble remembering after each session. Same thing with the counselor at A Woman's Place, except I think she called it incest, too, but it was all sort of . . . vague. Does that make sense to you?"

He said yes. Again, his affirmation pushed her forward. Stumbling over the words, she told him that she did remember her own screaming and a residual terror after each session. In the morning light, from the only window at which the curtains had not been drawn, her face became perfectly still. The stillness was in direct opposition to the hands twisting in her lap. She had, he noticed, an odd way of leaping from one thought to the other.

"At one point during my marriage," she said in a voice that became progressively more wondering, "things got so bad that I was treated for Premenstrual Syndrome. The same doctor who had delivered Page prescribed Valium and when that didn't work, he gave me Librium. The tests seemed to go on forever. I'd never seen so many doctors and needles and pills. No illness was found. But before it was over, they tested me for epilepsy and even though the tests were negative, Dilantin was prescribed. It's supposed to slow the rush of blood through your head. It didn't work. I couldn't stop being a bitch to Norman—that's my ex-husband; I couldn't stop feeling dizzy, or just blacking out."

The wondering voice had hardly faded before she started to laugh. The sound was harsh.

"You'll think I'm ridiculous when I tell you this, but I've got perhaps four or five memories up here." She pointed to her head. "That's it."

He assumed that she referred to the abuse. She reached out and seemed to hang onto the coffee table for support. Finally, she took a deep breath. Her words came out in a rush.

"My eight years are gone, I can't buy them back. But if the

6

counselor at A Woman's Place is right—that child abuse caused what I've been going through—and if incest is almost common-place with few good therapists to treat it, then aside from clearing up my own situation, I want to make a contribution.''

Her condition for taking on her treatment was that he would talk about it to everyone, to anyone, and the sessions were to be filmed for the eventual training of mental health professionals. It took him a minute to absorb what she was offering, the chance of a lifetime—to film a victim's therapy from day one. She explained her desire to break most victims' rule of privacy.

''It hit me for the first time when I went down to that library. All those children, keeping their mouths shut. I can't do it anymore. I'm tired of hiding and feeling dirty. I take three baths a day and still feel dirty. It doesn't go away. Lately, I feel as if every memory I don't have up here is boiling to the surface; as if it's close enough to touch. If I dared. I'm telling myself that I dare. My mother warned us as children, my half brother and half sisters and me, not ever to discuss family business.''

''Secrecy,'' he said, ''is incest's biggest friend. But I want you to be sure before you enter into anything.''

''I'm sure.'' She said it bitterly. ''I've been silent since I was two years old. That's one calculation I didn't need to spend time on. This will be a big step for me, one I need to take, or I'm not going anywhere. Land brokerage is a tough business; it's twelve to eighteen hours a day of dealing with people. Maybe it's always been a failing of mine, I don't know—but lately, I find myself constantly fighting the urge to shut this door and never go outside again.''

''You said you had four or five memories. Can you pick one and tell me?''

''I remember, quite clearly, being two years old. My mother and father and I lived in an apartment in the city. I can tell you the layout of the rooms, the furniture placement, the kinds of flowers my mother put everywhere—even the little pieces of caramel done up in small squares of cellophane that rattled when you unwrapped the candy. Just before my mother left my father, a man came to see her. I sat on the man's lap in the kitchen of that apartment, with two pieces of caramel in my mouth, and he smiled a lot. He wore a faded, soft red shirt that opened partway down his chest. I put my hand up against his chest to feel all that dark, feathery hair. And he smiled again and leaned further back in his chair. My hand was so small and the further back he leaned, the further the hand went down his chest. It got sucked below his belt. Warm skin down there and what felt like the soft bristles of an old hairbrush. It seemed to be a game we were playing, because he never stopped smiling the whole time. That's the man my mother left my father for, two weeks later.''

He wrote rapidly on the clipboard: Had the man been after the mother, or had he seen the child as easy prey? Some men instinctively ignored unattached women and looked for those with small children.

She'd certainly had no trouble with time factors, he thought. Her words had come out like bullets. Details about the apartment and even the candy and the way the man had been dressed were all things that her mother might have told her. However, no one but the child could have remembered so vividly what the man had allowed and thereby encouraged.

"That's all," the woman said, interrupting his train of thought. "Are you wondering if it's unusual to remember so clearly that far back? I don't have an explanation for it. There's nothing more in my head until a few months later, when my mother and I were living with him in the first farmhouse. I can't remember if things were clear, even then. For instance, when you are only two, how do you know where you will find someone, unless you've found them there many times before? But I knew without anyone telling me that day, just where the stepfather was. His family—his mother, father, and sister—had come out to the farm to spend the day with us. Just before dark, their car was packed up; they were ready to go back to the city and wanted to say goodbye to their son.

"Suddenly, he was nowhere to be found. So I went straight into the cornfield a little way from the house. Summer was ending, the cornfields were full; you couldn't see into them. The corn was high, like a green, swishing forest above my head. I remember the milky odour of the tasseled, drooping ears; the smell of the earth and the feel of it, dark and crumbling between my bare toes as I trotted along with a broken, two-year-old gait.

"It was darker between the rows of corn; the heat of the day was still wrapped in the soil under my feet and in the long green fronds. He was there. Lying between two of the rows, with his hands behind his head, waiting. He was uncovered. He always wore work pants and a shirt—his pants were down.''

A jittery, staccato laugh preceded the lighting of another cigarette, the downing of her coffee. The words were not totally clear because she cried through them, telling of being placed atop the stepfather's naked body, astraddle first his midsection, and then being moved lower. She described something flesh-coloured and curved, with masses of dark, wiry hair surrounding it. She said there had been a feeling of body warmth. Through it all, she used not a single word for either the male or female sex organs.

Short of asking her, he had no way to tell how far the first or second sexual encounters had gone.

"Do you remember any other occasions with your stepfather?"

"Except for maybe two other times, there are no clear pictures, only flicks against my mind. The flicks scare me and I cry. I can't stop."

"What you've told me, is that all you remember about the cornfield?"

"Yes. After I see his—" She stopped, unable to say the word. She was trembling. "After he puts me on top of him, there's no picture. Nothing."

He waited. Her movements had become erratic, her voice raspy.

"Why did that counselor at A Woman's Place say that it was child abuse? I hardly had anything to tell her."

"Perhaps your actions helped her to understand," he said. "Right now, I can see that you're terrified. I believe it's with good reason, and I'd like to help you."

"You're not saying that I'm overreacting or crazy? I'm willing to accept either one or both. Sometimes I feel crazy."

"What you've described can make a person feel crazy, especially if it's kept inside."

"You believe me." Again there came the jittery, staccato laugh. "But I don't think even that is going to help. There's something wrong here, and I don't know how to explain it."

Confusion, desperation, and fear; all were plain in her manner. She looked right at him, opened her mouth, and started to speak, then stopped.

"Perhaps it's best," he said, "just to continue taking what I call a psychosocial history. You've put down some dates and that's a help. But I need to know a little more about your life."

The person kneeling before him at that exact moment spoke as precisely as she could. Her eyes were on the daisies in the glass bowl. "I told you. I have four or five memories and a lot

9

of flicks against my mind. I'm in real estate because that makes me self-employed. I don't have to face job applications full of questions that I can't answer. Just a few months ago, I threw a census taker right down these front steps. Afterward, I couldn't believe I'd done it. He was very tall and big. But he came at me as if it were his inalienable right to interrogate me; he said there'd be a hundred-dollar fine if I didn't fill out his form. I was afraid that if I made a mistake, they'd think I'd done it on purpose.'' She frowned, as if unsure that she had made herself clear. ''My memory—you don't understand, do you? It's like that thing—remember that thing in the cornfield, the—''

''Penis?''

''Yes. That. I never saw another one of those, until I was twenty-four. I think I was twenty-four.''

''Were you sexually active up until the time you were twenty-four?''

''I don't know,'' she said.

''And after twenty-four?''

''I guess so. I don't know.''

''Is Page an adopted child?''

''Oh, no. Norman wanted a baby so badly. Page may be the one thing I ever did that pleased him.''

He looked at her. She looked right back at him, with a blank face. He knew by practised instinct that this woman saw nothing out of order in her conflicting statements.

The woman rubbed the burnt skin on her fingers, feeling the hot, smooth surface. There was no pain. The man across from her looked so pleasant—and confused. People often looked that way, as if they couldn't quite follow her reasoning.

His voice now had begun to reach her from a distance, mingled with thoughts that went through her mind like wandering strangers. There were too many thoughts and she ignored them. She didn't have to ignore his voice; she was simply no longer there to hear it.

The daisies were so pretty. She touched one of the petals and studied its thin green veins. The veins were like tiny, mysterious roads. After a while, the daylight in the room seemed to have shifted, as if it had grown much later. She saw him getting up from the sofa.

''Well,'' he said, ''I'll see you this Thursday. Don't feel bad. I'm not that good at directions, either. Here's the map I drew.

Follow it and you won't have any trouble reaching the university.''

The woman looked a little dazed. She held the map absentmindedly. He was noticing at the far end of the living room, a gallery lined with pictures. Reluctantly, the woman walked him to the doorway. She did not seem thrilled at his interest.

"They're bad." She looked embarrassed. "They should be burnt but I've never had the time. Among other things, I'm a very slack housekeeper.''

Not according to the cleanliness surrounding him, he thought. He moved from one painting to the other, admiring the style which ranged from a heavy to light palette, and from sledgehammer to finely feminine lines.

"They just seem to leap onto the canvas with no help from me. What I mean is, if they're bad and I know they are, I take responsibility for that, but their creation doesn't seem to involve a conscious effort.''

"Therapy has been known to loosen the creative flow. It can be the tapping of one's inner self.''

"Really? That would be nice. But I might waste a lot of time and money.''

He could not help staring. Her voice shocked him. It was that of a small child.

2

An odd increase in energy stayed with him for days after the interview. On a dozen occasions he found himself running when normally he would have walked. His speeding mind seemed incapable of sleep. He blamed the excess energy on the challenge the woman presented. Not only was she articulate and perceptive, she showed the tenacity to hang on and keep going.

Occasionally, he played the tape back. He told himself that perhaps pressure and tension had been responsible for the woman's memory block when it came to anything of a sexual nature.

While the woman had shown what he could only term a certain "richness" of manner and expression, no amount of rationalisation explained the child's voice. The tape recorder had been put away by the time he'd heard it. Afterward, only his own memory nagged him.

On Thursday, they had videotaped at the university. The woman had brought the yellow legal sheets. After a while, she'd seemed to forget about them. As in the first interview, she'd continued to refer to "people," and always on a note of apprehension or fear. He was careful not to let her see how that astounded him. She operated a real estate office with seven agents and negotiated contracts with a hard-nosed attitude, but he saw little belief in her ability to do anything without questioning her motives or painting the outcome black. Almost everything frightened her. Yet as a teenager, she'd left her mother with no idea where her next meal was coming from—and years later,

12

with as little preparation she'd walked out of an unhappy marriage.

During that first videotaping, he'd again heard the voice change from adult to childlike. He'd mentioned it to her. The woman had replied that she hadn't noticed any change. Nor did she seem to be conscious of referring to herself at times as "we." When he pointed it out, she'd said that very recently a buyer had asked the same thing. She'd told the buyer it was only a reference to herself and her seven real estate agents—what else could it be?

After the second videotaping, he looked more closely at the words "Distanced" and "Removed" on his clipboard. The woman seemed to be giving them a whole new meaning. There were times when she cried, but appeared puzzled by the tears on her face. "Distancing" from one's feelings did not mean forgetting what had been said just minutes ago. Yet very often, she did seem to forget. He had to keep reminding himself that she'd been tested for every ailment under the sun and that hers was not a medical problem.

Now, weeks later, he sat waiting for her in his university office. They were about to videotape for the third time. It had been impossible to take the usual psychosocial history. They'd only begun to delve, but he had never encountered a client with so few basic foundations from which to start.

From the age of two, she had lived on a farm, yet could not recall a single farm animal. Beyond vague generalities, she could not remember subjects taken in school, the clothes she'd worn, or the faces of her mother, her stepfather, or her half brother and two half sisters. When pressured to describe a single meal under her mother's roof or the sound of her mother's voice, the woman bent forward from her yoga position and cried in frustration.

She had an incredible amount of energy. In spite of her lack of memory after the age of two and her eighteen-hour work days, she had managed to hand him over sixty pages of typed journal notes, saying she guessed she'd write a book as they went along. He had applauded the effort. Finding the time to read would be another matter. With one eye on the clock, he bent to the pages she'd given him. She wrote:

Doctor Phillips, a decision has been made. Sitting down to compose anything of a personal nature has always made me physically ill. I don't think we can refer to you in these

13

pages as "Doctor Phillips," or by your first name either. Somehow it brings you and the authority you represent too close, and the sick feeling rises up. If you don't mind, another name has been chosen—"Stanley." I know it sounds like the name of an innocuous, lifeless entity. It is meant to. It will take a year or more to write this book through the journal notes, and we need a feeling of privacy for it. "Stanley" will keep you at a proper distance.

My stepfather said I was a liar ever since I can remember. So did my mother. Consequently, I suppose, I feel as if every word on these pages must be a lie, too, because the pages reflect my life with them. Having been told so often that one is a liar leaves one with the tendency to check every word twice, not only for veracity, but perspective. And I do question my perspective and certainly my right to say uncomplimentary things about my mother. Probably because along with calling me a liar, she described herself as a paragon of virtue. I believed for a long time that she was.

People gave me startled looks when I slipped and began talking even vaguely about life in those two farmhouses where I grew up. Actually, I only talked perhaps three times in my life and very briefly. Once I told a classmate that my stepfather was a bastard, that he shouldn't be permitted to walk the face of the earth. The classmate looked at me and she looked away and neither one of us knew what to say. I remember wanting desperately to continue, to tell her—and here I've got to tell you, Stanley, that my mind just stops at this point. The second time was to a man I'd been dating long after I left the second farmhouse. He was a very warm person with very good manners and extremely intelligent. We spent a lot of time together, in which he talked and I listened and learned to read things like *War and Peace* and Schopenhauer and Nietzsche. Anyway, I started to explain to him one day exactly what the stepfather was like. I don't remember how successful I was. I do remember that he held my hand and afterward we went for a walk in the rain and then we went to a bar and drank until they closed. I felt very strange that day. I don't know why.

The next conversation was with my husband eight years ago. He as much as said, "Shut up." He feared that my talking about what little the psychoanalyst had dredged up

14

might hurt his business and upset our daughter Page, who was only six years old.

Besides having so little to say, I simply felt numb. In fact, nothing really bothers me. I told you, I don't believe I have what most people would call emotions or feelings—just an awful fear, a guilt I can't define, and a sense of impending doom.

What I'm going to do, Stanley, is simply write it all down without regard for your opinion. You can make up your own mind whether I'm crazy or not. They said that, too, my mother and the stepfather, that I was crazy.

That second floor apartment where I lived with my mother and my real father—it seems like yesterday that I saw it all. Fish markets, shoe repair shops, ice cream and tailoring factories; all and more, were crammed in amongst the apartment buildings on a busy main street. I loved looking out the window into our back alley, smelling overripe melon and listening to the peddlers and rag men and vendors. Their voices carried up from the street every morning, mingled with the clop, clop, of horse-drawn carts. Car horns sounded rarely. Cars were for people with money and on our street there wasn't much.

Regardless of our lack of money, my mother insisted on good food. A neighbor lady gagged at the creme I drank from the tops of milk bottles. My mother said it made me healthy and she was right. Because there used to be a picture of me about a year old, sitting on my paternal grandmother's lap; plump and dimpled, with a mass of tiny gold ringlets and slanty, scrunched-up eyes.

Writing this, Stanley, is like peering into a child's mind and knowing how a brain operates only two years after birth. At two, all you're doing is watching. You don't know the meaning of the words "mother" or "father," or how those words relate to you. So I guess I didn't miss my father when we left him.

All I know is that we went to live on a farm, my mother and me, with the man who had put me on his lap that day. The farmhouse had dark brown shingles and white trim. It sat back from the road with a row of rocks on either side of the driveway. A huge old apple tree with a swing made of rope and a flat, splintered board sat to the right of the house. As soon as we moved in, my mother planted flowers

15

alongside the drive and the house, bunches and bunches of them. I remember the faces of the pansies, velvet bits of soft colour. They were pretty and I'm glad I remember them now. Because shortly after we moved into that first farmhouse, my memory seemed to grow more and more vague.

I do remember my mother telling me how my stepfather was kind and loving, did not smoke or drink, and faithfully brought home a paycheck. How, unlike my own father, he spent all his spare time with us, not off fishing and hunting and carrying on with other women.

Somehow, I don't especially admire those attributes in anyone now, and I certainly didn't as a child. In fact, all I wanted to do when my mother described his good qualities was break, smash, destroy, anything in front of me. She told me when I was older that my stepfather had been so good with me as a baby, that we wrestled and played and laughed for hours. I don't remember it. When I was four, she wanted to know why I couldn't be good instead of screaming and crying whenever he came near me. I don't remember my tantrums, as she called them. I do remember a boiling hatred inside myself.

A truant officer drove by the farm and insisted that a child my size should be in school. Kindergarten was strange and not entirely pleasant. I stole things. Scissors in particular. My mother made me take them back and 'fess up. That made me hate her as well as my stepfather. Now we have a pair of scissors for every room in the house and a really sharp pair for the bottom of whatever purse we carry. I can't remember where they come from, I simply know I don't *buy* them.

Sometimes I just didn't want to go to school. Once, when the sun had warmed up the floorboards in the living room, and my dolls were waiting to be played with (the stepfather was in the city that day, so playtime would be uninterrupted), I threw myself on the floor as the school bus drew up outside. Crying and kicking, I screamed a refusal to budge. My mother said I would go, by god, and she walked and then she stomped in retaliatory rage, over my prone body. I remember the shock of that moment. She said all the time that she loved me. I didn't feel loved. I felt her heels on my spinal column.

16

Late one night around that same time, I heard my mother's and stepfather's voices and saw a light on in the kitchen. My bed was in the darkened living room. I listened for a while. My mother commented that I might still be awake and my stepfather laughed.

"She's probably in there playing with herself," he said.

My mother told him, "Well, if you weren't after her all the time, she wouldn't know anything about that, would she?"

Stanley, something is wrong. All these years—and in spite of my vague sense of the abuse—I've felt that I had to keep my mother from knowing what my stepfather was doing. And yet I see that kitchen conversation on these pages. I must have known all along that my mother had always been aware of everything. But, Stanley, I didn't know. Either my memory is sporadic or I am one of those slow persons, just a little "off," perhaps, who can't quite get it together. I've only got one memory of that damned cornfield, and perhaps one or two incomplete pictures of my stepfather with me. So, exactly what did I tell my mother years later, on the day I left for good? I remember being in the kitchen with her, telling her something, but I can't remember what. Nothing is clear.

I'm talking now about the picture of a whole lifetime. Forced to look, I realise what you were talking about the other day, about how my memories must be somewhere.

You ask me for a psychosocial history and I try to answer you, but there is nothing to say. What do people have in their histories, Stanley, what do people have in their lives? I'm not stupid. I know what should be here, all the things that others have and discuss on a daily basis, concerning them and their interrelationships with friends and family and total strangers. That's what they have. So where is mine?

These journal notes are growing by leaps and bounds. Why are there so many pages and why am I at the typewriter every time I turn around *when there is nothing here*?

He laid the pages down, cursing under his breath. Her written words, "there is nothing here," were a repeat of what she'd tried to tell him in the very first interview. He'd heard panic in her voice then; he read it now, in the pages. Should he go on making allowances for pressure and tension, or take her statements at face value? She was exceedingly articulate. Assuming no communication problem, she literally had a few memories and what she called flicks, shreds—of a whole lifetime. The details, limited though they were, would then have to be coming from someone other than the woman. Might the woman be a multiple personality?

It was ridiculous to entertain such a notion on the basis of so little client contact. Besides, she'd been tested by experts. Someone would have noticed. Her family would have noticed.

And then he remembered what she'd told him last week: "I don't have what you'd call constant contact with anyone. Never have. Don't want to. People bore me. Small talk, chitchat, pleasantries; it's a pain. Nobody talks about ideas, concepts, the far-out, the impossible that wouldn't be impossible if they'd throw it around for a while, you know? So I run, I limit each encounter to a couple of hours. With Norman it was easy. He was always in the workshop grinding something to splinters. In business time is money; people don't waste too much of it on getting to know you."

The variety of her mannerism and expression melded too smoothly. Apart from what he saw as a woman at war with herself—one side frightened to death and the other frightened enough to run—no sharp delineation had ever materialised. Except for the voice of that small child.

He put the pages away in his briefcase and prepared to leave for the video session. Had the pages been in their original handwritten state and not fresh off the typewriter, his suspicions might have been confirmed. He would have seen the numerous different handwriting styles. The journal notes were being delivered up to him, not by the woman as one single entity, but through her people—the others of whom she was merely a "part."

Sybil and Eve had handed the world a bible on multiplicity. The Troop Formation was about to hand Robert A. Phillips, Jr., Ph.D., Psychotherapist, alias "Stanley," a much different bible.

18

3

Doctor Phillips had noted the continued use of "we" in the woman's writing. While "we" was still a puzzle, he understood how necessary his new name was: Stanley. He resolved to go along with it. In a recent seminar, another psychotherapist had reported that in over three years of treatment, a male client severely abused by his entire family had never addressed him by name. The man had felt threatened by the authority it represented. Doctor Phillips supposed that "Stanley" was better than no name at all.

The university's air conditioning had not been turned on. It was still too early in the spring. Prompt as usual, the woman looked up from the bench outside his office door. She seemed annoyed, not at the heat, but the way it had rumpled her blue denim skirt and precisely ironed white blouse. She put the lid on a large plastic coffee cup, set it and her red daily journal into a large carry-all purse. The purse and two orange floor cushions bound with heavy-duty string bumped against her thigh as she walked with him, down the hall to the video studio.

"I brought the cushions again." Her tone carried an apology. "You said you didn't mind them the last time. I really hate chairs. For some reason, they give me an awful feeling of imprisonment. You read the journal pages, how do you like your new name? I hope we haven't offended you."

"Absolutely not," he said, and looked at the heavy carry-all purse and the bobbing cushions. "Let me help you with that."

The woman juggled her things protectively. "No. I can do it. I wish this headache would go away. They're bad, the headaches. Nothing stops them. I take Tylenol, more for security than relief. Like whistling in the dark, I suppose."

"It sounds like migraines," he said. "They're very painful."

"No. The doctors ruled out migraines. And there's no pain."

No pain, he thought. Then how could she know she had a headache?

"I sort of sense the pounding," she told him, "but it's from forty miles away and that makes me nervous. Because I know it's coming."

"What's coming?"

"The pain."

"But you never feel it?"

"No. I told you. I never feel anything." She grinned. "But I stay so busy that maybe I outrun it. Think so?"

He wondered if the quantities of coffee she drank had anything to do with the headaches. She stared at him over the bundle in her arms.

"Nope," she said, still grinning. "I know what you're thinking. I drink around thirty-two cups a day. Maybe more. I stopped once. It didn't help."

The studio's front room was crammed with equipment. Several training students looked up at their entrance but went right back to headphones and clipboards. Beyond the front room was the control booth and beyond that, the video studio, sharply lit and barren except for a coffee table, two green plastic chairs, and a makeshift backdrop.

Tony, the video engineer, had been with the university for fifteen years. He was tall and thin with a soft voice, and had eyes that never looked at anyone with the interest that he showed in his equipment. While Tony talked to Stanley in the glass-walled control booth, the woman peered into her small compact. Vanity might be a sin but ugliness was unforgivable. It popped into her head, the long-ago conviction that she'd been born a mongoloid idiot. As a child she'd found it the only possible reason for having slanted eyes and an awful face. She'd felt that it might also explain her stupidity. Over the years, the idea had died away, but she still camouflaged each flaw. A good plastic surgeon could change things, but that would require a verbal admission of vanity and somehow, punishment.

As the word *punishment* entered her mind, there came a wave

20

of dizziness. She was seeing the studio for the first time, and with utter panic. The knowledge stayed with her only a moment: she wasn't looking at the studio; someone else was, and the panic belonged to that person. She tried to retain the reality of that; it flitted away. A second later, only a stern edict, something the mother had said time and again, nagged her: take responsibility for your actions.

Unable to recall what had just happened to herself, the woman stared at the video camera across the room. She knew that along with the decision to make training tapes had come the idea of punishment. If allowed to escalate, the fear would win. She could not envision going through the rest of her life afraid, and reassured herself again; her mother didn't know where she was and neither did her stepfather. She was a grown woman. What could they do to her?

Plenty, someone said.

Tony took the plastic chairs away. She and Stanley settled themselves on the orange floor cushions. Tony positioned the camera and signaled from the booth. Stanley led the woman into territory she had avoided in the first two tapings—her mother. Incest families were complicated. The abuser, whether male or female, was seldom alone in his or her efforts. Usually the "silent partner" played a secondary but important role.

"There isn't much to say about my mother." The woman looked uneasy. "Nothing daunted her; she could do practically anything. She was brilliant and beautiful—and told me that I was neither. She liked me to pay attention to her, but I seemed to drift. She told me I was a rotten child but I didn't grasp the scope of it until I grew up. She was good. She tried to make me good, too. I suppose I didn't want any part of it."

"Why not?" In the manuscript pages he'd read less than an hour ago, there had been an admission that her mother was no paragon of virtue.

"I don't know. I was bad."

"How did your mother react to that badness, as you call it?"

"She thought that if I screamed in pain, it meant I was paying attention. If I didn't scream, she'd lose count and hit me until I did."

What had, for a few moments, been a tougher expression now veered right back to a more vulnerable one.

"The mother hit me with her hands at first. Then she started

21

beating me with the strap, whatever was available. I used to yell 'I'll be good, don't hit me.' It didn't stop her.''

The woman kept her head down, staring at her hands. They had never, those hands, seemed familiar. The mother? The sudden strangeness of the expression yanked her to another level of awareness. Why had she said "the" mother? And why did the feeling sweep over her, that it was so appropriate?

Deep inside the Tunnel, that first questioning penetrated the walls of the Troop Formation. The threat posed by talking to Stanley—the first person with whom they'd ever shared so much and contemplated sharing more—the mechanism keeping so many unaware of each other since birth was a strong one, but the tremour had been felt. For a handful of Troops, the tremour was so strong that they recognised each other as being separate. For others, more insulated, only a question with no hint of the separateness behind it raced through their minds: Who is the woman?

Their voices echoed from one wall to the other and no answer came.

Of all the Troop members, only the Gatekeeper dared raise her eyes and stare down the length and breadth of the Tunnel Walls—to the deepest recess. The Gatekeeper heard his voice before she saw him and in fact she did not see him at all, but he entered her mind and soul like water seeping into a sponge. His reality came like a flood and his being was acid. A kind acid, to be sure; it at once coated and stripped her; cooled and warmed and abrased her. Knowledge.

The Gatekeeper wept, tears much like the confetti flicks with which the person before her ruled the Tunnel.

Old, *the Gatekeeper said to him.* You are old. I feel you, a thousand years multiplied, by every leaf on every tree.

Aye, *he said.*

She had never seen such a smile. She did not want to use the word "seen." It was ineffectual, demeaning to the experience.

I know you, *the Gatekeeper said.* I know your name. Ean. *She hesitated, grasping immediately that voicing his name was against the rules.* Who is the woman?

Not who, *he said, and the brogue in his voice was rich and full,* but what. Concern y'rsel' wi' that.

He was gone as if he had never existed, leaving the Gate-

22

keeper to gaze on the other Troop members and the danger that had materialised.

Three persons sitting in prime command had been wrenched from the surface depths of their Troop positions. It had quickly become apparent to two of the three that they were not alone—as they both had always supposed.

As quickly as she felt it, the Buffer denied the woman's presence on the orange cushions; denied, too, the other selves who were suddenly an overwhelming reality. Instead of abating through the denial, the horror grew stronger and the awareness finally took hold. She, the Buffer, was not alone, but sharing space with the woman on the orange cushions. Worse, there were others here. No matter which of the Troop members had ever, during the woman's presence, spoken at any time in the past, the Buffer had until now absorbed the resultant blows, thinking she was the only one and that she absorbed on her own behalf. Caught in the new awareness, the Buffer reeled. But not as in the past, from a massed series of blows. The emotional reactions of the other Troop members were now single and separate and piercing, as if a thousand tiny razor blades hacked away at her.

For the Interpreter, the woman's presence and that of the Buffer were computed quickly as being separate and apart from her own self. She recognised the need for them, hidden as it had always been. The Interpreter's job, without knowing where all the words originated, had been clarifying, in order to convey often convoluted meanings. It was in this instant and not before that the Interpreter knew that there were many sources for the words and that she, herself, was but one of them. She adjusted herself to the situation, and computed another flash of knowledge: it wasn't the woman on the orange cushions to whom Stanley was listening. Somehow, the Buffer sat in front of the woman, absorbing the blows, and speaking the words. The Buffer was catching whatever pain the knowledge behind the words might have caused the woman and deflecting it to herself.

With great difficulty because it was one of the most complicated aspects, the Interpreter saw that throughout the woman's life, there were time spans when neither the Buffer nor the woman were present. At those times another Troop member could move in and take over completely.

It made sense to the Interpreter. What she did not understand was the woman, herself. There was something very odd about her construction—her being. The Interpreter searched for words

23

to fit the mechanics of what she observed, and found them: the woman did not "lack" particular mechanisms; she had purposely been constructed to function without them.

And who was the other self, here on the perimeter of her awareness?

From a great distance, but closer to the woman than either the Buffer or the Interpreter, the Front Runner absorbed the individuality of her Troop charges. She identified them for the first time. Aware of their existence but not their identities all along, the Front Runner did not feel threatened by their presence. But she understood only today the true purpose of the woman on the orange cushions.

She wouldn't tell Stanley. Not by spoken word, and not in the journal notes being churned out each day at a rapid rate. Not wanting to interfere with the conversational flow, the Front Runner avoided eye contact with him and quieted her thought processes. She would not, as one of her duties entailed, throw out conversational bones today, to stimulate thoughts and guide proper conclusions.

Thus did four of the Troop Formation's upper echelon become aware of the existence of themselves and the woman—all as separate entities. In the deepest recesses of the Tunnel, the Irishman's counsel was his own.

The woman's words in the session would go on and the Front Runner would allow it because the Gatekeeper's signal far back in the woman's mind was clear: Continue.

The woman, oblivious to the Tunnel and whatever went on there, was crying.

She described the second farmhouse where she, her two-year-old half sister, her mother, and her stepfather had moved. It had been the summer of her sixth year. In the fall she would enter the second grade. Besides running their new, twenty-four-acre farm, her stepfather had worked in the city, thirty miles away. She said vaguely that he had been employed as some kind of factory worker, perhaps a machinist.

"He was crafty," she said. "I loved my new upstairs bedroom but sometimes you'd think he was gone and he'd be behind the staircase door, waiting. If my mother were near, I dared to squeeze past him on the stairs, hugging the wall. He'd sneer then and look innocently at my mother, asking why I was such a 'fraidy cat. If my mother wasn't inside the house I'd slam the door in his face and run back to the kitchen.''

"What happened when you were alone in the house with him?"

"I don't know. It's a blank. All I remember is when my mother was there. He was very big and quick on his feet. When he caught up with me, he sort of pushed his face right into mine and his expression—it was as if he knew something awful about me, some dirty secret that the two of us shared together. But I never talked to him if I could avoid it, hated even being in the same room with him, so there couldn't have been any secret, it had to have been my imagination.''

She talked, one memory leading to the next, all of them expressed for the next few minutes by a rush of words.

"We had a big, black, wood-burning stove in the kitchen. The fire in it never went out, even in summer. If my stepfather caught up with me in front of my mother, he'd grab me up in his arms and hurl me above his head over the stove. His hands were so big, touching me in places I didn't want to be touched. I used to wish those places did not exist.''

"You were six and your half sister was two," Stanley said.

"Yes. I think so. I've never been able to keep track of time, it doesn't mean anything to me.''

He asked if she meant that an inability to capture the sequence of many incidents in her life had left her with a distorted concept of time. She tried, but could not convey with words exactly what she meant, nor could she agree to any of his attempts to describe her feelings about time. She was vehement about it. He found himself fascinated at the erratic way her hands beat the air—rejecting the concept of time as it might apply to herself.

The cheekbones rose higher in her face. "Where was I?"

"In the second farmhouse. The stove.''

"Yes, the damned stove. It never got cold. It cooked all our food, heated the water for tea and baths and the dishes. At the back of the stove, instead of another griddle, there was a reservoir that was always full of more hot water. I remember the steam rising from it. When my stepfather hurled me above his head, I went up into the air. He'd catch me. Before he did, I'd look down at the reservoir of boiling water and pray to land anywhere except in those hands of his.

"When I was older, it got worse. He'd smirk and grab me, slam me into the wall. 'I'm going to get you,' he'd say, holding

25

onto me or some piece of my clothing. 'It won't be long now, you like this, don't you?' Something pushed at my mind those times. There wasn't anything to like. But his expression kept reminding me of something. Just like the ice cream did last night. I put a scoop of chocolate ice cream into a bowl and something so clear—as if I'd never seen it before—leapt into my mind. For you, Stanley, eating ice cream is an innocent thing—but have you ever noticed how those ridges from the scoop look like the skin on a man, in one particular place?''

It took him a minute to follow her reasoning. A man's scrotum.

"Shit," she said, abruptly. "I have to ask you, Stanley, where are these shreds coming from? I need to know, is this real? Screw Miss Wonderful, I'm scared.''

The woman heard herself saying the words. She knew they were tumbling out too quickly, but they didn't seem to belong to her.

Stanley didn't like the way her face and voice altered with every other sentence or how oblivious she seemed to the alterations.

"Miss Wonderful," Stanley said, "who is she?''

The woman heard him from a distance and struggled to surface completely. She didn't want to tell him that Miss Wonderful was only a voice in her head. So she muttered, as was true, only that her friend Sharon often called her Miss Wonderful because she acted at times like a professional hostess. "Stanley," she said, "if I don't get a grip soon, I might as well be back on the farm. What happens to those victims who aren't strong? Where do they put the weak ones?''

"Being strong is great, but you've got to learn to ask for help. Asking for help is a sign of health.''

"It's a sign of weakness!''

She began to cry and refused to take it further, rocking back and forth on the pillows, her eyes wild and glassy. Repeatedly, in lulling undertones, Stanley told her that she had every right to be scared. His low murmur through the sessions had grown familiar and she talked right over his words, knowing that whatever he said didn't need a reply; but that in the days following each session his monotone messages would reach her subconscious, save her in moments of stress. They were armour if she recalled anything while alone.

"Why don't I remember more right this minute?'' she

screamed suddenly. "When I told my mother I was leaving that house because of the stepfather, what did I tell her? The incidents were so vague, I could never be certain they'd really happened. But until I turned fifteen, 'tell her' rang in my head. I don't know what finally precipitated my telling her—or even our conversation. She didn't look shocked at all, just determined that I mustn't leave her. There I was, looking forward to a new life when she'd spent hers in as much filth as I had, paying him for the roof over my head, for the food that kept me healthy. She'd paid him with herself."

No, he thought. Your mother paid her bills with you. First with your body and very nearly with your mind. In spite of the anger he felt, Stanley kept his face expressionless, concentrating on his notes.

"My mother didn't rant or rave that day, she just said that I was to stay. Things would get better, she'd make him stop. It's impossible for me to believe that she knew what was going on."

As the woman talked, Stanley saw the conflict: a mother's harsh qualities weighed against the good—an inclination to accentuate the good and blame one's own self for the harsh.

Her mother, she said, pinched pennies all year because of a tight-fisted man who wouldn't give to his own children or wife, let alone his stepdaughter. The pennies at Christmas bought a wealth of gifts for the children; creatively, beautifully wrapped, even stacked artistically under the perfect tree.

Stanley began to get a picture of a woman, big bones and red hair and Irish-beautiful; a world-beater cook, seamstress, and laundress, who slaved over the cleaning, until the farmhouse glowed. A woman who haunted auctions to furnish that farmhouse well, on a budget tighter than Scrooge's. Someone who had the capacity, or was driven enough, to work night and day, not only in the farmhouse but in the fields as well, planting and picking crops. He caught a glimmer as in past sessions, of a deeply tormented woman who had perhaps been mishandled by her own mother and passed it down to her daughter.

There was more. It amounted to an inability on his client's part to see her own side or to speak in her own defense. Her mother had been perfect, she had not.

Stanley had listened. Now he laid down the clipboard. "You were not responsible for your mother's happiness or unhappiness. Your mother was an adult and her emotions were hers to deal with. You talk about how she scrimped and saved and denied her own needs to feed you, to give you nice holidays. But with your earnings from various jobs, you supported your mother, half brother, and half sisters, a long time before your stepfather eventually left.''

"I couldn't really earn a lot after school and lots of times I hurt her. I wasn't an easy child. I screamed and smashed things. I was a malcontent, whom nothing satisfied, one of those people who is happy with nothing and no one.''

"Or so your mother told you. You worked,'' he reminded her, "as a waitress every afternoon until midnight and every single weekend, during your junior and senior years. And your mother hurt you, didn't she? She beat the hell out of you. And she gave you to your stepfather; she handed you over to him.''

Stanley had purposely slapped it down in front of her, made it blatant and undeniable.

"My mother didn't know.'' The woman was crying.

"You told me she did.''

"Did I?''

"It's in your journal notes,'' Stanley told her firmly. "She knew what he was doing.''

The woman looked at him, confused. Stanley knew what he'd read that morning: the long ago kitchen conversation wherein her mother had told her stepfather that if he weren't after her all the time, the child wouldn't know anything about masturbation. How could the woman have forgotten it? But she must have done just that. Her blank eyes and face were too genuine, and the burgeoning terror they masked was something no one could manufacture.

Had he pushed her too far? So much had come out of this session. She'd held up this far and so many avenues had opened.

"Stanley? I remember something.''

Her face had not changed so much as it had softened; the voice was very young, the pronunciation very precise. It was older than the voice he'd heard in the entry foyer during the first interview.

"Tell me,'' he said.

"When the old barn burned down, the garage was converted. We took the car out and put the cow in there with a lot of hay. One day I was walking past the open door. The half sister lay there in the hay, all that black hair of hers spilling out. The stepfather had his back to me, he knelt between her bare legs, his pants were down around his ankles.''

28

"How old were you at the time?"

"Nine. I couldn't believe what I'd seen. When I asked her about it later, and told her I thought he was a bastard, she said she loved him, he was her father and she loved him. She was seven years old."

Stanley had what he thought of as a brilliant idea. The soft face and the very young voice told him it was brilliant. "And how old are you, right now?" he asked.

"Twelve. I'm twelve years old."

The voice had faded to almost nothing and Stanley had to lean over to catch the words.

"That's when I knew I had to be crazy. His own daughter loved him, people said it was wrong not to love your parents. Yet I hated him with a passion."

"You aren't crazy," he said, "and you've remembered one of the farm animals."

"What farm animals? We didn't have any." The woman was staring at him.

Tony motioned from the booth and Stanley reached out and touched her arm. "Time for the break."

He didn't know what else to say.

The woman headed down to the bathroom at the far end of the hall avoiding her reflection in the glass walls of the control booth. She could not, however, avoid her eyes in the lavatory mirror. At first glance, as she rubbed away the smudged mascara, her eyes were pale green and slanted. The colour changed then, almost to grey, and the slant became more oval. The eyes wouldn't shut; they remained open and stared right back at her.

4

OK, so you've got a tremendous need for coffee, which means caffeine, you've got 'we,' headaches with no pain, a sporadic memory, and somebody who tells you that she's twelve years old. Anything else?''

Marshall Fielding's voice crackled at the other end of the long distance line. Marshall was a researcher with his finger on the pulse of every happening in the mental health field. More than that, he was a very old friend whose judgement Stanley trusted.

''You're not laughing, you bastard.'' Stanley had one eye on his wristwatch, because the session was about to start again. ''There's plenty else. I saw the contents she dumped out of her purse one day. She lives by lists—she's got a list for every waking moment. Some of them are duplicates and triplicates of the same project but with variations as to completion. She's got an incredible memory before the age of two. After that, it's zip. Except that every now and then, details come out and I can't be sure what she remembers. She has no sense of time, no sense of direction. . . .''

There came a long silence at the other end of the line. ''Is she very creative?'' Marshall asked.

''Somebody thought enough of her work to give her a one-woman show. She once designed an entire art department according to a strict budget. That's another thing. Her work requires that she do cash flow statements on various income-producing buildings. Yet she has trouble with figures.''

30

"I take it then that this is a very productive woman we're talking about."

"Exceedingly," Stanley said. "Which leads me to believe that this can't possibly be multiple personality. She's never been debilitated, nothing seems to stop her. And I definitely don't see a neat parade of alternate selves who come out and say, 'Hi, I'm so-and-so.' "

"Go back to work," Marshall said. "I'll see you in a couple of weeks."

"And in the meantime?"

"She isn't going anywhere," Marshall said. "You're the first person she's ever had for that little trip into the deep forest. Now she's got an inkling that it's going to get deeper."

"Sometimes I don't think she has an inkling of anything."

"If it's multiple personality, somebody does."

Stanley hung up and ran back to the studio.

He lowered himself across from the woman and felt his ankles rebel against the position. One of these days he'd get the hang of it.

She began to tell him that as a child she had hidden under tables, behind the doors or the kitchen stove.

"I hated being with anyone," the woman said, "but I knew that I must never be alone and in full view. Whenever my mother did force me out of hiding, I stayed at her feet or at her side. I drew a lot with my school crayons. Then I'd lose track of time and panic. Where had my mother gone? And I'd run like the wind if it wasn't too late."

"Too late?" The woman's words had created a picture that Stanley didn't think she had ever examined fully.

"Yes," she said. "Too late. I knew there was danger, but I can't remember what. I want to go into the field of tall grass. Let's go. I'm ready."

He'd been trying in the first two weeks of therapy to teach her a method whereby with her relaxed breathing and his softened, singsong voice, she could hypnotise or "lower" herself into childhood recall. So far it hadn't worked. A tiny flashback of the field at the first farmhouse had been stirred up during the brief treatment with the psychoanalyst eight years ago. The flashback had triggered at that time an absolute terror for the woman that still persisted.

While he would have preferred to try for other recall, it was important that she develop faith in her own decision making.

31

"Very well, we'll go back," Stanley said. "You can stop at any time if you're not comfortable."

She started to count backward, from ten to zero. Gradually, her muscles relaxed. The drifting came slowly as always; it crept, taking her body but skirting her mind. Then it began as never before—the seeping into her mind of something she was unused to, a relaxation so strong that it was like a sedative. She knew she was going, and it was almost a relief. The final number, zero, escaped her mouth with a soft hiss.

The woman was no longer in the video studio, but in a field of tall grass. She smiled.

"The sun. It's bright. But it goes in and out of the clouds, it . . . does something funny to the grass. The grass is moving." Her voice was thicker, as if she were under anesthesia, and sounded very young. "Dress. I'm wearing a dress. The ground is—it's damp today. The grass is so tall."

"Who is there with you?"

"He's there. He's above me, on me." There was a shudder and her eyelids pressed hard together. "He . . . I can't see it."

"How old are you?"

"Two. I'm two."

Silence again for several minutes, a look of fear on her face and then, "My dress. It won't stay down. It keeps moving up above my waist and I keep pulling it down. I don't want my dress to go up." There was a whine in the voice, like that of a very little girl. "He is so big. I don't like this."

"We can stop if you want to."

"No." Still the childlike whine, but the words were more adult. "I'll get it, it just keeps floating back and forth, and the clouds move . . . he is so big . . . is it possible to feel disgust?"

"Oh, yes. Entirely possible."

"It's sweeping over me from somewhere. The dress won't stay down, he keeps pulling it up and I can't stop it!"

A low, howling sob began, mingled with a soft, childish weeping, as if she were crying two sets of tears. Unknown to Stanley, two sets of tears were being wept, and neither one of them by the woman.

Even under hypnosis, the woman neither saw nor experienced anything except the sunlight on the grass and the pressure of the stepfather's body on her own. Rabbit was a very young and un-evolved child who held the pain for almost the entire Troop Formation. Rabbit now re-experienced the act of penetration and was responsible for the howling sobs. Another very young child, undergoing the same act of penetration but on a "removed" level, wept more softly. One day as therapy progressed, Stanley would understand the phenomenon of two or more persons being present at exactly the same time. He would also understand how the woman, when she was present, and unbeknownst to herself, was only a conduit for other Troop members.

No words came in accompaniment to the terrified weeping, no verbal explanation of what was happening in the field of tall grass, to cause the fear and pain the woman evidenced. Stanley thought he knew, with or without words. Only one offender among the men he treated had ever admitted to raping so young a child as the woman had been in this recall. It had taken the man three years to face his guilt. His victim, his child, had been committed to a mental hospital.

The woman's throat muscles strained with the howling sobs. Stanley hoped they had not aimed too quickly at the field. This one area held what he felt might be the original, the deepest, root of trauma. After it, almost an entire lifetime of sexual memory had been shelved.

"Well," Stanley said, "that's very good. This isn't easy but don't be scared, it's alright. We'll stop for now, we'll count from zero to ten, and when you reach ten, you'll be here in this room and you'll feel refreshed. Are you ready?"

Haltingly, she went through the numbers. On the count of ten, relief flooded her face. Tears streamed.

"Why," she blurted as her eyes flew open, "is it so easy to get there now?"

"Because you are ready now." Stanley smiled.

The woman felt herself gripped by a sudden incomprehension. Certain words had formed in her mind but refused to be spoken. She wanted desperately, with no awareness of how limited her own view of the sexual abuse had just been, to thank Stanley for the breakthrough. Eight years ago, the psychoanalyst had let her see a brief glimpse of the field. She had run from the recall—for no reason she could fathom—and been terrified of that field ever since. Moments ago, however, the view had been larger and the threat of danger very understandable. The stepfather had been there.

But instead of thanking Stanley, she heard herself wailing the word "coward."

"You aren't a coward." He tried to catch her eye, but the blond hair blocked his vision. "Reliving actual happenings would

33

scare anybody. You're doing well, you're determined, and that's half the battle.''

"Those little flicks against my mind," the woman said, oblivious to his impression that she'd been aware throughout the entire recall, "they're coming faster now, they hurt, they're so ugly!"

"They're memories, they'll probably increase somewhat in the next few weeks."

"Is that what it is?" The woman laughed and sobbed, simultaneously. Her nostrils were heavy and swollen with crying. They felt strange; she felt strange—yet she did not feel anything at all, except a weird kinship to some trapped animal ready for slaughter. With no other warning, conflicting emotions began to war with one another. It popped into her mind that the emotions were actually the flicks of memory and that the pain they produced was only intellectual. It was not physical. Why, then, did her heart suddenly ache with a keening, biting, wrenching sensation and why wouldn't the damned tears stop?

"By the way," Stanley said, "I'll use this tape in class. It shows enormous progress." He stopped talking then, because as he looked over at her, he knew she wasn't hearing him.

"Dammit," the woman heard the snarl. "Dammit, why couldn't I see all of that stupid field? Why am I such an ass? I thought when I left the farmhouse that I was free of everything. But it's never stopped, I'm still running!"

"What do you think you're running from?" Stanley kept his voice noncommittal.

"Only one thing equals this guilt. I must have killed someone."

This was not the reaction Stanley had expected. Why didn't she express a direct verbal horror of the rape? Those howling, pain-ridden sobs—having just relived the rape, how could the guilt still rest squarely on her shoulders? Why hadn't she begun to transfer that guilt to the stepfather where it belonged?

His eyes raced back to his notes. There it was—immediately after coming out of hypnosis, she'd again referred to "flicks," not to a whole memory. How much of the field had she retained? Perhaps she was simply not ready to accept the rape; he doubted that he had been ready.

"Just offhand," he said, "who do you think you might have killed?"

There was no hesitation in the same young, precise voice he'd heard just before the break.

"The stepfather. I thought about it, a lot. But to kill somebody,

34

you have to touch them. I didn't want to touch him. If you used a rifle, you might miss and make him angry. Then he'd get you.''

"Jesus," the woman heard herself screaming in an adult voice, "why can't I remember when I saw that bastard for the last time? There's nothing in my head!''

Even as the adult voice spoke, bombarding flicks of recall and opposing emotions hit all at once. The woman held her head as if afraid that it would explode, and a shriek tore out of her mouth. In that one second, she saw a jigsaw puzzle with all the pieces flung into the air, helter-skelter. The pieces were a past that might have belonged to a stranger. No one piece fit side by side with another, nothing related to anything she knew.

Yet all of it, in fragmented form, seemed frighteningly familiar. So did the voice in her head. She heard it quite suddenly and was reminded of the mother. Somewhere in the very recent past, she'd heard that voice, but it had seemed like just another of those random, far-off—were they thoughts or voices? Whatever they were, they had begun, just before her visit to A Woman's Place, to spring up with no warning.

Stanley might not have been in the studio, seated across from her. The voice would not go away. Demanding, cruel—the woman listened, staring down at the orange cushions, feeling distanced, removed from Stanley's presence. Awful things were being said to her, mean, hurtful things, designed to wound, to impart the knowledge that one was imperfect, imbecilic, and worthless.

"It was bad back there on the farm," Stanley was saying. "It was bad, all of it, and you have a right to feel scared.''

But the woman heard through his words another voice, like that of a child, crying:

"No! It wasn't all bad, my crayons were good, they were the best part of growing up, *I want my crayons, now!*''

Stanley observed her over the clipboard. He tabulated what he'd seen and heard since the first interview, weeks ago. Little of it matched anything he'd witnessed before in his professional career. The woman knelt in front of him, her forehead on her knees, holding herself as she cried. When she finally raised her head, he noted the slanted eyes and thought that even without the makeup which had now washed away, they were oddly pretty. That thought was promptly replaced with another: this client might be beyond the scope of his expertise. Unless Marshall could give him some direction, Stanley had no idea to whom he might refer her.

5

Cigarette smoke drifted down the university hallway in the wake of students headed for Stanley's night class. He searched his pockets for Albert's number and juggled the telephone against a stack of papers that needed grading. Impatiently, he listened to the ringing as Jeannie Lawson, a first year student, waved to him from his office door. He waved back. He'd get to her later. Jeannie had yet to turn in her psychosocial history and he knew she'd come to beg more time. There wasn't any more time. The paper was due.

Finally, Albert answered the phone.

"Albert," Stanley said with no preamble, "what's the statute of limitations on murder?"

"You gotta be kidding." Captain Albert Johnson let out a howl on the telephone wire. "You're not talking cash or groceries, Stanley, you're talking homicide."

Stanley sighed. Anyone was capable of murder. All it required was to be pushed too far, and without a doubt, the woman had been pushed. More than likely, however, she was only expressing guilt. Her lack of self-esteem went far deeper than he'd suspected. Almost all victims had a fear that the "silent partner" to sexual abuse (in this case the woman's mother), would find out and despise them, as they despised themselves. Perhaps with the memory of the abuse so deeply buried in the woman's subconscious, the guilt had festered there, too. Until that which her mind could not accept had found an outlet: she was so bad that she must have killed someone—her stepfather.

"You wanna get off the line, Stanley? I got four phones going at once, thanks to you. My precinct isn't orderly anymore, it's a goddamned madhouse. Protective Services has been up my nose. What they want on initial and follow-up reports is that one of their staff should accompany what they call an officer trained in the field. Know what that means? I haven't got trained officers. I hand one of my people an incest call and they look at me like I'm asking for a moon shot."

"Albert, I've got some training videos for you."

"My officers fall asleep on that stuff. One of your offenders told me those films are cotton candy compared to what he put his kid through."

"I just made these videos myself, Albert, and they're not cotton candy. You set it up with your people, I'll be there. I'll even buy you a beer afterward."

"I haven't had one of them from you in three months. As I recall, that's when you talked me into being a clearinghouse for county abuse reports. Wound up tight as a tic tonight, aren't you? You on speed or something?"

"Something," Stanley agreed and hung up. Albert was right. Yesterday the energy had begun to fade. Today, during the session with the woman, it had returned. He'd even begun to document it, just to give Marshall something to laugh at. Where was Jeannie?

He caught up with her, halfway down the long hall. Jeannie was tall and slender with a wealth of pale brown hair that drifted across narrow shoulders. While walking, she kept her arms wrapped around herself.

Stanley had his suspicions about her. But it wasn't the kind of thing you asked about and Jeannie, unlike three of his other students, had never volunteered anything.

"Doctor Phillips, my counselor is a woman. Sometimes it's easier for me to talk to women. She's going to call you. For now, you said there were videos for this class. May I see one?"

"You mean of an incest victim? Sure. I've scheduled a video for next week, but if you can wait after class tonight—" Stanley knew his first-year student was itching to get away from him. In class she stayed pretty much to herself, spoke to almost no one, and avoided eye contact as if she were very angry or scared to death.

"I've heard she's local. I can't believe she's talking."

"Why should that be so incredible?"

"Victims don't talk," Jeannie said, "except for a handful, and when they do, they don't really say much. Nobody says much."

"This victim wants to change that."

"Lots of luck to her," Jeannie said. "I'll see you after class."

The students settled down, a few smokers lit up, and Stanley took his place at the front of the room. Jeannie, crouched deep in a navy jacket far too heavy for the month of May, was so silent that she might not have been in the class at all.

Stanley instructed in an even tone as usual, no theatrics because the subject didn't need them. Across the country, a number of educational facilities, enough to fit through the eye of a needle, were handling the subject of child sexual abuse and maybe, if it caught on, enough clinicians would be trained to treat its ramifications by the year 2000.

The students took copious notes, asked direct questions, and displayed, when the hour was up, expressions ranging from shock to studied casualness. From the back of the room a sophomore raised her hand.

"Doctor Phillips, next year my sister will follow me into this class. Will you be teaching it?"

"Next year," Stanley said, "this course may not exist. The funding for practically everything is being cut. Tape-record, take notes, and pass them on. Next week I'll be showing you video-tapes of an incest victim which were filmed last week and this morning. The woman you will see on those films made a request of me when we first began her treatment. She asks that after you have seen them, talk. Wherever you go and to whomever you meet. She does not care if her name or that of the company she owns is mentioned in your conversations. I have a request of my own. You're going to run into her in the halls here. Don't say hello, leave her alone for another couple of weeks."

As the students filed out, he sat Jeannie down in front of a small viewer and adjusted the headphones. Technicolor flashed in front of her face and there was no mistaking the woman's words.

Incest.

It had been one thing to have been trapped in her own mind with similar memories but to see and hear the woman displaying her own anger and fear was another. Jeannie pulled the navy coat tighter around herself.

"Those two farmhouses are there, somewhere," Stanley was saying to the woman. "You spent sixteen years in them. Suppose you just tell me whatever you do remember."

"Even if it's dumb?"

"Especially if it's dumb." Stanley smiled. "Sometimes that's the best place to start."

The woman gave him the little she remembered from the age of two. She insisted that nothing else existed in her mind until she'd been six and in the second grade in a little one-room schoolhouse. Her family had just moved, she said, to the second farmhouse.

"I was so scared."

"Of what?" Stanley asked her.

"The other kids and the teachers scared us. I liked the coloured paper, though. We used to make chains out of it and play wedding. The chains were the veils for our gowns. We used so much paper that the teacher locked it up." She paused and looked up from the floor, her face very soft and rounded, the eyes more slanted. Then cheekbones which had not been so noticeable for the last several minutes, seemed to appear again out of nowhere. "There are times, Stanley, when I don't feel as if this is my skin; it wasn't back then, either. Like the car accident in front of that one-room schoolhouse. I must have been in the third grade. We lived a mile from school, I was on my way back from lunch at home. A car hit me, knocked me down in the road."

"Were you badly hurt?"

"I didn't feel anything. I don't remember being hit, just some man bending over me, saying how sorry he was, and his car on the side of the road with the door open. He shook a lot. I felt very calm. That's all I remember. There wasn't any pain."

Jeannie could see Stanley on the videotape and now here in this room, considering that.

"All of a sudden, I'm in the sixth grade," the woman said, cutting three years out of her life.

Stanley pressed on. "You had half sisters and a half brother?"

"I don't remember them, except for bits and pieces. Everything is so vague—when it's there at all. Except the nightmares. I don't remember them, just the terror they produced."

39

"Scared of the dark?" he asked. "Too much dessert for dinner?"

"I'm not scared of the dark and I don't get sick anymore."

"Once you mentioned something about a cellar under that one-room schoolhouse and we never got into it, there wasn't time."

She started to bite her thumbnail and the face grew soft again, the cheekbones seeming to submerge. "It wasn't anything like the big school later, just three seniors, a couple of freshmen, some elementary kids, and me. I was in the third grade, so I must have been seven. Summertimes the teacher had flowers on her desk, lilacs from the big bush outside the window. In the winter there was the smell of our wet leggins and mittens on the floor register, and always, the odour of lunch-pail food and waxed paper.

"One of the freshman girls had a fuzzy pink sweater and fuzzy brown hair. I used to stare at the sweater because she had a chest. That impressed me. Everyone liked her; I thought it must have something to do with the sweater or the chest. During recess the smallest of us huddled in the snow outside the cellar door. Sometimes we put our mittens up to it, thinking we could get our hands warm. The furnace inside the cellar sent out blasts of hot air. One day we all stood outside, waiting for the girl in the pink sweater to come out with one of the senior boys. Everyone else stood around giggling, not wanting the teacher to hear. They thought it was funny, but I knew, Stanley, that those two were doing something wrong in there, something dirty and vile and evil."

The voice expressing in simple sentences a knowledge far beyond a child's third grade years, had struck Jeannie as odd. And familiar. She watched Stanley on the video screen, taking notes. Jeannie was taking her own notes and for her a warning bell had gone off.

"Did you ever have friends in school?"

"One. Later on in the big school. Her name was Helen, and she was big and tall and I hid behind her. But one day, she told a joke, and as she did it, she put out her hand to me. It scared me, her hand coming at me like that. Goodbye, friend." The eyes regarded Stanley under a fall of ash-blond bangs, and a smile slid to one side of the pale mouth. "The teachers tried to steer us toward making friends, then they insisted."

"And did you?" Stanley was asking on the videotape.

40

"Hell, no. By that time, we knew better than to do anything we were told to do. The stepfather told us to do lots of things."

Jeannie Lawson sat straight up in her chair. "We." The woman had said it repeatedly. The references, Jeannie felt, might not have been to the woman's classmates as a child, or to members of her immediate family . . . but to members of an even more "immediate" family. Jeannie ticked off the changes that anyone else might regard as simply part of an animated manner: hands that gestured broadly, that lay calm in the lap and then moved almost sensually through the tumbled blond hair; the voice that was never one but many; expressions that ranged from businesslike to street smart and childlike and all the gradations in between. The eyes. No one person had that many pairs of eyes.

This was a business woman Stanley was dealing with—someone who should be brisk and efficient; who gave orders and negotiated land contracts, someone who always had the upper hand. But Jeannie watched the woman going from that kind of person to another: one who displayed almost hysterical mannerisms and voice changes, there on the floor under Stanley's watchful gaze. Jeannie listened to expressions of what seemed to be of paramount importance in the woman's mind—staying hidden and isolated from human contact because she felt ugly and incompetent. And because each time people reached out to her, their motives were suspect.

Jeannie Lawson knew the woman's feelings and mannerism changes too well. They might have been her own a year ago.

Watching the woman go into the relaxed breathing, watching her face and body contort with the recall in the field of tall grass, was agony. By the time what had to be a small child began to scream for the crayons, Jeannie was screaming with her, in a part of her mind so scarred already that numbness fought with the pain. What Jeannie saw and heard reminded her of the few typewritten words of the psychosocial history Stanley was waiting for and which she had been unable to complete.

She had come to watch a victim who was willing to be filmed, using her own name, with no shadows and no voice distortion. Instead, she'd found not only another victim, but a mirror-image of herself—and her own case was termed "rare" by every printed word she'd ever encountered on the subject.

She turned away from the video screen with her mouth open and her eyes wide.

41

"You're working with a multiple for these videos? How in god's name did you find her?"

Stanley had been sitting there, staring at the screen, tapping his teeth with a fingernail. All of a sudden, Jeannie knew what he was going through; the same sporadic, suspicion/confirmation/doubt that had caused her own therapist to flounder.

"Tell me," he said, "how you know that."

At home that night, his mind whirling, Stanley tried to catch up with his client's writing. Again the pages were typewritten.

Stanley, with the psychoanalyst, it became impossible to go back, even under hypnosis. I wound up biding time by telling him about my mother reading to me, *The Five Little Peppers and How They Grew*, *Anne of Green Gables*, and *Little Women*, by the light of a kerosene lantern, while the wind howled outside and the snow blew against that first farmhouse, in great, swirling drifts.

There was so little of me anywhere, during that time with him. He increased the number of weekly sessions but it didn't help. I demanded to know one day, where all this had come from, my panic, the hysteria and guilt, over what? The unknown, terrible action that I could not remember, and the guilt, had to originate somewhere in childhood. I wanted to know, was ready to face, whatever had this much power over me.

He told me to count back, think of someplace I'd truly like to be, out of all the places in the entire world. I couldn't produce a single one. His voice got soft, slow, I tried and couldn't. And he kept at me.

It was a nice idea. Someplace you'd truly like to be. His voice went on, lulling, and suddenly in my mind, I let go for a split second and I was there, saying aloud, "Oh, a field of tall grass," and in front of my eyes, the very gentle breeze was causing the tall grass to move, to quiver—but there were yellow flowers in that field—*I couldn't go there!*

I fought so hard to get back, to be in that psychoanalyst's office again, out of that office, I remember screaming to someone, anyone, "Let me go!"

Norman, my ex-husband, says the doctor called him to come take me home that day, saying that he could handle anybody, but he couldn't handle me. I have no memory of that at all. I must have acted very badly, though. Norman says I kept screaming in the car, "No, no, I can't go there anymore, leave me alone." And Stanley? It just now hit me. There's more than one field of tall grass.

Stanley put down the manuscript pages. They'd probably been written a week ago. Yet even after today's revealing session, his client seemed almost as much in the dark as she had during the initial interview. Flowers represented both her mother and the guilt. Stanley recognised that, and he'd also known something else: anyone who conducted sexually roughhousing games over a hot stove, with a screaming, protesting, child, who could rape that same child, wouldn't stop at one field.

It was generally felt in the world of mental health treatment that brutal abusers like her stepfather were rare. But abusers, brutal or not, were seldom reported. Many of the men whom Protective Services turned over to Stanley for treatment had reported themselves. They'd had sexual relations with their children. That was horror enough. While all child sexual abuse was a physical act, a brutality—these men had *not* added the element of physical torture.

Jeannie Lawson had been a multiple as the result of sexual abuse and brutal, physical torture by her stepfather's teenage boys. Jeannie, and the woman whose condition he'd almost decided on, were supposed to be rare, too. Were they? What about the brutal offenders? Men and women who would never turn themselves in? Could there be more brutal offenders—and perhaps multiples, too—in greater numbers than anyone imagined?

The morning session had produced a fright that stayed all day. At bedtime it was still there. The sporadic awareness that had been stirred up lately, had struck her on a new front. She wanted to call her friend Sharon Barnes, but stood in front of the kitchen clock, scared because she could not tell what hour it was. It was either twenty after ten in the evening or twenty after eleven (in which case it would be too late to call).

What she really wanted was to simply drive the two miles to Sharon's house, have coffee and unload a measure of the built-up fear. But Sharon had a cat now, a sleek black cat full of curiosity and sensuous, prowling movements.

Hatred and fear of animals lay there for a second, naked in

43

her awareness . . . real this time, like a plastic monster come to life. She didn't know why the fear should be there.

The Gatekeeper waited. The woman's fear mounted. Only the whisper of the woman's breathing broke the silence. Fear began to take a stronger hold as her suspicions became less vague and therefore more real. The Gatekeeper gave the signal. And in the shadows of the Tunnel Walls, the Weaver bent to his task with nimble fingers. He gathered the threads of the veil that shrouded all and wove each one back into place. The woman's suspicion floated away. No longer able to feel the fear, she believed that it did not exist, had never existed.

She had always denied what her other selves gave through thought transference. Everything seemed like messages from her own mind. What made it so perplexing was that she didn't have the background for, or involvement in, much of anything, and often felt a wonder at the strangeness of what she received.

Now, while she stared at the wall clock, 10:20 just flew into her head. She dialed Sharon's number. They had, after all, been friends for thirteen years. Sharon did not make judgements; her sense of humour would certainly wipe out the sense of impending doom. The woman's hands shook and the words sounded far away but she came directly to the point when Sharon answered.

"Voices?" Over the phone, Sharon's sharp intake of breath didn't masque the anger and disbelief.

"They were real, Sharon. In the session this morning."

She hadn't expected Sharon to reject the idea completely. It took a minute to calm down because she heard the angry thoughts in her head, the anger rising at Sharon's denial. The woman tried again.

"Sharon, in this morning's session, I know it was just Stanley sitting on the floor with me, but there were other voices. In a peculiar way, they were in my head but they were outside of it, too."

"You listen to me! You aren't making sense. Holding it back all these years has been a terrible strain, that's all."

The Buffer had become upset. Nails, a Troop member who dealt with rejection, charged up front. Nails was now "sitting forward" in the mind of the woman who could still hear and operate, and therefore believed that the actions and words were her own. Even if she did feel "removed" from everything.

44

"Three of my agents quit," Nails said to Sharon and lit a cigarette.

The woman stared from a long way off, at the cigarette between her fingers and the one still smoking in the ashtray. People said she smoked too much.

"They quit just like that?" Sharon's voice reflected a panic the woman hadn't felt at all when three days ago, the agents had marched out of her office on Hampton Road.

The woman didn't hear Sharon's panic. She heard only that which Nails permitted.

"The agents couldn't deal with me," Nails said, "I couldn't deal with them. But in land and commercial real estate where everybody's the Lone Ranger, it doesn't matter."

"What about human companionship? You shouldn't be alone so much right now."

Companionship? The woman struggled to focus over a feeling of unreality, of having drifted off somewhere. In spite of her need to talk to someone tonight, companionship was not, had never been, part of her vocabulary. Her head had begun to pound. Rain lashed at the kitchen window as she hauled out instant coffee and found a cup, not sure when she'd turned the gas on. But the water had already come to a boil.

Sharon's voice droned on from a great distance. She asked the woman to reconsider and tell Stanley not to share the progress of her therapy with anyone he saw fit.

"You're not yourself," Sharon was saying, "give it time. Client-therapist confidentiality exists for a good reason. Revelation may help a lot of people and hurt you more than you comprehend right now."

"Forget it," Nails said. "The reason people get away with child abuse is that nobody talks about it. A librarian told us so."

"I care about you," Sharon said. "You're the one who'll get hurt with this exposure."

To the woman, Sharon's voice sounded hollow, as if she were speaking through an empty oil drum. There was no way to convince Sharon of how important the training tapes were, or to how many people they might make a difference. Sharon had never been abused. The woman hung up the phone, feeling drained. She'd wanted coffee, had she drunk it? The kitchen, except for the dirty coffee cup and ashtray, gleamed pristine under the track lighting. Somehow the house managed to stay neat although she never cleaned it much that she knew of.

45

Only when she felt one foot dragging ahead of the other, up the stairs to the bedroom, did the mechanical movements of her body become annoying and giant tasks undone flood her mind. Bills needed paying, the checkbook needed balancing, business letters should be written, lists made out for the week. And there it was again, the notion of being harassed, cornered. Why couldn't she be good, do the right things? Had she asked Stanley how long this therapy process would take, so that her life might finally have meaning and order? By working at top speed she might be able to cut the time in half. She prayed, using the term loosely, for she never prayed and despised the idea of it, that he could whip her into shape in three months. That would mean survival for her business life.

Exhausted, she crawled into a nightgown and then into bed. Her mind was so tired that sleep began moving in. Without warning, the mother's words came to her, "We get what we deserve in this world."

Nails drove these words away with a thought of her own: in spite of what the law said, and people paid lip service to, the stepfather had been worthy of killing. The woman sensed the smile on her face as sleep finally took over, but in her mind as always, the guilt brought by yet another self overrode Nails' message.

The source of the thought transference was not revealed to the woman and she tossed all night, battling random thoughts. At seven the next morning she awoke, wrapped in a strong and ugly terror. There would be a real estate meeting in two more hours and she had not typed the contract. Laughter sounded in her head as she fled down the stairs from the loft bedroom and started jamming paper into the typewriter. Fear erupted as she found a contract on the desk, already typed. Had she even been near the typewriter last night?

The Buffer, sensing an onslaught of more emotion than she herself could absorb, moved over completely and the woman was gone.

Catherine picked up the carry-all purse from the desk and slithered out of the nightgown she'd never liked. The fabric was opaque, the neckline high, and the sleeves long. She trailed the garment after herself, moving up the staircase with unhurried steps. Catherine never hurried, even when things got out of hand. And they were out of hand.

6

The second he walked into Protective Services that morning, he got a call from Martha Ryland, Jeannie Lawson's counselor. She introduced herself over the phone, in a voice that sounded friendly but professionally direct.

"Jeannie can't have told you much," Martha Ryland said. "Frankly, she still has an aversion to men. She's given me permission to fill you in."

Stanley remembered the little Jeannie had told him. She'd had multiple personalities; three to be exact, each one distinctly separate from the other. The abuse which had caused the multiplicity had gone on from the time she was seven years old until she turned fourteen.

"I can't begin to tell you," Martha said, "how rotten it was, or exactly how it screwed up Jeannie's life. She's now what her therapist calls integrated; in other words, all three persons have become one. Your class has done Jeannie a lot of good, she seems so much more open. Up until yesterday, she felt like a freak. There's just one thing. The woman you're treating now insists that you talk about her therapy publicly. Jeannie can't afford the same openness. I predict that one day she'll be an exceptional clinician, but exposing her background at this point . . . you and I both know what would happen. Her career would be over before it started."

Stanley did know. Adult child abuse victims in the work force were often regarded as "risky" employees, prone to falling apart

47

on the job. They probably weren't any more risky than other employees but the stigma was there. If a prospective employer should get wind of the added stigma of multiple personality, Jeannie Lawson could face an even tougher battle.

Which meant that he should call his own client and tell her that using the videos for training purposes was over. He felt almost sure she was multiple and if so, she would certainly not want it made common knowledge.

"How," Martha asked, breaking in on his thoughts, "do you feel about entertaining the idea of your client's being multiple?"

"I don't know, exactly. I've been wondering for a few weeks, but to me, the woman's symptoms aren't classic. Now Jeannie's pointed out things I was overlooking. As she said, once it's happened to you, it's easy to spot it in someone else."

"It still doesn't make you sure, though, does it?" Her tone had lost some of its professional crispness. "I don't envy you. I know Jeannie's therapist. At first she doubted everything too, the way a good clinician would. But when she weighed the evidence, as I suppose you're beginning to do, denying it was useless. Jeannie's therapist knew she wasn't schizophrenic or any of the other labels that had been pinned on her at various times by a number of other doctors and psychiatrists."

"Neither is this woman," Stanley said.

"It was eerie, listening to Jeannie describe that woman's tapes, as if she sensed a friend. She told me that during her therapy, none of her friends understood the multiplicity, and after a while she kept quiet. This is the first time that Jeannie has reached out to anyone. I view her willingness to go this far as a sign of recovery, and her psychosocial history, when she turns it in, will probably be something to behold."

Martha gave Stanley the therapist's number. Jeannie had alerted her to expect Stanley's call, and she was just as forthright as Martha. Stanley spent what would have been his breakfast hour going over what both counselor and therapist had said. Added to what he'd read of the little available information, certain concepts began to form; what few multiples there were, in general, operated in a world wherein emotions were "buffered" for them by their other selves. The selves, depending on how many there were and how damaging the cause of the multiplicity, handled what the first-born child could not. So that the degree of life which the first-born child might enjoy could range from a lot to a little.

If his client were multiple, it might explain her current state of confusion and mounting panic. A great deal might be the result of awakening emotions. If she'd never experienced them before except from a great distance, through her other selves, she might shortly become torn, wanting isolation because she felt strange in her new world—yet needing human solace for the first time. Would that solace be readily available to her among her friends and acquaintances? Stanley didn't know. One thing was certain. He had to get to her immediately, and cancel their agreement to use the tapes.

It was now 8:30 in the morning. The woman answered the phone on the first ring. He explained to her that perhaps they'd been hasty and that she should rethink her decision. A lot, he said, might come out on the tapes that she wouldn't want to be public knowledge.

"Like what?" she demanded. "I've hidden my whole life, mostly because I was frightened of what other people thought. What is it you're afraid people will find out from the tapes? That I'm crazy? My best friends tell me that. I don't care about my enemies."

"You don't understand," he said softly. "There are people who have no idea how the human mind reacts to abuse and they're all too willing to ostracise; worse than that, they don't mind taking bread out of your mouth in the bargain."

"Stanley, have you ever met a purchaser or a seller? You have to be crazy to be one. That's why I'm successful, so far. Those people relate to me."

"You aren't crazy," he said, and knew that if he went further, he'd have to say "multiple," and he wasn't ready to do that.

"Are you afraid that the mental health world will come down on you for exploiting me? If that's the case, I'll sign a statement saying the videotaping was my idea, which is the truth, and that I give you full permission to use everything as you see fit. I'll have it notarised. Whatever you think may come out on those tapes, it cannot possibly be worse than—jesus, there aren't words to say it. The fear just sits right here and eats at me. I don't know why it's here, when I wake up, when I sleep. I want it to go away. Maybe the tapes will make it go away for other people, too. It's worth a shot, isn't it? Stanley, I'm weighing forty years of fear against your argument, and you come out on the short end.

"Stanley," she said very quietly when he did not answer,

49

"regardless of anything else, I'm going to keep talking, and the next therapist may not have your expertise—or ethics."

"We'll go on, then," he said, "but I want you to know I'm wiling to stop anytime you are."

"We've got to hang up now, Stanley, or we'll be late for a business meeting. You mustn't worry so much. We'll be fine."

In spite of the May humidity that had seeped into Protective Services that morning, he drank his tea at break time, hot and steaming with two slices of lemon. The journal pages the woman had given him in yesterday's session warranted something warming.

Fragmentary pieces of time are coming back along with that old "catch yourself before you fall" feeling. That's as far as my mind will take me, only into, never beyond those little flicks of acknowledgement. I feel sometimes as if my head is going somewhere without me. The shadows tonight, the odd sounds in this house, are frightening.

My daughter Page loves shopping, with the enthusiasm of her fourteen years. It's an effort to block the fear long enough to pick her up from her father's house. I make excuses not to and feel guilty, but I'm scared to go outside this house.

Perhaps I should tell you. It probably doesn't mean anything but lately I've been hearing more than one thought in my head at a time. Perhaps I'm only talking to myself, but that name "Miss Wonderful" keeps popping up. Now there are other names.

Probably it's only my imagination. Or maybe before the gods drive you mad, they give you mind games to play. I hate games. The stepfather used to summon me and before I learned better, I used to obey. "Come and play," he'd say, "see the new game, little one?" He played games, the stepfather, long before I saw him starting out over the fields during the hunting season with the rifle in the crook of his arm, to shoot down the wild animals and skin and hang them in the barn. The animals he didn't shoot, he trapped and tortured. The acts aren't clear, only his expression as he did it. Before that, I didn't know how dangerous a man he was, or what an intense interest he took in the games. On looking back, he seemed an average adult when I was two, very tall, dark, crew-cut, burly; a man whose eyes

50

held tiny yellow lights when I got angry and refused him something. I don't recall his anger when I was small, just his ability to arouse curiosity in me.

Movement. I hate movement. Slow, from side to side, stop. Then start again. That thing. Curiosity. Touch it. I can recall the feel of it, the wiry hair around it, more than the thing itself. The picture fades then, grows bright for a moment, dims. The action is never clear.

Adding up the few memories of childhood that are here, the extreme panic doesn't make sense. Marriage was the same, Stanley. You want details. All I've got are vagaries, dim notions that I just couldn't be good all the time, either as a child or an adult afterward.

I seem to have done everything I ever put my mind to, even diametrically opposing things like art and math, at which I still believe myself to be inept. But I never should have gotten married. Norman's marriage to me was like a single piece of music that flits from a waltz to a disco beat, from that to a square dance, then roars into Ringo Starr on the drums and lo and behold, a Concerto in E-flat Major; a constant shock to all concerned. In trying to sort out emotions during that relationship, I discovered there weren't any. And for every statement I make to you, pointing out that or any viewpoint, I can give you twenty more, all in conflict with each other. They all belong to me and none of them belongs to me.

For that last statement alone, Stanley, the mother would have had me committed to hell. She always said that a person should take responsibility for her own actions.

Anyway, there I was, married, trying to be nice all the time because having watched the mother and the stepfather all those years, it seemed wiser to be the opposite of what they had been, what they believed me to be. Regardless, after years of single life, I hated being locked up with Norman. My niceness faded with the approaching birth of our child. Pregnancy made me feel dirty, as if I'd committed a sin. At the first sign, I hid myself inside the apartment in a voluminous white robe. It had been part of the trousseau, purchased to convince myself that I was passably attractive, and I wore it night and day to cover the biggest flaw of all.

Fear grew the moment that wedding ring went on. Hiding began to consume me. In stores, on the street, I stared straight ahead, looking neither left nor right, quaking when someone called my name. What did they want from me, what had I done wrong? For the first two years I shook all the time. I finally got angry and figured out what was wrong. I was bad, plain and simple. After all, Norman was a wonderful man, we had a beautiful child, everything in the world that others wanted, we had. I wasn't happy because I was bad.

Our daughter Page was born incredibly perfect and something incomprehensible tried to nestle inside me when I admired her. I wanted no part of whatever it was; she cooed, my mind shut off.

I was so preoccupied with my badness for those two years, that I'd forgotten I was ugly. I remembered and the tantrums began; I couldn't go near Norman. I smashed things and said things so mean and hurtful to him, about my concept of marriage, family life, about myself and the way I hated everyone. There were little flicks of time when everything was black—no vision, lost time, disorientation—but it didn't seem real and neither did I, nor did the doctors who couldn't find the problem. I slept a lot, Norman stopped talking to me. There was no way of telling what stray word might set me off. I raged when awake, needing to be more than an imperfect wife. One minute I was convinced that given the chance I could conquer the world, the next minute I was cowering in the apartment, doors locked.

Page and I went on picnics and stole flowers from a nearby park. The flowers reminded me of my mother; I hated them but for some reason felt it very important that Page see and touch beauty. All the while, some perversity, some ancient hope, ground at me. I cherished her individuality, that spark of independence no child should lose to life's restrictions and parameters. I went against Norman's wishes. I couldn't, wouldn't, train her to bow to discipline and respect us as parents, simply because we were.

Norman wanted her neat. Neat? I hoped she'd be herself—beautiful, free, sure of her own worth. And I kicked away stirrings inside myself. I liked her, so what? Other mothers spoke as if they'd invented the feelings I could not in all honesty say were mine. All I knew was that my ears ached whenever I looked at her.

The blackouts got worse. Right after the last one when they gave me the Dilantin, Norman and I really got into it. He was, as I have said, a quiet, kind man, and thoughtful, but he also had limits and I reached them one night, over something. He got up from the kitchen table, came at me, backed me up against the wall. In that instant when he lunged, glared at me with his face almost touching mine, I cannot tell you exactly what happened in my head. It was as if someone had taken it from me, bent it out of shape. It wasn't me anymore, it was as if I had been invaded.

I howled like some demented animal, waiting for the blow; childhood sat in front of me. A sound started in my throat. The sound grew, not so much in volume as in intensity, and reminded me of an animal, a small one, trapped and in pain. I was unable to stop that sound, couldn't really be making it, but it went on and on. Norman talked to me with a stunned expression and told me I was frothing at the mouth. Without touching me, he sat back down at the table and didn't say a word. The calmness of his reaction brought me out of whatever it had been, as though it had never happened.

So much for the marriage, Stanley. Not even that analyst helped. I left Norman. I left Page with him. I wasn't sure, you see, that I would be wise enough to choose a man after Norman who wouldn't try with Page what the stepfather had with me. That one idea was paramount in my mind but of course there were others—my anger and inability to do things right, to be a proper mother. For a number of years before the marriage broke up, I couldn't even undress in front of Norman, the idea of sexual interaction between us made me ill. More than that, I felt repulsed, angry, scared. It was no atmosphere in which to bring up a child, to taint that child with my own . . . Stanley, I don't even have a word for it.

Nothing has changed, nothing makes any sense. I look at Page and can't believe she's real, and don't know what I mean by that. I look at the paintings hanging on the walls here in this house and people tell me I painted them. I can't believe they ever came into existence. I look at me when I can bear it—I'll never be real, Stanley.

People at times tell me very pleasant things about myself. I find it all incomprehensible. I have no idea, for example, how I passed that four-hour real estate exam in forty minutes. I'm not that smart.

Stanley laid down the pages and called Jeannie Lawson.

"Help," he said, "right now before these incongruities all meld back together in my mind. I talked to the woman just minutes before I read these journal notes. She sounded very sure of herself and shoved me off the phone because she was about to leave for a business meeting. There wasn't a shred of fear in her voice. Yet in the notes, she's scared to leave the house. She also tells me that she has only a few sexual memories and they concern her stepfather. I have yet to hear her mention a direct sexual encounter with her ex-husband, yet in the notes, she refers to pregnancy as being dirty, a sin, a flaw."

"Journal notes." Jeannie hesitated a moment. "Are they hand-written?"

"No. She types everything out before she gives it to me."

"That's why everything melds together," Jeannie said. "If you were reading the journals themselves, you'd probably see the different handwriting styles. I had three."

"The lists," Stanley said. "I never thought about the hand-writing on the lists she took out of her purse. . . ."

Jeannie started to laugh. "I should have saved mine. I could have wallpapered a battleship."

"Who is talking when 'I' is used? Who is talking when 'we' is used?"

"Any other self," Jeannie said, "can use 'I,' and any other self can refer to the group as 'we.' There's a very peculiar period during the 'coming aware' stage, when 'we' is used and yet the other selves really aren't aware, or all that aware in some instances, of each other. It's sort of like a cloud in the sky and you feel moisture on your skin and know it's about to rain. It's that kind of forewarning, I guess. Am I making sense?"

"More than I've made on my own," Stanley told her. "I've been reading up on multiplicity but I have trouble understanding."

"What you're reading has been filtered by an editor, Stanley. I caught things in that videotape that tell me the woman is just like me in some ways, and not at all like me in others. Last week I felt up to reading *Sybil*, and I saw the differences between us. And the similarities."

· · ·

While Stanley dealt with his confusion in his office at Protective Services, the woman arrived across town at her real estate meeting. She was about to experience something for which no amount of prior therapy could have prepared her, even had Stanley been able to predict such occurrences. The woman, after today, would be more conscious of the Troop members' actions, and a very few identities would be revealed to her.

She seated herself between the purchaser and the seller; she identified which attorney belonged to whom and nodded to the settlement attorney. Instantly, time seemed to be going somewhere without her. She became aware that she had two cigarettes burning in the same ashtray in front of her, and that in her mind there was an awful lot of hilarity going on. Not only was there hilarity, there was tension, anger, distress, a feeling of inadequacy and an ego that knew no bounds.

One emotion seemed to be erupting over the other. Experiencing the battle and unable to make sense of the reasons for it, the woman knew that something awful was happening. Being suddenly aware that it went on in her own head, because no one else in the room appeared to notice anything, only increased her sense of unreality.

The eighteen-page contracts she had passed around the table became a blur and so did the faces of the men with whom she was dealing. She became dimly aware that someone inside herself observed everything very well, and that the meeting seemed to be going swimmingly. Then the purchaser's attorney, with whom no real estate broker in town could get along, began to gather the contracts and point out items he wanted deleted.

"If you do that," the purchaser told him, "I'm responsible for obtaining sewer and water."

With horror, the woman heard the hilarity inside her mind translated into words, words that were being spoken aloud.

"Lordy," she heard herself say to the purchaser, "I'm ridin' an ass to prayer meetin' tonight."

"What's that supposed to mean?" The attorney glared at her.

"That means," the woman heard herself saying, "that you're an ass and I'm going to pray for you."

The settlement attorney asked if they could continue without the verbal abuse and the purchaser's attorney said something about brokers who talked like snake-oil saleswomen. Eventually, laughter rippled around the table as everyone found themselves in mutual agreement over the contracts. That the strain should be ending, that the settlement would indeed take place, seemed to further aggravate the conflicting emotions inside the woman's head. She experienced a floating sensation as the room shifted. She shifted with it, horrified at her lack of control. From a distance, an overly wide and innocent smile slid onto her face. She heard more laughter, different from the men's. To her right, the seller's face wore a look of amazement. He steadied himself and glanced down at the blond head resting comfortably on his shoulder.

The Buffer moved aside then, but not completely, as Miss Wonderful smiled, wide-eyed, at every man at the table.

"Isn't that lovely?" she asked.

In her air-conditioned car a scant six minutes later, the woman's face was still red. She had to think of that blond head on the seller's shoulder as her own. Who else's could it have been?

The woman had just experienced and would continue to experience what only years of therapy would finally make sense of: during the meeting, Miss Wonderful had only made the woman "acutely aware" of her presence. Miss Wonderful and another Troop member were about to receive their signal from the Gatekeeper and "evidence" themselves.

Unlike other Troop members, the Outrider might consult and make mutually agreed concessions with the Gatekeeper, but she needed no signal to do anything. Part of her job was keeping sadness away and to do that, she had to be "around," or at least available most of the time.

The Outrider's voice in the woman's mind, as the car swung into heavy noontime traffic, was firm but only a voice.

Move over, I'm driving.

The woman refused to acknowledge the voice. Still embarrassed and more than a little scared, her hands on the steering wheel shook. Midway to the first intersection, she had to admit that somehow she was not driving. That awareness wasn't strong enough to allow total fright, but she didn't dare let go of the wheel in order to touch the rearview mirror. She wanted to. The adjustment everything seemed to need each time she got into the car, as if her height or posture had changed . . .

The Outrider reached out and turned on the car radio. The Pointer Sisters' "Slow Hand" began to play. As that song drifted into the wilder beat of Joe Walsh's "All Night Long," she smiled and turned the volume up louder. The music swept into the woman's mind, where she was making frightening connections:

careless hands on the wheel, cigarette dangling from restless, tapping fingers, the car shooting through traffic from one lane to the other although she always drove without changing lanes. The actions weren't her own.

With awareness still at a low ebb, the woman had no idea that the roads and landmarks were suddenly unfamiliar because the Outrider was in command. When the car pulled up at a traffic light, the woman looked out. She could not get her bearings. Reflected in the rearview mirror, the face of the driver in the car behind hers was familiar and ugly.

Now, said the Gatekeeper, and the Outrider loosened a soft rain of confetti into the dark Tunnel of the woman's mind. The stepfather's face came fully to her, but in shreds. And even in shreds it was too much.

The woman began to cry but the tears were already drying, as if wiped away by an unseen hand. Needles, a numbing, thousand pinpricks, the kind that accompanied heavy anesthesia, stung her arms.

The Outrider turned the volume up again. Time became strangely elongated. The watch on the woman's wrist was no help at all; it had stopped a moment ago. The music crashed in her ears while something pushed at the walls of her mind. At first she did not understand; when she did, the panic hit. The song, "All Night Long," even the longest version any radio station played, should have ended. In that moment, the woman knew, without knowing how or why, that someone's sense of time was different from her own. There came the sound of laughter. The Outrider went on as she had been, snapping her fingers to the rhythm, snake-level, belly-low, eyes shining, and she savoured her stretched-out sense of time.

The woman dared savour it, too, as she felt the Outrider's laughter and wanted to believe it was her own.

The Outrider vanished of her own accord. As the Buffer moved back in and immediately moved over, Miss Wonderful took her place. Happiness came in a flood, so excruciating that the woman wondered if her mind had snapped. A smile washed over her face in a giant wave. The smile obliterated all sexuality. With sexuality gone, so was the fear the woman had felt all her life.

Miss Wonderful had just evidenced her full self. It was all that she was, the complete absence of "bad." But there were two people in the car with the woman. The other began to evidence himself until, as with Miss Wonderful, the woman knew without knowing how, his name and his feelings.

They were both wrapping the full being of themselves around the woman, they were both inside now, more "her" than she had ever been. Yet they were separate from each other, and separate from her. Miss Wonderful's laughter flowed, right over the loud, intrusive music. The male presence exuded just that: maleness.

"Home," the woman said faintly.

No, Miss Wonderful said. *We've been good. Coffee. It's a treat and we deserve it, don't you think?*

The woman considered that as the car slid without her help through the next intersection. Miss Wonderful had made an ass of her in the meeting. But at the same time, the woman understood that Miss Wonderful didn't know what she'd done, she had no concept of anything but complete innocence.

Mean Joe did. Gigantic and quietly powerful, his presence was distinctly protective. As he continued to wrap himself lightly around the woman, she felt safe and trusted him immediately, without question.

Coffee. Miss Wonderful was still pleading. The car swung into the parking lot of 7-Eleven. Unable to lift a finger to prevent or alter a single movement, the woman found herself laughing with the two of them, and saw their reflection in the plate glass storefront as she got out of the car.

[She would tell Stanley in a session later that the "persons" reflected, advanced on the carry-out store with an unfamiliar stride; shambling, then perky; heavy, then lightfooted. The reflection was that of herself, then Miss Wonderful, and then Mean Joe. All separately. But together. She would tell Stanley that somehow they'd both made themselves instantly understandable to her as people, even if their reasons for being were a complete mystery.]

The 7-Eleven was crowded with noontime customers. She felt uneasy, going in with Mean Joe and Miss Wonderful and hesitated, sharing their laughter inside her mind. Mean Joe did not hesitate, he strode right in among the shoppers. Miss Wonderful headed straight for the coffee machine. Her smile to the cashier as she paid for her purchase was ecstatic. Mean Joe stood by her side, hands in his pockets, shoulders hunched, deadly quiet. He did not look up. He looked only from side to side and his eyes were slanted and knowing. The woman felt his simmering anger and sense of purpose.

Let somebody come near us, he was thinking. *Let somebody touch us, let 'em try.*

It was the first time the woman had gone into any public place without cringing, without being terribly frightened.

She didn't notice the strangest thing of all about Mean Joe. She did note how easily he and Miss Wonderful became friends during the short drive back home. Their conversation made her laugh but while going up the muddy driveway to the house, Mean Joe and Miss Wonderful exchanged their own thoughts and excluded her.

The 7-Eleven coffee cup sat on her desk in the gallery, along with the manuscript pages. Sunlight slanted through the floor-to-ceiling windows. It shot the gallery walls with long, thin shadows from the hanging ferns, and when the ferns moved in the breeze, the shadows moved, too. The woman shivered and flung the drapes shut. She took her turn at sipping the black coffee and placed herself at the typewriter, feeling words pour out from many sources to the fingers floating on the keys.

Miss Wonderful seemed such a fragile wisp and Mean Joe a removed, hulking, and ominous man with slanty eyes and the faint curve of a smile at the corners of his mouth. Their hold on the woman was not so much strong, as definite.

The room had grown darker, suddenly. The sound of spring rain beat against the gallery windows. Where had they come from, Miss Wonderful and Mean Joe, and where had they gone, just now? Shaken at being released from their grip, she wondered what to do. The next session with Stanley was so close, it would be silly to call him, and Sharon wouldn't believe a word of it. Someone reached out then and gathered the woman up as if in a warm blanket, for she had begun to travel a very lonely road.

7

In the woman's mind that night but separate and apart from it, a conversation took place.

Any Troop member who wanted to be a part-time Front Runner first had to travel with the Outrider, absorbing a working familiarity with the safety mechanism. So now as the Outrider monitored through the Buffer and the Front Runner, whatever reached the woman, a smaller Troop member sat, listening attentively and hoping one day to be chosen. She was only twelve years old, so there was a lot going against her. She did, however, have a sharp mind.

Why, *Twelve asked the Outrider,* do we have to be so careful, why can't we all just evidence right now and bring the memories with us?

We can't all do that, *said the Outrider.* Some of us are too damaged. Besides, there's always that dumb but justified word: caution. If we make a mistake, there's a lot to lose.

Ah, *said Twelve, beginning to see with an agile mind, far beyond the Outrider's words,* there are plans?

To be sure, *said the Outrider, smiling as her words bent suddenly under the cadence of the one who lived in the deepest part of the Tunnel. The Outrider knew he loved children. Twelve was still a child and possessed of what he treasured most—a flying mind.*

In every battle, *the Outrider continued in the borrowed ca-*

dence, there is something new to be learned; skills to be gained. This battle is no different. The soldiers tremble but they take up the sword and go. The woman, as well.

The woman is a Troop member then, *said Twelve, grasping the heart of the matter.*

This is true, *said the Outrider,* and her construction, irreversible as it is, was very necessary at the time of her birth among us. For this battle that construction will stand her in good stead. Do you see, now?

Twelve shivered. I see, but not alone. Someone is telling me. I feel cold.

Yes, *said the Outrider.* There are two cold places for us that we know of. One is the Well, a thing of this earth, this time. Olivia lives there—if it can be called that—and when she speaks, one grows cold with listening. The other place is not of this earth or of this time; its coldness comes from the one who lives in the furthermost reaches of the Tunnel.

I know and I'm scared, *said Twelve.*

No need. *Still the borrowed cadence beat, but with wings now giant and dark, on the Outrider's words.* He, too, is protection, although no man may say how.

On hearing Twelve's fright, the one who spoke through the Outrider prepared to come forward and calm her fears. As he readied himself, Twelve received his messages, a flurry of them, from the furthermost reaches of the Tunnel. Her head whirled, trying to keep pace.

You're saying a thousand things at once, *Twelve protested.*

Easy, *said the Outrider, feeling herself fading away and the reins being taken from her grasp. The one in the Tunnel held the reins now and his hold was firm. Twelve received his name and knew that if she said it aloud before it was safe, she would never be a Front Runner. His voice as he spoke held a slight brogue that Twelve did not feel was "borrowed" at all.*

Lay aside the fear and listen, *he said to her.* Take one lesson at a time or you will be lost. At this moment you must know, if you are ever to be a Front Runner, that because we are many, things happen to us in great numbers, all at one time. Sanity lies in separating those things, in dealing with them individually. Know now that there are those among us, calling out to be heard. They are small, helpless, dead ones—someone must listen to their voices.

The woman? *Twelve's eyes were wide with shock.*

Child, there are no lesser ones here. There are only different beings. *Suddenly, the brogue flourished heavily in every word as if he who spoke had thrown off all attempts at disguise.* The woman does n' feel pain now. The lack o' it is part o' somethin' planned a long time ago. But she will feel the memories we'll be bringin' t' her. When the time comes for our battle, the memories'll be the armour, and they'll be pain enough.

Twelve absorbed it, but she had done even more. Acceptance of what she knew now was not the Outrider, but the one who lived far back in the Tunnel, rode in her young eyes.

This person who is speaking, *said Twelve with great politeness,* is he the head of our Troop Formation?

Some say that it is so. *There was a smile beneath the brogue.* But there be no competition here. T'a man, we are equal as individuals. No one o' us could stand without the others; and even i' we could, we would n' want to.

Something awful occurred to Twelve. She had to ask because what she was receiving from this person who had replaced the Outrider was so peculiar, so all encompassing, so terribly without end, without beginning.

Are you what they call god?

No, darlin'. *The brogue was rich and the smile had widened to its fullest point.* Believe as y' will, but god, if he be a'tal, is not a single, far-off entity teachin' through fear those less than he be. There is nothin' t' teach. The knowledge is already inside each man on earth, merely waitin' t' be tapped.

Are you that knowledge?

Aye. Some say that it is so.

My god, *said Twelve.* What an enormous ego you have.

Aye. This is true. But I am no more than every man himself possesses. Therefore, I do not strut my ego. I merely use it.

Anne Dun from Protective Services, who accompanied Stanley, had a very nice but worn smile and soft brown eyes.

"It's very nice of you to do this," she said.

"I don't mind," the woman told her. She felt curiously adolescent, unperturbed, studying the precinct house. Captain Albert Johnson's domain was neat as a pin and the floors, big black and white linoleum squares, glowed with wax.

"If Stanley's videotape hadn't been so full of static, you could be home right now. If these police officers don't seem to be listening, don't take offense. They never listen. They answer phones, spit on the floor, and sleep during these presentations, but they seldom listen.''

Stanley walked on the woman's right, Anne Dun on her left. The room they went into was huge, with row after row of desks, and just as neat as the outside hallway. The men and women in uniform were neat, too. The woman felt it again, that curious adolescent bravado . . . the urge to giggle. Stanley's tape recorder got plugged in right away and he sat down next to her. The woman hated her own chair but had no choice.

Anne Dun didn't wait for silence to introduce them. Stanley was known by practically every officer in the room. The woman was not. After Stanley's brief remarks, she began to speak. Then that twelve-year-old feeling got very strong. There were times when her voice broke, times when the words seemed to tumble over each other. There was also the feeling of being removed. After a while, the collar of her blouse lay against her throat, sopping wet. In the back of the room, an officer felt the hair on the back of his neck rising.

"You ever heard a rabbit die?" he asked his partner. "The sound she's making. That's it.''

For an hour and fifteen minutes, there had not been a sound from any officer in the room. If anyone had spit on the floor, Anne Dun had not noticed.

The woman looked up to find an officer standing in front of her. His hair was snow white and his uniform crisp and straining against his chest. "Captain Albert Johnson,'' he said. "Friend of Stanley's. I always wondered, lady, why some people had to go through shit. Now I know. You gave me more today than I ever wanted to have, but I'll use it. You got guts.''

"That," said Anne Dun at the woman's elbow, "was high praise.''

Stanley smiled to himself. After today, all of Albert's officers not only knew for sure that two-year-olds could be raped, they knew exactly what the experience was like.

The woman went out to dinner that night, perplexed over what Anne Dun had said about the videotape. She would have to remember to ask Stanley why the tape had been scratchy. When she recorded notes at home, they were full of static. Even brand-new batteries and then a new tape recorder hadn't helped.

She stood just inside the restaurant door until the owner spotted her and led her to Morgan's table.

"You really didn't recognise my voice on the phone."

Morgan smelled of an exotic, male cologne. The sounds in the restaurant were muted, the lighting subdued, and the woman did not reply immediately. She was watching the blurred and shifting reflections of him in cutlery and crystal. Her mind shifted too, not a jarring motion, but rather like a car changing gears, smooth—except that she felt it strongly and wondered why it was happening.

Morgan waited for an answer. Under the table his knee pressed against hers; the Outrider smiled and pressed back.

"We speak to so many people on the phone all day long," she said, "that I have a tendency to become confused."

"Did you miss me?" he asked.

"Terribly. Your eyes are beautiful."

The Outrider spoke the words. The woman heard them and marvelled at the audacity. A sinking sensation ballooned inside and Morgan gradually came into better focus. During the last part of Morgan's phone call tonight, the sinking sensation had begun as she bathed hurriedly with uncommon euphoria, wondering at the transformation of her face. The excitement of feeling beautiful was now at peak force.

Dessert arrived. Orange peel held aloft by a serious waiter was drizzled with brandy and set afire. Spoon by spoon, mouthfuls of incredibly tangy-tart, bitter-sweet coolness, quivered down Catherine's throat. Catherine never surfaced in the Outrider's slum bars. But this was the elegant black and white decor, the mirrored walls and magnificent ambiance of "Churchill's," and well worth Catherine's time.

From a great distance the woman assumed that both the sensation of feeling beautiful and the words were her own. How much there was to say to Morgan on diverse subjects and how erudite she'd become!

Overnight, as it were.

The Outrider was making a joke but now the woman believed she had a sense of humour, too.

Later, in Morgan's apartment, the thousand startled reflections in the mirrored walls of the bathroom were unfamiliar to the woman. Again, there came a slight shifting and gradually, as if someone poured recognition into her brain, the room didn't seem strange at all. The voices were starting, though.

To hell with it, Nails said. *We survived before being dependent on Stanley and will again.*

64

The woman turned on the hot water faucet and began scrubbing her hands, hearing vaguely thoughts from a source she could not define.

I don't want to just "survive" any more. The voice of a twelve-year-old girl came from too far away and she sounded sad. *Besides, how much longer do we have before we start throwing things at Morgan and eventually drive him away?*

Lady Catherine Tissieu was appalled at the thought of anyone throwing anything at Morgan. Her nose went into the air. *Who would dare?*

We would. The Outrider grinned. She directed her words to no one in particular. *Every time we get into a relationship you think: It won't happen this time. This time I'll be good. But all it takes to start one of us ranting is the right word: family, church, religion, love—and somebody trying to force those things on us. Or the expressions "You will," "You should," "You must." That's all. Never learn, do you?*

Shut up. Bickering, bored Nails.

Morgan had the brandy poured and a hand of cards dealt when she came out of the bathroom, smelling soapy and looking damp. A game now and then relaxed him after a hectic day of dealing with his investors and their banks and everybody's idiosyncrasies. She was a strange card player. At times he doubted if she knew the difference between a three of clubs and the ace of spades because occasionally she still asked him, in a childlike voice. It had taken him eight games to teach her the intricacies of gin rummy. After that, she'd refused his instruction, insisting that she wanted to play it her own way. Since then, he'd lost regularly. What he didn't know was that while she wouldn't dream of cheating him, winning meant a lot to her and so she was employing a rather strong method.

The cards Morgan held were irrelevant—she concentrated on her own and what she needed to win. She did not understand how her "method" worked, nor did she truly believe that winning stemmed from that method. Had she been aware of it, she would have accepted even less, how little of the "method" was her own doing. All she knew was that she could stay his hand from the row of discards and direct it back to the face-down deck, so often that it amazed her. She could "visualise" whatever card she wanted him to throw; visualise it so often that it made her laugh.

He wound up, each time, fuming and incredulous at her

"luck" and stung by the smile she'd give him while tallying the score.

"How do you do that?" he asked, keeping the edge from his voice.

"I don't know," she said. "Or maybe I do but you wouldn't believe it."

"How much do I owe you?" Morgan ignored her statement because it was oblique and he didn't want to pursue it. Losing for the fourth time that night had irritated him more than he could admit.

"Can we take it out in trade?"

Morgan discovered that she was looking at him with the expression he'd found so disconcerting at dinner. It hadn't been what he expected of a woman in a public restaurant. But then she'd been a chain of surprises during the meal, drifting from the slightly puzzled, uncertain woman who sat down to dinner with him, to a witty conversationalist who moved with ease from reserved and rather dense, to sophisticated and urbane—to what he could only term "lewd"—the same look he was getting now.

He thought there had been other changes during the meal and the ride home, yet they'd been so subtle he couldn't be sure. How long had he known her now? This was probably the most time they'd ever spent together. All he was certain of at the moment was the narrow, slitted look she threw him over her shoulder as she headed for the bedroom. He followed.

After a very long while, the woman became aware that Morgan sounded like a balloon with a slow leak. His body had sunk gradually onto her own. She rolled to one side.

She could not ever recall studying a man's buttocks this way, revelling in the artistry of their contour. Morgan himself had been frightening from the first time she'd found herself in bed with him—a blank spot nagged her; she couldn't get past it. She started turning their relationship around, as if trying to find meaning in it, and find herself, too. All she found was the silence of the quiet, high-rise apartment and the navy blue sheets beneath her. She did not understand that for her, there hadn't been any more. Then or now.

The Buffer moved over completely. Ten-Four lay on the bed and counted her gains. By observing Morgan in action, her methods of negotiating had improved to the point where it astounded even herself. Ten-Four found Morgan's brain fasci-

66

nating. She wanted to snatch his mind from him and graft it onto her own.

Catherine, meanwhile, sighed in satisfaction. Morgan's bone structure, the way the flesh lay over those bones, intrigued both her artistic and practical sense. Morgan, Catherine had decided months ago, was no mere pretender to power. She'd gravitated to him from that point on, because something told her that she was very much like him, and that Morgan was therefore no threat whatever. He might have been if she'd desired marriage, but Catherine believed that marriage was a wasteland where a woman's mind was put on simmer until she gathered up her brains and finally divorced. What Catherine had wanted from Morgan was a man who looked marvelous in public, a little romance, a little ambiance—and to learn the skill of convincing people that she was invincible.

Invincible. Power. The words entered the woman's mind as the Buffer moved back in. The mother had had power over her a long time ago. Stanley hinted that she still did.

Yes, said a distant, younger voice than her own—*mother.* "I've got to teach you right from wrong. Pay attention: nice girls don't wear shorts, look at boys, think about sex, read bad books. They don't kiss, hug, touch boys on dates. Don't ever let a boy touch you, they only want one thing. Do you hear me?"

I heard her, the voice went on. "I'm your mother, you belong to me, you owe me the breath of life, you owe me everything."

Bull, Nails said. *Nobody believed any of that garbage.*

If nobody believed it, the Outrider grinned, *why did the fright keep growing? Why are we so mistrustful of all people and why weren't some of us, tonight, conscious of the sex act?*

[Stanley would ask months later how it was possible for the Troops not to know of each other's existence all these years when obviously they could, at times, talk to each other. The Interpreter would tell him that the Troop members had been speaking but not to each other. "It's a matter of thought transference, Stanley. We could hear each other's thoughts sometimes and didn't know where they were coming from. The woman, when she could hear them, simply believed they were her own."]

The woman wanted to get up from the bed and go to the bathroom, but an odd force pinned her next to Morgan. The voices became relentless. Somehow, one of them was directed at her.

Yes, this is a relationship. Morgan doesn't know how strange it really is, and neither do you. For you, there isn't any more.

The thoughts were in her mind, she had to be thinking them. Yet she knew that they never got inside her mind at all, were simply almost visible tonight, hanging outside some kind of peripheral sight that didn't belong to her, either.

Hey. Think about it. Morgan's strength lies within himself, not in his being strong enough to take something away from you. What is it that Morgan doesn't do, that makes you feel safe with him? It should be so obvious. What is it that makes Morgan so unlike the stepfather?

The woman's throat closed, the room seemed to tilt. Morgan reached out and pulled her closer. Staring at him in the semi-darkness, she felt something wet on her cheeks and tasted it. It was salty.

8

In Howard Johnson's, Ten-Four took a booth because the counter was crowded and she liked sitting alone. The breakfast she ordered was huge and appropriate. Within the hour she'd be walking lots, a term used by land brokers, meaning that you put on boots, gathered up the profit figures, and drove to the site. Usually the builder or the developer met you there and eyeballed the land from his truck. After making certain that you had spent weeks putting it together, he ignored the data. He either fell in love with the tract at first glance or he didn't.

Ten-Four had been the one to decide, after the required three-year stint as an agent, to open a company devoted to land and commercial real estate. She revelled in strolling an untouched piece of ground, of matching it up with the right buyer.

Today she was meeting one of the toughest builders in the metropolitan area. He might be cranky and eccentric, but he knew raw land and he called her the "land hawk."

The woman sat, fork poised over a plate of eggs, as Ten-Four's thoughts leaked into her mind. On her own, without Ten-Four "leaking through," the woman had no concept of real estate. For one peculiar instant, she compared her vast stretch of relatively empty mind—with what had to be someone else's very full mind.

She laid down the fork because her hand shook, and carefully removed the red journal from her purse. Red was hateful, a reminder of something unpleasant—she couldn't recall what. But she supposed that red did make the journal easier to find among the purse's scrambled contents. So many things got lost. Sometimes lost articles reappeared in strange places, sometimes she never saw them again.

She struggled to write down what she had just experienced, but sensed that another mind, not Ten-Four's this time, was doing the thinking and figuring for her—and that this wasn't the first time. Could that be? And was that her question or someone else's? For one tiny moment, the woman knew she wasn't a broker. What was she?

A humming began in her head, so strange, that she only wanted to get outside in the air, fast. She attacked her food quickly, because leaving food on one's plate had always made the mother angry. Why didn't the food she had just put into her mouth create a full sensation?

"For you, there isn't any more . . . ," the phrase she'd heard last night in the bedroom with Morgan, and denied so quickly, came back, as if in answer to her silent question. She faced the words. Somehow, they were related to the food and a lot more—to her life, to the relationship with Morgan, if that's what it was. Other women wanted husbands and children, someone to love them through life's happiness and trauma. What did she want? Nothing and nobody. With a mind so empty, and being constantly scared, nobody could want her.

The voice came as she paid the check and again as she got into the car: *For you, there isn't any more.* The phrase couldn't mean anything, but hearing voices had to mean she was crazy. One of these days, if she hadn't already, she would fall to pieces.

The humming inside her head increased; she drove and a shower of flicks began: tiny glimpses of the farm—trees, grass, the coolness of lemonade on a hot summer day, a fragment of someone's naked flesh, the smell of the stepfather's hot, sweaty body.

She needed to stay calm for the meeting. The builder was probably standing on the lots right now, impatient and angry. The car radio blared Fleetwood Mac's "Sarah," and the music scattered the flicks. The music wound itself around her mind; so did the knowledge that she wasn't alone in the car.

Two unseen children were about to make the woman "acutely aware," not of their ages, or physical characteristics, but rather their human emotions. The woman's awareness grew stronger as the car neared the crossroad and turned toward the remote countryside. Composure fled as the unfamiliar term "flatbed car" shot out of nowhere. The presence beside her was as real as the music. It cried and wiped its nose with the back of its hand. Another presence wiped its eyes with the hem of the woman's skirt.

She managed to determine that neither could be flesh and blood, but only the materialisation in the form of two unseen entities. The flicks had stopped whirling around like confetti. They'd merged, until a small but complete picture formed, of a flatbed car with rusted wheels and the wood of the body so old and weather-beaten that it must have been parked by the farm's hedgerow for years. The two tiny presences in the car beside her were crying louder at the image of the flatbed car. They seemed so afraid of the dark place under it. The picture faded. [The woman would not remember it or connect it to anything in her past for months to come.]

Another image came, an image she did remember and could connect to the past. The stepfather stood in front of the barn door, watching the first raindrops fall. Pitch-black thunderheads rolled across the afternoon sky. There was the sound of what? A zipper, opening. It was similar to the sound she heard each night, grinding her teeth through her nightmares.

The stepfather had something in his hand. Yes, it had definitely been the sound of a zipper, opening.

The small presence who had wiped her nose with the woman's skirt hem began to cry and then to moan. The sound grew into a howl, long and high and lost.

Ten-Four and Nails showed the lots to the builder that morning. When either of them became too tense or abrupt, as was their nature, the Outrider stepped in with a joke. They showed the lots and Catherine drifted in her own head, mentally designing houses and arranging floor plans with hidden escapes, private retreats. She designed, not according to building codes, but for safety from human predators. Some designs were hers, many came from the Troop members who lived behind her, ones who had never seen the light of day as it filtered through the tall trees over her head, and dappled the grass and stones at her feet.

Later that morning, the woman got out of her car only because the motor seemed to be shut off. With barely a sense of having been anywhere, she walked up the driveway to her house, placing one foot mechanically ahead of the other. The feet performing the zombie-like act did not seem to be her own. They moved mindlessly, as if getting there was all that mattered.

Once inside her house she bolted the door and headed to the powder room just off the foyer. The powder room, with all four walls of solid red brick, rose straight into the air, two stories above her head, where the walls met solid brick ceiling. The door was solid brick. The woman stood at the sink counter, washed her hands, and admired the hanging ferns suspended from the specially lighted ceiling high above. She felt very comfortable here, and safe. She even admired the framed lyrics from the song "Night Moves" hanging over the toilet, although she couldn't appreciate the humour of it and did not know where it had come from.

Catherine, who had designed that room for security, smiled into the mirror now. Unlike the toilet facilities at the farmhouse, this narrow powder room did not have a single chink in the walls. She knew because she'd personally supervised with the mason the laying of every brick.

Catherine looked with approval at her reflection in the mirror and shook her hair back over her eyes. Very nice. Lovely, in fact. But one had to keep at it or things atrophied. She strode out of the powder room and stopped to admire the foyer. She had chosen much of the furniture and wall hangings in the house. She had not chosen the single canvas hanging on the two-story brick column formed by the powder room.

This was a long, skinny composition; its component parts assaulted the eye and snapped the senses to attention. Glued-on string, hanks of rope, strips of old rags, twigs, coffee grounds, and dental floss covered it from top to bottom. It had been sprayed in white lacquer and, in spite of its contents, echoed forcefully against the rough texture of the bricks. Someone had thought the collage important enough to have installed a single track light that beamed down its full length.

Catherine admired it as a decorator's touch on an otherwise barren wall. Only the artist could admire its statement or the truth behind it [and that Troop member would not reveal himself for many months to come].

Intent on the manuscript, Catherine turned away. The stark white collage was no longer her focal point and the woman was able to surface. Each time she passed by the collage, she got an instant flick of hands, covered in a thick white substance, trailing

72

string and laying down odd bits of twigs and twine. That was all. She tried never to look at it. It was only a collection of junk.

The collage was bothering someone. There came a soft, low sobbing, as if a small child sat in a corner somewhere, awaiting punishment or witnessing some awful thing.

Hide. Pull everything down on top of you and hide. Both the small voice and her easy acceptance of the two unseen entities lay on one level of the woman's mind. On yet another level, that acceptance was directly opposed by hysteria over what Stanley might say and do when she told him. Curiously, the hysteria seemed dead-ended by the same mechanical movements ruling her feet. She plodded back to the gallery. To the typewriter, sit, switch it on. With no emotion the woman reviewed the manuscript notes: fear of going to the bathroom at home or in school; the eventual outhouse smell of her body as a result; blood all over the bright yellow dress in a coed gym class. None of it seemed real. Staring out of the tightly locked gallery windows into the darkness, the horror behind each of the scribbled notes rapped softly on her mind.

Someone very small cringed and the hem of the woman's skirt twisted. The wind had picked up, and tree limbs clattered against the shingles somewhere at the back of the house. Had the woman still been present, she would have been frightened.

Catherine didn't even notice. The manuscript lay in a snow-drift over the desk and a red oriental rug. Before picking up a single sheet of paper she unfastened the latches on the tall windows and swung them open into the backyard. She inhaled deeply. Fresh air was good for the skin. The smell of raw new earth and approaching rain hung on the incoming spring breeze. Mindful of her polished fingernails, Catherine typed:

The outhouse at the second farm was right off the wash-room that led into the kitchen. Jokes have been made, down through farm history, about outhouses. But they were serious business to the stepfather within the framework of his game plan.

Too early on, I suppose, I decided that his games were not for me and tried to evade him. Whenever he could not physically put his hands on me, he settled for watching. The idea of that was so awful to me that it was a long time before I could allow the strange sensation of being watched to seem even slightly real. But one day I stood inside the outhouse, noticing the slits between some of the panels. Outside, a large, dark shape unflattened itself from the wall and moved away. Curious because I could not believe what I was already thinking, I pressed my face close to the slits and looked out. The stepfather stood there on the garden path; he was grinning and his hands were in his pockets.

Presto. A new game had evolved for him. Eventually, I learned to control my body when he was home. I tried never to go to the bathroom, unless I knew exactly where he was. Sometimes he won. There was an opening beneath the little bench. From the outside the pail could be taken away for emptying. One day I sat down without looking. Something made me get up in a hurry; there was his face when I stared down.

"Gotcha," he said.

I still hate him. It doesn't go away.

A glitter had come into Catherine's eyes as her fingers flew over the keyboard. She was another of the Troop members who could not cry. The glitter increased as she typed, describing family life: the noise of constant battles, the hatred, and both the verbal and unspoken threats of killing. She wrote that sometimes the words hurt as badly as the physical abuse. So had the stepfather's smile when he'd taken off his belt to beat her. All smiles, she added, had henceforth taken on an air of unreality, of insincerity. She'd thought often about knives and shotguns and killing, and about being a boy. Boys didn't sit around, she wrote, with their legs crossed, waiting to be killed.

It annoyed Catherine as the words flew onto the paper, that she couldn't remember the lashings themselves; only her rage and inability to cry. She did recall the marks on her skin afterward, how they'd turned a funny deep blue with little red spots, which had been the pores of her skin, filled with blood.

The rage, she admitted, had been building inside her for years. It had not been confined to the farmhouses, but extended to everything, including school. Some teachers had been nice. She hadn't trusted them and pulled away or watched them suspiciously from a distance, sure that if they got too close, the niceness would change. Some teachers had hated her outright, and in the tiny schoolhouse, in the third grade, she'd bitten one. Furious, the teacher had taken a big piece of chalk and marked all her math answers "Wrong." A senior had stood up in the back of the room and laughed. He went to the blackboard, re-worked the problems, and arrived at Catherine's same answers, asking the teacher if his were wrong, too. Astounded, Catherine heard two separate thoughts in her head: One, she'd been right, and two, someone had defended her.

The woman surfaced with only the Buffer between herself and the typewritten pages. She did not know that she had what Stanley termed almost complete amnesia about her childhood and much of her adult life. Staring at the words the typewriter seemed to be producing, she sensed again the emptiness inside herself.

Why couldn't she remember school or birthdays or more than one or two flashes of Christmas holidays? Why couldn't she remember, more precisely, the family?

Family.

The gallery was dark except for the pale glow from the gooseneck lamp. Someone leaned over and spit on the floor. Someone else made the sign of the cross.

Come morning, the Outrider said to Twelve, *the battle begins.*

9

At dawn the woman awakened at the sound of rain pounding on the skylight. Her eyes focused. What she had first perceived as a dull grey haze filtering into the bedroom now seemed to be an integral part of it. Her mind seemed to be a dull grey, too, and when she shook her head, it didn't go away.

Now, said the Gatekeeper.

The haze remained, in the room and in her mind. She lay between the sheets, a full-grown adult, frightened and wary.

Now, the Gatekeeper said again and it flashed into the woman's mind—this was the way she'd felt as a child at the second farmhouse.

The Gatekeeper gave the third signal. One by one, they began to gather. The woman tried to avoid them by getting up from the bed but the feeling of their presence continued to hang in the dead air. She drew back under the covers, stunned and shaken. Five of them: Rabbit, Ten-Four, Mean Joe, the Zombie, Miss Wonderful. Five separate individuals surrounding her at this moment, crouched around the bed, "crawling" in some indescribable fashion under the sheets with her.

She scrambled for the pad on the nightstand. The pen had disappeared; a box of crayons sat in its place. With trembling hands, she composed a note to Stanley. "Please," she whispered, "let this make sense to him. It makes perfect sense to me and either that means I'm completely crazy, or I'm sane for the first time in my life."

76

Through the fine grey haze, the Gatekeeper watched the woman, carefully. The Gatekeeper knew how many Troop members were in the bedroom. Of the Troops present this morning, the woman had missed far too many. The Gatekeeper considered the process that had given birth to them all as individuals and had kept each one alive. The process, while as natural as breathing, could not easily be described.

The Interpreter, meanwhile, considered that which bothered the Gatekeeper, and finally, with a silent thought, explained the discrepancy: some Troops had only, in weeks past, made the woman "acutely aware" of their presence; they had not yet actually presented by the more potent "evidencing." And the Interpreter added, sometimes Troops might evidence to the woman in tandem, yet still be unknown to each other.

Having read the crayoned note without expression, although it was probably the most difficult thing he'd done in his professional life, Stanley hooked it carefully onto his clipboard.

The woman stared up at him from the bench outside his office, waiting for him to tell her what it meant. He was aware that the contents of the crayoned note could be termed hallucination— and she heard voices. Taken alone and at face value, those two things indicated a break with reality. But Stanley found the woman firmly rooted in reality, no matter how off-the-wall she sounded at times. The trouble with multiplicity, he supposed, was that to an outsider it did sound "crazy." The multiple might look and act, in some cases, like anyone else on the street, but inside the mind, it was another whole ball game. Another form of sanity. He began to comprehend just how scared his client was. What must it be like for a multiple to start making comparisons between the world he or she lived in and what society said was the norm? Especially when everything being experienced was real to the multiple, and so unreal to everyone around them?

"Well," he said. It was all that he could say.

"It happened. Maybe it doesn't belong on the videotapes, but you said you wanted to know everything. What should I do?"

The words were the woman's but the voice belonged to Nails and so did the face and body. Nails sat "up front" as she had from the moment the woman had entered the university grounds. Nails was absorbing from the Buffer the emotional blows the woman took, but only from the furthest distance possible. Nails didn't need to know that she and the woman were separate, or why or how the Troop mechanisms worked. She simply needed to solve a problem voiced by a worry that belonged to almost the entire Troop Formation.

Stanley heard the questions. Today's session and another later in the week would have to be navigated without help. Marshall Fielding would not arrive until the weekend.

"Well," he said, repeating himself without shame. "We'll just have to wait and see."

"No." Again, Nails voiced the woman's words. "I have seen. It was real enough to me. The five of them were there in bed with me this morning. They've been here all week, not flesh and blood, Stanley, but an overpowering presence."

Even as Stanley nodded to show that he understood, he knew that he did not. The woman's amazement at what had happened to her, in days past and this morning, was a direct reflection of his own stupefaction. For the benefit of the video camera he asked for an outline of the early morning experience in the bedroom and the feelings it had produced. Afterward, the questions came faster than he could follow with pen and paper. When he had fielded as many questions as he could, there was a moment of silence.

"You still say I'm not nuts?" Ten-Four's voice was sharp. Ten-Four acted on facts alone and wanted to know beyond any doubt that they were facts and not merely hopeful wishes.

"No. You are not nuts. Incest victims in order to survive the experiences of childhood sometimes live simultaneously in more than one world. We call that fragmentation."

Stanley took a breath and leaned back on his cushions.

"Fragmentation?" Behind Nails and Ten-Four, the woman wondered at the word Stanley had chosen as a stop-gap measure. In actuality what she heard, and even her hesitant acceptance of it, came from Nails and Ten-Four—even as, in the separate minds of all three, no one was conscious of anyone but herself.

The woman's awareness had always been sporadic. Very often it shut off because the thoughts of another Troop member took precedence; at other times the woman's mind shut off because another Troop member was completely present . . . and the woman was gone, vanished.

Right now, the three of them, partially surfaced, stole a look at Stanley. Nails and Ten-Four kept their mouths shut. Stanley was the expert here and they waited for him to produce a satisfactory explanation. He watched the silent figure before him and knew that the word "fragmented" was being poorly received. He found a pair of eyes beneath the fallen bangs and held on. If the conclusions he'd reached were valid, and if the few multiple case histories he'd read were applicable, then anybody could be watching him from behind that barrier.

"Different emotions within you," he said, "emotions you felt must not be expressed for one reason or another, compartmentalised themselves. They are separate from each other and you."

The woman shook her head. "No. Even if it makes me crazy to say it, Stanley, I tell you, they were people!"

He went over in his mind the names on the list she'd given him: Rabbit, Ten-Four, the Zombie, Miss Wonderful, and Mean Joe. They sounded like people and if the names were any indication, people who might have separate, distinct, characteristics. Still hesitant, he tried to give a definition of the term *fragmented*, knowing as he did, that it was a "trash can" term and that he was only biding time by using it.

"Well," he said, "perhaps it felt that way to you. If they were—are—by whatever definition, people, as you call them, that's one thing. More than likely, they're separate emotions which you perceive as separate persons. Each one of them, or rather each emotion, may have lived in its separate compartment all these years, walled off, in a manner of speaking, unaware that there were others. Which may explain why you haven't been aware of them."

Stanley wondered: While attempting to explain "fragmentation," had he just given her a partial definition of multiple personality? In his training as a therapist, Multiple Personality Disorder had been touched on lightly, as an afterthought. It had been regarded as a topic unworthy of full instruction.

"If no one dared to look over his or her individual wall, then how did Mean Joe get into the carry-out store with Miss Wonderful that morning? Have you ever heard of two of them operating in tandem that way?"

The point was legitimate. Neither Stanley nor the woman was familiar enough with the process of multiple personality to have figured out that in therapy, "leakage" occurred after a certain point and to varying degrees. Among the Troop members, only the Gatekeeper had observed through the Interpreter, how the "walls" had been worn away just enough for Miss Wonderful and Mean Joe to break through to each other in the car that day.

Mean Joe had been born of a single-minded purpose, to protect the most vulnerable Troop members. Miss Wonderful's innocence put her at the top of his list, so their instant recognition of each other once their barriers had come down was only natural.

But "leakage" aside, Stanley's small bank of Multiple Personality Disorder information rattled around in his head, incompatible with the image of three separate entities roaming through a 7-Eleven store. Again he came face to face with the term *hallucination*, the perception of sights and sounds that were not actually there. Might it be true that within the realm of multiple personality, the sights and sounds were actually there? He silently cursed Marshall Fielding and whatever was delaying his promised arrival.

"There isn't that much information to go on," Stanley hedged.

"If you'd been in the car with me, if you'd been in the bedroom this morning, it was as if they'd created that grey haze especially for their coming-out party, something to hide in while they made themselves known to me."

The woman's soft, hesitant voice went on, laying out the truth of her own reality, in spite of her dismay and the fear that he would lock her up. It was time, Stanley knew, to define the problem once and for all. She'd come to a point where answers, even harsh ones, would be easier to live with than more unknown terrors. But a premature diagnosis of multiple when the problem might lie elsewhere could damage therapy progress, perhaps irreparably. His job at the moment would be to encourage and help her define her own reality.

"You may be quite right," he said. "Perhaps they are people."

The scene came abruptly but she could not place the incident in time: The breakfast in Howard Johnson's and what had felt like awakening inside somebody else's mind—the awareness that her own mind was empty in comparison. After two false starts, she tried to convey to Stanley exactly what the experience had been like. His face revealed no disbelief, but he didn't understand. Then she saw his willingness to listen and, with no comprehension, to accept what she said as being valid to herself.

Distracted because her head felt bigger than it should (almost as if she were a child carrying an adult's head on her shoulders), the woman attempted to deal with what amazed her so thoroughly: Stanley believed her on faith alone. She reflected and finally, because the patterns were so ingrained, had to regard his faith with high suspicion.

So did Nails and Ten-Four, each one from the seclusion of their individual minds, and each one still unaware of the other. No one present at this moment, except the Gatekeeper, knew how accurately the Interpreter had judged the process this morning: right now, more than three persons hovered around the woman, yet were unaware of her and of each other.

The session had begun on a note of disruption and revelation that continued; memories were dredged up and spewed out in tones of guilt, fear, and heated rage. When pieced together the memories gave Stanley a partial understanding of the woman's childhood—and the reasons why as an adult she avoided human contact. He watched the body, face, and voice switch, in the same smooth meld as in previous sessions, from one attitude to the next. No identities were revealed to him. But he felt more strongly that behind the smooth changes, separate and distinct identities did exist.

Apparently the stepfather's voyeurism had not been confined to the outhouse. He'd managed over the years to watch covertly as the child had bathed in a tin tub in the kitchen; as she changed into a swimsuit at the nearby lake; and even to peer up at her from a filigreed floor register in her bedroom. The child had reacted violently to the invasion of her privacy and had been severely punished by her mother for the resultant "uncontrollable tantrums." Stanley probed, wanting the woman to see whatever feelings her mother's punishment had caused.

Ten-Four's tougher voice replaced the woman's and both were unaware that it had happened. "Hey," Ten-Four said. "It's hard to think mean thoughts about a mother who trimmed the crusts off the bread for your school sandwiches."

Ten-Four told Stanley something else the mother had done, that forever made complaints against her verboten: To earn money for lean winters she had prepared fruit for canning at the adjoining farm. The mother's fingers, numb with cold water and sticky juice, had clutched a paring knife she could barely hold onto.

The bitterly self-protective shrug Stanley saw just then belonged to Ten-Four. "I can't eat canned peaches or apple sauce anymore. I still see her sitting there . . . summer dusk in upper New York State could be very cold, especially when it rained. There'd be water all over the barn floor. The mother would sit

81

with her feet in the water, leaning down into the crates of fruit, bent over in that awful position. She did it to feed us, give us Christmas presents.''

"That's very nice," Stanley said, "but did your mother protect you from your stepfather?''

"Sometimes. In the beginning, she yelled at him. But he got crafty, he started camouflaging his moves.''

The face relaxed as the woman surfaced. The voice changed from tough to bemused and while her sentences flowed smoothly after Ten-Four's, the words were spoken with more hesitancy. "My stepfather," the woman said, "would pretend to be doing something very innocent when he was really spying on me. That way if he were caught he could claim immunity for his actions. So I stayed in my room, away from the floor register and the windows. But that made my mother angry, first because it was so cold and I was prone to flu and strep that lasted forever, and second, because she couldn't keep track of me. I didn't feel the cold. I drew or read under a heavy quilt. 'I know what you're doing up there,' she'd yell. When I sassed back and demanded to know what she thought I was doing, the speech began: 'I gave you the breath of life . . . if it weren't for me you wouldn't be alive.' ''

Stanley had seen the change rippling across her face and body. She'd started cracking her knuckles; it sounded like rifle shots in the video studio.

"In my head," she told him, "I'd feel hatred at her words. My mother hadn't done anything wonderful for me. What made bringing a child into the world such a class act? It shocked me when I found out later that everyone didn't live the way my 'family' did.''

"You couldn't go to your own father for help?''

The nostrils were flaring now. "Not," she said, "without making the mother loathe me more.''

Catherine, who had merely voiced words through the woman for the last few moments, now materialised. Catherine had been speaking, for a more damaged Troop member, thoughts and feelings held as a child; a child who had lived until now behind Catherine.

She'd screwed her face up, and Stanley expected her to shriek. She did not; the facial muscles struggled fiercely and then relaxed, and Catherine in her spokesperson role described the isolation of the farm, of snowbanks taller than a man's head; days verging into weeks without transportation, the total silence when nothing moved across the winter landscape. Her only knowledge of people in any season, she told him, had come from the movies the paternal grandmother took her to each summer and from school, where she'd been carefully invisible, going silently from class to class and shrinking from close contacts.

"The best times growing up were when I was totally alone, at the rock in the back field of the second farmhouse. The rock was huge; it had a deep indentation in the middle, so deep you could barely see over the edge. I hated the snakes. They lay around on the rim of the rock, basking in the sun. Once you made it to the center of the rock, you kept an eye out for the snakes and any human being sneaking up on you from the house at the other end of the farm."

"You've mentioned disliking snakes on other occasions. What else frightens you?" Stanley was busy writing on his clipboard but had noticed the change of voice, gradually taking on a rougher and less sophisticated tone.

"What else? Water and animals and high places. They aren't just frightening; they strike terror in me. Most women are afraid of spiders or lightning or something dumb. Spiders won't hurt you and neither will lightning if you're careful. But these other things? Hey, run for your life, man."

The manner in which her forearms rested loosely on the bent thighs, the way she leaned forward; it was the body language of someone physically fit, who did not fear physical violence. It was also tough and rather unfeminine. But in the eyes glittering behind tumbled bangs, there was terror.

Just before the break, he was given a description of the nightmares that had taken over twenty years to fade.

"I wanted," the woman said, "to get down on my knees in thanks; I didn't believe they'd ever fade. All I remember of them now, aside from my stepfather standing on that ladder naked with his head in the attic opening, were the parts where he chased me for hours, stark naked, gaining on me, finally close at my heels, looking at me, saying *nothing*. No words. Every night was the same. Darkness, the whole house asleep, just the hall light burning. My eyes shut tight, not to open for anything until morning. Because the sounds always began, the creak of a floorboard, a soft footstep. The total fright, the fear that squeezed my heart the whole night long, the sweat pouring off me. I'd wake up screaming, Oh, jesus, where was my mother?"

Her hands beat the air, up and down and sideways, making a frantic sign of the cross. "I don't know when or why but my stepfather was forbidden to come into that bedroom; something about screams . . ."

"Who was screaming?" Stanley laid down the clipboard.

"I don't know, but it didn't stop the footsteps, the whisper of a presence in that dark bedroom, the hand following my body under the blankets, pausing, resting. I had to have imagined that. I didn't ever dare open my eyes to find out, and it went on for years, until I was fifteen, I think. Every night I'd just roll over, pretending to sleep."

Stanley consulted the clipboard. She'd said that she awakened, screaming; then she didn't know who was screaming. Could there be two people here, very similar to each other, so similar that he noticed no change? Stanley caught sight of Tony's face in the control booth, turning into a masque of frustration. He glanced back at the woman in time to see her face contort, the muscles under the skin swelling.

"I hated being home, hated being in school. It was like whoever looked at me must know all about me, all about the 'family.' Whenever the school bus neared our door, I prayed it would blow up and release me or that the house would burn down with all of them in it. Every last one."

Something was wrong in the control booth. Tony was twisting the dials furiously. Tony had managed to patch the most scratchy of the tapes so far, and still searched for a flaw in the equipment that didn't seem to exist. Stanley kept his pen flying over the clipboard, jotting key words while his eyes tracked the woman's movements.

"If I protested anything," she was saying "the stepfather denied it and the mother went along with him, pointing out that I was an idiot. They both said, each in their own way, that I was unfit for much of anything. That's how I thought of me, too; there was nothing I could do right! Nothing I said or heard or saw, seemed to be right!"

She cried. Stanley asked if she'd like to sketch for him the layout of the second farm. The drawing, as it progressed, was crude. The woman's face was blank. Her hand gripped the pencil above the sketch pad as she outlined the farm's boundaries. The mailbox at the road, the two big poplar trees on either side of the driveway, and the house itself were put into place. At the walnut tree on the front lawn, the pencil paused. It started to tremble in her hand. There was still no expression on her face. The tremble continued as she sketched in the garage, the chicken house behind it, and a narrow creek running across one of the fields. She outlined the barn with apologies. She could not, she said, "see it" at all. Stanley noted that in sketching the hedgerow leading back to the orchards, the trembling wasn't just in her hand but her whole body. After the corn crib and the field of tall grass had been delineated, the pencil shot over the pad to draw another open field lying just outside the back orchard. The field was surrounded on all sides by a dense hedgerow of thick bushes and tall trees. The pencil paused at the opening along the hedgerow and then, just inside it, began to draw a circle. Stones were being sketched around the circle.

"What's that you're drawing?" Stanley asked.

The eyes were wide open, staring, and the words were spoken through teeth that chattered. He could barely decipher the first answer. He pressed her, not sure if he should be pressing anything at the moment.

"A well," Sewer Mouth said, "a miserable, shit-assed well."

Stanley called for the break and went to speak with Tony, who waited to speak with him until the woman was gone.

"Fragmented, huh?" Tony bent over his dials, frowning. "I'd like to know why this damned equipment only goes haywire when the two of you are in there."

10

The session resumed. Stanley had never felt so inadequate with any client before her. What kept him going was having read somewhere that treatment for most multiples (provided they really existed)was a guess-and-go situation.

A rigidness of attitude gripped the woman so hard and so often that he wondered why it did not strangle her. The rigidness bothered him because it sprang from her fear and guilt, both of which had grown to enormous proportions. Her occasional blank face bothered him, too; it was reflective of what she'd told him about waking up in the middle of someone else's mind, with her own mind quite empty.

The face across from him now wasn't blank. The expression was the same one that slid into place whenever the subject of family was brought up. She looked so haughty. He wanted to ask her name. More than that, he wanted her to volunteer her name. In other multiple case histories the personalities did not just appear, they introduced themselves.

"He," in reference to the stepfather, had dominated the conversation. Stanley decided to do something about it.

"No one will know whom you're talking about if you don't call the stepfather something besides 'he,' " he said.

Prior to the break and for the last few minutes, Catherine had been verbalising sporadically. Part of her job was to hold her own rage and that of several other Troop members. The excess was filtered up to the Big Three, of whom Black Katherine was felt to be the reigning power. Until pressured, Catherine hid whatever emotion she retained for her self behind a cold and lofty exterior. In pressing for identification of the man whom the Troops despised, Stanley had unknowingly forced Catherine out of hiding.

"What would you like me to call him?" An eyebrow shot up.

"How about 'my stepfather'?" Stanley asked.

"I'm not related to anyone." Being forced to identify with the stepfather as someone related to her when she knew he was not, was tantamount to picking one's nose in public. Aside from his tackiness, he had been evil. It was something one could feel whenever he walked into a room. Except, of course, when relatives visited (either his own or the mother's, and sometimes even the child's own father and paternal grandmother). Then the stepfather's evilness vanished like a cloak he shed at will.

The idea of being part of any family, in view of the one she'd grown up in, was anathema to her. For all Catherine's sophistication, she could not control her ire—or the feeling that someone right inside her mind was crowding up against it, shooting straight past, yanking the reins from her grip. And Stanley pushed it just a hair too far. . . .

"But the other children were related to you by blood," he said, "by your mother's blood."

One of the Big Three glared at Stanley and spoke through gritted teeth. "I have no mother. Family? I'd like to see them all bloodied before my eyes. We are related to no one. And that's final."

The outpour of rage stopped as quickly as it had begun but while it had lasted, Stanley would have sworn he'd never laid eyes on her before. One thing was clear: if there were other personalities here, they did not consider themselves to be related (as the first-born child would be) to a flesh and blood family. It appeared that "family" was considered by at least two of them to be an ugly institution.

And again, because he didn't know what he was doing, his floundering produced results. "But Page is your daughter, you're related to Page."

"I have never been married," Catherine said. "I've never been pregnant. What do you take me for, a fool?"

The woman was staring at her cup, muttering over how cold her coffee had become. The muttering ceased and she was suddenly almost screaming.

"Did I kill him? Oh, god, why can't I remember? In the car the other day, I kept trying to remember, and I heard—you won't believe it."

"Yes, I will believe it."

"Murder is an awful thing, one shouldn't laugh! But along with wondering if I had murdered my stepfather, I heard myself laughing and doing an imitation of W.C. Fields, then Marilyn Monroe, Mae West, and Scarlett O'Hara. I can't imitate anyone, Stanley, so where was it coming from? There was laughter and the idea that Fields, Monroe, West, and O'Hara all have similar voice characteristics. Then my mind just went blank. I couldn't direct it anywhere, it was empty. If I did kill my stepfather, whether I remember or not, I've got to pay!"

"That sounds just like something your mother would say."

"Well, she was right!"

"She wasn't right. Your mother ruled by fear. She convinced you that you were so bad that you could only survive at her side—for whatever purpose she wanted to use you."

For a split second, someone beat on the woman's mind with joy at how clearly Stanley perceived the mother.

"You got up and walked away from your family. That was healthy. Yet you persist in feeling guilty for having left your mother to her own devices. And you seem so frightened of your rage. But it's warranted and you have to keep letting it out. I just saw a good deal of your rage; I applauded."

"You did? I was angry?"

"Yes, you were."

"When?"

Stanley looked at his watch. "Just a few seconds ago."

The woman looked at him as if she'd misunderstood his words.

"You told me," he said, "that you were related to no one."

"Isn't that funny? I don't recall saying such a thing to you but I've felt that way. Well, most children believe at one time or another that they're adopted or something. Except that I'm an adult now, so why hasn't the notion just been put away?"

Why, indeed. According to Jeannie Lawson, the selves had a certain speech pattern that, up until now, he'd considered only briefly. Relatively sure that the woman was present and verbalising, Stanley decided to explore, by a backdoor method, the suspicion that suddenly grabbed him.

"Was your mother affectionate with you?" he asked.

"The mother said that if she showed me affection, the stepfather would say she played favourites, that she was cheating his children. I don't think I ever knew that hugs were part of a mother-daughter relationship until one day, when she hugged me for the first time, in front of a total stranger. I remember being shocked. I guess I was thirteen.''

Who the hell was sitting here? Stanley had assumed for the last few minutes that this was the woman and, by the natural order of things, also the first-born child. But she had just said "the mother."

He asked her about it.

"Did I say 'the mother'? I know that's wrong. I should say 'my mother.' One should do what's right.''

If it's right, Stanley thought to himself. "Don't I hear you saying 'my mother' sometimes?''

"I guess so. I do it because I'm supposed to, but sometimes I slip.''

Stanley stared into the blank face in front of him. Marshall, he thought, would arrive none too soon. This conversation was turning into Abbott and Costello and their "Who's on First?" routine.

He tried another route.

"Did you draw for me in the sketchbook just before we took our break?''

"Did I bring the sketchbook?'' The woman held her skirt aside and looked down at the floor. "Do you want me to draw something?''

"Do you remember telling me about the second well in the back field?''

"What second well? We only had one, by the kitchen door.''

"My mistake,'' Stanley said. If he went further, they'd be into the well business and neither of them was ready for it. Something had gone on in that back field. The woman in front of him right now did not remember it, and probably for good reason. What concerned Stanley more at the moment was that, just like an alternate self, she did not consider the mother as her own.

The woman wished the dizziness would go away. Her skin had broken out in a cold sweat. There seemed to be nothing inside her.

From deep in the Tunnel, someone heard the silence in the woman's mind. The Gatekeeper gave the signal. The Buffer sat

up front now, allowing the thoughts of another Troop member to
flow again through the emptiness of the woman's mind.

"Did I do something wrong?" the woman heard herself asking Stanley. "You look at me so funny, what did I do wrong?"

"Not a thing," Stanley said.

"This is a lot like being back home. I was always scared I'd done something wrong. I spent a lot of time being scared that the mother would see the special badness the stepfather hinted we were capable of. Was it so horrible that he couldn't say it out loud? Why didn't I remember it? Why was he at me, everywhere I looked, trying to do things to me, touch me, force his fingers . . . but things he did are coming back now."

The voice had been a peculiar mixture of adult woman and small child. Stanley gave up tracking the differences between "my mother" and "the mother." The expressions were too intermingled as the woman rocked back and forth on the floor cushions, gaining control one minute and losing it the next. She was recounting the crawl along the kitchen floor with the stepfather atop her protesting six-year-old body. Her mother, at such times, continued her cooking at the big black stove and seemed oblivious.

" 'Somebody,' the mother would say to no one in particular, 'is going to get hurt if you continue to play that roughly.'

"The game at that point was at my mother's feet, me trying to get away from my stepfather's body on top of me, he with his hands over my mouth to shut off the screams. My mother said that over and over, 'Somebody is going to get hurt.' "

The outraged and tormented expression remained but the face became rounder. The voice and demeanor were unmistakably those of a very small child.

"Didn't the mother know it had already happened?" she asked Stanley.

Neither the woman nor the Troop member speaking were aware of it, but the amount of rage being suppressed might have fired a missile. The stepfather's inhumanity, his dehumanisation of the small child, had never been forgotten or forgiven. It had merely grown to astronomical proportions and was now, as in the past on too many occasions, evidencing itself as energy. Tony stood inside the control booth, his frenzy indicating more trouble.

The woman surfaced and rubbed her arms. She was freezing. The coldness seemed to accompany a childlike feeling inside herself. The woman was leaning forward from her yoga position and laying her forehead on her knees with the suppleness of a fourteen-year-old gymnast. When she sat straight up, both hands were buried to the wrists in ash-blond hair, her face red with emotional strain. There were no pauses between the words, they tumbled out of her mouth. She spewed hatred for everything and everybody, including herself; denied the worth of whatever she had accomplished, or might accomplish, in her lifetime. Her eyes remained, for the most part, veiled behind the bangs.

"I tried to run away," she said. "There were transient workers on the next farm. They laughed a lot, I could hear them when the wind was right."

Stanley heard the child's voice but so faintly.

"The transient workers," he said casually, "how close to your farm did they live?"

"Ooh." Soft eyes, wider and more lively, sparkled at him under ash-gold fringes of hair. "I don't know. This far." Her hands came together, moved apart. "Music," said the same childlike but suddenly lispy voice, "it was pretty the way they sang, and do you know what?"

"What?"

"He was my friend, that black boy. He made the mother smile a real smile, bringing me home up on his shoulders that day I got lost back there behind the apple orchard. She smiled and said what a nice person he was to do it, can you believe that?"

"Yes, I can."

"I can't believe that. She didn't like anybody." Her mouth turned down at the corners. She stared at Stanley and bit her lip.

"Was that your mother who smiled?"

"I used to call her that but she wasn't, you know."

"If she wasn't your mother, whose mother was she?"

"The big one's mother, I guess. But it was a secret."

"What," Stanley pressed, "was the secret?"

"Us," said the small voice, and she pointed at herself. "We were the secret."

"I see. Are there many of you?"

"I don't know. There are a lot of voices. You won't like some of them. Some of them don't like me. I can't tell you why. If I do and she hears me, there'll be trouble."

"And who is she?"

"The big one." She skipped neatly off the dime, diverting her attention to the songs the transients had sung at night behind

91

her farm, and gave him a short stanza in halting, childish sing-song, of a nursery rhyme half-remembered. " 'Lazy Mary, won't you come home . . . ,' only we didn't sing it that way. We sang it, 'Crazy Mary.' That's what they said she was, the big one."

Stanley recalled again the names on the list the woman handed him in the car this morning. Five of them, added to the voice of a very young child in the woman's foyer that first day, and this new one who must be around three or four years old. There must be others, too, because on his clipboard he'd been tracking changes that could not be confined to these seven.

"Tell me," he said, "about, uh—Mean Joe."

Her face lit up and she clasped her hands as if they were fat-fingered. "He protects me. Mean Joe is nice. I hear his words and then I can . . ." she hunted for a word, couldn't find it, and looked as if she wanted to cry in frustration.

"What happens when you hear Mean Joe's voice?"

"I can see him even if he isn't there. That's not what I mean, but I don't know how to say it."

"You mean his voice helps you visualise him? I know that's a big word." Stanley tried again. "It helps you see him?"

"Yes." She giggled.

"How long have you known Mean Joe? How many years?"

"I never knew Mean Joe." The small voice sounded petulant. "I never knew he was there, but I knew he was there."

Stanley looked at what he'd written on the clipboard and then at her. "Who are you?"

"Me," she said, and when he looked puzzled, she pointed a finger at her chest.

He leaned over to peer into the eyes that had glazed over so quickly he wasn't sure he'd seen it. The cheekbones were popping back up beneath the skin. It wasn't a child's face anymore.

"That's a pretty dress," he ventured, watching carefully for the reaction.

"This?" She looked down at the full-sleeved, sheer blouse, the pale mauve skirt and vest. "I love the jeans, they're more comfortable when we film. But today, I don't understand why, I felt determined to be feminine." There was a bemused set to her face.

"That must be a nice feeling."

"No. It scares me. See these earrings?" She flipped back her hair to expose two golden hoops. "My mother said hoop ear-rings, makeup, and shorts denoted looseness. I don't know why

92

I'm wearing them today or the clothes, either. They make me feel uncomfortable. As if wearing them makes me bad.''

"That is the dumbest thing I ever heard you say.''

"Really?''

"Dumb,'' Stanley said.

"Oh. Well,'' the bemused look intensified. Stanley, by calling the mother's opinion about the hoop earrings "dumb,'' had given Twelve the courage to push all the way past the woman. Twelve's face was innocent of adult emotion. "I always felt it was dumb, but that's what the mother said. See this lipstick we're wearing? Pale, isn't it? Bright lipstick scares some of us. Once, back at the farm, we bought a lipstick. We sneaked it. Purple. Put on a lot of it.''

"I imagine that was pretty, too. Purple is a great colour.''

"No. It was ugly. And that other one came out and smiled into the mirror like she'd done a bad thing and didn't care. When you do bad things you've got to care.''

"Otherwise?''

"You're going to hell, that's what. The mother said so.''

There came only the merest whisper of change and Stanley knew the woman was back.

"Stanley,'' she said, and her words bore no relationship to lipstick colours or hoop earrings. She was obviously worried about something else entirely. "I was so sure I had everything under control the other day but I went on appointments, grocery shopped, all with a silly, sixteen-year-old smile on my face. When I caught sight of myself in the mirror, I looked different, gleeful. I was warm with people all day, caring, ridiculous. Around five o'clock that same afternoon, somebody else took over and again I felt different. That's the way it happens, they just take over. They take me. I'm them. Am I crazy? What do I do now?''

"My sense is,'' Stanley said, laying down the pen, "that they will be getting stronger, coming out by themselves. You may not have as much control over them anymore.''

He tested her again with bits of memory revealed in the session. She looked at him with blank eyes and the beginning of a worried frown, unable to connect herself to what he was saying and too polite to dispute him except on one point.

"I control these people?'' she repeated. "How can I control them when I didn't even know they were there? I feel like a lunatic. How can I go out in public this way?''

He'd taken a risk by sliding the hint of multiple personality into his previous answer. He didn't think it disturbed her or that she'd even caught on.

"How long have you been going out in public up until now?"

"Oh, jesus," Sewer Mouth said. "You mean I've looked like an ass all these years?"

She agreed to call him if things got too hectic.

Stanley went back to his office to get ready for his next class, feeling that his energy was boundless. He worried that it was a mistake to wait for a reinforcing diagnosis, not to trust himself. He hoped that when the time came she would understand that he'd been doing it for her own good. "Her own good." Her mother had said that to her constantly, and he knew the revulsion it summoned up. When the time did come, he'd better have other words ready.

11

The hallway outside Stanley's classroom door resembled a bus terminal. Students clutched tote bags and brown-sacked lunches, they leaned against the walls and sprawled on the floor of the narrow corridor. A dark-eyed woman with raindrops caught in her black hair sat rearranging the contents of her purse into bright plastic envelopes, all neatly labelled.

The retired Air Force captain watched her thin fingers whipping among grocery receipts and cancelled checks and odd makeup items. He knew her name was Pamela; she appeared to be in her twenties but little mean lines were already forming from nose to mouth, and a frown wanted to settle into her forehead.

"Wouldn't you think," he muttered out of habit because all of Stanley's students muttered, most of the time to themselves, "that if a course simply required a man to go downtown, visit a few porno shops, watch god knows how many skin flicks, outline the working parts of, say, three hundred self-pleasuring instruments . . ." He paused, seeing the tight look on Pamela's face, the way her thin neck was grasped by the high-collared white blouse. Inundated by his own words, he knuckled a pair of tired eyes. His classroom attire, tan chinos and a sweatshirt, was soggy from the spring rains lashing the campus.

"That he should be able to pass?" Beside him on the bench, Pamela laughed with no humour. "Of course not. Phillips isn't content with the mechanics of sex. He wants to delve into one's shyness about discussing those bloody field trips; he wants one's whole life history on paper; he wants to know how one feels about prostitutes and pimps, as if I feel anything about them. How could I? They're not part of my life-style. The more I hear in this course, the more I think that sex should be banished from the face of the earth. I think this course is giving me migraines.''

"But you can't say it isn't interesting." He was startled by her vehemence and tried to hide it by watching her fasten a bright green envelope shut.

"Interesting? I'll tell you this," she spoke the words as if they were red hot and her tongue was sizzling. "I wanted, actually wanted, to be a therapist when I signed up for this course. I must have been mad. The human animal in my estimation is beyond redemption and to spend forty hours a week treating that irredeemability is perfectly ridiculous.''

"The red-light district got to you, did it?" The captain smiled. "That isn't the whole world.''

"I wonder." She glared and gathered her purse and her books, and she marched ahead of him into the classroom, where Stanley waited beside a large video player.

The room had begun to fill with students and the odours of wet fabric, lebanon bologna, and peeled eggs. Pamela placed her thin body on a bright blue plastic chair. Her notebook with its carefully tabbed pages mocked his collection of jottings, all scribbled on various scraps of paper and held together by a rubber band.

"He's got tapes today," the captain whispered.

Jeannie Lawson, bundled in a tan raincoat, tried to creep past the two of them with her head down. The Air Force captain said hello. She gave him a hesitant smile. In plain clothes and as an invited guest, Captain Albert Johnson strode in and took his seat near the back of the room.

"The tapes I'm going to show you this morning," Stanley said, "concern another aspect of sexual relationships. The woman you will see in these tapes is a client of mine. She is not unusual, although I felt she might be when I first began working with her. Since then I've learned a lot about incest aside from what I already knew as a therapist treating male abusers, and so has she. You may feel that her situation is bizarre, that it is unreal. I assure you it is not. She has lost the greater share of her memory, she suffers from what might be called migraine headaches, although she feels no pain whatsoever. She claims to have no emotions or feelings, yet she expresses a wide range of both.

"Yes," he said, seeing the puzzled faces before him. "The woman is a dichotomy. She may also be something more."

Jeannie Lawson, still in her coat, shot him a questioning look and he nodded at her. She sat down quietly and removed the coat but kept it draped over her shoulders. She was seldom without a coat in public.

"Current figures on sexual child abuse," Stanley went on, "are now at a definite twenty percent of our population, or fifty million. This year at least four thousand children will die from sexual child abuse and another three million new victims will be added to the rolls. Remember that these are reported cases only and that both men and women sexually abuse children, although women are not usually reported. Usually—mistakenly—it is felt that sexual experience for a young boy, with his sister, even with his mother, is macho or a joke—certainly not traumatic. Many offenders I treat, however, might not have sexually abused their own children had they not been abused by their parents, siblings, or some close adult authority figure. Some victims experience more trauma than the particular victim you are about to see, some less—dependent, it is believed, on the severity and the duration of the incest. In any case," Stanley looked over the class as he turned on the video player, "this is what it's all about."

The woman sat to his right on the screen. Initially, she was the perfectly controlled business woman as she described having been in her mid-twenties and wondering where babies exited the human body, insisting that as a child she had no idea what a penis looked like, and no memory of ever receiving candy or money for sex. That done, she got into what she called "flicks against my mind," protesting that they had grown in the last few weeks, not only in number, but in duration and content.

"I'm scared to think of the hedgerow nearest the house, of the chicken house or the fields. There was never a day of peace, nothing was safe. I was fifteen when I dared complain to my mother the first time, to tell her I couldn't spend one more day in that house, that I was leaving. About the only thing I recall when my mother and I confronted my stepfather with those years of hell was that he broke a broom over my back in his rage. He hurled a bowl of fresh made apple sauce at someone. That day, his killing instincts went full-throttle. I knew that if he got his hands on any one of us, he'd choke us until we had no more breath. My mother held him off with the rifle; she explained in deadly quiet tones that he had to leave.

"At some point afterward my half brother, who was twelve, found a small hole carved in the door of the closet separating my bedroom from that of my mother and stepfather. There was a pile of old sawdust on the floor under the hole. I felt shock, and then I felt dirty and immobile."

The woman paused for breath, searched for control and found it. "I was so ashamed. I just shook, realising that while I hid in my room all those years in what I believed was privacy, my stepfather had stood there on the other side of the wall, peering through the knothole. In short, the bastard had made himself privy to my every movement."

She shrugged and shuddered at the same time. "Right now, what bothers me most is the pink thing in the flicks. It's there with all that wiry brush around it and it seems to pertain to me, and yet it doesn't. The flicks won't stand still long enough."

"What pink thing?" Stanley asked innocently, and she tried to describe her stepfather's male organ with a look of utter helplessness. Her hands balled into fists and she pounded them on yoga-positioned kneecaps.

"It's like the animals, we lived on a farm, we had animals. I know we did! But I can't remember a single god-damned one, and I know they were there. I hate animals, always have, always will, something about animals and my stepfather and me, but every time I think of them or him lately, I run, I go crazy. You want me to say that word, well, I will, I'll show you I can do it!"

She couldn't.

Captain Albert Johnson, along with the students, wanted to get up and yell, "Penis," but he, like they, sat watching her adult face, still puzzled over the reference to the animals, and then realisation hit the class like a shock wave.

Albert marveled at the woman's ability to tell Stanley about naptime on a quilt as a three-year-old, and in the face of her inability to spit out the word "penis," a few minutes ago, now to describe so explicitly her mother's anger at her infantile, but driven, masturbation practices.

"My mother put me down daily for naps. She sat up in a chair, reading her magazines. I guess I was three, I don't know. What I was doing seemed normal, but looking back, I realise that for me it was a frantic sort of thing, all-consuming. And it made her furious. She said I'd get pregnant. She screamed and she hit me; for some reason that one activity frightened her badly but I couldn't stop.''

The woman put her head down but raised it almost immediately. "Some complete asshole," she told Stanley angrily, "wrote a story and in it, he said small children don't feel sexually aroused. Was he wrong, or was I abnormal?''

"He was wrong." Stanley was writing furiously on his clipboard. "Children are capable of sexual arousal from birth, and if someone else is instructing and encouraging as your stepfather was, the need to masturbate can become an obsession.''

Albert thought he'd seen her face change drastically twice so far. Now it was almost purple, a masque of rage. She swung to face Stanley. The bangs flew back for an instant, revealing a pair of eyes so deadly that Albert recoiled.

"I'm trying," she hissed, "to tell you the obscene first; I figure that way the rest will be easy. Like the vegetables we hate. Eat the shit first, right?''

"Right," said Stanley, and uneasy smiles rippled across the faces of his students. Her voice, raspy and hate-filled, tore into the outhouse and her stepfather's face at the opening under the bench and how after that she couldn't force herself to use the bathrooms in school, preferring, one day, to sit in a pool of menstrual blood in a coed gym glass.

When she described her stepfather's face, positioned between an open pail of body refuse and her bare bottom, a silence fell throughout the classroom.

"I never told anyone that, can you imagine?" She snarled and cried simultaneously, her face glistening with tears. "I've been married, for christ's sake, and I never was able to tell that to a single soul, including my husband.''

She began a stream of cursing. As she got to "tit-toothed, prick-faced, pious, piss-ant bastard," the black woman seated to Albert's left let out a deep sound of appreciation.

"Right on, girl.''

Albert had to agree. At the precinct house the woman had stupefied his officers and detectives, but her presentation had been mild in comparison to this one.

"As a teenager, I got strep throat, flu, some really rotten colds. It bothered me being out of school so often, with a temperature, on the living room sofa, not up in my room. After each illness, I'd wonder what he'd done to me when my mother went out into the fields or to town, shopping. My memory is blank.''

''He was so goddamned big,'' the woman was saying more calmly, but with controlled rage holding her features together, ''no matter how strong I became or how tall I grew, he was a mountain and mean as a snake.''

She turned her attention to the day when she played alone in the spring mud by the tractor parked on a knoll in the truck garden, and the tractor slipped and slid over on its side, on top of her.

''They were all in the house, my mother saw it from the kitchen window. My stepfather came out and stood over me. I couldn't open my mouth to ask for help. I knew . . .''

''What,'' Stanley prodded gently, and the wild green eyes flared.

''Favour for a favour,'' she whispered. ''Like I could read his mind. If I were able to paint his face, they'd give me a scholarship to the Sorbonne. He was a maniac, I saw it in his eyes. He grinned and he stood there, and he didn't lift a finger. How did I know what he was thinking so clearly, and why can't I remember it?''

''Do you remember anything after you saw his face that day?''

''No.'' She seemed ashamed of her answer. ''It's like trying to remember the rest of my life. Nothing is there.''

Jeannie Lawson put her head down on her desk and when she lifted it seconds later her face was drained and expressionless.

A sense of fear emanated from the disheveled woman on the videotape as she battled to control herself, placing a hand over her mouth for a second, pausing to stare wild-eyed at the floor. When she looked up a smile had replaced the twisted, pale slash of her mouth. She mentioned the headaches, how much worse they'd become the moment she'd sat down to write the journal notes, the amount of Extra-Strength Tylenol she took daily to absolutely no avail.

''They're strange headaches,'' she said. ''They hurt but they don't hurt.''

Albert didn't know what to make of that but he estimated that Tylenol in such big doses could lay a horse low. Didn't she read directions or warning labels? He remembered her face that day at the precinct, and how he couldn't describe it afterward. It made him want to cry suddenly, to reach out and lift her bodily from the torment of the video screen. She wasn't mature, wasn't a business woman but something else entirely. His policeman's mind wanted to know what. He listened to her talk, in that strangely childlike voice, about the black boy bringing her home from the orchards. Albert wanted to find him and wring his neck. But where else could he have brought her? Where else did abused kids go but right back to face more of the same?

An hour had passed; the video player was shut off. Pamela raised her voice to carry over the commotion.

"This woman," she said, "speaks so concisely at the start of each session. She obviously has a logical mind. Admittedly, this is hard for her. But somehow I expect by her initial appearance, at least until she falls apart after ten minutes, a more orderly presentation of facts. I suppose I need orderly recall to grasp what went on in those two farmhouses. Isn't there some therapy method that you could use to bring the memories out in chronological order?"

"Like the steps in a cake recipe, Doctor Phillips."

It was the first time Jeannie Lawson had ever spoken in class. Stanley acknowledged her sarcasm by the briefest flicker of a smile.

"What I mean is," Pamela was not oblivious to Stanley's quick smile or the surprised eyes of the other students, "the therapist has enough problems without trying to sort out the order in which these atrocities occurred. Why does she skip around so much?"

"Because," Stanley said, "for this client—to put it mildly— there are sore spots she's never talked about before. Nor have these tapes been edited for any kind of logical progression. They're one of a kind, unique in student training, just as the manuscript she's writing will be unique when it is published. Do any of you realise how unconducive therapy is to orderly thinking on the part of a client under fire? The intensity stimulates a kind of free association. So a lot comes out, much more than if I tried to structure thinking to any great degree. There's nothing 'neat' about psychotherapy. You might say that it holds up a mirror to a life being probed. As therapists, you may find eventually that no one's life is orderly."

"Deliver me from the profession," Pamela snorted. "I'm signing up right now for a course in library science."

General laughter broke across the classroom.

"Doctor Phillips?" A young woman with her hair in a frizz

of pale gold tapped Stanley's arm impatiently. "When your client was pointing out in her sketchbook the different locations of outbuildings at the second farm, her hand paused sometimes. Her voice would catch, and then she'd go right on with it as if nothing bothered her at all. I'd be interested to know if the stepfather did something to her in each of those particular places. They really seemed to upset her. One of them was the well, not the one by the backdoor of the second farmhouse, but the one way up in the back field. What could a well have to do with child sexual abuse?"

"I don't know," Stanley said. "She doesn't know at this point. If any of you read the recent article in the paper about the two-year-old boy in Virginia who was beaten by his parents and died, you'd know that for him, the instrument of his destruction was a long-handled wooden spoon, in and of itself an innocent kitchen implement. The well seems innocent too. But something tells me that there was nothing innocent about anything on those two farms."

"I hear," a well-muscled young man, who wrestled for the university, spoke up behind Stanley, "that those parents will get off with maybe a one-thousand-dollar fine and no jail sentence. How can that be? In fact, whenever you read an article about kids dying from child abuse, more times than not the person responsible gets off scot-free."

"Our laws have not caught up with what we as clinicians know to be the true state of affairs. The general feeling among the public is that children are possessions. If you want to mistreat them sexually and/or physically, then feel free. But your question brings up an interesting point. The two-year-old boy died. This woman probably endured a lot more; her abuse went on until she was sixteen. But she didn't die and she didn't become psychotic. Can anyone here tell me how she survived?"

"She's obviously strong as hell. Or nuts." The student wrestler's hands dwarfed the notebooks in his lap. "Wouldn't you have to be nuts to survive?"

"Not necessarily." Stanley had been watching Jeannie Lawson and now, like a mother hen seeking to protect her young by distracting the enemy, Stanley moved further away from her. "The human mind is a strange and wonderful place. But there are those who possess minds that I can only call 'wondrous' and those minds do survive atrocities without falling prey to insanity. Can anyone tell me how?"

"You tell us," the Air Force captain said.

"One thing I hope this course will give all of you, no matter what profession you go into, is the notion of questioning. Of being open to all avenues, no matter how far-fetched they may seem. Does anyone here, after seeing the tapes today, have another conclusion besides insanity?"

Jeannie Lawson raised her head from her chest and looked Stanley directly in the eye. "You questioned her at the end of those sessions," she said. "It was almost as if she hadn't been there most of the time, because she really didn't connect with your questions. I got the feeling that very often she was almost humouring you, trying to be 'good' by pretending to know what you were talking about. Her voice changes, movements, and attitudes during the filming were all so different. If she has no memory, as you've said, then where is all this recall coming from? Multiple personality, if we're searching for a label here, comes pretty close to her situation."

"Does it?" Stanley looked innocent. The class was over. He watched his students gathering up their belongings.

"Multiple personality," said a student at the classroom door, "is rare. Your client is a business woman. Her competence doesn't tie in with the disablement that multiple personality caused people like Eve and Sybil."

"Ah," said Stanley. "Boxes, compartments, niches, neatness, chronological order."

The student made a face at him and laughed. But she hesitated a moment as she turned to leave. Some of his students were destined one day to be excellent therapists. Their minds were open, questioning, perceptive. Others were there only for what they saw as a relatively easy credit. After viewing the tapes, what they had in common today was a single desire, rippling quietly in the minds of some, spoken aloud by others, firmly felt but just as firmly repressed by still others: "Kill the bastard." The thought had been precipitated by the woman's videotaped agony, exacerbated by Stanley's reminder of the little boy who'd died in Virginia, nurtured by other reports they'd heard on television, and in some cases brought to the surface by personally remembered abuses suffered as children.

It would not occur to any of them for a long time that they'd been unable until now to voice true rage even for the major trespasses against themselves. Or to wonder why they'd needed to see what had been done to someone else in order to feel their own pain.

"Killing," snapped a twenty-seven-year-old woman whose features were normally pleasant and placid, "is too damn good for him."

Stanley filed her comment, and all others, away in his mind for that time when his client would be close enough to her own feelings, and have enough memory, to express her own justified anger. What, he wondered, would she say and do when the time came?

One person in the classroom grinned and was not shy about it as she listened to the opinions being spewed out around her. She seemed to have grown taller, more upright, inside her raincoat. Never during her lifetime had she thought that anyone cared enough to feel angry—as outraged as her classmates were—over things similar to those that had happened to her. She'd believed, before therapy, that she'd deserved it all and more, and had no right to complain, cry, or fight back. After therapy she'd felt alone, and numbness had set in. She looked around the classroom today, felt a wave of unaccustomed emotion and decided it was genuine within herself: affection for other human beings and a lot less fear of them. For a moment she just stood there with students brushing or bumping against her in an effort to get out the door and on to the next class. Body contact no longer seemed a threat; in fact she almost welcomed it.

Stanley noted her emotion and laid a hand on her arm. He smiled and Jeannie Lawson did not move from under his grip. A wraith in white knee socks and hanging, damp brown hair, she shot him a conspiratorial glance and then was gone.

At lunch with Stanley afterward, Albert's mind was as full as his plate. "That silent, easy, yoga position, what does it indicate to you, Stanley?"

"That I'm younger than she is, and I need help getting off the floor. I've seen her sit like that for two solid hours. Sometimes she can splay those legs out, one to each side, and sometimes it isn't exactly a yoga position. When things get rough, she kneels with her forehead on the floor. We cut out the chairs, one week into filming."

"When I saw her today, it reminded me of something. She sits easy on the floor, but not with the attitude of someone born to it, just someone who's been forced to it for a long time, so long that it becomes second nature. Maybe you don't get down-

104

town a lot, Stanley. Watch the shoulders of the street people. The Vietnam vets hold themselves the same way, at least the ones who went through the high crap. Like they need their whole body compressed underneath them, controlled.''

''Control is what I have to break her of. That and a lot of other things. I'd like to get her to the point where the self-esteem can operate better. She's going to become a full-fledged recluse before this is over.''

''What does she mean,'' Albert asked, ''about the headaches that don't hurt?''

''Defense mechanism, it looks like, highly developed. To her mind, nothing happened if there was no pain.''

Stanley could not know how overly simplistic his answer to Albert was, nor how convoluted the real answer and what wide ramifications it held for society as a whole. Albert accepted Stanley's reasoning without understanding it fully, and charged ahead, asking the questions uppermost in his mind.

''Her face changes, so does her voice, from one emotion to the other, as if she's fifteen people all at once. Sometimes with all the 'we, us, our, they,' I couldn't follow her. Was that student serious about multiple personality?''

''I'm checking it out,'' Stanley said.

Just about the time Stanley's lunch with Albert broke up, his client exited a business meeting. She had no idea how she'd gotten through it, or this morning's session, either. How could sessions and business hours pass so quickly and how could she come away with so little memory?

The rain had washed the air clean. For a moment its freshness seemed to hang in her face like a balm. But as soon as she took a deep breath, wanting to enjoy it, something in her mind moved, almost as if her brain had given way. And then she saw it on the sidewalk, a clear puddle that reflected what she believed was her own face. Except that the features staring up at her appeared to have been preserved in a block of ice so that they were not three-, but rather one-dimensional. Only the eyes had depth—they were concave, nothing more than eye sockets, really, and a deep, burnt-sienna colour, as if rotted. Seeing the face did not scare her. What made her tremble and gag and run like the wind for her car, heedless of the blaring horns and screeching tires, was the beginning of a hideous memory.

Stirred in this morning's session by mentions of a well, and revived now, far back in her mind, by the one who had lived through the experience and "died" from it, the memory took shape. Just as quickly, it was whisked away.

For you, there isn't any more. The words were screamed aloud by the Troop member who seemed to run alongside the woman in her own mind; a Troop member not really alive, but only a long-dead vessel, hurling scars from behind her ice façade.

12

The sun had come out. The memory of the face reflected in the rain puddle this morning had almost receded. The woman stopped with Page at a restaurant for dinner, where the odour of seafood and corn on the cob activated recall. [The woman and Stanley would discover that smells even at the most inopportune times had become a catalyst to recall.] The flicks began, fleeting shreds of memory, a thousand tiny knives of emotional pain. No flick was big enough to peer into and she was grateful but she could not order food. Her stomach had knotted. Page's meal was served; she broke open fried shrimp to expose fat pink meat. The fragrance wafted into the woman's brain. Flick.

Across the table, Page went in and out of focus. Her almond-shaped blue eyes and strawberry-gold hair, her young giggle seemed unreal. The woman tried to steady herself and heard laughter, realising that she had to be making the sound. Page was laughing, too, nearing the tail end of a conversation.

The woman could not connect to the childhood incidents Page sat there recalling—things that a mother should have remembered. Page kept talking and laughing. The woman could no longer hear even shreds of conversation. Instead, a bittersweet emotion rose up. Eight years ago when she'd left Norman and Page, running had occupied every waking moment. She'd been unable to bear the closeness of another human being. And now? Business appointments were kept short; she lived alone. It seemed to work. She visited her daughter and took her on outings like this one. Over a feeling of suffocation, she was unaware that invading Troop members who were bringing their emotions to her were so numerous and so in evidence that she was being crowded out. She continued to fight back, determined to inspect the fourteen-year-old sitting across the table, drinking Pepsi. The harder she looked at the young features so similar to her own, the less relationship Page had to her.

Mother. What did the word mean?

Someone within the Troop Formation screamed a thought. The battle for primary position raged. The emotions of the other Troop members took their signal straight from the Gatekeeper and the walls of the Tunnel rocked. Page's face, flesh and blood, the image of it and all it should mean to a mother, penetrated.

Why, the woman cried silently, urged to sadness by unseen minds inside her own, did I ever leave you?

Pain came from a long way off; so did Norman's angry and then defeated look. There was a wavery reflection from the black surface of the coffee in the woman's cup. Rain puddles. This morning's terror was back. The voices in her head started up, bringing panic and a sense of danger. Two faint glimmers of knowledge hovered out of reach. Curious at first and then only fractionally more interested than frightened, the woman grabbed for one of them: Page was not her child, Page belonged to someone else in the Troop Formation. She grabbed for the other thought: The memory being forced on her today, the strange face gazing up from the sidewalk, had nothing to do with puddles. It had to do with reflections. Puddles were somehow merely allusions, a device being used in an indirect manner, to prepare her for the eventual reality.

The woman had just fitted together two parts of an enormous puzzle. But like all knowledge she'd gained in her lifetime, it would be fleeting, sporadic, and not truly hers. It came, like all else, from her others. The woman avoided glancing at her coffee cup for the remainder of the meal, avoided, too, the cutlery and crystal. The restaurant lights caused reflections in them—as in almost everything she would encounter for months to come. She sat there, believing that the power to deny what she'd just learned was hers. Stanley had said that she controlled whatever went on. She'd assumed that he meant subconsciously. Was that true? A small voice told her it wasn't, that Stanley as well as she had a

108

lot to learn—knowledge that wasn't printed in any book, but which would be gained the hard way.

The woman discovered a half hour later that she was home and the restaurant incident had blurred. No matter how short the stretches between each visit, Page always spotted something new. Usually it was new to the woman, too. This afternoon, while inspecting the white collage in the foyer as she always did, Page found the worm farm in the glass aquarium. The sight of it gave the woman a roaring headache, followed by a sense of annoyance, then fear.

They watched a horror show on television with all the drapes drawn, so that eerie shadows flickered in the loft bedroom. Page dragged clothes out of the closet and paraded in them, in front of the mirror. The woman kept her eyes on the television screen, not seeing the movie and afraid to look at the dresses Page flung onto the bed. The colourful, bold fabrics and designs were unfamiliar.

"Mommie, you can wear anything. I like this dress with the slit, but I hate those blouses with the bows. You know everything, what do I do for stretch marks?"

Page, like most girls her age, dieted too much, and weight fluctuations caused stretch marks. The woman smiled, hearing from a distance, in a voice that sounded strangely familiar, an odd remedy for stretch marks and an exercise to keep them away "forever." Page laughed but her elbow hit the mirror. It tilted at an angle and the light reflected . . . the woman screamed. The memory flung like snowflakes into the Tunnel left her with the impression of dampness, rough circular walls, and the sound of other screams. The moment lengthened.

The Gatekeeper's signal was heard. The Front Runner, the Outrider, and the Buffer moved as one. With quiet determination, they blocked the tiny glimmer of light that threatened to penetrate the walls of the Tunnel. And the Weaver wove in furious haste, as he had been weaving since the restaurant incident, closing strand by strand the gap through which the woman might have seen too many things.

There was an objection. The Gatekeeper, satisfied that she was correct, always correct, precisely so, raised placid eyes to the Buffer, and the message was passed from one brain to the other: Don't question me.

The Gatekeeper went on with her work.

• • •

Catherine, feeling the Gatekeeper's mind probing for her own within the Troop Formation, answered. With veiled eyes and a wry smile, she shot forth in the loft bedroom, the shears in her hand. She considered nothing to be perfect in and of itself, without experimentation, change, alteration. Catherine had never loved anyone. She did, however, have a knack for listening, for digging into people's minds and laying out truths which they might not otherwise have discovered, or believed, about themselves. People either loved her because she showed an interest or hated her for suggesting they might be imperfect. She frightened some because under her hands they tended to look and feel great, and that attracted more attention, which some didn't want and weren't ready to handle.

People believed that Catherine was: wonderful, irreverent, phony, sophisticated, creative, sporadically impossibly dense and incredibly brilliant, hysterically funny, boring, self-centered, and a truly giving person. What they didn't realise was that while Catherine seldom failed to show up in most social gatherings, she never showed up alone and never stayed very long. She found it dull.

Page sensed the change in body stance and facial features, the air of fun in the room that emanated from Catherine's narrower eyes and broader, more relaxed mouth. She dumped the dresses on the bed and clung to Catherine's hand.

"Mommie, are you going to alter my states?"

It had long been a joke between the two of them, and Page giggled as the shears moved across the red-gold hair. Being called "mommie" was no joke to Catherine. She hated it. Motherhood? Far above her, Black Katherine spit into the wind and cursed all mothers and the horses they rode in on. It was her favourite curse.

The shears went click, click. Red-gold hair dropped onto the white carpet. Page squealed and swung her head. The angular cut showed off newly exposed cheekbones.

"You're beautiful," Catherine said and took the small face between cool fingers.

"You always tell me that. Am I, really?"

"Truly," said Catherine, bending to the pull of a mind far back in the darkest corner of the Tunnel. "For all time and beyond." And her thin, cool fingers flew into the pots and powder dishes and whipped softly back and forth over Irish pink

110

skin. They brushed mysterious shadows above the cornflower blue eyes and turned the brows into graceful, soaring feathers.

"You're beautiful, too, mommie. Do I take after you?"

"Of course." Catherine pretended she did not hear the "mommie" and spent the next half-hour instructing Page on table manners: "Never butter a whole slice of bread, only a bite at a time; place the knife 'like so' on the edge of the plate, no noise as you eat because it's gross." Catherine made it all a game, and Elvira supplied the teenage expressions, "gross, awesome, totally," since Valley Girl was big at the moment.

Page had school the following day and the woman had her usual Monday business appointments. Late that night, they packed Page's things and carried the bags to the car. In the darkness and the silence surrounding the house, Page shivered. The woman loved the solitude here at the end of the dusty lane, and the absence of other house lights.

There were things Page did not understand but which she accepted as "mother's way." Aside from the secluded house, one of them was Nails' guarded habits. Nails always drove Page home.

"Why are we on this road?" Page hung out of the car window with the radio on full blast and hoping for a 7-Eleven Slurpy. If they continued on this road, they would not pass 7-Eleven.

"Never take the same route twice, Cupcake. That way, nobody can keep track of you."

"Like in a spy story, mommie?"

"You got it, Cupcake."

"Mommie, why are you smoking that funny black thing?"

Nails did not reply. They weren't too far from their destination. She was already dousing the headlights and, to Page's displeasure, turning off the radio. Moonlight tipped the trees with blue silver and gave Page's face a mature look. The child was growing up, Nails thought. The car glided down the street with only the moonlight in front of it, a lonely courier carrying precious cargo. One block from Page and Norman's house, Nails stopped the car. She made sure there were no vehicles on the street, no one she did not want to meet. Satisfied that all was safe, Nails continued on to the driveway, parking in deep shadow away from the street lights.

The woman watched Page enter Norman's front door, and she waited in the car until the lights went out. Who had washed Page's hair and made her chocolate cake all these years?

Not you, you unmothering bitch.

The woman cringed as if the remark had been addressed to her. She was still unaware that before some Troop members evidenced fully to each other, they exchanged gossip, solace and warlike barbs, each one believing that all thoughts belonged to him- or herself. With Page safely back in her father's domain, she drove home by the dark of the moon, knowing that she'd discovered an infinitesimal scrap of emotion all her very own. It was sadness. And someone laughed and said that was too bad.

Because for you, there isn't any more.

Each time she heard it now, there was simply a flicker of pain and a tiny, quickly disappearing edge to the meaning that never lasted long enough to sink in. Or was she avoiding it? Stanley said she was avoiding many things. Stanley was a wise man for whom trust had begun to develop. She sensed truth behind the words "For you, there isn't any more," even if she could no longer pin down what she'd learned in the restaurant with Page. Because of that truth, she knew Stanley had missed or was avoiding something, too. Did her situation scare him as much as it did her? She didn't know. But she stopped the car by the side of the road and laid her face on the cold steering wheel. Did she want a whole lifetime this way, frightened of herself and everyone else?

If she told him he was mistaken about the fragmentation, he'd hate her. But something more was wrong here, dreadfully wrong. It wasn't just fragmentation. Page's hair ribbon lay forgotten on the front seat beside her, a length of silver in the moonlight. The woman's face began to change and the one who held the excess of Troop emotions started to cry.

Stanley turned up the air conditioning in his townhouse and picked up the latest manuscript pages. He could not sleep; the energy after this morning's session propelled him onward. The words of an old instructor came back to him: "Don't push the river . . . the mind is a river with its own undertow and very deep currents. It's nature's miracle; a strong, protective, protected entity. Push it too far and too fast ahead of itself and you're asking for trouble."

But he'd better find answers for the woman, soon, or her fears would topple her. Could those fears be lifted long enough to complete the repair job he'd begun as a therapist? Some of his colleagues to whom he'd recently mentioned this case expressed grave doubts that the woman could ever be fully mended. Certainly not, they said, enough to lead a "normal" life.

Stanley wondered, each time anyone stressed "normal," just what the word meant when applied to this client. Aside from a desire for less stress and fear, her mind (and theirs) would spit on the word "normal." It was too narrow, too limiting an expression for the wants, needs, desires, and capabilities that surged forth in the sessions. His job would be pushing her not to strive for normalcy, but to dare to reach beyond it.

"What have you been up to?" Morgan's voice was muffled against his shirt front as he fastened thin gold links into the cuffs.

"We'll tell you," Catherine tied the belt to her green robe tighter around her waist.

Downstairs, with two snifters of brandy on a tray in front of them, Catherine leaned back against the arm of the sofa. She let her mind stray over his impeccable tailoring, his masculine good looks, and his air of power unfettered by self-doubt or weakness of purpose.

The woman didn't know there was a war on: Catherine sat hoping Morgan wouldn't muss her hair or smudge the expert makeup with one of his slow-moving and, to her, annoyingly damp kisses; Sixteen yearned to be touched, caressed, warm; Twelve perceived in him a father figure and wanted to listen as he talked and smoked, reminding her of the child's father years ago. The woman stood outside it all, wishing the off-balance feeling would go away, and wondering why there was a sudden compulsion to tell him all, and risk rejection.

Because, the Outrider said, *we expect rejection, we'll work hard to get it, that's the pattern. Morgan is too close these days, his eyes are warmer, his touch softer. That's scary. Go ahead, tell him how broken and strange a force we are. Paint him a picture of what his life will be like if he gets any nearer. His business is bigger than Norman ever dreamed of for himself— Norman couldn't take exposure, how can this man?*

Not just one thought thrashed in the woman's mind, there were the thoughts of over twenty Troop members present just then. The thoughts came and they multiplied, because for each Troop member Morgan didn't call up a few fears, he called up many. The woman looked back at the spinning fragments of her life. A future based on continued silence meant that nothing

113

would change, she'd never be safe. The room didn't seem to stand still and her head was crammed with voices and a roaring sound. Again she felt an awful determination to get Morgan away from her before he wanted something it was not possible to give.

The words she heard herself saying weren't clear, only the essence of them. She saw Morgan's almost unwilling tenderness and then his controlled withdrawal. It wasn't any different, actually, than when she'd tried to tell her classmate years ago.

She handed him his coat because it was the thing to do. Good hostesses, Twelve whispered in her mind, did that when they sensed a guest was ready to leave.

His leaving would be a final act; Catherine knew it and found it amusing. Catherine's sense of humour put her above scenes. Morgan was a gentleman. At the door, he did not take her in his arms. He laid a tender kiss on the end of her nose. His eyes were warm as always, but conveyed little beyond finality. "Stay the way you are," he said.

The woman went back up the staircase to the loft, got into bed, and stuffed her head under the pillows. She should be feeling something. There was nothing except the ache in her ears and the faint sound of voices, unidentified by names. She listened.

It was very nice while it lasted, Twelve said.

Perhaps. It was Catherine's voice. *Tell me. Is there anywhere a man who talks and strokes, in tandem?*

You won't let them talk, the Outrider said. *Everyone isn't an Einstein and you can't stand stupidity.*

At least he didn't wave his working parts at us. Twelve sounded hopeful, as if by giving Morgan points, the outcome might change. But of course there wasn't any hope, just a cold draft in the room, created not by the rising winds outside, but by Morgan's absence.

No, he didn't wave his working parts at us, Sixteen said, *he wasn't what anyone would call threatening. Morgan was a passive lover.*

The Outrider, knowing that for someone in the Troop Formation, Morgan had been anything but a passive lover, let out a scream of hilarity and turned up the radio. "Slow Hand," the Pointer Sisters' hit record, played loudly and long. "I want a lover with an easy touch, I want a lover with a slow hand . . ."

The infinitesimal kernel of emotion discovered only hours earlier as being sadness, pulsated, nudged out yet another kernel. The woman with her head under the pillows wanted to scream. She got up. She poured a glass of white wine, hoping that if she read for a while it would make her sleepy. It did not. The gallery bookshelves teemed with volumes ranging from mystery stories to classical literature to poetry and the occult. They'd all been in her hands at one time or another and some were duplicates or triplicates. She could not have quoted the story lines in any of them, but her other selves could and frequently did. The books were arranged in no particular order. The Troops did not like categorisaton.

With another glass of wine, the woman made out a list of duties for the following week: cleaning the house, getting her clothes in order, and maintaining a "decent" personal appearance. How strange that she bought so many cleaning items and used so few, and that her dresser boiled over at times with makeup items that she never used. Her ears were vibrating again.

If you cry, Nails said, *I'll break both your arms.*

Around 4:00 A.M., tired of staring at the ceiling, she got out of bed, consulted the list, and stumbled downstairs in the dark. The house around her beckoned with moonlit fingers. It smelled faintly of mice and cookies she couldn't remember baking.

She loved this house. How much longer would it be hers?

First things first, the Outrider said, and the surge of energy lifted the woman almost bodily and carried her to the typewriter. Another hour or two, and dawn would break. Inside the gallery, shadows hung, impenetrable even by the 150-watt, gooseneck lamp.

Shivers took hold; her fingers paused on the keyboard, another mind forcing the action she could not instigate. She turned the stereo on, not because she wanted to, and by the time dawn had crept up to the gallery windows, she'd outlined a land contract for a business meeting that afternoon.

She didn't notice the crumbs from a toasted cheese sandwich scattered among the typewriter keys, or the notes written by a forceful new hand in the red journal. She was too busy dealing with a chocolate craving. She beat it into the kitchen, for Morgan's supply of sweets. They'd been there last night, now they were gone. A green garbage bag, neatly tied, sat at the back door.

In the bathroom for the first time that morning, she got a glimpse of her swollen face in the mirror and nearly fainted.

Seated in the dentist's chair a scant hour later, she burst into tears before he had a chance to lay a hand on her.

"Don't yell at me," she sobbed, "we know you will."

The man's tender, fatherly concern surprised her.

"Oh, god," the woman said, laughter rising over the tears, "what's wrong with me?"

"A little hysteria, a lot of infection. I told you last time. Bone disintegration is caused by pressure, strain, tension. This has been going on for at least fifteen years. It drains your body of vitamins, depletes you; don't you ever get tired?" The dentist consulted his chart. "You've had this since you got married. Have you been brushing with the baking soda and peroxide? You look like a squirrel. Doesn't it hurt?"

She tried to tell him, with her mouth full of steel probe, that she never got tired and nothing hurt. The same compulsion she'd felt with Morgan last night had pushed to the forefront. The words weren't any clearer this time.

When she'd finished, the dentist stared down at her. "Your therapist calls that 'fragmentation'?"

She admitted that, yes, that was what Stanley called it.

Outside the dentist's office, the sun burned bright on her face. Mean Joe ambled along, his wary eyes moving from side to side. Miss Wonderful did not need to "see" Mean Joe. He had always been there for her—sentinel keeper, warrior in a silent cloak. She knew only that in his shadow she was safe. Her smile grew wide in the June sunlight.

Nobody knew that incest created basket cases, because nobody talked about it. She'd already told Sharon; now she'd told Morgan and the dentist, two outsiders. Miss Wonderful would tell anything, rather than keep it inside. With her mood of celebration at full steam, she spied a street vendor with a cart of flowers. But whereas Miss Wonderful perceived the vendor as being safe because he was a lot like Mean Joe, and the flowers as simply golden and beautiful—the woman regarded him as the enemy, a stranger, and the flowers called up a field of tall grass and lurking danger.

Miss Wonderful's thoughts seeped through to the woman and gradually the idea of beauty overtook danger; she felt secure, then miraculously happy. The street vendor, a tall black youth wearing a red beanie, smiled at her. In a voice that sounded like an ocean of raw silk, he quoted a price and extended an armful of flowers. His presence, the beauty of his wares, were strong

116

messages. Three very small Troop members responded and their thoughts seeped through to the woman. She did not even wonder why she was so at ease with him or why she felt so faintly childish, counting money into his big, roughened palm. The daffodils nodded yellow heads. Their pungent, earthy odour tugged at something way, far back in her mind as she buried her face in them and got into her car.

Two days later, with the swelling all but unnoticeable, the woman made her way on unsteady legs beneath a sheer skirt of bottle green that clung damply to hot, wet skin. At the open foyer doors, laughing guests chatted, waving paper napkins at each other and swatting flying insects.

"Makes twice in one month that I've seen you," Sharon cried, "is the world coming to an end?"

"Sharon, which charity are we attending?"

"Cancer, heart, whatever." Beads of perspiration clung to Sharon's upper lip, her red hair hung limp on her shoulders. "I wanted to get you out of the house. Your friends are calling me, saying that you never go out, you keep the answering machine on and they can't reach you."

"I'm busy."

"You're scared. We're all scared of something; you can't let it immobilise you." As if to press the point, she handed the woman a glass of champagne. "What are Stanley's plans for you, do you know?"

"Eventually a face-to-face confrontation with my stepfather, letting the chips fall where they may."

"Why not? He deserves it. Take a gun with you. Want crab or lobster?" Sharon was cruising the buffet line like a pro.

"Because." A giant Waterford punch bowl directly in the woman's line of vision had caught the sunlight in its thousand crystal cuts, and the reflections were dazzling . . . there was that same dead face, the idea of water in her mind. She looked over her shoulder and spoke too loudly in Sharon's direction. "My stepfather is twelve feet tall."

Sharon's full plate tilted in her hands. Why was the woman's face so smooth, so rounded, so . . . babyish, and how could she point her toes in that way? "Ssssh," she hissed.

"No! He scares me."

"Norman called me," Sharon said, trying to change the subject and unable to find the way. "He's convinced, finally, that

117

this therapy is good for you. 'Under the circumstances,' whatever that means. But he's got some fantasy that your problem is a sort of sexual coup d'état that has yet to be remembered—a single event.''

''Would that it were. I keep getting this image of a day-to-day horror back there on those two farms. Stanley says hang in there. I swear it's killing me.'' The woman smiled, brittle and bright.

Sharon found them a table near the band where conversation could be drowned out, and they sat. Sharon spoke into her wineglass. ''It isn't like you to get down. Think happy thoughts and you'll feel better. I promise.''

''Yes, I'm calling you. Wonder of wonders, right?''

''Astounding,'' Stanley laughed. ''Bad night?''

''The pits, man. I don't think anyone we know knows how to talk about this, the nitty-gritty of it. We tried yesterday afternoon, with Sharon.''

''And?''

''Couldn't get through to her. She likes us to smile. We can't always do that. When we stop smiling and try to unload, it makes her uncomfortable. And to me, the unloading sounds like complaining; I stop before I get started.''

''Work into it gently,'' Stanley said. ''Try telling whoever, how bad your headaches are, see if they accept that, and then work up slowly to something else, like your toothache. Everyone understands those two things, pain-wise. From there, you can get into what's really bothering you. People are so used to your strength, it probably shocks them to see you in this situation. But if they can't accept this situation, that's their problem, not yours.''

''My teeth don't hurt and neither does my head.''

''Pretend,'' Stanley told her.

The reflections, having begun, continued. The woman's fright, each time she saw them, grew. And deep in the blackness of the Tunnel, the Troop member whose emergence the reflections heralded huddled soaking wet and icy cold. Her essence, so wrapped in pain for too many years, sensed the mind that probed for hers with a message she'd thought never to hear: It's safe. We've made it safe. No one will get close again. Even Morgan is gone.

118

Remember the flowers? See the paper? See the crayons? It's safe. You're free, now.

Olivia, the one the other Troop members would shortly refer to as "The Well of Creativity," was coming alive; not as the dictionary defined "alive," but rather as it was defined within the mechanism of the Troop Formation. And to a man, within the dark Tunnel, there was a scurrying, a making of comfort, a paving of the way. For Olivia would bring with her untold artistic abilities and a horrifying reality.

13

Marshall Fielding had called last night. He'd be here "sometime today," but not in time for the woman's session. So what Stanley carried in a brown paper bag to the university that morning had been purchased for two reasons; one, to occupy and therefore calm himself and two, as a lure for the children whose names he wanted to learn.

His client showed up for the session with an angular haircut that swung from forehead to nape of neck in a severe swath. Not many women had the face for it. As she settled herself on the orange cushions, Stanley wasn't sure that she did, either, except for moments when he wondered why she ever wore it any other way.

Stanley handed over the brown paper bag. "This is for you," he said.

"Me?" She sat there, an adult in emerald green blouse and trousers, with hammered silver earrings and two bracelets that clinked smartly. All her sophistication fell away as she opened the bag, stuck her nose in, and shrieked. "Oh, god, how did you know, aren't they beautiful!"

She snatched out the dark-green and yellow box and flipped open the lid. Embarrassment overtook enthusiasm as the crayons spilled into her lap. Her nose went into the air, she looked very haughty; then her shoulders hunched protectively. The changes were rapid; another followed as she asked, puzzled, if she was crazy or was it normal for victims to have memory blanks.

"Normal?" Stanley asked. "Just because something happens or doesn't happen to others has nothing to do with being crazy. Don't you love your daughter's uniqueness, her very special individuality?"

The green eyes were frosty. "Love is a fallacy," one of the Big Three said.

"There is right now," Stanley told her, "a ten-year-old victim who has no memory of incestuous experiences with her father. Yet we know they happened. After three years of private therapy, Protective Services took over her case, and they are at their wits' end. A twenty-four-year-old woman in one of my classes has just now emerged from successful therapy. It took her four years to remember. One day, if you're willing, I'll arrange a meeting between the two of you."

Stanley didn't elaborate on how similar she and Jeannie actually were. The woman started to cry and asked if the other woman were well now, and happy.

"Whatever that means," Stanley said. "She's putting her life back together. She gave me a message for you. Said to tell you that it gets better.

"Jeannie," Stanley said, trying to make things more real for her by using his student's first name, "watched several of your tapes."

He saw it sink in. She might be listening, but he suspected that the crayons occupied the attention of someone else. The hand began to move over the sketchbook, clutching a fat purple crayon. He'd seen the woman's absent-minded drawing before, but the flowers erupting today were loose and flowing, their shapes more imaginative than the stilted daisies with which she usually decorated either the red journal or the sketchbook.

There was no way for him to know that in the woman's mind, the creativity he saw on the sketchbook pages was being unleashed through another Troop member. Someone had begun to chant, Make it pretty, paint it green, yellow, red, purple. Let it be a flower. Let there be a lot of flowers. The woman didn't hear the chant and Stanley could see no expression in her face.

"Very well," Stanley said, "let's relax here."

"Thank you for the crayons."

Lamb Chop's voice was tiny. Stanley grinned. She took sly whiffs of the waxy crayon odour. Suddenly the soft voice gave way. Without warning, it whipped back and forth among other voices, a three-, a six-, and a ten-year-old, to a hard-nosed

121

twenty-five, and back again to the first childlike tones. Except that a lisp had now materialised in another child's voice, fleeting but definite. The woman's face changed so rapidly during the voice fluctuations that Stanley gave up tracking its cheekbone angle, the slashes of pale mouth, the nostrils that alternately flared, compressed, widened, and pinched themselves together.

The voice and facial changes belonged to various individual Troop members, each one motivated by the air of safety which Stanley had manufactured with a three-dollar box of crayons. One by one, they looked out from behind the swing of blond hair and, just as quickly leaped back into hiding. Although he asked repeatedly, no one would give him a name. As things calmed down, he heard a single voice, good-humoured and unflappable. The female speaking did not introduce herself.

"I never associated the words 'daddy' or 'father' with the stepfather. I totally refused to do that. He had rewards for himself and one of them was cruelty. Toward us, animals, people, it didn't matter."

"We call that evil," Stanley said.

His air of agreement had reached past Elvira, to Twelve. Stanley would learn to recognise her intense warmth of manner, the lilting voice, and a pair of eyes that sparkled like sunlight on water.

"Nobody ever said that to us before. You agree with that definition of the stepfather? You'll have to, or you won't believe a single thing we tell you today or any other day."

"I believe you."

Twelve told him that the stepfather stomped new-born wild baby rabbits to death during the spring plowing each year. One day, the half brother managed to save one. He'd carried it home, wiggling and scared to death, and put it in a cage in the washroom along with the family pet, a big white bunny. At dinner that night, the stepfather sat there laughing. Then he got up, watching everyone's face, and opened the washroom door. Both rabbits lay dead in the cage.

"There was too much screaming and fear during any meal; you were never sure what would happen next. We all screamed, but that day with the rabbits, I remember the half brother's most of all. The stepfather beat him unmercifully. He kept yelling at him, 'Be a man.' Did he want his son to be cruel and sadistic, the way he was? The half brother wasn't effeminate. He just didn't know how to be like his father."

122

Catherine now spoke her own, the woman's words, and those of another Troop member. The woman heard the words and realised that letting them out today had a relatively calming effect on someone. For her, what had lain shrouded in her mind over the years sounded familiar and brought back the old terrors.

"The stepfather looked on mealtime as a battleground. He'd give even his own children such scornful, loathing looks. He'd chew his food in a slow, sloppy way, because he knew it made me sick. He'd sit there laughing while my mother insisted, 'Eat, damn you, I grew this food in the garden! I canned it, I cooked it. It's hot over that stove but you wouldn't know that, I do everything for you!' Just thinking about that now, I want to get up and run out of this room, I want to scream and hit something. But fury or tears created a kind of joy in him. He'd stare at me and smile. If my mother left the table even for a second, he said things to remind me that I was stupid, odd, crazy, useless. He jeered and calculated what it cost to feed me. Even today, as an invited guest in someone's home, I can't ask for a second helping of anything."

She told Stanley about stealing food to eat outside the house. Until turning thirteen it had been possible to hide her appetite, but that summer the cellar walls needed rebuilding. Both her muscle structure and appetite had grown as she and her stepfather lifted boulders down from a flatbed car.

The woman's hands shook at the mention of the flatbed car, and her eyes darted from side to side. Her face took on a curious, listening attitude, as if she heard things outside the studio. She gave Stanley a list of leftovers filched from the kitchen cupboards.

"Cupboards, cupboards, hide," the words left the woman's mouth in a chanting lisp. She winced and went right on. "Once I ate jelly doughnuts from the two-week-old baked goods we bought for the pigs. The doughnuts smelled like the burlap sacks my stepfather brought them home in. When my stepfather caught me stealing them, he called me a sow, a fat, greedy pig."

The face Stanley saw from the corner of his eye had almost "melted" as if there were no bones under the skin.

She started to repeat "cupboard" over and over, holding her head in her hands and uttering a low, moaning sound. "Oh, damn, oh, hell," she was weeping and cursing, "where is *that* coming from? There were cupboards in the pantry at the second farmhouse and cupboards in the kitchen. I smell mice right now.

I see a tin can, we used to nail the lids over the mouse holes; it's dark in the cupboards.''

"Did anyone put you in the cupboards?" Stanley was casual.

"No," the lispy, small voice told him, "I hid there, behind the pots and pans."

He didn't recognise that voice or the quickly changing features that had accompanied it. "Were you playing in the cupboards?"

The answer came in a rough, adult voice. "Hell no, man. We were scared."

"Night and day . . ." Elvira, whose name he didn't know but whose voice he recognised, along with her abandoned body language, sang the words in an alto, to a Southern baptist beat.

During the break Stanley made a phone call to Marshall's hotel. The message read to him was, "Be cool, see you for drink 3:00 P.M. today." Stanley clenched his hands all the way back to the studio. Ever mindful of his instructor's "river theory," he pushed the woman harder, reminding whoever glared at him that they didn't have enough recall at this point, that if someone, anyone, would only elucidate on what was termed the "flicks against my mind," they'd get further. Things grew more confusing. At one point he heard what seemed to be the woman, explaining her mother's interrogation tactics; how she'd held her daughter by the hair of her head, alternately yanking and screaming questions. The woman sounded bewildered, as she tried to name what she'd done to cause her mother's rage.

Brat, who was eight years old, simmered just behind the woman. Brat seldom appeared in public, she was too volatile, unable to stand still long enough, to understand much except the rage inside herself. Her rage expressed itself in tantrums, instant and full-blown at any cross word. For Brat, the world and the people in it meant torture, misery, degradation. She remembered the agony of being accused and punished by the mother, while being guilty of nothing. Neither she nor the woman had committed the overblown "crimes" the mother had ranted about. They had simply not been present at those times.

Unknown to Stanley, this young Troop member's confusion, her feeling of dehumanisation and long-suppressed anger had now welled up. Identical emotions swept throughout the Troop Formation, and he spent the next fifteen minutes like a spectator at a hockey game, viewing a composite picture of how not to raise a child.

Stanley decided to bring up the subject of Mean Joe.

"Once his size and power is clear, Mean Joe can be scary to people who don't understand him. We've written about Mean Joe in the manuscript pages."

"I'm sorry," Stanley said, wishing he had a name to go with a voice. "I don't think I read it. Tell me."

"You don't read very fast, do you?"

"Not as fast as you write," Stanley told her, thinking of the growing backlog of manuscript in his office.

"You'll have to shape up," For once, Elvira wasn't laughing. She told Stanley that Mean Joe had blown the mother's mind.

It occurred to Stanley that if Mean Joe, a male, had presented the mother with a boy's more aggressive attitude and behavior, then she'd have been startled, to say the least.

"Usually," Elvira said, "we got beaten and worse, when we crossed the mother. But then one day Mean Joe was there, I mean he was just there. Things turned around after that. Of course, Mean Joe couldn't be there all the time but when he was, watch out. The mother didn't dare smack him. People look at Mean Joe today. His voice, his size, it scares them. But Mean Joe wouldn't hurt anyone unless they tried to stomp on one of us. Besides, the Peacemaker is always with him when he's out, more to calm whoever he's talking to than to protect them from his wrath. Mean Joe isn't a wrathful person."

The Peacemaker, Stanley thought, someone who made peace in Mean Joe's wake, another of what seemed to be checks and balances in a complicated, internal process? He chose to ignore the reference and question something else.

"Somehow I get the impression that you enjoyed the mother's discomfort. You're smiling. Did you enjoy it?"

Elvira disguised her scrutiny of him by listening in her own mind to the Talking Heads do a drawn-out version of "Take Me to the River." That way if Stanley broke bad, if he chastised her for enjoying the mother's misery, she could just fade into the music. She couldn't be hurt if she didn't hear him. Nor would she ever tell him anything else. The music in her mind ended. She took a shot.

"Yeah," she said. "I enjoyed it. No excuses, man, I hung on every yelp out of her mouth. Like a really great piece of music, you know? Something that sinks right into the old bones!" The pleasure on her face was plain; she punctuated it with a sound that might have made Little Richard envious.

Stanley laughed and by so doing, became less the enemy, more the-possible-confidant-being-tested. She still wouldn't give her name but she would, throughout the balance of the session, give the names of several other Troop members, their activities and fears. Let him guess, she thought, that's all he's doing, guessing. He can't kill what he can't specifically identify.

"Reading was safe," she said in her street-smart way, with the music in her mind going full blast. She recited snatches of poetry having to do with moonlight. One of them was "The Highwayman," and she did not stumble over the words. The imagery of a renegade highwayman travelling on a moonlit landscape yanked Stanley back to his high school *Prose and Poetry* books. Her voice, aside from an ever-present bravado, was almost wistful and quite reflective. Stanley was sure, however, that more than wistfulness and reflection lay behind it.

"The mother hated that romantic streak in us. One night, Sixteen, when she was thirteen—Does that confuse you, Stanley?—leaned out the bedroom window. The moon was full, so pale a blue, a colour no one can mix, no matter how hard we try. It washed over the countryside that night; quiet, no movement anywhere. We smiled to ourselves. And the next morning the mother hissed: 'Did you sleep without your nightgown on last night? You know that's not nice, the rule is you sleep in your nightgown, you keep your clothes on at all times.' And the mother didn't look at us but kept her eyes down and got very quiet and then nervous, telling us that we had no control, that we'd never had any."

"Us?" Stanley couldn't resist it. He knew the person in front of him wasn't referring to the half brother or the half sisters, but to herself and the others with her. It was like asking the rain why it was wet. She looked at him as if he were dense and said that it was only an "expression." But wariness haunted the eyes; he sensed a withdrawal in the body movements, caution behind the good humour. Immediately there was another change.

The laughter came in giant, unrestrained waves, washing over the woman's body long before it reached her throat.

"Why am I laughing? What did I do wrong those times? I wish I knew." She held onto her face with both hands, trying to ask over the hilarity why her mother had hated her so much. But her jaw dropped and the voice became sluggish, the words thick and forced.

126

"Do you want to stop now?" He kept the concern from his tones.

"No! But there's something wrong. My arms are full of needles, the room is swaying and my head roars, Stanley, I feel as if my hands are moving in molasses!"

The only thing he could conclude was that some sort of chemical imbalance had taken place within her body—too many persons coming and going all at once and, in the process, somehow tripping the delicate balance. He watched her fighting to regain a footing, struggling to tell him, over the continuing laughter, that her mother had never failed to drive her back into the "hole" and make her cringe after an outburst.

"She treated me at times," the woman said with the same thick voice as before, "as if I were a wild thing in a cage."

"Maybe it seemed that way to her," Elvira smiled. "Mean Joe could scare the mother just by looking at her. She thought Mean Joe was wild but he was just different. The drummer he listened to did a mean beat and took no crap from nobody."

Behind the words there was an unyielding sense of humour, the ability to hang on, unperturbed. The mind producing the slang expressions was quick; it would give only so much at a time and no more. Stanley knew he was being tested with the few sentences about Mean Joe and did not press it, fearing to destroy the progress already made. Spurred by his reticence, she leaned forward to ask if he liked chocolate chip cookies dunked in scotch, Francis Bacon's paintings, and rock music. Sensing the opportunity to create a bond, Stanley took a deep breath and said yes.

Elvira smiled to herself under the angular swath of hair that partially concealed her eyes; Stanley really wasn't a bad sort. Trusting him or anybody, though, could be a mistake. Well, what the hell. She snapped her fingers to a silent beat, moving her body from the waist in a short burst of amazing abandon, telling him about "that woman's," meaning the mother's, criticism of Elvis Presley's "lurid gyrations." The mother, she said, had been horrified and threatened to "shut his mouth for good" by turning off the television set.

"Are you talking about your mother?" Stanley asked.

"You can't play that game with me, honey," Elvira said. "That was never my mother."

Her next words reminded Stanley of the white collage hanging in the woman's foyer. First her voice and then a number of others

127

told him of a national art exhibit in which their high school had participated. Apparently they'd turned in over a hundred and fifty entries and won awards for all. But one particular water-colour of a tree, their first attempt at the medium, earned them a coveted gold key. He felt a shudder at hearing the description of the tree—eerie, cold, and twisted into itself, standing in yellow moonlight on an empty moor. The roots, he was told, could not be discerned from the branches, because they intermeshed, clinging together. Somehow he felt the symbolism was linked, client to tree. Had whoever painted it understood what they were painting, had they done it intentionally? "Does anyone paint anymore?" he asked.

"Thirty-eight paintings in two months' time last year, for a one-woman show. In acrylics. Did 'em all, right in the middle of full-time real estate."

Silence. The woman's blank face made him uncomfortable. He asked who painted.

"We don't know," Twelve said. "When one of us begins, sometimes one of us is creating. But at other times it's as if someone here, someone we don't know at all, takes over. Whatever goes on the canvas then, comes from that person. Catherine paints all by herself and she writes, always in a wry style, very sophisticated and cryptic. She wouldn't let anyone guide her, except . . ."

"Who guides Catherine?"

"I can't tell you. When the time is right, Catherine will tell you herself."

Silence, and again the withdrawal.

"I hear the mother had what might be called an enlightening tongue," Stanley prodded. "Is that true?"

Elvira proceeded to mimic remembered phrases.

"'I didn't have to give birth to you; I chose to and it's a debt never to be forgotten or escaped, do you hear me? I want you to act like a lady, walk without sashaying, lower your voice, speak up, act adult! What are you smiling at, why are you frowning, what are you doing up there in your room all day long, why can't you be good, why are your grades so bad? You think life is hard now, wait until you get out in the world and you'll know what hard is! It's a cold world out there. What are you crying for, keep that up and I'll give you something to cry about!'"

Elvira described the first date, a prom. The dress for it was long and white and the motherly chat beforehand turned into a

128

diatribe on what good girls didn't let bad boys do. To the mother, all boys were bad; so were the girls who went out with them. The lecture didn't dim Sixteen's joy and astonishment that a boy had actually asked for a date. But the stepfather found out about the date, and grabbed her in the kitchen one night. Enraged, he said that if she went to that prom, he'd tell the boy she was a whore.

The woman surfaced just before Elvira's last words, looking the way she felt: off-balance. "For weeks before the dance," she said, "I wanted to die because stepfather's actions just didn't make sense to me."

"You had no idea what he meant by 'whore,' in relationship to yourself, you didn't understand why he didn't want you to date, to be with a boy?"

She doesn't know. Stanley wrote it down on the clipboard, digging the pen into the paper. If his assumptions were correct, here was the heart of Multiple Personality Disorder. Her eyes at this moment, no matter what knowledge various other voices had imparted to him this day or any other, were empty of that knowledge. They reflected only the shock he'd seen growing in the last hour, the surge of disbelief at what her vague suspicions had to mean.

It seemed that one minute he heard "her" stating point blank the stepfather's intentions, as if "she" had some recall of the incest and the events surrounding it. The next minute "she" would break into her own conversation, exhibiting no knowledge at all about the stepfather or anyone else in the family. At those times, what he ran up against was a blank face, a doubting look, an unawareness of things discussed in past sessions or even moments before.

Catching which person was the woman and which was another self; delineating when the woman vanished while speaking a whole series of thoughts or merely, in some instances, a single sentence, was a chore he didn't think he'd mastered. How was he to determine exactly how much she knew, when he could not always determine which one she was? The face in front of him bore the look of confusion, unfamiliarity with her surroundings. For a moment he doubted that she knew her own name, or would understand if he asked her. He was silent, unwilling to disturb the vulnerability, the fear he was sensing.

"Stanley," she didn't seem conscious of the tears on her face, "this is the first time my stepfather's face, his expression in the

129

kitchen that day, has ever been clear to me. Why did he act like that?"

"Whore." The word was said by a small voice and repeated. But then the voice changed and wet green eyes looked up at him. The voice carried a note of desperation and self-doubt, asking if he'd ever treated a victim who didn't cry.

"No, not one," he said, and told her that her childhood was bizarre, that her stepfather, and possibly even her mother, had been "sick." He hoped the woman heard him; it had become difficult to pick her out in the crowd.

Shaking with exhaustion, with eyes gritty from mascara after more than a solid hour of crying, the woman drove home from the session, hating the traffic and driving between tractor trailers and buses with her eyes shut. Each time no crash occurred, she gasped a sigh of relief. She'd been driving for many years and didn't understand how her record could be perfect when she was such an imperfect, frightened driver. She'd told Stanley about her driving. He hadn't known what to say.

Today's session, like all the rest, had been almost completely enervating, a result of unconscious straining to remain "surfaced" and in control. The woman struggled daily for that same control, unaware of what she struggled against. The sessions totalled three hours a week, and the recuperation time afterward ate into a calendar that never contained enough days in any one month. Eventually she would wonder why her days were so crammed with scheduled events and duties that seemed only vaguely to transpire; then she would laugh at the obvious answer. She wasn't laughing now. Her entire body ached, her head roared, and always there was that awful sense of imbalance, the feeling of imminent danger, the fear of unnamed things. All of it was mixed with the certainty that any second she would topple over.

Summer was in full swing; a hot, humid blanket covered the countryside, baked her front lawn, and threatened to burn the grass trying to grow there. On her front porch she fumbled with the house key, wanting to get inside where things were more familiar, where she could throw off the effects of the session. But from the corner of one sore, gritty eye, she saw it, movement at her feet. The key lay forgotten in her hand.

Lamb Chop bent down, slid to hands and knees, fascinated by the earthworm making its way across the front porch. Gently, she guided the worm onto the palm of her hand. She had always loved them. Twelve had a whole bunch in the big aquarium in the living room. Lamb Chop would have brought the worm inside and added it to Twelve's collection but the edict had gone out: no strange worms; you'll destroy the chemical balance.

A half-hour disappeared somewhere; time seemed to do that, drift away like vanishing smoke. For a second the idea of smoke hung in the woman's mind . . . then came the smell of it, burning leaves. She saw the stepfather, the flatbed car, saw the hiding place under it, understood for the first time that the flatbed car was an open trailer on which the buzz saw had been hauled around the orchards so that tree branches could be pruned. Why was the stepfather waiting as she got off the school bus, why was she getting off here at the orchard instead of the house where the mother would have an afternoon snack ready?

The second had lasted too long; in the Tunnel, the Weaver's fingers flew, blessedly overtaking the woman and the screams coming out of her mouth. She found herself, moments later, listening to static on the radio and searching for a lamp that would light. The bulbs blew so often, perhaps the wiring had grown faulty. But then she'd lived in a lot of places and the light bulbs always blew fast. At the back of her mind, knowledge formed and was swept away.

Go away, leave me alone, I hate you. Why did that expression pop into her head so often, along with an almost childish anger and a feeling of dirtiness? She stood in the kitchen, two brand-new seventy-five-watt bulbs in her hand, anxious to replace them before dark. The words were repeated. As with all else, she'd assumed, on hearing them in the past, that they were hers. She didn't know what they meant. She'd simply lived with them, noting vaguely now, after two months of grinding therapy, how they coincided each time, with certain events. Sometimes it was a flick of memory, or her perpetration, real or imagined, of a social gaffe, or someone discovering her mistake at one task or another—it never dawned that immediately after hearing the words she could not sit in a chair but had, in order to perform any task, to kneel on the floor. At those times, she shook and there was the sound of hysterical crying.

Now as always, she tried not to listen to the banshee wails, tried to continue without interruption the task at hand. The small fingers rapping on the walls of the Tunnel that were her mind, went unnoticed.

Go away, leave me alone, I hate you. The words kept echoing in a small, fearful, crying voice. And again she felt the unknown danger. Along with the knowledge of her own cowardice because she didn't dare to wonder what the small voice was terrified of, the woman trembled as she went from room to room, gathering lamps. She sat them down on the kitchen floor and knelt, with hands that shook and eyes that were too full, to put new bulbs into each socket. She did consider for a moment the extraordinary amount of money she spent on light bulbs and batteries.

14

No question. She's a multiple. I've counted at least seven of her in thirty minutes. So what's the problem?''

Marshall Fielding turned away from the video screen. Stanley had purposely avoided, all through drinks at the airport and the ride to the university, any mention of the woman. Stanley preferred to let Marshall see for himself, from his vantage point as researcher in a complex field. It was now six in the evening and neither of them had thought of dinner.

"The problem," Stanley said, "is that she doesn't always jibe with what I've been reading."

"And she won't. We've barely touched the surface of how varied multiplicity can be. These people are unique, Stanley; they've got their own patterns and if double or triple the amount of case histories were recorded, there'd be areas in most of them that wouldn't match. We know very little about this phenomenon."

"Mental health," Stanley sighed, "the inexact science."

"That's why I'm not in your end of it, remember? Can't take pain too close up." His dark brown eyes were level and serious behind the affable smile. Marshall was not a big man; in height he reached just below Stanley's nose. His body, wiry and compact in a tan, summer-weight suit, gave the impression of fitness and no wasted motion. "I'd rather chart the researchers, watch the clients from a distance. And watching them isn't always what the movies lead us to expect. On the other hand, these persons here have only known you two months; they may be a little reticent, sort of feeling you out. The tapes show a very smooth transition from one person to the other, and sometimes I don't even see a transition, I simply hear more than one of them verbalising at the same time.''

''Today's session was the strongest it's ever been in that regard, but you've no idea how I wanted a second opinion.''

''Well, this is it—multiplicity, full blown. Whatever you've researched, pretend you never read it. Multiple personality isn't always materialisation after a great struggle. By that I mean all multiples don't necessarily turn red in the face or seem to fade away before the changes. That may happen in the case of this woman, but so far on the tapes everyone has been relatively cool about it. I daresay her friends probably don't notice many changes because they are so smooth, and to some, she just seems moody or excitable.''

Marshall had already given the manuscript a cursory examination and asked if he could have a copy to study more thoroughly. ''If the title means anything, Stanley, you've got trouble. I know you don't hunt, but the scream of a wounded rabbit is the one sound you never want to hear again.''

Stanley told him that the officers in Albert's police precinct never wanted to hear it again, either. He outlined the oddities and the most intractable problems he'd encountered with his client.

''She's as confused as you are right now,'' Marshall told him. ''Regardless of her strength, as she gets deeper into therapy, this smoother type of personality 'switch' will frighten her more. She may be coming in on the tail end of some of the switches already, or even in the middle at times. If so, she 'hears' snatches of conversation from a distance, whether it's from outsiders like you or from the other selves. She may know periodically that she's here or later that she's been here, but it will take a certain trigger or a series of them to remember even vaguely what was said. And if any one of these persons starts revealing deep sore spots, she won't remember what they've said at all. It may not be a matter of remembering; she may not have been there in the first place.''

Stanley told him how the woman kept a daily journal and tape-recorded at home.

''You realise, of course, that the others are participating in those efforts? You're not used to their world; you tend to think of everything as originating from a single source, when in actuality the sources are many."

"It's a habit I'm trying to break myself of," Stanley said. "I'm just now realising how little memory my client has, and that I'm not even sure which one she is."

"You may never even have met her." Seeing Stanley's expression, Marshall gestured at the video screen. "C'mon, Stanley. I'm not saying that you haven't; I don't know. But think about this whole multiplicity process; its purpose is to protect the core, the original, first-born entity. These people can't do that if the core is out wandering around all the time."

The tape rolled on. Marshall tried to make Stanley understand that he'd simplified what was a convoluted, unique-unto-itself process. Nobody, not even the experts, were sure they'd even scratched the surface of the mechanism. She, or whoever, sat there before them in full colour, her face and body reflecting a mind-bending range of emotion. Eventually, in the middle of the trauma and then an outburst of rage, "she" made an aside to Stanley that set the two of them laughing.

"Somebody," Marshall said, "has a true sense of comedy. The wit is sharp. It ranges from a gallows humour to a sophomoric naïveté but if I had to guess, I'd say most of it is coming from a single other self. One of them is playing games with you, testing your perceptions." Marshall shook his head. "There's so much diversity in these tapes. You're lucky they're willing to be filmed, but it may take a while to delineate each one."

He continued to watch. "You just asked a question and she couldn't remember. There, she did it again! She can't remember what you said just three seconds ago. Obviously three seconds ago she wasn't there."

Marshall's attention was riveted to the videotape. He watched the woman talking to Stanley, as her face, her body, began more obviously to shift and change. Seated there on the floor Indian-fashion, her face had lost the masquelike look of a second ago and was relaxing; her eyes had softened and become wide and innocent, her mouth the rounded "o" of a small child. The voice dropped to a whisper and she smiled, trustingly. After all this time, that voice still made Stanley shiver.

"Oooh," there was a giggle from the screen, "she's coming, I feel her, she's here, right now."

"It's a child," Marshall said. "You've tapped the well, so to speak. Behind this child, there are others, just as small and

135

probably far more damaged. She's a façade for them. I can almost feel it. See the way she holds herself?"

Stanley did and he didn't. Either Marshall had become a romantic over the two years since they'd seen each other, or an exposure to multiplicity had honed his senses. Stanley watched the screen, trying to absorb the action with Marshall's faculties. The child gave herself a final hug and seemed to melt away. An older but just as innocent and lilting voice emerged, along with eyes that held nothing but happiness and wonder.

"Who is that?" Marshall demanded. "Which one of them was the child talking about?"

Stanley swallowed. "Miss Wonderful."

Marshall grinned. "The names are sometimes a trip. And I'll bet you thought they'd call themselves Martha, Jane, or Henry."

Marshall yanked the tab from a can of Pepsi and told Stanley that he could forget his usual six-months-and-out-into-the-street routine. "No telling how many persons this woman will wind up with. Funny, isn't it? A good shrink would give his eyeballs to get hold of a multiple personality because statistically, we're lucky to find two bona fides in a professional lifetime. Notice I said 'statistically.' Yet when you see it in front of your face, in a real, live client . . ."

Stanley nodded. "The sadness," he muttered, "is incredible. For me, it outweighs the discovery."

"Hey." Marshall raised a black eyebrow as wiry and mobile as his body. "I'm an optimist. I think to myself, Better to find the problem, no matter how old the client is, knock it out, give them some good years. And Stanley, you'll be giving good years to forty or more of her."

"More than forty?" Stanley was thinking of Jeannie Lawson and her three separate selves.

"From the tapes and the manuscript, your client is a candidate for the higher numbers. We're discovering that between fifteen and thirty-seven is the median; beyond that, nobody knows. In Los Angeles right now there's a man with two hundred, and at a very prestigious Ivy League university a young woman with one hundred and twenty-five is studying for her law degree. As to your client, when the incest starts that early, two years old, and it continues over the years with a close authority figure, not the guy down the street, you're talking prime multiple personality breeding ground. Of course, you've first got to be talking gifted child, at least that's what we've found in most cases. Multiples are born, the majority of them, creatively brilliant. But for those stripped bare by child abuse, the brilliance is fractured, hidden from view. In the case of this woman, you throw in a very peculiar mother and you add a maternal Irish grandmother steeped to the gills in catholicism. It had to make for an exceedingly restrictive upbringing.''

"Her mother had broken away from the church. The children never went to church." Stanley frowned.

"It doesn't matter. The catholic influence was, and is, still there. I noticed that nothing is capitalised in the manuscript if it's even vaguely reflective of religion. There's a lot of deserved hatred for all authoritarianism there, and for the church in particular. But there's conflict, too. Someone on those tapes today made the sign of the cross, over and over.''

"I told her two weeks into therapy that before becoming a therapist I was a minister. Come to think of it, the reply was a little strange. It took about thirty seconds of consideration and then she said, 'We forgive you, Stanley.' ''

"Whoever said it wasn't kidding but at least you're outside this group's ring of fire. That good old Irish grandmother, if my estimation is correct, was mean as hell, with the beads tucked under both arms and a tongue like a puff adder. They visited her often; she could have pumped gallons of sin and the devil into that kid over just one weekend. Then they all troop home to the farm and mommie takes over where grandma left off. You don't forget catholic training easily. So mommie, fallen away from the church or not, could have planted more ideas of sin and retribution into an already tortured little brain and, presto, this kid's got no place to go.''

"So she goes into her mind. She splinters," Stanley said.

"She not only splintered, she pulled out. The human mind can only be pushed so far before it refuses to deal with the garbage. Some of these persons probably got started at two or three and if her stepfather took an immediate liking to the situation, which I'm sure he did—I mean, that guy had her locked up like private stock—a lot of the others were born shortly thereafter. We'd better find a sandwich, Stanley, you'll need to keep your strength up. You've got what I'd call an increased case load.''

"Must you cackle that way?"

"I'm a very adjusted guy, I go with the flow," Marshall's tone behind the grin held a deep sarcasm. "As I was saying, certain ones become damaged along the way, they stop developing. Others are created to pick up the threads. The damaged ones remain, but usually their replacements are a lot more aware of the world through established knowledge; a form, if you will, of previous experience.''

''While the client remains in blissful ignorance.''

''Sure, except that thirty years later she finds herself in a wall-to-wall brick bathroom. Your clues, the only two you need, are the amnesia and the headaches which resemble migraines. Forget the manner in which the persons emerge, or the overall operating pattern, MPs as a rule have got their own individual patterns, and survival is uppermost in their minds. Stanley, these people are the survivors. If the world blew up tomorrow, guess who'd walk out of the rubble? Unless, of course, they commit suicide first, and nobody has those statistics.''

''Is it settled?'' Jeannie asked over the phone.

''MPD,'' Stanley replied, ''your diagnosis and mine.''

''Stanley, could you possibly be right, that if incest and physical and sexual child abuse is so prevalent, then multiple personality may be prevalent, too?''

Jeannie and a math professor and his wife joined Marshall and Stanley at a restaurant that night. Jeannie hadn't gone anywhere socially in over two years; she seemed grave and silent. Fortunately the place wasn't crowded; not so many eyes watching her, but she wished she'd been able to keep her coat on. She felt lost without its voluminous folds. She wished her counselor could be here, but it didn't really matter. Jeannie still had the sharply retentive mind of one of her former ''selves.'' She would write out a report later and add it to her thesis material.

Marshall was saying that according to Frank Putnam at NIMH, Stanley had handled his client with professional aplomb: he had given encouragement, never a feeling of rejection, no matter how strange she might have sounded. He had planted posthypnotic suggestions in her mind as to her worth and instead of downplaying fears had told her that she had every right to be scared out of her senses. Marshall outlined the kind of therapy multiples could expect as a rule, and the math professor's wife made a sound of annoyance and disbelief.

''You sound as though proper treatment for a multiple is practically unheard of. You mean that if I came down with multiplicity my chances of surviving therapy would be, say, ninety-percent negative?''

"For one thing, you don't 'come down' with it, but, yes, those are your chances. Provided of course that someone could diagnose you in the first place.''

"Is there anything in particular that I ought to watch out for?'' Stanley asked.

"Watch out that you don't kill her.'' Marshall's tone was sarcastic. There was silence at the table. "I saw a multiple killed once. Not in the strict sense of the word, of course. Her therapist did it. She had what I can only call a 'flying mind.' The goddamned thing soared, Stanley. It flew right over the garbage that bogs most of us down in this world; her own situation aside, it sliced like a sabre, straight to the heart of any problem. Of course she wasn't doing the slicing, it wasn't her mind that was soaring. One of her people was a bona fide genius, the kind you see once in a lifetime. Her psychiatrist tried his damnedest to force her—them, her other selves, to integrate. He wanted to see one 'well-rounded, whole' person. I think in many ways the fragmented aspect of MPD scared the hell out of him, especially when he saw things he couldn't comprehend, ideas he couldn't have conceived himself in a million years. There was so much beauty unfolding in that woman, and she had such a long way to go—her people getting to know each other fully, exploring themselves and her, showing their wares, if you will. They never had a chance.''

"What happened?'' Stanley laid down his fork.

"Nobody knows. The last time I saw her, the psychiatrist had managed to convince himself that he'd fused two of her selves and was aiming at the other one hundred and fifty of them. I'm not saying that integration can't be a damned good thing for a lot of multiples. But it wasn't good for her, and he kept trying to fit her into a mold. Multiplicity by its very nature wasn't made for any mold yet conceived by man. I watched her for over a year, growing more and more confused and less productive. It was as if she were right back in the middle of the experiences that had caused the multiplicity in the first place. He had re-created a restrictive environment for her. She just disappeared one day. Gone. Multiples are good at that. Some could hide in the middle of main street, name tag and all, and nobody would find them.''

Jeannie had been trying hard all evening to stay behind her

disguise of a student researching her thesis. She hoped the strain she felt at her next question would not give her away.

"Do people believe you when you talk," Jeannie asked, "do they believe that multiplicity and the complexity of its process really exist?"

"Ask Frank Putnam that question. The guy has contributed more toward understanding in the area of MPD than I'll know for another five years and in some learned circles they still spit on him. When Putnam was researching schizophrenia, he discovered that the term didn't fit all the patients he encountered. That led him to research the multiple personality cases recorded since the early 1800s. His final documented conclusion was that ninety-eight percent of the multiples on record involved repeated and severe incidents of child sexual and physical abuse. Incest seems to head the list, culprit-wise. For better or for worse, multiplicity may not be as rare as we think—only misdiagnosed. All I can say is, I hope Stanley keeps doing what he's doing. At least he won't harm her. Or them."

"Putnam." The math professor frowned into his dinner plate. "I've heard that name somewhere before, on television, I think. It was a documentary on a man with five personalities. The actor, David Birney, was superb, and I'm sure they mentioned Frank Putnam's research at the end of the show. I remember thinking how close to schizophrenia the symptoms were, and how severely they'd hampered the victim's life. But you, and correct me if I'm wrong, don't seem to regard MPD as being highly debilitating, as it was for Sybil, or even as a 'mental illness.' "

"It depends on the multiple," Marshall said. "In the case of Stanley's client and the young woman studying for her law degree, yes, they're going through hell, and yes, their lives have been damaged, but for them, MPD has also been a high-level coping mechanism. Their people have carried them through one accomplishment after the other, allowed them to exist in a world that is frustrating and sometimes impossible, even for the 'sane' among us. Think about it. No matter what, Stanley's client has lived with her rage and it never erupted against society; she isn't on welfare or in a mental hospital."

The woman stared right back at Stanley and then at the wall. Finally she spread her hands out in front of her and looked at them for a long time, as if she'd never seen them before.

"Multiple," she said in a shaky voice. "*Three Faces of Eve, Sybil.* I never wanted to read those books, never wanted to see the movies, either. What I've heard about them seemed so far-fetched." She didn't add that just the mention of Sybil or Eve called up ideas of science fiction and was, to her, somehow frighteningly repulsive.

Her voice changed abruptly; so did the look in her eyes, and Stanley had the impression that whoever was trying to get out held her in a desperate grip. He saw the laughter coming, long before it burst out of her mouth.

"What am I laughing at?" She raised her hands and pressed them to her cheeks, hard. "I knew back then that things were bad; I can't remember them, can't believe they were as bad as people described Sybil's situation. Were they that bad? Is that what you're saying?"

"What do you think?"

"The reactions of your students to the tapes, Sharon's expression sometimes, even Norman's, tell me it's possible. But they must be wrong. Whatever else, there was never . . . penetration." The word had come out of her mouth as if someone had strangled it. "Never. I was a full adult, far from that last farmhouse before I knew what a, uh . . ."

"Penis," Stanley said.

". . . what that looked like. Ugly, ugly word."

With the differing facial and body language, he found it impossible to hold onto the single image he grasped of her at times. She tried to tell him over sobs that alternated with barely restrained nervous laughter, about the pink thing nestled in wiry brush. As usual she could not say any word aloud if it was connected to herself and described human sex organs.

Stanley didn't need his notes to remind him that someone did remember penetration in the cornfield at the age of two, or that they had howled with remembered pain during the recall. Simple denial was not the issue here. The issue was that while other selves might remember many things, the woman did not.

"With or without penetration, which never happened to Sybil, by the way, even what you've remembered so far could cause multiple personality." Stanley handed her a cup full of hot coffee. She stopped crying and drank. When he launched vehemently into pronouncing the words "penis" and "vagina" and describing sex acts, perverted and otherwise, in an attempt to blast away some of her mental cotton batting, she merely stared

141

at the floor. It was apparent that while she acknowledged the words on one level, she couldn't repeat them.

But all of it was having an effect. Inside her mind, something shot up like mercury heated at the base of a thermometer, rising to a point far beyond her own vision. "You're telling me," snapped a harsh voice, "that incest caused multiple personality, that because of it, I'm not alone in here, I've got to be part of a goddamned group? The stepfather did that to me? The bastard, if I had him right now, he'd be a dead man."

For the person speaking, the rage at discovering close "neighbors" went on for the next ten minutes. Stanley didn't even stop to wonder how he would feel under the same circumstances. He had enough trouble envisioning the woman's world. As the rage dissipated, he brought up the subject of imaginary playmates.

"I never had an imaginary playmate," the harsh voice told him stubbornly. "I wanted to be alone, got that? Totally, one-hundred-percent alone." A shiver went through the hunched shoulders. "I never 'saw' myself doing anything, good or bad. What little memory I've got of those two farmhouses does not include an imaginary playmate."

"You keep on asking," the voice had softened and slim fingers buttoned and then unbuttoned the high-necked collar of the white blouse, "if I heard voices as a child. No, I didn't. I never heard voices until I began putting journal notes together for the manuscript. One night I was walking from the kitchen to the gallery, putting coffee on. Someone whispered my name. That voice was real, Stanley, and I was all alone in the house. Am I crazy? Is that what multiple personality is all about?"

"How did she take the news this morning?" Marshall stood with Stanley in front of the university, his arms loaded with duplicate files of the woman's manuscript. Students went by, laughing, scuffing their shoes on the cement sidewalk. There was a smell of fresh-cut grass in the air. It all seemed very normal.

"She thinks she's crazy. I wish you were in town with me on this one," Stanley said.

"I don't. Particularly not this one. I read more of her stuff last night. The similarities to my friend are rather chilling."

"I've only had time to read fifty percent of what you've got in that box. My schedule is worse than ever and, outside of the

142

sessions and for a few days afterward when I'm energised, I'm exhausted."

"No kidding?" Marshall pretended surprise. "Better get yourself some vitamins. You know, this manuscript, putting so much down on paper, is dangerous to a multiple's sense of crime and punishment. If I were you, Stanley, I'd be busy hanging onto every scrap. Somebody in there writes with a very old hand and the symbolism, especially toward the end . . ." Marshall's face clouded over and then the smile was back. "Listen, give Putnam a call when you get the chance. And let me know what's happening. One more thing, Stanley. Sometimes during the most productive period, a multiple will panic for no reason. No reason the shrink can predict, that is. They start fighting it, they run."

"I'll watch her, Marshall."

"You better. And watch yourself, too."

Marshall waited by his car until Stanley had gone through the doors of the Humanities Building. He wondered, in view of what he had observed on the tapes, how long it would take Stanley to catch on to the most bizarre aspect of all—an aspect that professionals didn't often risk talking about, even among themselves.

15

The next session moved faster than Stanley had anticipated. From the beginning, the sketchbook had sat in her lap. Right in the middle of one of the woman's blank-faced stares and a large bunch of snapdragons erupting under a pink crayon, he encountered a small self who told him that as children, "if you were smart, you didn't write anything down and you didn't draw anything, either. The mother would get you."

At that, she burst into tears. He hadn't learned to determine which child was which. But whenever creativity through painting or drawing, or the written word had been mentioned today, someone tiny wept buckets, holding her right hand protectively cupped inside her left, and sobbing words that sounded like "hot stove."

Stanley instantly thought of the big black cookstove in the farmhouse kitchen and moved as if to pat her arm. He had been too quick; she reared back as if he had struck her.

"No skin," she wept and continued to crouch over the hand in her lap.

"Who are you?" he asked, and watched another change take place. The attitude of the figure before him now suggested a teenager, laid back and in control of the situation. Without knowing it, Stanley had reached Sixteen, who was shy only in romantic situations.

"You shouldn't do that," she said. "The child can't bear to

be touched and hardly anybody here will say their own name aloud to you.''

Stanley asked if there was a reason; she told him her job was only to be around when the little one was out. Immediately her features seemed heavier, the brows lower on the forehead and they appeared fuller, as did the lips and cheekbones. The voice was husky.

Stanley was informed that in days of yore, soldiers came out single file, in full view of the enemy, and were shot down, one by one. Giving names, the husky voice said, was tantamount to giving someone control over you.

"The little one," the husky voice went on, "was trying to tell you that the mother burned her drawings and everything she ever wrote in the big cookstove. The little one made the mistake of identifying herself with her work, and the mother held her hand over the front griddle one day. It taught us a lesson. Don't identify yourself.''

"Why," Stanley asked, "would the mother do that?''

"Almost anything one put on paper was interpreted by the mother to have a sexual, forbidden meaning. The little one never grew after she was burned, she was too frightened. Others of us continued to create but there was a fear about quality that wouldn't rest, the feeling that we'd be punished. We kept everything away from the mother. Only when an art teacher noticed our class work and insisted that we enter a competition, did we all drag out what we'd hidden.''

"You received over one hundred and fifty awards," Stanley said. "Didn't so many convince you of your talent?''

"No," the husky voice said, and Stanley heard the merest hint of a rich brogue, "the mother, strangely enough, took us into the city to receive our acclaim. She acted proud, but we didn't believe her. Not after what she'd done to the little one. We felt shock at so many awards, especially since no one else in our high school had gotten a single one. After the shock wore off, we told ourselves the judges were only in a good mood, the best artists in the state had probably neglected to enter, etc. In short, the awards weren't worth the paper they were printed on.''

For several minutes, the actions had been masculine. Whereas the smaller selves often wiped their tears on the hem of a skirt, and one of the older females licked her tears with her tongue, this one brushed them off with the back of his knuckles.

"Don't stare at me that way, just listen. Someone is speaking

145

through me, someone far back in the Tunnel. It's my job to let him through.''

"He's a man," Stanley said. "I can hear it. Are you a man, too?''

"Are you?" A faint smile twitched at the corners of the heavy mouth.

"Something happened since the last session," Stanley said, "to make the little one surface with those memories about the stove. What was it?"

"The other day, the woman saw the face of the Well in a rain puddle. Now the Well's memories are surfacing—so, too, the memories of the others around her. In a manner of speaking, the Well of Creativity has been awakened. Before her death there were certain others, learning, absorbing her talents. When the Well died, their growth stopped, too."

Stanley asked if the Well had a first name. There was no response. "The child who just told me about her burned hand—is she the Well, and what is sometimes called the 'core'?"

"Never. Your journey to both will never end."

The Troops had begun to trust Stanley more than he realised. Most members would never trust anyone enough to part with their own individual names in face-to-face conversations. But Stanley was about to receive one name that would encompass the whole of their operation. The heavy brogue in which it was announced called up for him visions of the greenest land on earth.

"Y' may," the husky voice said, "call us the Troop Formation, f'r that is what we are."

The Front Runner sensed that for the one in the depths of the Tunnel, the conversation had ended. She readied herself to surface. The Front Runner never slept. Various other Troop members who were practiced enough at front running under her direction might sleep, but never the Front Runner. Her duties were inner circle in nature, and her ministrations were performed constantly, close-up, eyeball to eyeball.

From the husky-voiced male who had been talking, the switch to the Front Runner was fluid, without apparent strain. It took place like the ripple of horseflesh in strong sunlight. The Front Runner saw Stanley smile to indicate that he acknowledged her presence, with or without her name.

"How," the Front Runner asked Stanley, "do you think personality is formed?"

"No one knows, exactly," he said, "or at what stage of life it begins to be formed. Some insist that personality is fixed in the womb by one's genes; others say that we 'learn' our personalities as we go through life. I don't think the answer is readily available or that there is one single answer."

"For the sake of argument, let's envision within each individual human being a tiny, utterly priceless core, containing one's own persona, or personality, one's own self. And let's say that during the formative years from birth to seven years old, the core is open and very vulnerable."

"Done," said Stanley, entering a dialogue he sensed the Front Runner enjoyed.

"Even with the torment that began at two and continued on a daily basis, ripping that core in half, we've heard you express dismay at the amount of disjuncture present. Precisely what do you mean by disjuncture?"

"I suppose what I mean is the necessity for so many of you. No room is left for the woman. Where is she in all of this?"

"We are a necessity for each other, not a luxury or a whim. Individually, each of us have certain memories. As some of us begin now to put the top layers of memory together and evaluate the evidence, a certain knowledge emerges. As the Front Runner, the duty to inform you is mine. Our core, what should have been one person, is split in two. One half is a 'child,' and the other a 'woman.' The two halves are so damaged that the child is little more than an infant mind. The adult half is so unevolved that, were we to describe her condition, you might be skeptical. We can only tell you what we observe. Neither of our cores, 'child' or 'woman,' exists in the outside world."

On the one hand, Stanley was elated. The Front Runner had given him her name. Good manners in this case dictated that he not acknowledge the introduction. On the other hand, he was horrified. Nowhere in other multiple case studies had there been more than one core. What kind of parental guidance, under what guise, from what corner of hell, produced damage so severe?

Furthermore, how did the information he'd just received apply to the woman who had initially asked for therapy?

In her careful, watchful way, the Front Runner stole a look at him. She was aware, although his face was placid, that the news rocked him, but he was not her main concern. Her duty lay with the Troops, with the woman. Given the limitations of the English language, problems loomed ahead in translating for him the exact mechanics of her duties and the Troop Formation's inner workings. It was possible, sometimes, to override another Troop member and pass information to Stanley, using nothing more than her thoughts. In reading the expression in his eyes, the thoughts behind them, and applying just the slightest pressure when he did not receive properly, the Front Runner had thus far been able to convey meaning. But passing information was one thing; would Stanley be adequate to the task of receiving what was to come? Would he be willing to receive all of it, as regards the Troop Formation's inner structure and working apparatus? There were Troop members living behind Catherine and the Outrider, whose identities might never be discovered; Troop members whose minds had never been explored because their thoughts lay on a plane that left them isolated; they might begin to express their views but no one to date had known how to respond. Would Stanley be different, as the Front Runner sensed that he might; would he know enough to ask and pursue the right questions when he did not understand? And would he, conversely, ask too much, too soon? .

For all her strength, both of self and of purpose, the Front Runner felt a sliver of doubt at the advisability of the therapy.

Hi, ho, the Outrider laughed inside the Front Runner's mind as she passed her own silent thought, *In for a penny, in for a pound.*

The Front Runner paused to wonder why that one had ever been chosen to perform a high-echelon task. Probably because she was more than she seemed.

"Behind whom do those Troop members live?" Stanley asked, looking at his notes because the question had just popped into his head. He assumed that he'd written it down somewhere.

The Front Runner had the grace not to smile. "They live in the shadows where it's safe," she said. "For one, they live behind Catherine."

Having said as much as she wanted to for the time being, the Front Runner removed herself, but left what the Troops would someday define as a "marked conversational trail."

"Stanley," the woman said as she surfaced abruptly, "I don't think my mind works the same as yours."

"Of course not." Stanley laughed, right over the distraction he felt. "Your mind is unique and so is everyone else's."

"That isn't what I mean. I have thoughts in my head, just like other people. But their thoughts are connected to feelings.

148

What I've got are only the unconnected thoughts and feelings given me by other selves.''

"Alright," he said, "is someone giving you thoughts and feelings now? Who is giving them to you?''

"They are. My other selves. The voices I hear through the thought transference are from them to me. Not from me to them.''

For the first time, he knew how very removed she was, even from the horror of the concept she presented. A grown woman who, if her statement was valid, had never lived a single moment of her own life. Perhaps, on the other hand, he'd misunderstood.

"It's a weird place up here." She was alternately pulling at the blond hair and tapping her skull. "It's so hard to explain one's own mind.''

"Try," Stanley urged.

"I've told you, or at least I hear myself saying it too often, that when someone screams at me as my mother did, or when I even suspect that someone might, I go away in my mind.''

"By what mechanism? Can you tell me how you do that?''

"No. Because I don't do it. It just happens.''

"Where do you go?" he asked her. "When it happens, what goes on up there in your head?''

"What goes on?" The woman stared at him for a moment. "Stanley, when it happens, I'm not here. There's nothing in my mind except when they give something to me. Right now they're giving me the words I'm saying to you.''

The woman did not understand the meaning behind what she'd just said. She'd said it because another Troop member "gave" it to her and yet another Troop member sat a long way off— puzzled as to the exact meaning as it pertained to herself. The woman on the orange cushions was silent and growing uneasy at the disbelief on Stanley's face. Her unease vanished. She might have been shrieking in the dead silence, so fast and furious were the motions made by the individual facial muscles. Her body strained against the seams of her clothing, the muscles knotting and unknotting.

No previous change had been as harsh as this one, nor had the struggle among her people been so fierce. As features one after the other bent under the onslaught, another person turned to face him. Stanley asked for a name. Silence.

"Do you have a name?''

"You may call me the Interpreter. The differences between

149

the Buffer and myself are vast and complicated. The Buffer stands between the woman and the outside world, absorbing emotional and physical impact. She also absorbs any stray knowledge the Weaver cannot reweave from her mind. The Buffer cannot reason as well as I. She is more emotional about the past because she operates on an emotional level and I operate on the cognitive. I am trying to make this very simple.''

The voice of the Interpreter was devoid of emotion, not like the ragged, erratic sound of the Buffer, who would join future sessions. The Interpreter's eyes were tranquil with a hint of humour, they did not flash with anger or widen in terror. Indeed, her body language conveyed self-confidence and lack of fear.

''You want to know what happens in your client's mind. Her mind is only a tunnel, an avenue to each of us when we choose to enter or ''flood'' it, on occasion. The opening of the Tunnel or avenue is a choice—and you can be sure it is made wisely at all times. The Gatekeeper is the one who makes the choice.

''When the avenue from one or more of our minds to that of your client is opened by the Gatekeeper, we send memories. You know what confetti looks like: little, shredded fragments of coloured paper. We send your client memories, seldom in whole segments, but rather in those shreds; a flurry of them at times, swooshing through the avenue of her mind. To give her or most of us the whole picture at once would be too dangerous, it couldn't be coped with. Our pain would be too great.''

''How can you be sure of that?'' Stanley asked. ''Perhaps everyone's strength is greater than you know.''

''You say that with no concept at all of what's back here. I will give you an example. When a child is tortured, as we were by the stepfather, the child cries. The mother hated crying; to her it was a sign of weakness. 'Be strong,' she used to say, 'and if you don't know how, I'll show you, otherwise you'll never make it in that world out there.' The mother took whatever nightmare things the stepfather tortured us with, and did some torturing of her own. To make us strong, she said. It worked. Some of us are very strong—and stripped of human emotion. Others have no emotion and are weak. The woman is in yet another category. I cannot tell you more. I can only trust you to accept what is said, and hope that you will use caution in working with it.''

The Interpreter saw that Stanley was willing to try and understand what she'd given him so far. One day she might lay out

150

the rest. It was far more complicated and involved the efforts of the entire Troop Formation and the state of the cores. What would he say when he discovered the monstrous number of Troop members that clustered around that double core? Worse, could he, could anyone, understand the intricate, convoluted, but essential mechanism that protected that double core?

"Who," Stanley muttered over his clipboard, "is the one with nothing in her mind? The one you all refer to in the manuscript as 'the woman' or 'the client'?"

The Interpreter gave what might pass for a smile. "She has no other name. Someone had to operate in the world with no memory of the abuse. The woman is merely the tool of the Troop member who, among other things, directs her as the façade."

The Interpreter felt the reverberations of Stanley's inner anger and saw him pushing it aside, plunging ahead.

"In all the case histories I've read on multiplicity," Stanley said, "there is one among the other selves who knows everything. In the case of the Troops—would that person be the Buffer?"

"No." The Interpreter spoke carefully. She was receiving information from more than one Troop mind and as quickly as she caught the words she juxtaposed them for Stanley. "The Buffer only sits in most instances in front of the woman. When one of us moves in, the woman is gone and so is the Buffer. In most instances. So you see, the Buffer couldn't know everything."

"Who does?"

"I do not have that information as yet." She judged his face, inside the tailored Vandyke beard with its sprinkle of grey among the dark brown hair, to be kind; his eyes were alive with intelligence and humour and the anger that had crept to their surface. He looked to be the sort of man who could take anything in stride. Eventually. There was so much that she should be telling him, would be telling him, were it not for the warning signal being sent precisely then from inside the Troop Formation.

A pinpoint of light, for which the conversation and the Interpreter's strong, innermost thoughts had been a catalyst, had suddenly entered the woman's brain. The light was noted and immediately blocked, but the warning continued to sound.

Not yet, *said the Gatekeeper.*

The Interpreter agreed, and, as was the custom, sent a sound-less acknowledgement. From far off, blanketed inside the protective mechanism, a faint cry echoed and was silenced.

The cry echoed and once more it was silenced.

Sleep now. The words came from far back in the woman's mind. They were not directed to her at all, but to the cores. They did not come from Mean Joe this time, but from the one who waged his battle in the darkest recesses of the Tunnel.

Later that night, Stanley reviewed the session. One of Marshall's remarks came back to him. "Regard yourself," he'd said, "as an invited guest in a foreign land. The customs and the life-style may not be your own; they certainly won't be your reality. But we don't know zip about the human mind and who's to say, exactly, what the criteria are for human existence? When you're in their territory, you might learn more by bowing to the East."

All Stanley knew as he looked at the mountain of manuscript, read and unread, was that he'd have to change his perspective if he ever hoped to achieve full understanding—or to determine exactly where the "woman" was, within the scope of the Troop movement. He didn't want to take literally the description of her as it had been given in today's session. Yet when he turned that description over, examined it, it seemed to make more and more sense.

16

With a lot less to go over than Stanley, the woman reviewed the session herself that night, and brooded. She could not recall having said much. She shuffled manuscript pages under the gooseneck lamp, focusing her attention on scattered sentences and doubting the words. Was any of it true?

All this and more, someone said.

Several minutes later the woman surfaced again. She held the same batch of pages in her hand, but over twenty were now missing. Unable to think what she had done with them, she cried. Stupid people lost important things. The pages were irreplaceable and nowhere to be found, although she spent the next half hour searching everywhere.

The woman did not know that the manuscript held messages born of more than ninety minds, each one determined, desperate that the story be heard. Many of them were too young or too damaged to speak aloud. For one Troop member, the twenty lost pages had been her only hope of retribution.

The woman knew only that she had done something wrong. The harder she looked for the pages, the clearer it became that they were gone. Her mind could not identify their contents. As she ripped open the desk drawers and flung other pages about, a hailstorm of confetti burst into the Tunnel. The confetti gave up only shreds of recall. It was enough, however. She began to cry.

· · ·

From the depths of the Tunnel and yet not, because the walls were vertical this time and cold and damp, someone stirred and cried out in utter agony. Shoulders hunched, Mean Joe moved instantly, on silent, monstrous feet. Catherine moved too, anxious to keep her secret. It was too late. She felt Mean Joe's searching gaze as he followed the cries to their source. A child atremble with flesh so icy, so damp it might have been a fish out of arctic waters; Mean Joe knelt in the Tunnel tide and swept it to him. For one brief moment when the wet green eyes opened and locked with his, he knew her. His own eyes grew angrier— not at this sodden, quivering bundle of humanity, but at their mutual tormentors.

The green eyes saw him and shuttered closed against a fleeting recognition. As with a mummy preserved for a thousand years from the harsh light of day, the green faded. In a whispering flash of time, all that was left were two emptied, concave depths of deadened burnt-sienna.

Catherine of the worldly attitudes, the wry sense of humour, Catherine whom nothing ever touched or tormented, uttered against her will a strangled cry, half-felt, half-remembered. It was her own and yet not, enmeshed and yet separate from the frightened wet bundle Mean Joe held against his chest. Catherine's mind fastened on his and sent a steady stream of messages. One of them was gratitude, held in her own eyes that mirrored exactly those of the creature Mean Joe had taken to him.

In the Tunnel darkness the cries grew louder; pain escalated, threatening all those within. The cries became a single shriek. Mean Joe captured the sound, muffled it against a body so tremendous that all reverberations were silenced. His hands, like huge butterfly wings, caressed the face of each tiny charge. With a mind that held a stone-cold rage, Mean Joe called out to another Troop member and was answered.

The Recorder moved forward and sat, mind unleashed under the gooseneck lamp. Her lips were pursed, her brows drawn with the strain. Her whole body tensed with the breath she took in, and then she relaxed. The words formed and flowed, one by one, from the mind of the Recorder through to the hands of the woman sitting at the typewriter. Letter by letter, thought by thought, the twenty pages were re-created. Deep in the Tunnel, the cries subsided.

The Well of Creativity slept. And her name was Olivia.

"Even the mail scares me. Always has, I don't know why. I'm not sure I've ever opened any mail. Isn't that silly? I'm tired of being scared of everything. It means that in the long run I can't ever win."

"That's right," Stanley said. A kind of ingenuous wonder hung in his client's eyes. What did she mean, she never opened the mail? Everybody did. It was like death and taxes.

"I get the feeling," she said, "that I'm doing things wrong all the time. It isn't just the mail, either. I can't relate properly to people. I can't be like them. I don't have feelings or emotions of my own; when a situation calls for responsiveness, I'm lost."

"You weren't brought up to use the feelings you were born with, but they are very strong within you, and hidden."

"I never felt them. Once, in grade school, the boy I had a crush on broke his arm. I looked all through myself but there was no emotion. I remember that day; I was very puzzled."

"But you had a crush on him. Wasn't that an emotion?"

"In a funny way, the crush wasn't mine, either. It was sort of borrowed."

Stanley knew the woman was gone again, and that someone else sat here, discussing herself as if she were a total stranger. He found that many Troop members did that; it was another way of hiding. A pink tongue circled the mouth slowly, moving at the same pace as the fingers that had begun to twine a lock of hair round and round. Purposely, Stanley made no comment. The time wasn't right to say that having no emotion was just as dangerous as having no sensation of pain. Without pain there was no valuable warning signal when the body suffered from a physical ailment. Without emotion, one tended to act, minus regard for the feelings or desires of others—and it eliminated the need for love. Would anyone here ever openly admit to wanting love and affection? So far he'd heard it expressed obliquely, in convoluted terms, as if they were afraid and unsure of its meaning. He asked now if she'd ever felt loved. The answer was no. He thought it came from the woman.

"People," Stanley told her, "have had close relationships with you. Norman, Sharon, your daughter . . ."

"No, not close. I always felt a terrible lack of love in any relationship, unless I was good—a pliant, perfect person. I didn't feel anything for them, not really. It wouldn't matter if everyone died tomorrow, that's how much they affect me. I'm telling you

155

the truth, Stanley; not just to get a rise out of you, but to explain what's going on inside me."

Stanley knew that in adulthood, abused children often turned a deaf ear to any avowal of love. Nor could they, themselves, avow it.

"Sometimes," he said cautiously, "when we don't feel worthy, we can't give or receive anything. To someone laboring under a feeling of low self-esteem, love is completely unrecognizable and therefore unattainable."

"Please," she said, "try to understand. I don't want it, even though I hear myself saying or thinking at times that I do. I'm empty. When I say all this to you, it's confusing because I feel so far away and because so many different thoughts go through my head at once. I can't be sure of anything when that happens, except that I'm so scared."

"Once you've absorbed and accepted what your people are trying to tell you, once the denial period is over," Stanley said, "and I can't predict how long that will take, whether it's months or years, you'll feel many things. All kinds of emotion will be real for you. Love, passion, happiness . . ."

"The word 'feel' doesn't apply at all."

"You may be receiving everything on an intellectual level only." Stanley wanted the layers to peel back by her own efforts, but it couldn't hurt to peel back a few himself. Eventually she would make her own way and grasp her own realisations. "Emotions aren't harmful to us, they serve a useful purpose. They're a human ventilation system. By experiencing all—the good, the great, and the worst of emotions—you will also be able to relax. Along with that will come a new 'sight,' a view of yourself as lovable, worthy. Your mother and stepfather took that away from you so early on that to construct any other image was impossible. Once your 'sight' is changed and their picture of you has been destroyed, new pictures will form. You'll have the ability to act as yourself without the need to construct a pliant persona that changes constantly, merely to fit whatever others want of you. Some of that anger will be able to get out."

Stanley also figured that the woman wasn't the only one listening and others could benefit, too. The woman couldn't tell him that she had never "constructed" anything, and that while she recognised the anger in herself at times, it was not hers. He would think she was simply denying responsibility.

Green eyes blinked rapidly and the woman shivered. "I've

got to tell you something because it sits right here in my mind. Except for what you call these other selves, I'll be alone for the rest of my life. The best part, Stanley, is that it won't even bother me.''

The switch this time didn't take very long. It had been gathering momentum for several seconds. It looked strange, her sitting there like that, childlike and bemused, and all the while those sensuous movements—hair being caressed between long fingers, the mouth taking on a plumper, less narrow line. But before he could readjust to the obvious differences, both the childlike quality and the more womanly movements faded.

"Holy, unmitigated shit," said a gravelly voice, "how do we get out this black hole?"

"Shit is not holy," Elvira said with a smile, "excrement is holy."

Stanley ignored both the comment and the voice change. If the others wanted to talk, they could introduce themselves. "You get out of it by letting your people out," he said, "by relaxing enough to let us hear what they've got to say. Your people hold the keys. They hold the memories you don't have."

Each person who emerged from cover of the Troop Formation brought into the woman's awareness (or at least whatever awareness the Weaver allowed, for however long he allowed it) an oddity, a peculiarity, all their own. In the case of Olivia, the Well of Creativity, her creativity, long stored and newly awakened, became a heated, wondrous thing. Night after night and at odd moments during the day, the woman would see a pattern in almost anything and Olivia would promptly slide a completed painting into her mind; unique, individual—and sometimes upsetting. She brought more than individuality. She also brought memory, not in bits and shreds, but in "trays." The Well of Creativity slept these days, but no longer only in the dank well which she had occupied since her death at the age of six. In some strange fashion, she now also occupied another sleeping place—close in the tuck of Mean Joe's shoulder from where, perhaps, her essence was near enough and safe enough to make current contributions to the recall.

Tray by tray, Olivia slid each night into the woman's dead-tired mind an image of cylindrical stone walls and the odour of water long held captive at the bottom of them. It was a dank

157

smell and hung during the daytime in the woman's nostrils. She could not get rid of it.

Olivia slid other things into the woman's mind. One of them was the notion that there had been an old well up in the back field of the second farmhouse. The woman did not believe it when in one of the sessions, Stanley took out the sketchbook and showed her the drawing made several months ago. The well had been sketched in very carefully just at the corner of the hedgerow.

The woman screamed that it was all a lie, that there had been no well other than the one by the kitchen door. But the sketchbook remained embedded in her mind along with a growing fear and for some reason, a much-heightened repugnance of anything vaguely resembling a snake. She could not drink anything unless she avoided looking into the glass or cup; the reflections were terrifying.

Olivia, the Well of Creativity, slept on. But the "essence" of her was very busy nonetheless.

Full of fear and renewed hope, the woman marched about admiring summer. Meanwhile, various Troop members took full pride in saying aloud "incest victim" and "multiple personality" to friends and relative strangers alike. They knew, as the woman knew only when the Weaver allowed it, that both were tags that applied to themselves like the clothes in their closets, the driver's licenses and social security numbers. But Twelve, feeling marvelously adult, picked her audience carefully, trying the term MPD on Norman first.

For a moment he didn't say anything. Then he swore, a rapid string of obscenities, the same kind that made him furious when Sewer Mouth started up. Twelve paid him rapt attention, disappointed when he stopped for breath.

"I don't believe it," he said. "Yes, I do believe it. It makes more sense to me than anything else I've heard. As a label and, yes, I know you hate them, it gives me a viewpoint. I never had a clear viewpoint where you were concerned. Our lives were simply chaotic. Now I damn well know why."

Twelve had always been kind. And mannerly and at times too pliant. She hung her head, thinking that would mollify him, and then she looked straight up, right into his eyes. "Listen, Norman. I'm through apologising. I was having a rough time, so I left. That's all I can tell you."

Twelve heard the words coming out of her mouth. They

weren't hers, but she silently thanked whoever gave them to her, because they increased her feeling of adulthood. Norman, on the other hand, wondered why her voice tonight was so young, her attitude so innocent. She could do that, it seemed, swing from adult to child and back again. It made him nervous. Then he remembered; she'd just told him how she could do that. In the middle of wondering if she were doing it now, he began to sweat.

"Everyone has bad times," he said, wiping both palms on his handkerchief. "They work them out. You wouldn't work anything out, you hated me."

The woman had surfaced in the middle of Norman's words. "I don't remember that," she said. "Page wants to come over this weekend. Is that in line with your schedule?"

"You asked me once tonight and I'll ask you again; are you dangerous?"

The woman gave the only answer she had. "I don't know."

On hearing the news, for someone in the Troop Formation was determined that they should, friends did not quite turn their backs; they inched away. To them, multiple personality meant insanity and they could not accept or connect that to this astute, articulate business woman. They spoke to her of vitamins, taking a vacation, and, most of all, putting the incest behind her. They told her not to dwell on it, that she must get on with her life. They did not understand that they were talking to many people, not one; nor would they believe it.

With the woman's letter in one hand and a double gin in the other, Morgan called from sunny Spain, to ask if she didn't think he could make her happy. He did not ask what the experience she was going through was like, or if she were scared and miserable, or how it affected her sex life. He did demand to know if she hadn't been ecstatic with him, if she couldn't be ecstatic again. She hung up on him. It wasn't worth an argument. Three days later she was trying to memorise a brand new, unlisted telephone number for herself, and figure out when she'd had the time to change it. Sharon accepted the new number with disgust and said the woman would be sorry later, that bachelors like Morgan were hard to find. "Impossible," was the word Sharon used.

"What are you doing? If you don't want him and you don't want anyone else, what do you want? You don't look well. Life

159

is too short to be lived this way. Maybe some time off from your job and away from this house would change your perspective. Honestly, I want to help you but I don't know how."

The anguish showed in Sharon's pinched face.

"Everything will be alright, Sharon. Stanley says it just takes time. He doesn't say how much."

The woman awoke that night, entangled in a nightmare that included a face frozen inside a hoar-frost block of ice; a face so smooth and unlined that it might have been a one-dimensional painting. It wasn't. The name "Olivia" echoed in the woman's mind, over and over again, and with it, another Troop member sent her a message. She listened and began to understand, finally, that her pain was too evident to her friends, now that she'd learned to say ouch. Her friends, like most people, shriveled when pain entered the picture. She resolved to cool it with them and concentrate on the immediate. On winning.

Stanley called an extra session in the middle of the week. She'd lost weight, was increasingly tired looking and on edge. He took her, almost literally by the nape of her neck, pried her eyes open, and tried to make her look fully at her own hatred and the emerging reasons behind it. For, in spite of the evil things recalled, she still insisted that she couldn't believe it.

"There's only one time in my mind when I did fully believe it," she said. "And even then, all I remember was knowing that I had to get away from that farm; that if I stayed, the bad things would go on and on."

"What bad things?"

"I don't know," the woman had begun to wring her hands and her voice came out in a low-pitched scream that ended on a note of embarrassment and desperation. "The only thought in my head was, Get away, you've got to get away from this place. Well, the chance came and I remember being determined to take it. I think I was thirteen. My father had been away in the war and then he'd stayed on longer, training pilots. The day he returned my mother gave me permission to walk up the road to the bus stop alone to meet him. The difference between him and my stepfather was so apparent that morning. While both men were big, my father was taller, more broad-shouldered, with curly dark brown hair and warm brown eyes. He came swinging down the road, happy looking and handsome in his Army uniform. When he hugged and kissed me, I couldn't stop crying. He asked me, "What's wrong, tell me. If anything is wrong, I'll change it. I'll take you away."

"So you told him?"

"Are you crazy? I couldn't. He looked too clean. I was too dirty. I knew that if I told him, he'd hate me, it was too shameful, all of it. For another thing, when I was four and he came to visit, my mother used to hide me under the bed and tell him that I wasn't home. I used to cringe with my nose in the dustballs, knowing that she was lying to him. Lies are bad. It was as if I'd lied to him myself. How could I ask him a favour in the face of such deceit? And do you think he would have believed me? I hardly believed it myself. If he had believed it and taken me away from there, another bad thing would have happened."

There was silence, except for the sound of tears. Stanley had taken note of the childlike words and voice, interspersed with the more adult tones. Someone very small clung to the idea that she was to blame for everything, including the lies told by a mother determined not to let go of her child.

"I'd have been hurting my mother, breaking my promise to her if I left, not that there was anyplace to go. She said my father was bad, shiftless, lazy, a womaniser; that if he took me away to live with him, I'd see his real side. She told me there'd be his mother to contend with, too; her rules and regulations and no freedom at all. And of course if I ever left, my mother would die. In that one moment with my head on my father's shoulder, something else went through my mind, too. She and my stepfather had told me so often that I was stupid, that to make up my own mind seemed dangerous. I couldn't trust myself to tell my father anything. I guess incest victims have to get past that, before they open up to anyone. Feeling dumb, I mean. I had to get past it with you, Stanley, and I'm not sure I really have."

Her nose dripped. He handed her Kleenex. Mucus ran into the tears and the tears ran into her mouth and down her chin.

"You're doing very well," Stanley said, "and you're not dumb."

"That sounds nice, but someday they'll cart you away because obviously your perceptions are twisted."

He heard what sounded like real laughter and then she started to cry again.

"It's a good thing," she said, "that I don't miss my father

161

and don't care if I see him again. I did a bad thing in high school and he'll never forgive me. I didn't invite him to graduation. It would have made my mother angry; she let me know that she'd supported me and that my graduation was her honor, not his. You don't do bad things to people, Stanley, and expect to get away with it. No. My father wouldn't waste spit on me, today, let alone extend a welcome.''

She refused to buy Stanley's conclusion that her father bore no grudge, that there was nothing for him to forgive, and that her mother had been cruelly manipulative. She was up off the cushions and at the door, carry-all purse in hand.

"Break time,'' she said.

17

Tony gave the signal from the control booth. The woman wore a look of embarrassment.

"Before we get into this," she said, "I need to ask you something. These dates, these calculations, they just come into my head. How can I be sure they're right?"

"Doesn't matter. Most of us are eighty-percenters, meaning that utter perfection is not our boss. You, or someone in the Troop Formation, strives for one hundred percent, and you drive yourself nuts doing it."

"Stanley, it's the only way I know. The mother—"

"Screw the mother," Stanley said.

The woman gasped, with shock and then with grudging admiration. She laughed. "You'll go to hell for that."

She began to speak, grimly but with a detached air, using first person singular, because that, along with various calculations, was what someone far back in her mind gave her.

"I have no idea how my father arranged for my mother's permission, but when I was between six and thirteen, I tasted the freedom of two weeks each summer, during vacations with him and his mother, my paternal grandmother. They lived together in a two-bedroom apartment up over a Jewish delicatessen.

"My mother warned me each time beforehand to behave myself, that grandmother was a stickler for manners and neatness, that she wouldn't put up with my nonsense; one false move would send me right back home. On my first visit, the neatness was obvious. Grandmother's kitchen got scrubbed daily with strong bleach; the floors, the windows, all the appliances glowed, not with wax but with her scrubbing and polishing. On Saturdays she got up before the sun to begin the wash; pre-soaking, pre-sudsing, then the bit with the wringer, squeezing my father's shirts and each white towel or sheet twice, hanging it all on the clothesline that ran on pulleys from the apartment to the next building. But she let me sleep late and I'd wake up to the smell of fresh coffee and frying bacon.''

The woman did not look at Stanley, she talked to the floor. ''I slept with my father for those two weeks each summer. It was nice. He had a double bed, and I lay curled up against his back under the covers, counting the glories of the day, looking forward to the next one. No matter what my mother said about him, I loved my father; he was mine. A wonderful man with a hearty laugh and big hands that took my small ones in his. I liked that. My father made me feel as though I was a good child.

''This is so clear to me, as if it were yesterday; so is the shame I felt for years afterward. There lay my father, warm and protective beside me. He and my grandmother and I had just come back from a marvelous dinner in a restaurant. We'd discussed what we'd do tomorrow; the downtown zoo and the sea lions and shopping in the art supply store.

''I recall exactly, because it is burned into my brain, the sentences floating in my mind just before sleep: 'My father is such a wonderful man. He loves me and I love him so much.' My hand stirred under the blankets, found my father's back. I hugged him. Funny, but at that age there was no conflict of emotion; just one-line reasoning, clearly defined. As I lay there, I knew I adored him, wanted to give him something to express my pleasure over all the goodness he'd given me that day. I knew what it must be. My stepfather demanded and enjoyed the same thing.

''I told myself, I wouldn't do this for my stepfather, just reach out and offer this, because he's vile and nasty and I hate him. My hand found my father. Right there. And I squeezed. My father didn't respond positively. He took my hand away, moved away, lay on this tummy, and went to sleep. I don't know if I drifted off then, because I was almost asleep anyhow. I don't know how I felt the next day or how he treated me.

''My grandmother took me into her bed for the rest of that visit. I never slept with my father again. I lay with her the next

164

night, reading and eating Oreo cookies with her; there were crumbs in my grandmother's bed, with the sheets so tight, the linens smelling of talcum and lilacs. I never forgot her kindness but the memory of what I had done burned so bright. I was bad, Stanley, you can't say I wasn't. How had I gotten to be so bad when I wanted to be so good?''

''Baloney,'' Stanley said, wishing that his casualness would take the pain out of her face. ''Most men are taught to express love only with the penis. Same thing you were taught.''

''Are you serious?''

''Never more,'' Stanley said. ''And with that attitude, men have a tough time convincing women they're worth more than a one-night stand. But we don't wipe out childhood training if we don't understand it first. You're beginning to understand what most people never do.''

''Why don't you ever laugh at me, or just tell me I'm crazy? Everything I say to you can't make sense.''

''You aren't crazy and I'm afraid it all makes sense.''

''Nobody else ever told me that. You mean I might be right, sometimes? Can that be true?!'' She sat hugging herself and grinning but quickly, almost with guilt, turned to the business at hand. ''My grandfather said I was right, a lot. I loved him, did I ever tell you?''

So far, Stanley had a long list of things and people the Troops hated. He dug out the infinitesimal mental list of things that were loved and added her maternal grandfather to it.

''My mother and her mother, his other daughter and his two sons—talked about him in whispers that never reached his ears. He wasn't to their liking, not the average, grey-haired gentleman who held grandchildren on his lap and nodded tenderly over sticky fingers. He was tall, with flaming red hair and cornflower-blue eyes and ruddy complexion that said outdoors, and pubs and brawls. He could do anything, including steal all the very expensive wood he loved to work with. On his good days, he built my grandmother's house and made the furniture, hand-rubbing it and the pillars he'd carved for the staircase. Otherwise he was gone, taking his Irish fighting spirit off to some down-town bar, and that sat ill with the family. Once he got so drunk for so long, he spent every nickel of the two thousand dollars that would have paid off my grandmother's mortgage. Somehow I loved him all the more for that bit of bravery in the face of my grandmother.

"Grandfather saw my feisty side as it marched to the cadence in my own head; the one that looked him directly in the eye and said no or yes as only I pleased. That's when I was a baby; and after I was maybe ten, I never saw him again. I don't know where he went. Just away.

"The story was that on my mother's side, the women had been servants—maids in some old Irish castle before they came to this country during the potato famine. Grandfather had been a carpenter. Listening to those stories from the top of their staircase, their voices thick with brogue, drifting up to me in the shadows—it was fun but not as much fun as being with my grandfather. In fact, the stories were vague and so was the brogue, but I'll never forget him.

"We used to sit on the front porch, everything dark and quiet with a soft breeze—I liked to watch him. When he noticed that the rattling of his newspaper infuriated me, he did it again, laughing. His eyes were kind and full of spirit behind the laughter, and I knew that. So after I'd punched him with a small fist to let him know I had spirit too, he'd give me a sip of his beer. But only when no one was looking.

"We'd sit there together, content. The adult remarks from inside the house carried to us on the breeze; gossip, bits and pieces of who in the family was a scoundrel, a tramp, a boozer; how my Uncle Tom was headed for Sing Sing sure as we sat there; and how could Uncle Bill have married that silly twit who dyed her hair blond? Anybody could see she was a black-haired Italian. And if my Aunt Katherine didn't shape up, she would go down in family history with a scarlet letter on her bosom. Who had she taken up with now? Knowing looks were eventually exchanged between grandfather and me. We'd get up, go out past the railroad tracks for a walk, an ice cream cone. It was the last time I ever felt truly safe with anyone. Grandfather didn't know how bad I was; and I feared nothing from him. Grandfather hated the stepfather; he seldom visited us on the farm."

Who had been talking? Stanley didn't think it was the woman. He said how nice it was that the Troops have known an appropriate male role model.

"Appropriate?" The voice was a growl. "I don't want to hear that word; it sucks, man. Appropriate. It grates on my nerves; it's an insult to my intelligence. Exactly who is the high chief of 'appropriateness'? If everybody in the damn world ran around considering how 'appropriate' everything was before they took action, we'd be back in the Dark Ages.''

Even without a name, he recognised Ten-Four. ''Are you a man?'' he asked.

''Hell, no, I don't go for either sex, got that? Sex is a waste of time. First you got to figure out who you want, then you got to figure out if they want you and if the whole thing is 'appropriate.' You wind up, in any relationship, spending all your time wondering what you're doing wrong and when you'll get caught at it and spit on. Screw that. Give me a boardroom full of men, let me see the whites of their eyes while I'm dealing the deck. The only way you can ever beat a man is in business, where they're flat-out dumb.''

Stanley wiped the smile off his face and consulted his clipboard. Names or no names, Ten-Four hadn't been the only one speaking this time. He'd also spotted Nails and a hint of Sewer Mouth, and knew that somehow, even the one referred to in the manuscript pages as ''the Outrider,'' had been verbalising. What had set them off? The incident with the natural father, obviously. He was unsure of the Outrider's origin but something told him that for Ten-Four, Nails, and Sewer Mouth, the trauma of that incident might have ''given birth'' to selves of their nature; a trio who eschewed sexual relationships, either male or female, and henceforth channeled all energies into work and business. Stanley ignored the cold look he was getting and the conversation continued. The voice, full of barely restrained anger, belonged to Nails.

''When grandfather went away, I began drawing a wall of silence around myself, tighter than before. People say my powers of concentration are terrific. They aren't. I just honed to a fine art the ability to shut out unpleasantness. Go ahead, scream at me. I'll never let you know, provided the game is begun correctly, that your words hit home inside. But if I begin the game incorrectly, then it's all over. Adrenaline surges through my body, enough, it seems, to let me lift the Empire State Building in a single heave. In that moment, I'm like Mean Joe; we both know the strength of which we are capable, the leashed rage within. And so we're smart enough to treat it gingerly. With respect.''

The pain in her face had faded. First misery over the loss of her grandfather, and then rage, had replaced it. Whoever this was, she wouldn't, perhaps couldn't, weep. The word "game" had been spit out, as if it tasted vile.

"During childhood the power to shut things out got me into deeper trouble. A simple request from the mother to go down to the cellar for a bucket of coal would find me standing in the cellar twenty minutes later in absolute fright and frustration, while I tried to remember, was it coal or eggs she wanted? No matter which I decided on, I was wrong.

"Or the morning my stepfather turned extra rotten, and wouldn't give me privacy as I got ready for school. I didn't want to look at him. So I shut him out of my mind along with my mother's voice. As I went into the kitchen, sleepy and not yet alert, she'd told me, 'Please use the bucket on your left, to wash your face.' The bucket on the left was full of well water, the one on the right, fresh creme from that morning's milking. My stepfather stood in the kitchen doorway, watching me with a smile. He scared me. A few seconds later shaking my head, blindly trying to rid myself of creme in my nose and eyes, I couldn't see which one of them hit me. Don't tell me I was good, Stanley. I did wrong, bad things all the time. Creme cost money. My mother worked hard; my mistakes cost her plenty."

"What did they cost you?" Stanley asked her.

"No. I can't go along with you. It all seemed normal to me, the way we lived. They were right and I was wrong. They said so. Except when I went with my father each summer. My mother told me not to get any high-flown ideas; but that's when my life began to look odd. For those two weeks, things were totally different. By the end of the two weeks each summer I exploded with guts, courage, determination, and with candy, new clothes, books, art supplies—and too many new debts. Believe me, whatever you get in this world, you pay for."

Stanley was being bombarded with new information faster than he could sort it out. Once more he'd discovered that the person speaking bore no resemblance to his client as he thought he knew her, yet she spoke in the first person singular.

"Bad debts," she said, grimly. "There was guilt because the half brother and half sisters hadn't gotten away to enjoy what we had. Once we got back home it was hard to sit around enjoying the spoils, knowing we'd made out like bandits. Except that anything we showed up with enraged the stepfather. He broke what he could and threw the rest away."

The woman seemed to emerge then. Stanley knew she hadn't

heard a word of the conversation. She talked about her father and having loved him enough to eat everything on her plate, pretending to be blasé with cauliflower which she wouldn't touch at home. "He said once that I'd look good in a feed sack, that it didn't matter what I wore. I was shocked and couldn't believe him. I learned from those visits that unless I behaved like the perfect child my grandmother and father would hate me, and if I seemed sad or told them one word of what went on at home I would never be allowed to go there again."

"How did you figure all that out?" Stanley asked.

"My mother told me."

"I see." Stanley saw too well.

They both agreed on one thing; some of the tape recordings she made at home were scratchy, barely intelligible, and his own from the session were sometimes not much better. Tony still had problems with the video sound and picture. The woman looked bemused, then skeptical; her eyes changed colour as a smile crept over her face, but it was directed at the floor. Stanley waited for someone to say something, anything. They didn't.

Back home, the woman trotted into her kitchen. The top of her skull began to thump and she closed her eyes against an ache of impossible proportions. If she had ever felt anything vaguely resembling pain, it had been that ache through the years, at long distance, as a sort of "threat." She gazed out the window into a backyard draped in whispering emerald ivy over a sea of white gravel. Easy things to care for. One did not need to leave the confines of the house in order to tend them. No reason for sweating with hoe and bug sprays, exposed to strange eyes.

She made two slices of toast and slathered them with sweet butter and wild blackberry preserves. Standing at the window holding a cup of steaming tea, a hanging fern from a rafter high above brushed the back of her neck. Shadows darted on the walls and danced closer to her taut body. Hot tea spilled onto her hand from a cup that rattled in the saucer. She felt nothing.

In the Tunnel, the Gatekeeper gave the signal.

The signal had been a strong one; the Troop member whom it had summoned was bearing down with the whole of his being. The woman fought back, lifting the teacup to her lips and trying to smile. It never materialised.

169

Ivy blew in the garden outside, the leathery leaves brushed and rubbed against each other. The sound, muted as it was through the window, did not penetrate the detachment she acknowledged but did not feel.

In the garden, a squirrel shot under a pile of dead leaves that trembled atop his quivering body. Inside the house the woman stood stock still, gazing out at nothing. Inside her mind there was nothing. No memory, nothing. She had no experience with which to compare that lack; no emotion of her own with which to feel terrified, or even annoyed. For a very small second in time, she looked out of the prison of her own space and knew that except for when the others gave her something, she did not exist.

All during the latter part of June, the reflection in anything liquid drew panic around her neck like a terrorist's rope. An approaching animal, no matter how small or innocuous, even the sight of one in a magazine, brought on a frenzy of repulsion, of sexual aversion. She had no hint that these episodes were connected to the child abuse. Her own instincts were useless in deciphering the meaning behind them: first because she had no instincts of her own, and second, because the incidents behind the terror had not happened to her, but to the other selves. Selves who were only now getting ready to paint a fuller picture of life in the two farmhouses. Olivia II, the Well of Creativity, would paint the first one and thereby reveal, among other things, the depths of Catherine's long-held secret.

The Troops wrote through her and around her. They wrote whether she was "present" or not. They were determined to see their efforts in print, to dissolve the mystery and myth surrounding both incest and multiple personality. The pages grew, based on notes made and scenes written, during the night, on lunch breaks, and while waiting for builders and settlement attorneys. They mushroomed at the hairdresser's, while Catherine called for a pale ash-blond colour and Ten-Four confused things by demanding brassy, harvest gold.

The woman did not resent the long hours as much as her inability to stay awake and participate. But even as she laboured among them, anxious to keep pace, the words rang in her head, night after night. *For you, there isn't any more.*

One day the woman would realise that she did not even go to the bathroom. Her people ate; they went to the bathroom. Such

170

knowledge at this point in therapy would have cut her adrift. Those who knew the truth were wisely waiting to tell her.

For now, the woman listened to television commercials extol the virtues of Preparation-H and Ex-Lax and wondered why she didn't need either. The closest she'd ever come to dealing with body functions had been the time during a very long car ride when she'd noticed an odd discomfort and found a Tampax inside herself, still in its cardboard tube.

Once more, a vague premonition of disaster seemed to be following the woman. She took her fright to Stanley one day and listened to him carefully. Afterward she couldn't remember what he'd said but in the following days there were brief moments when the terror did recede, and she half-believed that it would all get better.

What little the woman did comprehend of the stacked manuscript pages in the gallery escaped here vaguely puzzled mind, like wood-smoke in an open field.

The minute but significant cooperative force building up between herself and those Troops who had now evidenced was double-edged. The daily bombardment of their individual natures on each other occasionally flooded the woman, along with each one's desire not to attract attention. Each one believed that his or her behavior was perfect—and that the others needed to tone it down, shut up, or go away entirely.

The amount of energy spent in sessions and everyday life dealing with the other selves was enormous. But a stronger, more compelling energy kept building up. If not singing to rock music on the car radio, the woman found herself dancing to the living room stereo, wanton and with a carried-away feeling so pronounced that it frightened her into a more concentrated hiding than every before. Terrified that one of them might escape in public, she denied even the possibility of it, and someone laughed. The sound was unpleasant.

The Outrider evaluated what the Buffer and the Front Runner were reporting on a daily basis and knew that the woman, because of her construction, still operated at safe distance from the truth. That distance was a straight line, leading directly to Troop members whom no one wanted disturbed.

When the phone went dead one morning, it popped into the woman's mind how frequently she must lose complete track of time. How long had bills been paid in three- or four-month increments because she couldn't open and read the mail? She looked in the checkbook; its contents were too scrambled. The calendar in the kitchen stared back, indecipherable.

At midnight she paid the phone company a call, stuffing the envelope into the night depository. The "under cover of darkness" operation pleased Nails. The woman scuttled home. Unable to sleep, she sat at the typewriter, watching manuscript pages pile up, until three in the morning. Finally, she crawled into bed. She'd been cold since noontime, shivering over steaming cups of coffee in an effort to find warmth. The temperature in the loft bedroom was 72 degrees, yet she huddled under the big downy comforter and three blankets, with skin icy to the touch. The premonition was alive again.

Under the tent of bedclothes, by the tiny beam of a tensor lamp, she began organising a stack of what appeared to be sloppily written manuscript notes. The handwriting had shifted more than a dozen times. It went from neat up-and-down strokes to letters that dangled above and below the lines, to a chicken scratch that danced into a flurry of curlicues. The woman stared at the handwriting, appalled by the messiness.

A voice sounded in her mind. The premonition of doom, stronger than before, had raised goose bumps on her arms. Everything the mother had warned against became a litany. She was sloppy, fat, stupid, incompetent, prideful, greedy, selfish, and cowardly. The litany lengthened to include the chaos her life was in, and proved both the validity of the mother's warnings and her own chaotic condition. Stanley's ego building, all the armour he'd tried to build around her, fell away. The mother won, the stepfather won, she lost. Worthless and doomed to hell, the tears were cold on her face.

The Outrider took a look at her. The irony was that this person who had so little—whose construction didn't even allow for the actual consumption of her own food—should be so necessary to what happened, or did not happen, to the cores. The Outrider felt as if she were walking a high wire every time she tried to give the woman something while making sure the cores still slept.

The Outrider moved. Selecting a handful of confetti, she knitted the shreds together, piece by piece, and prepared to let them fall in a single veil. Under the blankets the woman's breath was frigid. Her fingers, lifeless cold stubs on the black pen, moved over the pages with a will of their own. The Outrider let go of the veil. In the name of the one who had experienced what the

172

knitted confetti shreds represented, the Outrider made a silent apology to both child and woman.

Into the woman's half-awake mind fell an image of cylindrical rough stone walls and a quavering reflection in the water below. A sense of movement gripped her; she became dizzy. Long, thin, living shapes rushed at a downward angle past the periphery of her half-sleeping mind.

She shivered, and inside the Tunnel walls there was only silence and the black water beneath her dangling feet. Over her shoulder, the stepfather's face appeared in the reflection, along with a third face that looked like her own and was not.

Then another image and it was so clear. The woman sat straight up, the bed covers flew off with her momentum. She was screaming in a loud, shrill voice, shaking like a leaf in a high wind. The screams went on and in front of her eyes the snake lay on the bed, large as life with a scaled body, tan with black markings. Except that there wasn't one snake, there were many and they weren't on the bed now. They rained down on the tiny creature hanging in the well, the child who swayed back and forth in some kind of contraption, made by man, that only the devil himself could have contrived.

18

Dawn came into the loft bedroom. The woman untangled herself from the sodden and rumpled sheets. Wet stone walls and a swaying motion . . . she hung onto the bathroom door for support. She brushed her teeth with two kinds of toothpaste and gargled with Listerine, but the taste of well water remained.

Dazed, she dressed in whatever lay at the foot of the bed, but the bright blue blouse and the white slit skirt were not what had been laid out the night before. Exhausted but still in the grip of last night's raging fear and the coldness that had settled into her bones, she drove to the university.

She walked into the session that morning and spent a half-hour telling Stanley that the second well did not exist. Stanley watched her; he couldn't envision anything to do with a well that might have torn her apart this way. He kept pressing because if she didn't unload and face it, the fear would grow, and possibly explode outside a session. She was unshakable, her face frozen and blank. During her fourth or fifth disavowal, the adult voice grew tiny and tears rolled down over what were no longer high cheekbones but the smooth and rounded face of a child.

In the dead essence of Olivia II's six-year-old mind as she surfaced and began to speak, things were as they had been on the day of her "death." As she sat playing in the field at the second farmhouse, there came the call of a far-off bird, his song heavy with summer's inertia. The sun beat down on the hedge-row that surrounded her on four sides like tall green fortress walls. The leaves were silent in the windless heat, and perspiration matted the pale curls framing her face. A giant daddy-long-legs crept up a blade of grass near her bare toes. She watched his spindle legs, bent in the slow-motion, stop-and-go walk that took him precisely wherever he wanted. The actions mesmerised her, claimed the attention she had been giving to the shards of coloured glass in her lap. They had been lovingly collected. One was a deep, navy blue that had once been a whole drinking glass, the other was ruby-red, a fragment from a heavy service bowl. She had more, pried up from the soil in the area where the stepfather burned the trash from the house.

Regardless of the treasured glass and over a strong sense of apprehension, her eyes were riveted on the spider. Her mind soared for a moment, then focused. Unaware of what she was doing, the future course it would take, she memorised the spider's motions, refined them. She was, in effect, "giving birth" to the seed that would eventually become Grace, the Zombie. The Zombie, not the child, would walk out of this field today.

The child didn't know that and yet she was suddenly doubly afraid, as if a chill wind had sprung up. The daddy-long-legs's motions had carried him up the blade of grass to where its tender green tip lay against the rock rim of the old well. The child moved, too, from the heat of the earth, and hoisted herself up next to him, feeling the stones cold and hard under her haunches. Her bare dangling heels brushed against rough stone walls and she saw the reflection of herself in the blackness of the well water far below.

Her mind swung, from the glittering blue and red glass in her hand, to the spider, and back. Somehow the sun glinting on the shards of glass and the spider's lazy motions became a single energy source, compelling, enveloping—and still, above that energy, separate from it, she was afraid.

The shadow that had been there for some time moved in front of her, lay directly across herself and the spider, too. The stepfather, no longer a shadow, moved into her line of vision, carrying the planks with which he would reseal the well, now that he'd finished whatever he'd been doing. He carried something else besides the planks, she couldn't see what it was, he'd hidden it behind his back.

"Come play," the stepfather said, but Olivia II had learned a lesson from what had happened to her predecessor, Olivia I. She prepared to flee. Before her feet hit the dirt, the stepfather grabbed her and she saw what he hid behind his back: a crate, the kind that lettuce or carrots were packed in. The slats were thin, held together with wire, and the crate was open on two sides, forming a sort of swing. A rope had been attached to it.

The "dead essence" of Olivia II screamed on a far-away note that plunged straight down Stanley's spinal column.

The woman surfaced, shaking her head so hard that the tears flew. "No, I won't believe it; nobody can make me! There was only one well, by the kitchen door!"

She was suddenly shoved aside. Olivia II had seemed to speak from the depths of irreversible damage. The child who emerged over the woman showed signs of that same damage, except that hers was voiced in near-hysteria.

"Oh, yes, there was a well in the field," the second child sobbed. "The stepfather put Olivia II in the crate and hung her down."

"Do you know why he did that to her?" Stanley felt as if he were choking.

She held her fists together in her lap; the sobs were racking, and she talked in a sort of lispy baby-talk. She seemed ashamed of what had been done by the stepfather and petrified to tell. The woman's denial had made her furious; enough, Stanley thought, to force her out, this child whom he had never seen before.

The child replied over wilder sobs that the stepfather had been angry over a refusal to play "that dumb game." She had no concept of how long the torture had lasted. She was far more determined to tell him something else.

"Snakes," she screamed, "he knew we hated them, he found a lot and threw them down the well on top of Olivia II!"

The child cringed with every word she uttered and gripped both hands together between her knees.

"Olivia II died in the well," the child sobbed. "She hadn't been around long enough to have anybody to take over, so Catherine did it. Catherine is her adult mirror-image."

Catherine, Stanley thought, who hated the idea of motherhood, had become an adult stand-in for a six-year-old dead self.

"Who are you?" Stanley asked.

"Olivia I is dead, too, because of the stepfather and what he did to her with the pink thing, and because the mother walked on her. She was four years old. From Olivia I, there's just me left. I'm her child mirror-image."

Stanley asked what her name was; she howled that she didn't have a name, didn't want one.

"Who," Stanley asked with a dry throat, "took over as the adult for Olivia I?"

"The Outrider."

In the control booth Tony's expression was unreadable but his hands flew over the dials in a frenzy of outrage. Stanley didn't know what to do with his own outrage. He signaled for a break.

The university hallway was silent. Only a faint murmur escaped from the classrooms on either side and his footsteps had a hollow, lonely ring. The night cleaning crew had left the odour of Lysol hanging on the linoleum floors; it made his eyes water. He tried to imagine, but could not, what might have gone through the child's mind as she'd hung there in the well. The screams in the studio today and the wild sobbing . . .

"Kill him," the students had said. Again Stanley wondered what the woman would decide to do when she had possession of full memory? She didn't believe the well existed, but someone had drawn it months ago in the sketchbook. Marshall had been right. There were other, smaller, far more damaged selves behind the first child who'd evidenced on the videotape that day.

Shocked to the point of nausea, Stanley again took his place across from her in the video studio, unaware that more puzzle pieces were about to surface. The woman sat with blank eyes and frozen features, giving no sign of distress over the children's recall. Only when prodded did she disclose the 2:00 A.M. "nightmare." She insisted it was simply a bad dream.

Stanley listened to the denial. He doubted if she would fully experience any of it, at least for a long time to come.

After the break she fought not the label but the actuality of multiple personality.

"I can't even buy nylons anymore," she sobbed. "Somebody doesn't like them. When I get home from the store, the nylons I buy are gone. It's probably Mean Joe and he won't talk."

"Or someone very small," said Stanley, "someone who is too young for nylons. Here. A friend sent this to you." He handed her a package done up in red-and-white flowered wrapping and tied in red, crinkly ribbons. She tore away the paper to reveal a second green-and-gold box and a sketch pad. For all the joy on her face, Stanley had expected, at the least, a fur coat.

Laughing and crying simultaneously, the woman read the

177

words Jeannie Lawson had written: "Do not confuse childish with childlike. Someone inside you is very young and wants to play. Please try to believe that it does get better."

"Are you telling me that she's a real multiple, that there's somebody like me around here? Is she experiencing these same things; is it hell for her? Please. Is she real?"

Stanley gave assurances, wishing he had a few for himself. From the very moment they'd sat down to film this morning, he'd felt it, the surge of energy, the forward momentum, the feeling of being "high." It happened every time he was with her, but today it was particularly noticeable. Sometimes it took him several days to "come down" again. It seemed to be tied in with Tony's periodic complaints about the picture and sound quality.

With the opening of the gift, the energy in the room had grown. While Stanley pondered to himself, unwilling to give credence to his suspicions, the energy continued to emanate from many sources: Mean Joe peering over the woman's shoulder to check out the present safety-wise; Catherine, who loved all gifts, admiring the wrappings; a number of children eyeing the crayons.

It was no wonder that the woman asked if Jeannie Lawson were real. With all the Troops members coming and going over the crayons in her lap, the woman felt unreal herself, and disconnected to anything or anyone.

Stanley explained Jeannie Lawson's final integration.

"Integrated. That means everybody is 'one'? Before that, did she sound as crazy as I do? Is she really like me?"

"Jeannie wasn't crazy. Nor was she mentally ill or insane or whatever other label most people use. Her other selves were protecting her. I suppose to an outsider the way they went about it might seem unusual."

Not crazy? Forces inside the woman for which she had no name burst and sent fresh tears. Someone stuck a nose into the brilliant crayon colours, peering at Stanley and crooning. The sound was that of a child, content with an old and familiar toy.

"It's like an underground movement, isn't it?" The woman spoke, oblivious to the crooning. "I've never met Jeannie but she's more real to me than I am."

She folded the wrappings, neatly, precisely, and hid them in her purse, trying to involve herself in the session she hadn't wanted. She expressed concern about almost every waking action, showing Stanley, in effect, an adult who did not trust herself or her ability to cope with anything or anyone. The crayons were tumbled helter-skelter across her lap. Mean Joe emerged briefly, slant-eyed and unverbose. The eyes were a deep hazel, his body language angular and masculine. He did not announce himself. The woman only said that she "felt" him, the same as in the carry-out store that day with Miss Wonderful. The smile on the woman's face grew wide as she uttered the words. The cheekbones vanished.

After the emotional impact of the first two children in this session, it was almost a relief to see the third. It was not the "dead essence" of the same child who had described the field and the well, or the child who had emerged afterward, only slightly less damaged but angry and informative. Yet the voice held a tiny hint of a lisp.

The terror and pain were back in the woman's face. Like a small conjurer, the third child called up the name of her protector.

"Mean Joe," Lambchop said, "is a mountain. We call him Mean Joe Green now. Did you know that, Stanley? We call him Mean Joe Green 'cause we found out the other day that he's black."

Stanley had been wondering for weeks, stumbling over clues to Mean Joe's precise characteristics. The mother didn't give approval easily. The Troops knew that. Yet she had smiled at a young black boy from the farm behind theirs, for delivering her lost child. Had the mother, unknowingly, thereby given "permission" if not for the birth of another alternate self then at least for his colour?

There was another consideration. The stepfather had been white. Did any white man consequently frighten some Troops so badly that this hulking protector whom the children called Mean Joe had to be black for them? Or had Mean Joe himself made the decision? The question addressed MPD as a process and Stanley reminded himself that no one knew exactly how it worked.

On the cushions, Lambchop jabbered, picking up one crayon after the other, lining them up neatly on the white skirt.

"Mean Joe Green," said Stanley, smiling over his clipboard, "that is a big man. Big enough to protect anybody, I guess."

"I'll draw you his picture sometime." The face looked sad. "When I get to play."

179

"Don't they let you play?" For whatever reason, this child felt safe enough with him to stay for a while. Then he saw it: her body stance beginning a slow transformation from a free-moving child to one who huddled into herself and regarded her surroundings with terror.

"I'm not allowed." Damaged or not, the lisp was pronounced, unmistakable.

"Well, what kind of games did you play when you were little?" Stanley wanted to yank his tongue out. This Troop member was still little. "Back then," he amended.

Silence.

A tremour shook her. She tried to tell him how old she was, counting on her fat-fingered hands. She cried in frustration when she got to six and couldn't go any further.

"But you sound even younger than six," Stanley objected.

"Time," she said, still crying and beating the fat little hands together, "time just . . ."

Her eyes darted, she held herself as if she hurt, like one who expected blows, not hugs. Grinding down his reactions, Stanley clutched his old edict: Getting caught in a client's emotion is a trap. He swallowed and reached back into his mental notes, to a past session. "Time stopped? Are you telling me that time stopped for you?"

Stanley couldn't decipher her words. Something told him that while she had nothing to do with the well incident, her development had been cut off completely but for other reasons. Where had this child been all these years?

He asked her. He couldn't tell by her movements on the cushions what was happening.

Within the Tunnel walls there was a burst of panic. Certain informed Troop minds surged to the forefront, intent on a single act—to protect that which was now in grave danger. The child struggled with Stanley's question, her infantile mind awhirl with the implications. But even as she struggled and grew more terrified at the answer, she felt them: Troop members massing, drawing the Tunnel walls tight around her.

No one in the Troop Formation understood how it had happened. They only knew that the particular child in front of Stanley was the child core's mirror-image. She had put herself in jeopardy and themselves along with her.

Catherine's eyes flew to Mean Joe and they were wild with

pleading. The Front Runner and the Buffer jockeyed for a position that would give them purchase, a means of surfacing quickly over the wandering child. The Gatekeeper gave the signal.

Mean Joe moved.

Stanley sat frozen on the cushions, knowing the child's eyes were turning darker, becoming hazel and slanted above the high cheekbones, and that suddenly the figure crouched there was very, very masculine.

And in the child's moment of extreme panic, Mean Joe wrapped her within himself and took her away. Back to the place Stanley would have given anything to discover.

"Where are you?" Stanley prodded, but the face remained blank. "I'm here to help you. Unless you talk to me I can't help you."

During the break, Tony asked Stanley if the little one had been putting him on with Mean Joe Green.

"Anything can be," Stanley said.

Back on the floor for the second half of the session, Stanley took note of the woman's quiet tone, the withdrawn body stance and blank eyes.

"I'm blessed," she said. "No matter how bad things were as a child, it was always possible to hang in there until the next day, the next year. Why do I say that when I can't remember what happened, just that I hated the farm?"

"One day you will remember," Stanley said. "All of it."

"Shit," the woman said. "Hell, crap, and damn." At least she heard herself saying it. She said she was sorry and looked contrite and then there was nervous laughter. "I don't think too many other victims are as lucky as I am. Something always saved me. I found you, Stanley, just when I thought that my mind had snapped. No," she added, seeing his thoughtful expression, "I may be blessed but it's got nothing to do with god or the devil either if they exist, and I doubt that they do."

"For some people they do," Stanley said, testing the water.

The eyes glinted and the jawline hardened. The quiet tone vanished.

"I spit on those things," said Sewer Mouth, and she mimed the action over her right shoulder.

"I suppose," Stanley groped for a handle, knowing of the upbringing by a mother and a grandmother steeped in catholicism, "that if religion were stuffed down your throat as a child in the face of the other things going on . . ."

Sewer Mouth's rage was expressed and thus vented, by means of cursing. She often ran into people who did not understand her rage and could see no good reason for such a filthy tongue. It seemed to her that their disgust over expletives which were perfectly natural to her was a denial of the reasons for them—reasons which she'd never explained to anybody except for a few abortive attempts.

A family living together in peace and tranquility or even an uneasy truce was one thing. But a family of six, living with hatred and the threat of each other's daily rages, was another. When the mother went to the fields or was preoccupied with household chores, Sewer Mouth had found a way to cope with the screaming and the battles between the half brother and half sisters.

Incapable of swatting anyone into silence, first because she would be beaten into retreat by the mother or the stepfather, and second because her rage frightened her, Sewer Mouth learned to use her tongue. It did not draw blood and could be employed freely without the threat of bodily injury to anyone, herself included. Her anger, while frightening, was always safely vented through the cursing.

Seeing by Stanley's face that he did seem to understand her anger, Sewer Mouth considered dropping her defenses.

"God," Stanley was saying, "doesn't mean much to someone who lived the way you did. The thought of any salvation outside yourself must have seemed laughable. You've been taught to trust and depend on no one."

"Why don't you look at me as if I'm a leper?" Her voice was a rough whisper. "Can you also accept my feelings that all parents stink? That they're vengeful, even the best of them, and that no smile they show you is real? Does that mean you can also understand that I hate kids, that after I left that farm I never wanted to see another diaper or a bottle of formula, or hear a squalling infant?"

"It makes sense to me," Stanley said.

"I wanted to be alone! But everywhere you looked there was another kid—the half brother and the half sisters—screaming their lungs out. I wanted silence; they yelled and tormented me. I still don't want to see, hear, or smell anybody, ever again. Someday I'll find a way never to have to be with another human being. I think about it night and day; there must be an island somewhere, or a mountain, with no damn people!''

"I'm afraid there isn't," Stanley said.

"Well, I won't accept that," Sewer Mouth told him grimly. "I hate this life. I hate everything. Ask me," her voice was a low growl, "what I don't hate. It might be easier for me to tell you what I don't hate.''

In the gallery that night, the woman stared at the debris. The manuscript, through three rough drafts in a sea of white paper crumpled, stacked, stapled, and pinned to the walls, stared back.

Hurry up, bitch. You're wasting our time.

"I'm hurrying!" she screamed, convinced that if she replied as her mother had always insisted, the voice would go away. It didn't. Neither did the sudden smell of her mother's body. The odour was something she'd loathed as a child. It had stuck in her nose periodically, ever since the second farmhouse. Each time it returned, the woman experienced, as now, an extreme aversion and the desire to simply be dead.

"I'm hurrying!" she screamed again.

If you can't keep up, get out of the way completely!

It was not her mother's voice. That much became clear. It was one of her selves with a voice that sounded the same. How one of her selves could have such a voice, perhaps be like the mother . . . the idea terrified her.

She looked, dumbfounded, at the glass of milk she held to her mouth. The impression came that someone else was drinking the milk and remembering a tin cup on the farms. That person wanted a tin cup full of milk now; not from a carton, but fresh from the cow. The woman set the empty glass on the desk very carefully, as if that other person's hand had just touched hers.

19

From the woman's upraised right hand dangled a flimsy bit of nylon and skin-coloured lace. Happy-hour patrons undulated like a shifting sea of sardines in the long, narrow barroom, more intent on their two-for-one purchases than on her underwear. On her left, seated in full sight of the dangling bra, Ben Purceval, an architect she'd known for years, paused and looked away. He was a nice man, a trifle confused right now, but apparently determined to finish his discussion. The woman had no idea what the discussion had been. He wanted to know if she intended to go off with someone named Thornton, as soon as he returned from the men's room.

"Who?" the woman asked from a great distance, trying to count the empty glasses on the bar in front of her. She had obviously been there for some time consuming a boatload of scotch, yet she felt nothing. The neat paisley blouse she had put on this morning was still partially buttoned and a memory of outrageous laughter sat in her head along with the notion that she must at some point have taken the bra off beneath the blouse by pulling the straps down through the sleeves. Why? And who was Thornton?

What god-awful things had she done in front of Ben and in front of the faceless Thornton while downing a quart of scotch? More than three of her selves fought to speak, to turn over the evidence. There in her head, someone was wryly amused; someone else was not amused at all. There was one who did not

184

speak; it was as if he sat in the shadows of her mind in the depths of the longest, blackest tunnel ever created. Shaking, the woman gathered up her purse and lighter and cigarettes with hands that couldn't stuff everything out of sight fast enough.

"I'm going to get cigarettes," she lied to Ben and beat it through the crowd and out the door.

It had to be late afternoon or early evening by the sun's position in the sky. She finally found the car at the far side of the parking lot. A bag of groceries was on the front seat, sodden with defrosting foods. Guilty over the careless waste of money, it never registered that she had grocery shopped just before lunch that day. She dumped the contents of her purse on the hood of the car, heard the keys rattle, and took a deep breath. Admiring herself for a calmness she had little to do with, she avoided her reflection in the rearview mirror and drove home double-quick.

Elvira smiled all the way and played the car radio with a vengeance.

It was not until the woman removed the paisley blouse at home and saw in the mirror a pair of naked breasts that she went wild with fright and a curious, cold, panic. It was only then that she really began to believe that in a public bar she might have acted like a whore, actually undressing, exposing herself. What else had she done? What kind of woman was she to do these things? Why couldn't she remember taking the bra off?

She remembered other items of personal clothing that seemed to come off in odd public places for no reason. It had always been possible, she realised suddenly, to remember afterward the particular garment, but not the act of taking it off. The sense of having been in those odd public places was vague. Somehow she got the feeling that there were more of them than she knew.

Stanley would only laugh if she told him. He would explain that taking a bra off under one's blouse did not constitute undressing in public. Stanley was too lenient. Her mother would have gone on for hours, days, weeks, the harangue would have been endless.

The odour of her mother's body was suddenly there in the bathroom. The woman shook as she found the skin-coloured bra in the bottom of her purse. Without looking, she flung it into the clothes hamper and slammed the door shut. The smell of her mother's body would not go away.

The woman fled down the stairs to the foyer powder room and scrubbed her hands and face in hot water and strong yellow

185

soap. Clean, spotless, freshly pressed no matter how long or hard she worked in the house or the fields, her mother had not been careless about hygiene, so where would the smell come from? Anger, fright, and disgust, all self-directed, lay just at the edge of the woman's awareness. She wanted to feel them for herself this time, not second-hand, as she was beginning to suspect was the case. She tried. Nothing happened.

She put in a call to Stanley, trying to stop shaking. She lit a cigarette, forgot its existence, and immediately lit another; tried to make the stereo work, and when the static began, kicked it and played "Smoke on the Water" in spite of the crackling sounds. Never had she wanted anyone to return a call so badly.

"I can't go out," she told Stanley when the phone rang twenty minutes later. "I never knew why I couldn't. People invited me; I didn't have the time; I was so busy. I've lived my whole life this way. Well, after today, *I know why*!"

Stanley pointed out firmly that she had to break that hiding habit a little at a time.

"You're not the one left sitting in a public place with your bra in your hand!" she screamed.

"Don't wear one," Stanley told her.

In the gallery an hour later with the gooseneck light trained on the manuscript, the ache in her ears had reached an unbearable state. In the last two days she'd consumed three-fourths of a large bottle of Extra-Strength Tylenol. The medication didn't dull the ache in the least; it only left a residue of grit in her brain and slowed down her reaction time. Regardless, ten seemingly disembodied fingers were flailing the keyboard. In no time at all she'd caught up on the pile of notes. By staring at the clock for a long time, she estimated another two hours before meeting Page; just enough time to tape the memories that had been captured in the last five days. She pressed the recorder button. Once she caught on to what was happening she couldn't stop it. Smells. In towering waves they hit her: the perfume of flowers, all the myriad kinds her mother had grown, along with the heady odour of wild pink primroses, followed by the rich, thick stench of manure from the area where the barn had once stood at the second farmhouse.

Suddenly, as if she'd been given a brand new palate, her tongue was assaulted with the taste of her mother's cooking, her Irish mother whose hand with seasoning had been expert and creative. The woman sat in her own gallery over thirty years later, tasting a long-simmered corned beef brisket, braised onions and new potatoes fresh out of the field, sweet corn and wild pheasant done to a turn, fried rabbit and squirrel. Yes, squirrel. Her grandfather had cooked squirrel one day as a treat for her, and she'd loved the gamey taste, the fact that he'd taken the trouble to fry up a special dish just for her. How old had she been? The image of tiny fat hands flew into her mind. The woman smiled. But not for long.

Flick. The image of the old barn; why had it burned down? Why could she never picture the outside of it, much less herself inside the weather-beaten structure that had certainly been there when they'd moved into the second farmhouse? How old had she been when it burned? She didn't know.

The confetti grew in volume and gathered momentum; it became a hailstorm, and each tiny shred made that flicking sensation against her mind. The flicks did not halt long enough to peer inside them, when suddenly there was the musty-smelling pantry at the first farmhouse. The first farmhouse had no electricity, no refrigerator. Mice lived cosily in the pantry, dashing out for the bread and cereal stashed in the kitchen and the other foods that were kept cold down in the dirt cellar. The door from the pantry had led directly down to the dirt cellar.

The woman remembered now how cool it had been there, even in the heat of summer. How the black earth of that dirt basement had crept between her bare toes as she'd stood fascinated by grey drifts of spider web. Sometimes when it rained, the door from the cellar on the side of the house would be left open. Occasionally a raindrop would hit the spider webs and fascinate her all over again. All the colours dancing in a tiny raindrop, caught undisturbed for a moment. It would occur to her then to wonder if somebody could go away in a raindrop— except that by being in a tiny drop of water, one was trapped there for any predator. Just as the little bugs were trapped for the big spiders.

Right after a rainstorm, the mother duck and her four young ones trooped in a loud formation past the cellar door at the side of the house, snatching drinks from the puddles as they went. Somehow the ducks, of all the farm animals in the world, never frightened her. Except when she watched their long necks and was reminded of snakes. Then she hated ducks, too.

At this moment, however, more than thirty years later, what she hated most was the door that led from the pantry down into

187

the cellar. The confetti was no longer whirling about, it was standing still, and the cellar door with it. Flick. The image didn't go away and in her mind, with a childlike curiosity that the woman had just become aware of, she dared to go forward, down the darkened, creaking, wooden staircase. Cobwebs drifted at the corners of the low-ceilinged, stone-walled room. Dust coated the stones and rafters. Once at the bottom, feeling the hard-packed dirt between her toes, she waited.

The misty grey giant stood silhouetted against dim, mote-laden light from a small dirty window set high in the stone wall behind him. His hands were big on her tiny thighs, slipping inside her cotton pants, stroking her flesh.

Three. She was three years old.

"Sssh," he said. "She mustn't see us. Isn't this nice?"

And his hands took her own two hands and ran them over the pink thing protruding from its nest of black, wiry, bush. In the darkness of the cellar, with the feel of those hands sweeping over her, the woman, caught up in the ancient memory, cursed and swore; but the recall, once started, wouldn't stop. Sexually aroused, painfully, erotically stimulated in her own gallery with the gooseneck lamp casting ugly thin shadows on the walls, she felt the stepfather's hands over and over again.

The curse words Sewer Mouth lent her, a thousand of them, were being spewed in anger at the sexual arousal. They flooded the inner recesses of the woman's protesting mind and were as vile, as rotten as the woman had always believed herself to be.

The woman sat there in the gallery, little more than a baby; she dared to peer into the flick no longer. The desk tilted as she pushed her chair away from it and papers went sliding to the floor along with the gooseneck lamp. She stumbled as she ran on tiny, small-boned feet, with baby tears a translucent shimmer before her eyes. She kicked open the foyer closets and grabbed for a sweater, desperate to run; this time for good. Even flying out the front door she knew: this was why incest victims stood mute, why they hid themselves away in terror and why, with few exceptions if they appeared at all, it was from shadows as dark as the knowledge that followed them.

Somewhere in the back of her brain she must have known all along that there had been pleasure along with the pain.

Yes, dummy.

Along with the voice in her head came a thought that was bound firmly to it; they sat together in her mind, separate from

188

her. Then they weren't separate anymore, they were one and she was a part of both voice and thought: *Kill him, kill the bastard.* The sexual arousal was not, it seemed, only a thing of childhood past but a thing of the present. This minute the arousal gripped her—recalled by what she'd forgotten too long ago or by what one of her people had experienced for her? It didn't matter. She herself was the whore the stepfather had called her in the kitchen that day. This was what he smirked at all those years.

The woman wanted to put her two hands between her legs and tear the offending flesh away. Kill it, too.

Once born, of course, the notion wouldn't leave. An hour later, it had just become more appealing. Kill him. It sat in the woman's head as she tried to note the time on the dashboard clock. But then she remembered and referred instead to the small travel alarm clock that now went in her purse, everywhere she did. The dashboard clock no longer worked and neither did any of the wrist-watches, from Timex to Piaget. Once repaired, they all promptly went haywire again and now lay useless in a dresser drawer, useless as this car's electrical system. The fuses blew constantly although no mechanic could ever point out a reason. Lately she hadn't bothered to replace the fuses and now the cigarette lighter, the dome light, the seat belt warning buzzer, the door locks, and the dashboard clock were all inoperable. In addition, the engine refused to turn over several times after stopping at 7-Eleven on the way to the video studio and she'd been forced to walk across the campus to meet Stanley. No mechanic had been able to point out the problem there either, and always after several hours the engine ran properly anyway.

Whenever she considered what it all meant, the question arose immediately as to what was wrong with the stereo, the radios, the television set, and every light bulb in her house. Next she had to question why, if she were in anyone else's house too long, their lights began to flicker, their stereo started to crackle.

Someone slid it into the woman's mind for her: 9:00 P.M. By midnight, Page would be back from a school field trip, packed and waiting by her father's door. The planned weekend of "potting around," as she and Page called it, free of appointments and business phone calls, held little allure. Much as she wanted to see Page, the recall in the gallery had stripped the woman bare. She could not look forward to Page's youthful exuberance, the long jog through the shopping malls, and worse, sitting in a public restaurant, while attempting to ignore the cellar recall and

189

the pulse that had started to beat between her legs. Shouldn't she be able to enjoy Page without the intrusion of such garbage? The barrage of thoughts grew by one more: the woman felt cheated.

Sewer Mouth's rage burst, and she slammed the steering wheel with a doubled-up fist. The horn did not blare; it was not working either. Elvira reached over and turned on the car radio. Manfred Mann began to wail.

Would there ever be enough time with Page? One day—and she felt the decision come from nowhere and watched her fingers beat out a heavy rhythm on the dashboard—therapy would be finished and life back on an even keel. Much as she wanted to see no one, to hide and work on the manuscript this weekend, the idea of Page waiting with a crestfallen face by her father's door negated the urge to hide. But the cheated feeling welled up again . . . and Sewer Mouth promptly bludgeoned it. Sewer Mouth batted people away like bugs on a hot summer night and zeroed in on workloads. Sewer Mouth had focus and a mind that could stop all other emotion while she produced. The woman experienced the guilt that eighteen-hour workdays created to the exclusion of all else. Page had been an exclusion all these years.

For now, in lieu of a whole weekend's solitude, the woman pulled into the 7-Eleven parking lot. Before picking up Page, she'd settle for taking a cup of coffee home and drinking it, alone. Someone laughed at the word "alone," but the laughter was far back in the woman's mind. Streetlights cast long shadows through the car windows and she added "car wash" to the ever-present list of things to do. The windows were filthy with fingerprints and stained with nicotine; they let in only a grey, fogged light.

The better not to see us by. This time both laugh and voice were closer but the woman heard neither. She was trying to get up the nerve and the energy to get out of the car. "Junkyard Dog" played on. Through Elvira's mind, the song made the woman smile. What could be meaner than a junkyard dog? The words had a protective ring, warning away the bad guys. Once she'd heard herself tell Norman that it was her favourite song, replete with the finest expression ever coined. Norman had told her that she had a twisted mind. She'd tried after that to keep the radio volume down and not mention parts of any song to him. He had been serious and even angry and she had not been successful. The volume, it seemed, was always too high and the

190

catch words of everything from Tom Waits's wailings to the Fifth of Beethoven sprang out of her mouth at will. Norman had retreated into a silence that grew almost poisonous over the years.

The woman observed, as she dragged herself across the parking lot and into the store, that one foot seemed to be going nicely ahead of the other, no matter how lethargic she felt or how she cringed when anyone looked at her. But as she poured coffee into a paper cup, the movements were rigid and quick. Desperate, almost.

The stepfather and the cellar recall of twenty short minutes ago had not died down. It hit her again as she spilled steaming black coffee on the dashboard in her haste to start the engine. A biker holding a bag of Half-Smokes and a giant Pepsi yelled out to her and then he whistled. The woman froze. Was he crazy? That went for Norman and Morgan, too. What did they see in her? What was wrong with them that they'd find her worthy of time or attention? Even with all the hot coffee on the way home, there was no warmth. The stepfather hung in her mind: the cellar recall had made him real. Until the Weaver wove the recall right out of her head.

Back at the house, so tired that putting one foot ahead of the other was an effort, she stumbled at the kitchen door and began to cry. The sweater resisted all efforts to get it off, it was too full of static, clinging to her like a white shroud.

We're not through yet.

The smell of her mother's body was back, along with the overpowering desire for tea. Hot tea with cream fresh from a cow and two teaspoons of sugar, a bowl of tomato soup, and a bologna sandwich, fat with butter and Hellmann's mayonnaise, with all the crust trimmed off. *Hot tea.* Boiling, scalding, hot, hot tea.

The woman began to scream. Even as the first sounds left her mouth, she was trying to run, stumbling up the staircase, scrabbling at the bannisters for leverage each time her feet lost traction. She clutched the baggy skirt and blouse around a body that had become so thin that the arms and legs seemed like unfamiliar sticks. Sticks that could not run fast enough or hang on tight enough to protect her against anything.

The screams went on as she watched hot water pour into the tub. A cup of steaming tea rested on the tub rim, she had no idea how it had gotten there. Still uttering screaming, sobbing sounds she gulped the tea while kneeling on cold white tile.

Somebody yelled and began to curse. Someone else laughed and urged her both to stay on her knees and get into the tub. Somehow the words "Grace under pressure," as the laughing voice kept using them, referred to the zombie-like movements the woman knew she was making. None of it made any sense except in blinding flashes of recognition. She could not stop screaming.

She obeyed the laughing voice without question, had to because the zombie-like movements that were not her own, carried her forth anyway. She lowered her body into the hot water and felt her feet slide under her. Now she was crouched there, surrounded by soap bubbles and tears and the mucus dripping into a cup of hot sweet tea. There wasn't enough strength in her body to wipe the tears or the mucus because she felt as if she were operating with the comprehension of a six-year-old; as if someone had just beaten her to within an inch of her life, as if she were being punished. But punished for what?

Get those feet under you.

And yet another voice spoke in the woman's head; it was heavy with some sort of foreign accent which she immediately denied. The voice questioned her in a friendly, conversational way, asking why she sat so often with her knees under her?

"I don't know!" the woman screamed.

And someone slid it into her mind then, like a tray of rich pastry that her mother used to bake, and she watched the picture from a distance that would never again, as long as she lived, be far enough away.

The second farmhouse and she was six years old. The stepfather making a tent of the blankets, she positioned between his legs, roughhousing, as the mother called it. The first-floor bedroom, the bedstead with the chipped white paint, and sunlight on a winter day streaming in the tall windows, glinting on her mother's auburn hair as she worked at the sewing machine by the foot of the bed. The stepfather's laughter and his knowing look, the mother's tight-lipped expression.

Blankets slipping with the force of activity, no longer a tent in front of the mother's eyes. The anger in those eyes now directed to the child, not the stepfather. The pink thing in the wiry bush bobbing back and forth.

The teacup hit the white tiled floor; dark liquid splashed on the yellow bathmat. Another tray slid into her mind; the pastry this time was as rich as the first and more difficult to swallow because the picture was too clear. Sweet hot tea rose in the woman's throat. Still six years old and seated this time on the living room floor in front of the stepfather, again on a winter's day. Another round of "roughhousing," his legs in old green work pants spread wide in front of her. She imprisoned between his legs, her feet just touching him where the legs met in a V. Sounds of a zipper opening, other quiet, stealthy movements. Her small feet now held between his two hands that guided them to the V; her head being snatched from above and her face slapped. The smell of her mother's body, the bleach she used on the clothes, mingled with a softer smell of woman, some kind of face powder and deodorant, but still paramount, the odour of her mother's flesh itself, that only a lover or one's child could identify.

The tray slid again, pushing time forward a notch. Her mother that same night, eyes narrowed into slits at the child sitting on the floor in one corner of the kitchen. Everything curiously still. The mother's voice breaking the stillness, shouting an order: "Get those feet under you. Sit there, don't move, you don't move until I tell you."

Time passing, legs beginning to cramp.

"Get those feet under you."

The skin on the child's ankles beginning to puff and turning deep reddish-blue as the circulation was cut off.

The pain.

The woman didn't understand how she drove to Page's house and back, or how she kept the smile on her face. Page got ready for bed. The woman kept busy by unpacking Page's suitcase and hanging her clothes in the closet. The pulse between her legs continued to beat. She wanted to vomit. *Kill him.* It was crammed in among all the voices roaring in her head. The unbalanced feeling, the sensation of falling grew worse each time "Kill him" surfaced. The idea grew steadily more appealing. By the time she'd stashed away Page's underwear and the books she'd brought along to study, the image of the stepfather's imminent death was full-blown in her mind. Blood from his gaping knife wound and the bullet hole in his twisted face materialized as Page watched her from the big bed under the skylight.

Page, pajama-clad and excited, talked about a school field trip as she snuggled in the bed. Strands of strawberry-blond hair caught in the white eyelet pillowcases; her eyes were glowing as she asked if they could get away this summer. Would they? The woman didn't know. Things happened around her, not through her. She made plans or believed she did, and then they changed as if the reins guiding any outcome were held by someone else.

The woman hoped that her face did not betray the thoughts leaping in her mind. She tried to straighten up the loft, with her head turned away from Page's view. The thoughts were too exquisite (''exquisite'' was Catherine's word, just as the murderous thoughts were Catherine's too, but the woman didn't know that) to wait until she was alone. The smell of blood in her nostrils, the excrement from the stepfather's burst intestines stuck under broken fingernails that were ragged from full and glorious battle. . . . She put aside the intestines just long enough to gather up Page's blue jeans and T-shirt from the floor, and to stick her tennis shoes under a chair.

Where had Page's pink ruffled pinafores and lavender hair ribbons gone? Gone away with the little-girl voice and the wondering eyes. Promises, too many over the years since she'd left Norman, crashed to the floor between Page and herself, all broken. Not mercifully forgotten, just broken.

The roar of voices in the woman's head made the stepfather's intestines glow bluish-red. A lovely, hellish colour. It grew in her mind, that colour, until it ignited and burst in the mind of Black Katherine. Now it wasn't just voices inside the woman's head, there was also Black Katherine's banshee scream that first, at its lowest ebb, blended with all the other voices. It reached a crescendo then, and hurled itself on to a fever pitch. Black Katherine was beside and inside the woman, her being personified by gritting teeth and flashing, glaring eyes.

Now do you understand why you've got to hurry, bitch?

For a reason she could never afterward identify, the woman understood that the voice referred to the recall that had been brought to her in the bathtub. No, if it could be helped, she'd just as soon not see any other child go through that. Did her others really feel that the book would do that much good? That it could, perhaps, stop mothers from punishing the child, instead of the abuser?

''I always understood,'' the woman said silently. ''Somewhere inside me I understood, without knowing you were saying it.''

Do you know me? Do you like me? A number of troop members would say the same thing Black Katherine was saying, as soon as they emerged. Revealing themselves was painful. Few believed they could be liked. Black Katherine had been sure of her reception today but she asked anyway.

The woman stood in the loft, appearing quite normal to Page's sleepy eyes, while protesting silently against too many marauding thoughts, none of which were her own. But even as she summoned up the iron will to deny, the solid irrefutable presence of Black Katherine blocked it. For one tiny moment the woman stood facing all that it meant, all that it would mean, and then Black Katherine drifted away as if she'd never been there.

Page had turned out her reading light. The voices in the woman's head died down and some of the off-balance sensation left as she fell onto her own side of the bed, pulling the sheets up to her neck. The darkness held welcome, the promise of escape through sleep. The woman believed tonight's recall was all over so she didn't react too badly when the trapped, smothered feeling that Black Katherine's words had given her moments before came right back. The fright when Page leaned over and planted two kisses, one on each side of her face, was something she couldn't turn away from.

Affection is dangerous. Affection is always followed by pain. We've always known that. Now you know it, too.

That night, as Page slept peacefully beside her, the woman's others brought her something else, something she would fight over with Stanley for many months to come. They slid another tray into her mind: the memory of her mother with a pair of shiny silver clippers in her right hand. The other hand grasped a hank of the half brother's hair. The mother didn't just cut his hair, she applied the teeth of the clippers to the base of his skull and cut until there was a wide bald ribbon of scalp showing, from the base of his neck right up over the top of his head and on down to his forehead.

"Did your mother cut the children's hair?" Stanley would ask her when she told him later.

"Yes," the woman had to answer. "But I must have been hallucinating that night. Why would my mother do such a thing for no reason?"

"Was there a good reason for any of the abuse that took place?"

The woman would be unable to answer, aware by now that her standard, "Because we were bad," was unacceptable to Stanley.

"The half brother wasn't bad," a small voice would speak up then. "The mother was mad at everyone that day. The half brother had begun to notice girls and he wanted a new shirt. He was growing and only two shirts still fit him. The mother got tired of his hounding, she wanted to teach him a lesson. Just like she taught all of us."

Stanley would remember the times in the last two months when the woman had mentioned gagging at the sight of anything silver and shiny. The recall that had made her ill each time had finally surfaced. She was making progress.

Nobody had told him about the recall in the cellar. So of course he couldn't know just how much progress.

Lamb Chop cried in the darkness of the loft that night, while clouds scuttled across the face of a pale dead moon. Mean Joe let her cry. Sometimes people had to do that without interruption, without being shushed to death and told that it was alright, things would get better.

Lamb Chop had been rattled since the last session. First, hearing the "dead essence" of Olivia II in the well, then seeing Olivia I's child mirror-image, and finally having the "dead essence" of the other child emerging almost on top of her . . . it had been a lot to handle.

"They were so different from me," Lamchop sobbed in spite of the yellow gumdrop Mean Joe had given her. "What's wrong with them?"

"They're dead," Mean Joe told her.

"I was scared. Am I dead, too?"

"No, you're not dead, and everybody's scared."

"Even you, Mean Joe?"

"Especially me, and I'm supposed to be the strong one. You could do us all a favour."

"What's that?"

"Make up your mind how you want to spell your name. You write Lamb Chop, Lamchop and Lambchop. It's never the same. You confuse whoever is typing the manuscript."

"Too bad," Lambchop said. "That's the way I like it."

Mean Joe reached over and put another gumdrop, purple this time, into her waiting mouth.

The child folded her hands across her chest. The gumdrop slid around on her tongue. "Your skin is pretty, Mean Joe. I wish it were mine."

Lamchop closed her eyes. Her steady breathing indicated the beginning of sleep. Mean Joe quit smiling. The fragrance of Opium perfume drifted up from the pillowcases. He lay in the darkness thinking about Olivia II, who had died in the well. That day not so long ago when the woman had first seen the face reflected in the puddle of rainwater and the well recall had started for her, Olivia II had come to life again. But life by what definition? Mean Joe shook his head. Could dead people scream? Olivia II had ceased to be over thirty years ago in the well at the second farmhouse. When he'd reached down into the Tunnel that time and scooped her up from its dark, wet depths, she'd lain in his arms, a sodden bundle of long-dead flesh and bones.

But there in the session today, there'd been that tiny voice. She'd finally won. She'd said what she wanted, until her essence had run out of steam, and Olivia I's child mirror-image, terrified and angry, had finished it for her.

Mean Joe laughed in his silent fashion and his eyes in the moonlight were cold. Did all dead souls, the wronged ones in particular, somehow manage to pass their messages in voices that could be heard long after they were gone forever? Or were the sins of their tormentors simply buried with them, never to be known?

Was there some high-flown intellectual concept that allowed for the possibility of such a phenomenon? Mean Joe, if he'd put his mind to it, could have come up with a thousand high-flown intellectual concepts. But since he'd been born at the second farmhouse, his job had been as today—only to protect. He left, for the time being, intellectual concepts to people like Catherine, who, when she wasn't simmering with suppressed rage behind a cocked eyebrow and a deceiving smile, was busy leaping on her own flaws and those of others. She leapt with both feet and a red-hot determination, as if flaws were base and only perfection, or at least change, would make her world safe.

He did not blame her for the rage. She hadn't as a child been able to explore her world with the freedom of physical or mental movement that her creative talent needed to grow. She hadn't even been able to go past the stepfather on the staircase without the man's hands on her. Once, when she had been five years old, the stepfather had grabbed her off the stairs as she'd tried

197

to get away from him. He'd gripped the top of her head with one hand and jammed the other right up her vagina. Holding her aloft with her feet just touching the stair treads, like a human Popsicle with his arm for a stick, the stepfather had laughed and dared her to run up the stairs ahead of him.

No wonder Catherine craved mobility, larger-than-life accomplishments, and power. Beside him in the darkened loft, Lambchop sighed in her sleep. Mean Joe reached over and removed the last shreds of the purple gumdrop from her mouth. Olivia II, the idea of her, continued to roam his mind like a vagabond warrior searching for a battleground. Mean Joe thought about Olivia I's mirror-images: one, the child who had emerged, lisp and all, in the session today, just like a ghost—and the other one, Catherine, the adult. The child mirror-image had never grown, never would. As for Catherine, she had called out to him in the session with more human feeling, more passion, than he'd ever glimpsed in her before. Catherine was no hypocrite. In those pleading eyes she'd let him see a message not totally altruistic. She'd been thinking of her own skin as well as that of the sleeping cores, who lay directly behind and right in the path of the child who'd finally emerged with the strong lisp—the other wandering, ghostly, child core's mirror-image.

The woman would never awaken, she had no mechanism for it. But she would become fully aware of her true state and look herself in the eye and probably scream. Maybe he was using the wrong expression, Mean Joe thought. Maybe it wasn't a question of the woman becoming aware, because the message had been passed to her a hundred times: "For you, there isn't any more." He'd stood at her shoulder as she stared out at the squirrels that day and realised that she didn't exist. No word for the state of her mind in that one moment really fit except the word "nonexistent." Because as she stood there for that one brief moment, he'd made sure that no Troop member passed her anything to divert her attention from what he wanted her to know: no problems, no emotions, no feelings, no nothing, had passed to her from anyone, including himself. And she had grasped the reality of her state of being; he had felt it. Except that she was like a lamp with its cord unplugged from the socket. That's how much it had affected her.

But the woman was being bombarded these days; it would continue. The battle was on. The one who lived in the deepest part of the Tunnel had said that this Christmas would be the high feast to end all high feasts. Mean Joe shivered, knowing that the plans being contrived, re-evaluated, and recontrived, had nothing to do with tinsel or fancy tree ornaments.

Beside him, Lambchop stirred. The cores cried softly, and from a long distance away, the one who slept in the well began to scream.

20

The Troop Formation now fell into four categories: those who had made a conscious decision to speak more directly to each other and to the woman by thought transference and aloud to Stanley and to outsiders; those who had been pushed to do so against their will by emerging recall; some who spoke only to each other and not to the woman or Stanley; and a few diehards who chose to lurk in the background, as yet "unevidenced" to anyone but themselves.

Many Troop members had operated their entire lives on a verbal and physical level that still remained unknown to the woman.

For those Troops who were aware of each other, the experience ranged, after the initial shock and anger wore off, from joyous acceptance, to nitpicking at each other's shortcomings, to rage and disgust. Facing some Troop members through thought transference or the more potent "evidencing," the woman was aware at times of a kind of wonderment; she almost wanted to count their fingers and toes the way a mother might when presented with her newborn child.

That motherliness was not her own. The Troop members were giving her, as they always had, their recall and their feelings and reactions, because she had none of her own. They gave her only what they thought she could handle. The Tunnel walls rumbled frequently with preparations to give her more.

By late June, the preparations fell into place as the woman

stood on a street corner, trying to decide if it was safe to cross. For her, streetlights were in a category with math, clocks, and calendars. A light drizzle had been falling and now the humidity moved in, making her blouse stick to her skin. She smelled the cigar smoke on the man waiting next to her and determined that she would cross when he did. That was the last she saw of him.

With no warning, two separate entities invaded her mind. One was a silent, far-off figure; the dead "essence" of someone whose birth and death had happened simultaneously and long ago. Adult core. The words, without meaning, slid into the woman's mind. The "essence" of the adult core remained for a moment and the woman felt as if their two minds had been joined, as if she herself floated into the vast, empty space of them both.

The second entity's emergence was only the cry—of someone locked out of Troop Formation experiences for sporadic, but long periods of time. This entity was almost as empty as the first. And then the woman "received" from it, frustrated, fearful, wondering; and the emptiness was filling up with not more than five memories of an entire lifetime and confetti shreds of the rest. The woman had believed those five memories and the shreds were hers, and if not, what did that leave her?

In the Tunnel, he waited and stayed the Gatekeeper from giving the third signal.

Darlin', *he said to the woman,* y' have now received the essence of the two who sit nearest you. Are y' up t' receivin' the third?

His voice was so strange, so bland, as if before it reached her ears, he somehow filtered it through time itself. There was not a hint in that voice of the person behind it. The woman trembled and he said things to her in that bland voice that she could not comprehend, but the pain of experiencing both entities, the silent, far-off adult core and the one who had been locked out for so long, had taken her mind in a giant fist and wrung it. The emotional pain grew and flooded her.

The second entity, darlin', is the source o' all your own emotions and thought. The second entity shields the first. Y' are more empty than either o' them.

The woman, her mind joined with the second entity and feeling as she had all her life, that one's bewilderment and emptiness knew he told the truth. The other Troop members held their

201

breath. But that truth plunged straight through the woman's brain like a bullet and sped off, leaving nothing but disbelief and denial in its path. When he asked again if she were ready for the third one to evidence, the clarity of his silent thought became a call of outrage heard through the Troop Formation ranks.

He knew it wouldn't work this time; she would have to be devoid of anything given to her by other Troop members, and their outrage blocked his efforts. But he forced the woman to listen to her own mind; forced her to hear the dead silence of it. And then she knew who the third one was—and inside herself she ran like hell and the Weaver ran with her, snatching away all that the Tunnel darkness had given her.

Mean Joe waited in that lone, fleeting moment, ready to absorb any blow which the Buffer could not handle. His two giant hands, beneath which there was no terror, went out to the woman.

We all have to evidence sometime, *Mean Joe said.* Paideia, the Greeks called it; the transference of knowledge. When one of us evidences to you, you receive what we are and at the same time, we receive and know ourselves, too. Even the most infinitesimal among us can evidence. There aren't any words to express some of us, except to say that nothing is something, too. You need to keep that one idea, hang onto it, because your turn is near.

With no idea how she'd done it, the woman saw she'd not only crossed the intersection but had navigated a very big parking lot and was sitting in her car. The radio played full blast. Hurriedly, instead of turning the volume down, she rolled up the windows. The Outrider laughed and the woman was glad of it. Harsh afternoon sun streamed in, slanting across the dashboard, making her eyes water. Or was that someone else's tears? Numbness had set in.

Knowing himself to be a full-fledged bastard for the act he was about to perform, Mean Joe seized the advantage.

He signaled and the long-dead image of Olivia I inserted a piece of recall in the woman's mind . . . she was almost three years old and in the first farmhouse kitchen. Walls and floorboards rattled with the gusts of icy wind. The room filled with raw winter light glinting off the snowbanks outside. The high chair in which she sat was made of varnished maple with a yellow duck painted on it. The tray held a dish of gritty cereal

202

and a tin cup of milk. The hand coming toward her seemed giant in size and covered with little black hairs. In the hand was a silver baby spoon with a curved handle, a gift from her mother's mother; in the spoon, cereal on which Karo syrup floated, golden, pretty, ugly.

Why was she imprisoned in this high chair to eat her breakfast when memories of sitting down at the kitchen table for various other meals, at this same age, were suddenly batting her from every direction?

The high chair tray was lifted then, and the woman knew why. Tiny hands were bound to the arms of the high chair. Karo syrup, the taste of it in her mouth—Karo syrup not floating on a spoon of cereal but coating the long pink thing that nestled in the wiry bush. A small voice in the woman's head, crying. *Go away, leave me alone*.

The long pink thing bobbed up and down; the hand with the dark black hairs gripped it, pushing it at the child's face, aiming it at her mouth. The small voice wailed in the woman's mind. It was the same one she'd heard that night in the bathtub, during memories of the games the stepfather had played right in front of the mother and for which the child had later been punished. Her mother wasn't in the kitchen though, not today. Something told the woman that her mother was busy elsewhere, giving birth to the first half sister.

Because the woman's mind was open now, because Mean Joe knew with this recall that Olivia I had her pinned like a fish on a hook, wriggling and screaming protests in her own brain, he let Olivia proceed. Right into the woman's helpless mind, he allowed the insertion of one more picture.

Sunlight shot through the slats in the barn, although the barn itself was hazy. The dust motes were much clearer, dancing in the hot summer air. It was the crate that really got her, sitting off to one side, but looking as if it were often used. Wooden, with metal straps around it for extra support; a very strong crate, strong enough for a man to stand on. No sound at all in the barn and then she heard the cow bleat, heard the stepfather grunt.

That was all because Mean Joe let the picture fade and he even took the sound away. So she didn't know why her screams should be louder than the music playing in the car. Or why somebody should be trying to tell her that the screams weren't her own; that there was a very good reason why all recall seemed like a movie of someone else's life.

Mean Joe did move then, assuring her as much as he dared that the image had meaning, that the wooden crate and the cow had a definite purpose in the stepfather's games back at the second farmhouse. On hearing his words the woman did not move. She stood like a stone with dread rising in her throat until it formed an ice-cold knot.

Suddenly, June was gone and by the middle of July, the woman felt nothing except the dire need to hang onto herself, counting minutes by the clock to make sure that no one else stole her time. To what purpose, she had no idea. Stanley had been beating his brains out to help her overcome the lethargy.

The presence of her people, now that more of them had come forth, was inundating. The woman became confused. The more she wondered what it was that she wanted, or needed, or was, the more determined they were to tell her what they wanted. The woman wondered what her own purpose was.

We'll let you know, they said.

On most days, she worked on the gallery floor except when typing, knees folded beneath her. The small voice cried out as she worked: *Go away, leave me alone.*

At times, for no apparent reason and with no prior warning, the woman found herself down on those same knees, rocking back and forth, sobbing. Depression grafted her tired limbs together and immobilised her so badly that there were times when she barely moved except to drag herself to the sessions.

Someone dumped it into her mind one day that in view of the irrefutable evidence of the Troop members, her denials sounded stupid. To the woman, the Troops and the incidents sounded at times unreal. The media had not yet begun to publicise child abuse in all its horror. So the woman might well have been alone, although joined in a pitiful alliance with countless millions of other victims.

But as Norman was quick to point out to her, other victims kept their mouths shut; they did not allow their therapy to be filmed and shown at a large university to a student population that asked Stanley questions, like: ''Freud says that children secretly want sex with their parents, couldn't she be fantasising?'' or ''She reacts so hysterically, could she simply be menopausal?'' or ''She's just one of those people who overdramatise things; can child abuse really do this much damage?''

Stanley reported such comments to the woman in an offhand way, checking her reactions. He wanted her to be aware and prepared for the day when someone would make such comments to her face. He also reported to her on those students who watched the videos and thus found the courage to report their own childhood abuse to him.

On hearing that those students were now getting treatment, the woman cried with relief. The other selves urged faster completion of the manuscript.

"How can the bastards be so dumb," Sewer Mouth raged. "Do they think that female children of twelve are menopausal? And what about male victims? Are they menopausal, too? Screw Freud and the horse he rode in on!"

From a distance the woman heard snatches of Stanley and Sewer Mouth's conversation. The language, the anger, were frightening, and told her that Sewer Mouth at least was real. The woman knew she could not have changed or prevented a single word that had been uttered.

Occasionally, listlessly, when not consumed with terror, the woman picked up such evidence of her other selves and turned it over. Immediately, thankfully, the bizarreness of it would leap into her mind, allowing that evidence, as if it were flawed merchandise, to be put back on the shelf.

For the woman, July did not mean beaches and languid sunning. Paying 25 percent interest on a recent business loan had depleted the savings, and three settlements, whose proceeds would have carried her nicely for another four years, were shoved into limbo. Land purchasers were scared, afraid that inflated housing prices would not hold. The banks weren't lending to any builder who wasn't liquid, and few builders had been liquid for a long time now. The career for which Ten-Four had struggled so hard was going down the tubes. Real estate companies were closing.

Nowhere could the woman find the energy to plot alternative and necessary job changes. *Loser,* said a raspy voice. And it was true. Moving out of the house and leaving everything she loved about it loomed ahead, if the bills were to be paid by renting it out. Pressured beyond the ability to cope, she stayed away from television news as well, for fear that it might loosen her fine-edged grip on sanity. One Friday morning, the horoscopes, the only thing she read these days except "Hagar the Horrible," stated: "Your mental stability is suspect today." She cancelled the subscription to the *Washington Post*, killing her last media connection.

The mail she didn't read, stored in over twenty paper grocery bags, disappeared from the cupboard one day soon afterward.

Coward.

The woman winced at the voice that sounded like her mother's. She didn't miss the mail, but the receipts, records, and notes, the extraneous baggage of a life she hadn't lived, were gone, too. Everyone kept such things; people said it was required. Elvira, who pressed closer these days along with yet another formerly distant self, replied, *So what?* The woman shrugged. Whatever she could, ought, must do, seemed to have lost its hold on her. Most people would have been shocked at her lackadaisical attitude. The woman, having experienced little but fear and an overpowering compulsion to "do right" all her life, felt only a hesitant relief.

"Thank you," she said to whoever might be listening.

You're welcome, they said warmly. *See? We are all cooperating here. You didn't think we could do that.*

The idea of being cared for and the newer, relaxed pace seemed suspect and their charms paled quickly. Sewer Mouth took her gripe to Stanley.

"I'm starting to feel smothered. I'm capable of running my own life, I always have been and always will be."

"They have been with you a very long time," he said. "They have your best interests at heart."

Sewer Mouth couldn't bear it. She leaped right over the woman's half-surfaced presence and snarled. "That statement sucks. It's a bloody platitude. I'm suspicious whenever someone tells me junk like that. As for this 'other self' business, this 'process' as you call it, I hate the whole damned thing. It scares me."

"Why does it scare you?" Stanley did not smile. He wanted to because Sewer Mouth, adamant about not giving her name, was one of the most easily recognisable Troop members.

"It means," she growled, "that the only private place I ever had to myself has been invaded by strangers, and I'm not alone anymore. I hate it!"

"Why do you hate it?"

The woman, receiving only fragments of the conversation, wondered at the carefully withheld smile on Stanley's face, at his constant Whys. Couldn't he follow what she was saying? Or was he distracted or responding with smugness at some stupidity of hers? In her exhausted state, all she could do was watch his mouth carefully, trying to hang on as she studied the thought moving in her head. It came out of her mouth with no effort on her part and the clarity of its meaning amazed her.

"People who get close," she said, "can kill you."

Finally, Stanley thought, they were getting down to it. No matter how strong she grew in business, her personal life would always be nil unless she did understand. She would always run at the idea of closeness to anyone.

"People can kill you?" he repeated. "How can they do that?"

She started to speak but her voice broke and the changes were happening so quickly that Stanley kept missing them. One minute he was looking at the woman and the next he wasn't sure who sat in front of him. The only thing he knew definitely when the voice broke was that his client was gone.

In her place behind the bangs sat a woman with apple-green eyes. The outer edges were ringed with a thin line of black and in each center was a tiny, dead-black iris. It would take Stanley years to figure out that this self was Black Katherine's mirror-image; created to go where Black Katherine could not, to deal as Black Katherine could never deal, because her rage was too great. Black Katherine was one of the selves who would forever remain in the darkest shadows of the Tunnel, secluded and on guard. One day, in a retrospective mood, Elvira would tell Stanley that the Junkyard Dog of "Bad, Bad, Leroy Brown" fame, had nothing on Black Katherine.

"Are you aware," the apple-green eyes bored right into Stanley's, unblinking, "that there is a nun in our midst? Her name is Sister Mary Catherine, and sits clicking the beads all night and calling out, 'Harlot!' She prays. We can hear her. Have you any idea what Sister Mary Catherine is trying to deal with?"

"A nun," Stanley said. It was all that he could say.

"Sister Mary is on the edge." The voice held no emotion. "We don't know exactly how to keep her from that edge, when so much of a sexual nature is being hurled at her."

While the person seated in front of him spoke of concern for the Troop member she called "Sister Mary Catherine," her tone reflected no concern whatever. Neither did her eyes. There was something not quite right about them.

"Sister Mary," the voice went on while the eyes stared at him fixedly, "finds the sexual recall difficult. I gather that having been a minister you can understand her problem, but she's driving some Troop members crazy with her bleating."

"And you," Stanley said, "how do you feel about Sister

207

Mary's reaction?'' He had figured out what was wrong with her eyes. Aside from the unusual apple-green colour and the fine thread of black at their edges which reminded one of an Alaskan husky, they were utterly without human emotion. She looked as if she could kill without remourse; and as if the loss of her own life would concern her even less. In her whole attitude there wasn't a shred of humanity. Stanley was finally frightened.

She did not answer his questions. She made statements with no change of expression, matter-of-factly, as if she did not care one way or the other what he thought.

''You don't like me,'' she said flatly. ''I'm not here to be liked. Some of us don't even like each other. But there is one thing we all have in common—our individuality. While no Troop member will accept Sister Mary's beliefs, to a man, we are determined that she, like the rest of us, be allowed her own space. No matter what she represents.''

''I take it that you mean the church.''

''We know that for every nun, priest, and pope you turn over, there's restriction underneath. The church leaves us cold, it's full of dogma that chains up the mind and cuts off growth.''

''If Sister Mary bothers you so much, how is she going to have space within your ranks?''

''Sister Mary will have to learn to take her beads elsewhere and pray in silence. The woman goes out of her mind when she hears the chanting.''

''Perhaps it comforts Sister Mary.''

''Nothing comforts Sister Mary. The sexual recall is anathema to her and there's no escaping it now. She'd like to stop, turn back. But it doesn't work that way.''

She observed Stanley's pen moving resolutely over the clipboard.

''Yes,'' she said tonelessly, ''write it down. The nonsense has got to stop. Sister Mary has her place in our structure. She earned it by rejecting the stepfather's sexual demands. Sister Mary, because of her religious leanings, has been greeted by heartfelt scorn among us; yet she's the one who said no to the stepfather. Of course she wasn't the one who paid; Rabbit took the pain whenever the stepfather lashed out.''

The word ''pain'' had an effect. Perhaps her words had triggered what started to happen then, or perhaps the Troop member trying to emerge heard them and reacted. Up to this point, she'd merely sat there, eyes unblinking, shooting bulletlike sentences.

208

She did not, as in the case of some of the Troops, straighten her hair or fidget with a bracelet or even move an eyelash. At the word "pain," however, there was a flurry of activity, in both her eyes and body, as if she were warding off something or someone.

He watched the effort it took to keep her footing.

"You want a name for me," she said, as if nothing had happened. "There are blank spaces on your clipboard because you think that eventually I'll give you my name. I won't."

The change this time hadn't seemed to materialise fully and there was still only the hint of another Troop member behind her. He'd contemplated earlier the possibility of two or more persons within the Troop Formation being able to share exactly the same space at one time. Now he was positive.

"Pay attention." She leaned over and rapped smartly on his clipboard. "Someone is hitting on me. You know that, you can sense it."

"Yes," he said. "I can." It always gave him an eerie feeling when Troop members anticipated his unspoken thoughts. Had Marshall not mentioned that research was showing that gifted children were familiar with the paranormal, with precognition, he would have discounted each incident.

"I'm going to talk fast," she told him, "there isn't much time. Those who sit in the front lines must consider the total welfare. I will never be a Front Runner; it is not my nature to care about anything or anyone. Having no scruples, morals, or other impediments, I'm more capable in certain areas than any other Troop member."

Stanley did not interrupt; she did not give him a chance. He wondered if he would ever get used to her eyes.

"I'm only here," she said, "to ensure that our Troop Formation remains intact. The stepfather told us every time, 'I'll kill you if you tell.' The mother said for any infraction of the rules, 'I'll kill you if you do that again.' The little ones believed them both, because the parents' actions reinforced their words. The children are petrified now because, to them, breaking the rules by telling in the manuscript or by talking to you means death. Their fears and ours are being transferred to the woman. She believes the fear is her own. But she will only have to experience what we lived through."

Her rush of words caused Stanley to ask quickly how she felt about telling after all these years and especially in such a permanent, public way.

"I don't care if the whole story is carved in cement and hung outside the United Nations building. The mother stressed the value of one's reputation. 'It's all you've got,' she used to say. 'Protect it. Once your reputation is gone, you're dirty for life.' Well, our reputation will have to rely on its own merit. On those two farms we followed the mother's advice and never said a word because that would make us 'dirty.' Our silence only protected the stepfather.

"You're wondering," she said, "what other purpose someone like me serves. I am also the safety mechanism between Catherine and the Big Three, the means by which Catherine siphons her anger off so that she operates in the world without killing anyone. If wishes were deeds, Stanley, there wouldn't be a living soul within a hundred miles of Catherine."

She told him how the rage was siphoned off. Even with the change already taking place, she managed, hurling one word after the other.

"I'm a filtering process," she said. "Catherine feels the rage; it's red-hot. By the time it's filtered through me, it's still potent but the urge to kill is deadened. Do you see now? Read it in my eyes, Stanley. There's more than one kind of 'dead' in this world."

He said that the Troops had survived, that they had a chance now at many things. He started to name them. But the thin ring of black around her eyes had disappeared and the twin dark centers had widened. She was gone.

"Survival? To what end?" The question was asked woodenly; the shoulders hunched as if a weight rested on the back of the seated figure. "Life starts at birth and continues until death takes us away. There is no happiness, no joy; only the illusion of it."

"That's a pretty bleak picture of life," Stanley said. "What about the joy that children bring to a parent, or that lovers bring to each other?"

"None of that means anything. Life begins, it ends. In between, people lie to each other and create misery."

"Don't you love Page?"

"I love no one. One Christmas, we sat at the front window and wished that the father would drive up and take us away from there. He never did."

If the previous pair of eyes had bothered Stanley because of their lack of human emotion, these bothered him because of their lack of hope. They were empty, as if the life had been drained out of them.

"People leave you," the wooden voice told him, "and they never come back."

The Troops could scorn familial affection and with good reason. But behind those empty eyes lay both the desire for love and the death of all reasonable hope for it. Given the proper circumstances, this Troop member was a prime candidate for suicide. Except that she did not display enough energy to lift a finger, let alone do herself in. Was the compartmentalisation strong enough to seal off the suicidal one, whoever she was, and prohibit her from acting?

To the Troop members who were listening in on that session, the comments and attitude of their lifeless fellow member were puzzling. No emotion, no interest—who was this? No Troop member seemed to know.

Someone who did know reached out and, very gently, led the Suicidal Warrior back to where it was warmer, safer. That someone laid strong hands across the shoulders that were rigid, as rigid as if a last sleep had already begun. And the song heard that night in the back of the woman's mind was an Irish lullaby, the kind that old warriors used to sing—to young warriors fallen in battle from wounds so deep they would not recover.

21

Released from what had been the lethargy of the Suicidal Warrior's prolongued evidencing, the woman experienced again the high energy level of the other Troop members.

Stanley had been busy the last few weeks, jotting questions about two cores and a woman who did not think for herself or consume her own food.

Finally, he called Marshall, long distance.

"The strain on the woman is awful," Stanley said, "sometimes she just shakes. I'm trying to figure out who she is."

"I don't know," Marshall said. "But one thing is certain. She isn't the first-born child."

"I keep hoping she is and that I'm just taking things too literally. . . ."

"This is their world, Stanley. They've got ways of dealing. As to the cores and their exact location in that throng of humanity, you're close now, you'll figure it out. Have you noticed that spring holds a great significance for the Troops? I think that's when the first-born child died and probably both cores were born in that same moment. The Irishman is the one who rocks me. By nature, he's a high-handed giver. I sense him choosing a day in time on which he's going to make a major move. The bomb has been activated. I'd say you've got about four months and the bomb's going off. Whammo. A Troop gift, a celebration."

With the same sense of impending upheaval as Marshall, Stanley decided that a dose of logic might be in the Troop's best interest. The woman had told Stanley some time ago that pride, guilt, fear, and cowardice were her biggest problem.

"You're not too proud to ask for help," he told her in the next session, "you're too scared. Pride in one's accomplishments is nothing to be ashamed of. Pride in one's appearance isn't cause for ridicule, but you can't even comb your hair in front of someone or shop for a new dress, for fear you'll be thought of as vain. You aren't vain, you aren't proud, you're terrified that you're ugly and that someone will notice."

He'd known he couldn't reach everyone with his statements today. But he smiled when a haughty look shot across the features in front of him. Catherine might not regard herself as ugly, but she did have other hang-ups.

Catherine, who shopped, as the bumper stickers said, until she "dropped," so that she would never look unfashionable, took heed. Stanley's words had also made her remember writing on the flowered wallpaper of the second farmhouse, in complete darkness so that no one could decipher her literary efforts.

You should be proud of us, Elvira yelled at the surfacing woman who heard and understood through Catherine, *you're hanging in there, and we're helping you. Go for it, bitch.*

"Bitch" was said not in a derogatory way, but as a street language paean, the kind of invective that is hurled with a sense of humour—not to wound or impede but to rally one's friends to higher horizons.

Pride. Viewing now through Elvira, although the woman wasn't aware of her because Elvira had yet to evidence fully, some of the word's power to frighten was gone. She examined the measure of trust she'd felt between Mean Joe and Miss Wonderful; between Mean Joe and the few children who'd evidenced; she herself and even Stanley being trusted at times by them. Whenever Stanley pointed out the progress, she'd been blind to it. All she'd seen were the number of steps remaining and she berated herself for being in this situation.

"As to the guilt that's been transferred to your every action," Stanley said, "one day you'll realise the guilt isn't yours. And the real coward in all of this is your mother."

The woman slept fitfully that night, hearing Stanley's words repeated in her mind, and sensing, but not privy to, the awful awakening process going on around her.

• • •

Twelve, knew the Irishman was up to something. She sat at his side, watching the Outrider move around the Troop Formation. Both the Irishman and the Outrider seemed to focus on one far-off, silent figure.

Am I right? Twelve asked the Irishman, hardly believing what she absorbed from him.

That silent figure is the adult core, *he said.* Were she ever t' evolve and need t' move freely in the world, the woman is what she would wear as a new skin.

Twelve sat mulling that over and wondered why the Irishman was preparing the woman for something that would never happen.

Not in this world, *the Irishman told her,* but the next.

Twelve ignored him. It was macabre . . . true, the woman, incapable of her own thought or emotion, was merely a conduit for everyone else's. The Buffer sat in front of her just in case anything at all might leak through to the sleeping cores.

And then, almost before he spoke, she knew the reason behind his plan. The potential child and potential adult cores had slept from the moment of their birth, unaware of anything. Their mirror-images could not verbalise or understand the concept of the sex act, beyond fondling. Neither could the dead first-born child. As to her child mirror-image—Twelve didn't know what she knew or understood. Which brought her back to the woman.

Go carefully, Twelve, *the Irishman told her.* D'not let y'r thoughts through t' anyone else. When one o' us expresses emotion too strongly, that creates a kind o' residue which the Weaver must take away, lest the cores or their mirror-images be harmed.

You're playing games with real people, *Twelve whispered.*

Nothin' on earth will change the woman's structure. Right now, out o' all that he's taken away, the Weaver is weavin' a temporary kind o' second skin o' memory. When the signal is given, the skin will be in place. 'Twill be an awful moment, but when 'tis here, the Weaver'll weave for the cores and their mirror-images alone.

There is, *said Twelve,* more than a hint of the Machiavellian about you.

T' be sure, but as Front Runner, y've got t' take y'r guts in both fists and fly w' the devil himself. Such behangidness creates a taste o' time and all the warriors down through it. So. Are y' flying w' me or are y' layin' low?

I think, *Twelve said,* that I'm too young to be hanging out with you.

No, child. Y've got the mind o' a witch and an Irish warrior's backbone.

All this preparation, *Twelve said,* what's it for?

F'r Christmas, darlin'. The time o' the high feast.

That same night, moonlight flickered in the loft bedroom, through the leaves and branches of a very old tree hanging over the skylight. The one in the Tunnel depths sent a barrage of preparatory goodwill and a generous sense of his natural hospitality. Almost as if the woman were a visitor on his territory.

While struggling into the white flannel nightgown, her mind shifted, almost as if someone had tilted it abruptly. Rabbit's whimpering sounds produced a hail of confetti.

As the storm halted, a sudden flick against the woman's mind stood still, longer than ever before. The flick, intricately beclouded as it was, revealed that there had been sexual contact with the stepfather past childhood, into teenage years.

The idea shocked the woman. She looked at the bed twice before seemingly nonexistent muscles allowed her legs to move forward and spill her onto the mattress. Suspicion hidden in the marauding thoughts of other Troop members had told her over the years that the abuse had not stopped until the stepfather had left the house for good. But each time they'd erupted, the Weaver had taken those suspicions away. What he'd always left was nothing more than the idea that sexual contact meant lurking and spying and fondling. Not penetration. And not past childhood.

Faced now with the knowledge that as an adult teenager there had definitely been sexual contact with the stepfather enervated her beyond anything she'd previously experienced. She burrowed into the quilt, torn between seeking the darkness under its folds and wanting to strangle herself with it.

A child was too small to fight off an adult demanding sexual favours (and again in her mind, that meant spying or fondling) and might be just too scared to refuse someone who could turn mean in the blink of an eye. But a teenager?

Elvira moved to the surface, humming snatches of any song that appealed to her as being sufficiently "snake level, belly low," using her humour like a synthetic adrenaline against the woman's fading strength. The woman heard it all vaguely but, crushed by the idea of her own inadequacy, was unable to move.

Elvira tossed the inadequacy right out of the woman's mind and pointed out strength and, again, the idea of progress. The cellar recall was definitely progress, but there had been a second farmhouse. Rabbit's whimpering grew. Grimly, Elvira's humour reached the woman, spurring her on. Relaxing the way Stanley had taught her, she got her breathing synchronised and started the count back. Rabbit, having evidenced to her fully, was no longer a voice. The woman addressed her by name. And Rabbit was down on the front lawn of the second farmhouse, leading her to the smudged cellar window. They were inside, passing the rows and rows of gemlike canned goods: corn and carrots, peaches and strawberries, cherries and plums, and even the beef the mother had salted too heavily that year. The produce in the clear glass mason jars with grey metal lids was testimony to the mother's countless hours at the big black cookstove, to her hours out in the fields and orchards, tending and picking. It was also, even in the dim light, like having the mother's glinting eyes following her own and Rabbit's progress through the cellar.

Damp, musty smells, and the old fuse box high on the stone wall to her right and another window dead ahead . . . but a tall figure was silhouetted before the window, blocking the light. In a deadly silence, contrived by his own stealthy movements, the stepfather's hands moved out and took her around the waist even while broad calloused fingers worked at her white cotton pants, separating fabric from flesh, from the space where thighbone met pelvis. And she rode the pink thing forward and back, no more than five years old now and less than six. She should have known better than to try the recall on her own again.

Because right on the heels of it, so fast that she couldn't avoid the blow, came another flick. This time it wasn't a child but a teenager and there was the stepfather, and the flick wouldn't let go; it showed her, made her feel, the two of them entwined in some kind of crazy position and the look on his face and worse, what was happening to her own body right now, to her mind, and the stimulation became a flood. . . .

The screams and the tears mingled with undeniable sexual arousal and the broken dishes surrounding her now. And how had she gotten from the loft to the kitchen, with the teakettle shrieking madly on the gas burner and cigarettes burning in the ashtray?

On the following afternoon, the woman told Stanley about the cellar recall. In shamed tones, she explained the physical reaction it had caused. Someone else told him about penetration. Stanley listened as the woman berated herself because she couldn't remember ever defending herself against the stepfather,

216

told him that somehow the knowledge had been passed to her that there had been sexual abuse into her teens.

Stanley wanted her to say it clearly. The woman paused, looked at the floor, and wrung her hands. She couldn't seem to open her mouth. Finally, she told him that the stepfather had "sexually related" himself to her.

She couldn't tell him, because she had no mechanism for understanding or expressing such a thing—that beyond "fondling," her own mind held nothing. For her, the degradation stemmed from the stepfather's fondling.

"A teenager," she said. "And I let him do those awful things. What does that make me?"

"Manipulated. That's what it makes you. Nothing more."

Relief, secondhand from Sewer Mouth, took hold. The woman heard herself swearing as the coffee sloshed out of her cup. She swore and cursed and ranted. Stanley planted posthypnotic sentences, in haste and fury and a pride in her progress so deep that he was almost embarrassed.

"Bastard," she screamed, "I hate him! The feelings, I can't discount them this time; I can't say I imagined the recall, it was too real! I was aroused, an animal at five years old—what am I talking about? I was an animal long before I was five!"

"He manipulated you. He was the adult. You aren't to blame."

"I understand you," she screamed again, "intellectually I understand and agree with you, but part of me doesn't understand a bloody thing and I want to kill him!"

"It's easy to comprehend something on an intellectual level, but you still have to battle it emotionally. You've got to take it slowly."

Stanley knew that to a certain degree, she was embroiled, finally, and ready for the next plateau. The words, "rode the pink thing back and forth," could mean only one thing. But he'd heard the change of voice as penetration had been mentioned. Did the woman understand that the act had occurred? She'd screamed out, "I want to kill him." Did she understand the implications of that either?

Sewer Mouth sat and continued to curse, using words Stanley had never heard before, even when he'd treated abusers in prison; she had variations on cursing that astounded him. In the control booth, Tony had forgotten sound quality and was eagerly writing it all down.

Based on what he'd heard in other sessions, Stanley suggested that they try for attic recall.

The woman balked. The first farmhouse had no attic, and one would have needed a ladder to get into the one at the second farmhouse. No ladder existed in her memory, only a terror of them and attics in general. But Stanley was adamant.

"Rabbit," he told her again, "may hold the keys to many things. Would Rabbit like to help us?"

"How are you going to get Rabbit to come out?" The idea seemed stupid. "I can't call any of them. I don't know how."

"I want you to concentrate on relaxing. Relax, take in the air, let it out." Stanley's voice droned on, insisting that she keep breathing and relax.

Control, Sister Mary hissed in the woman's mind. *Keep it. This will only be disgusting, dirty, and vile.*

Stanley called Rabbit. The woman was too far into it now to come back. She began the count at ten, moving backward number by number, hearing voices in her head demanding control. A strain more mind-bending than any other time tore between the voices in her head and the voice on her left that was Stanley's. She drifted past the final count of one, lost and unable to cooperate.

She hesitated, bereft.

Listen and watch, *he said in the thickest of brogues.* Escape, like denial, creates its own places. But the woman does not know that. She believes herself t' have no options except t' join us or Stanley.

But they are the same, *Twelve said slowly,* so why bother to give her a third option?

The woman must choose her own colours.

You, *Twelve laughed,* are a bastard of the first water.

You, *he said,* are learnin' the language.

Without any warning the woman was in a part of her mind in which she'd existed all these years, away even from her own selves—and had never known at all.

It isn't really yours, darlin', except that everythin' is yours, just as everythin' is ours. Do y' like the riddle? 'Tis no riddle, 'tis fact; each man among us has his own and only as the spirit moves the man, not as the man is moved against his will, does the sharin' become a positive thing, an enhancement if y' will.

• • •

The space, vast and comforting, shut Stanley out. It shut everything out. The light. Wonder filled every fiber, she felt every last particle of herself and she felt nothing. It was that kind of space. Quiet, a haven of it, shimmered unending, brilliant white. Not a glimmer of light, distant and easily ignored, or blazing like a beacon, or light framed in a friendly window on a dark night.

This light flowed forever and it consumed the space before her—everything without end. Without beginning.

Y' don't have t' go back. The choice is yours.

The woman smiled and nodded. Time had lost all meaning and nothing existed except the complete wonder of her mind, bathed in the excruciating white light. Free and drifting she wandered, smiling and content within a blinding brilliance. Her selves might have been on another planet; they could not hurl anything at her. Stanley might have been on another planet. He certainly wasn't up here, and could not reach into the light to pick and prod at shreds of memory, knifing through them to expose the rot.

She felt her own drool on limp fingers.

On her way to the ladies' room, she passed the control booth, marveling at how quickly the time had gone in this first part of the session. How long had she been up there in the white light? It never occurred to her that it might be out of the ordinary, or even extraordinary. It seemed so natural, now that she'd experienced it.

Tony's voice, conveying worry and frustration over another loss of sound, an extensive one this time, floated past her ears. Tony was complaining that the equipment had been completely overhauled since their last filming; it had been in perfect working order. So why, he wondered to Stanley, hadn't it worked during this filming session?

In the Tunnel, Twelve shivered. The white light, *she said.* How did you do that?

The woman did it herself, *he answered.* I only told her that she was able.

You gave her permission?

Merely encouragement. 'Tis better sometimes than a full

round o' ammunition. And now she's got a thing all her own, a crutch for the journey just ahead.

Elvira could not resist. "All god's chilluns," she sang, "got somethin', and somethin' ain't plenty for me . . ." and she took off running in the Tunnel darkness. Sister Mary Catherine's beads were clicking at her heels.

Under light hypnosis, the woman smiled. She made it this time with Rabbit, up into the attic, through the dark hole in the upper hallway ceiling of the second farmhouse. Suddenly she was surprised to feel her stepfather's arms around her middle, to feel the pressure of those arms; and when part of her mind rebelled at that, another part whisked the rebellion away.

He was helping her, he said in a low, husky voice. "Sssh. Touch it. Touch it," he said. She heard him clearly as she squatted, unleashing the pink thing to let it move and swell.

Silence. The emotionally painful reality was the very familiar smell of the attic, the thin, faint whisper of light filtering in from the eaves. It was the pink thing in front of her face. The stepfather moved it for her now, his voice encouraging. He placed her so that the pink thing abrased her flesh in that one particular spot her mother had forbidden her to touch.

The woman wanted to cry for help, but her mouth was closed over the words and would not open. The hypnotic state weighed her down. Or perhaps it was only guilt that made her feel so heavy. An eerie, far-off, wailing sound came closer and, as it did, became first a moan and then the keen of an animal trapped in the woods. The seams on her blouse threatened to split under the strain of muscle swelling along her arms. She grabbed at her throat, trying to quiet the sounds she couldn't be making.

"Calm, calm, Rabbit." Stanley's voice at the woman's side was an incantation but neither Rabbit nor the woman could respond with calmness. Stanley began the count back, from zero to ten but Rabbit had difficulty with sequential numbers. The woman, unable to shout "Help," willed it instead, and help came, to Rabbit who mouthed the numbers one by one, stumbling all the way.

Gradually the wail subsided in the studio, but the woman still trembled. Stanley's eyes were on the clipboard. It served no useful purpose to let a client coming out of that kind of hypnotic recall see the therapist's reaction.

It seemed to Stanley that Rabbit was the only Troop member

220

who expressed remembered pain. Especially the pain of what had obviously been penetration in the attic recall just now.

The woman sagged on the cushions. Her face was changing rapidly from awe to disbelief, to a helpless kind of terror, to rage and then embarrassment. Stanley noted her exhaustion. It was a difficult session for him as well. Her long withdrawal during the first half of it had forced him to wait interminably. He had no idea why she'd done it or why she'd come around so well after the break.

As to her embarrassment, a student had asked after viewing one of the tapes if it had anything to do with the era in which the woman had grown up. Stanley had replied that young incest victims today went through the same agony in the face of sexual recall. Victims, he'd said, including males, choked at expressing the degradation and dehumanisation they'd felt as children at the hands of supposedly trusted adult authority figures. Adult rape victims, he'd added, went through it, too.

At times he found it amazing—how everyone wanted to pin a victim's reactions to sexual child abuse on anything but the abuse itself.

Recall was getting easier for her to achieve, if not to deal with, but each time another memory surfaced it tore to shreds what little self-esteem he'd built up. He wasn't sure what capabilities belonged to her and what belonged to the Troop members. At this point, all he could do was "patch" and hope he was aiming at the right wound.

He pointed out to her her numerous accomplishments, her high energy level, her powers of concentration. He'd done the same thing before and knew it would take many repetitions to sink in.

"I know what you're saying," the woman told him. "But worthlessness sits right here in my brain; the idea of it blocks everything else. I get so scared that by losing control each time the recall surfaces, I'll go to pieces. I'll wind up a bag lady."

"There isn't any danger of that," Stanley said because he had to; it was part of the mending process.

"I can't operate the way I'm supposed to when the recall hits. I get tired," she whispered.

"That's alright, of course you're tired. Others aren't." Stanley said it, hoping the others didn't become tired.

Shoring up finances and choosing another occupation seemed to be on everyone's mind today. Ten-Four didn't give Stanley a name, she just barged into the conversation and began to talk, keeping her eyes hidden behind the bangs. She outlined all the jobs she'd gotten over the years, without benefit of a college education.

"Until we got into real estate, we were cheap labour. Now we can't afford the office rent; we can't even afford to renew the broker's license. But there's got to be something we can do, even if it's becoming a housekeeper for someone."

Ten-Four bit her thumbnail and frowned. Stanley watched her without knowing her name. She appeared competent to survive almost any financial disaster. He suspected that apart from harbouring a deep resentment, she did not become involved in disasters. As the woman emerged again, the resentment was gone. As she spoke, Stanley caught a glimpse of what her world was like. For her, none of Ten-Four's conversation existed; she was still on the topic of being tired.

"I slept a lot in high school," she said. "I was so afraid that I wouldn't graduate. I still have nightmares about it."

"Or," Ten-Four said, "we could become a waitress, except that after being a real estate broker, people would recognise us. There'd be those looks."

There seemed to be no way around one huge problem. Stanley wasn't the only one who recognised it. Some of his colleagues told him that night at dinner for a departing fellow professor, what he already knew: the Troops had survived because the memories were compartmentalised, so that no one had to endure the whole picture. What kind of chaos, they asked, would be created by consolidating all that memory?

Several of them suggested a series of drugs that might dull the woman's reactions; some recommended hospitalisation.

Two days later, Captain Albert Johnson put it more succinctly.

"You can't dance her through therapy fast enough to outrun the consequences of all that memory, Stanley. Something's going to give, long before she'd mended. It's nature's way. First you get the wound, then you heal. While you're healing, though, you remember the gunshot and the bastard behind it. Your client isn't a cop, she didn't get her wound in the line of duty. She's going to want redress."

22

Albert's comments stayed with Stanley and bothered him every time another plateau was reached. The platcaus were a natural evolutionary flow; therapy at work. But each one brought recall that heightened the Troops' anger and reinforced the validity of Albert's theory.

"I hear myself saying 'I,' Stanley," the woman told him one night over the phone, "but there's no way to explain how I . . . am just not speaking. It all comes from behind me, through me. I can't separate me from them, except to say . . . it isn't me, it's them."

He believed her. He tried to understand. When he did, he heard the tears and another voice.

"We've always run at the last moment, from violence of any kind," Sewer Mouth said. "But I gotta tell you, things are changing. I figured out that there's a part of the recall when it hits that's just plain sadness. Because inside each flick is also a memory of how beautiful those farms were and what life could have been like without the mother and the stepfather. Sometimes the beauty just flooded you: summer grass, the hedgerows alive with sweet wild cherries and strawberries; raw earth, the smell of celery growing. Winters, like a white blanket covered in diamonds, and we skated on the big pond . . . in the fall you smelled apples and wood-smoke and saw all the little animals getting ready to go underground and you wished you could go with them. Every Thanksgiving we went into the woods and gathered moss and pretty leaves, red berries and pine cones, for the centerpiece on the dining room table. But spring—you had to catch your breath. The apple orchards burst into bloom overnight. The fragrance would hit you one morning and you'd lean out the window and there they'd be, apple trees turned to pink lace with a thousand bees buzzing.''

Stanley heard Sewer Mouth's intake of breath, her amazement at what had loosened inside herself.

''There's an apple tree at the first farmhouse,'' she said at the other end of the line. ''I never want to see an apple tree again in this lifetime. I think I want blood, Stanley. I want to see it flow. I want that bastard as dead as some of us.''

''Bloody shit,'' said Sewer Mouth to Elvira. ''Our names are down on the pages now. Shit.''

''Sad but true,'' Elvira said. She began to hum new words to an old Alfred Hitchcock theme song. ''The worms crawl in, the worms crawl out, in and out of the monkey's snout. . . .''

The combination of Troop anger, fear, and sadness over the loss of their anonymity still did not fade. Elvira hummed another favourite to the tune of ''London Bridge Is Falling Down'': ''Lizzie Borden took an axe. . . .''

''Shit,'' said Sewer Mouth.

And so it went. In the midst of what they felt was their world being torn apart, some Troop members called for caution and a slower pace, afraid for the woman. Mean Joe, of course, had known all along where the real need for protection lay. He hunched his shoulders these days, like a Pittsburgh Steeler blocking the New York Football Giants en masse, and his eyes were flintier than ever.

But no matter who among them screamed caution, other Troop members would not be held back. Memories by thought transference came to the woman and, with the Weaver's help, vanished. Until one day something stuck and allowed the other self who held that memory to break through and voice it clearly. The woman came into the session, muttering about hennaed hair and sausage curls. Through the eyes of another Troop member, she was seeing the stepfather's mother very clearly for the first time. As the picture grew in detail Stanley knew they'd uncovered clues to the stepfather's background, to his upbringing as a child, and possibly to his adult proclivities as a child abuser.

''Alma, my stepfather's mother, is as clear to me as if she

224

were sitting here. A heavy woman, soft, no muscle tone at all; she overflowed the seams of sheer, flowered dresses. She wore black, high-heeled shoes with bows and glittery, fake jewelry. Her mouth was plump and slack, a big blotch of purple or orange lipstick.''

The woman described a kind of mutual flirtatious, doting attitude between Alma and her son. On the other hand, Alma seemed to ignore her daughter Velma, a younger, morose version of herself. Alma's husband had been silent most of the time, too. Alma's husband, son, and daughter waited on her hand and foot.

In the initial interview, the woman had written the stepfather's first name on a piece of paper for Stanley. As if to have it pass her lips would be an act of self-defamation. Only two other Troop members had said the name aloud since then, and both times it had been in scathing tones. The woman did not use his first name now. She outlined a relationship between the stepfather and Alma that sounded more like lovers than mother and son; a relationship that excluded Alma's daughter and husband.

The woman appeared oblivious to the meaning behind her words as she described the stepfather's fawning behavior toward his mother. When Stanley pressed for further details, she could only recall that the stepfather and his family had been holy rollers. She told Stanley about one "prayer meeting" when they'd knelt, pressing their faces into the seats of chairs.

"It made me sick, it was so hypocritical an act, my stepfather praying," she said. "He was a pig."

So, Stanley thought, in the minds of the woman and the Troops perhaps anyone who prayed henceforth was a pig, a hypocrite, capable of the stepfather's same actions. Thus associations are born. The woman actually looked ill, as if she would vomit. Her skin had a greenish tinge. She plowed on, telling Stanley about family gatherings, at Christmas, Easter, and Thanksgiving holidays.

"Smiles," the woman said, still with a listening tilt to her head, "the relatives hated each other but they all showed up for the holidays and my mother's cooking and they never stopped smiling once."

Her father, she said, brought his mother. The stepfather's family had shown up, along with the maternal Irish grandmother and sometimes an aunt if she wasn't too busy with a new affair. A maternal uncle came to visit whenever he was not in Attica prison. The relatives whispered among themselves, behind each other's backs, and kept on smiling.

"The Irish relatives talked knives to your face. They are volatile in the curses they laid on each other, and every other word was 'jesus, mary, and joseph.' Alma and Velma complimented my mother on the dinner, but they whined to my stepfather later that the food had disagreed with them. Alma tended to feel faint a great deal, and the stepfather would run to her all day, adjusting things to her liking . . . as if he loved her. I can't imagine him loving anyone. Like when the bed springs creaked in his and my mother's bedroom. I wondered how my mother could even stay in the same bedroom with him. The idea of it made me sick."

Stanley knew that she expected his disapproval at having described her family in such a way. But Stanley cheered silently, glad to see a measure of justified anger. He spent ten minutes supporting both her anger and her hostility.

It seemed to pay off. The woman elaborated on Alma's attitude toward her grown son; what a perfect child he'd been, sleeping with his mother in thunderstorms, when "daddy," as Alma called her husband, was away working with road crews. Alma praised him as being a perfect child, always spotless, with long sausage curls. Just like a little girl, Alma had noted proudly, squeezing his cheeks and kissing his hands.

The woman remembered how the Irish grandmother had then uttered something about lunatics.

A child's voice began describing Easter baskets and chocolate rabbits, and the colouring of eggs. The tone was plaintive; Stanley asked if someone were sad. By now he knew Lamchop by her voice alone but still she wouldn't give him her name.

"Holidays," she said, "are special. We don't celebrate 'em anymore. They're for families."

The face turned, at the mention of families, from child to angered adult, and Sewer Mouth spit over her right shoulder.

"One day," she said, "we'll have collected somewhere, a whole room of spit. We'll take it to hell with us."

Sewer Mouth ranted, enmeshed in her hatred for families and for holidays, especially Christmas. Stanley tried to steer the session toward a clearer picture of the woman's mother. Eventually the woman surfaced again, but only listened to the words she seemed to be speaking.

"It's so difficult to remember more than bits and pieces. I still

226

don't understand why, but I remember loving her deeply when I was very small and then hating her when I grew into my teens. At some point, I shut her out entirely. All that's left now is ambivalence. She was beautiful with auburn hair and hooded green eyes and the most marvelous bone structure. Her cheekbones were high, her nose thin and well shaped.

"I could never figure it out. When I was two, she was only twenty-one and brilliant, yet she hid herself away with the stepfather. From reading her poetry and other writing, I knew she didn't belong in that house with him. One of the worst times, when my stepfather really showed himself, was a Christmas where I can't remember opening any packages at all. The preparations made for that holiday were stupendous. Company was coming—an outsider, a playwright my mother corresponded with. He'd seen some of her work in a magazine. I wonder to this day if he had any idea, sitting in our living room in front of that beautiful Christmas tree, what really went on there? I wonder if with all his literary flair, he could have described the screams or the madness or the perversion?"

Stanley knew she'd forgotten he existed. Here she was, describing madness and perversion. Yet he had to wonder if it really sank in for her.

"It was the first time I'd had a chance to observe my stepfather's behavior around a man other than my father, with whom he was simply brooding and silent. How my mother got the nerve to invite a stranger into our house, I don't know. Maybe she was just desperate, finally, for company. It was obvious that the man's presence antagonised my stepfather. As my mother brought out her writing, he started to prowl the room. But then the playwright had found her poetry, tracked her down, and made his way to our farm; he'd walked the mile from the corner bus stop in heavy snowdrifts, just to speak with her.

"That part was exciting. I watched it from a corner of the living room, trying to be still, to listen. But writers are observant, and he noticed after a while how my stepfather circled them. He was beefy and sullen looking anyway, and that night the brutal look in his eye kept growing. The playwright tried to include my stepfather in the conversation; all he got was a sneer.

"My stepfather was literate but his reading material had nothing in common with my mother's writing. He used to hide magazines around the house: *True Crime*, *True Detective*, that sort of thing. They were full of gruesome, bloody, debasing things

227

the newspaper didn't print, like women lying in ditches with their skirts up over their heads, blood gushing from wounds, children chopped up and flung into the bushes, people hacked and bludgeoned.

"He had a lot of pocket books, too. I've always been a reader but after the first one, my curiosity died. They weren't about vampires, which I adore; they even went beyond mass murders. The sex scenes described a world where men and women were treated like animals.

"That night with the playwright, the hair on the back of my neck began to stand straight up. The house felt so quiet. When the playwright stood up to go and said good-bye to my mother, he told her that she was gifted, that he'd enjoyed the evening. It was both a relief and an awful realization; our house was empty of almost the first stranger who'd ever stepped into it.

"When he was gone my stepfather raged, he said vile things to my mother. She got the beating of her life. He tore and pounded and broke things. That night long after the screams got fainter, we could hear something heavy thudding into the walls.

"My mother didn't come out of her room for days afterward; when she did, she'd stopped speaking to anyone. She sat day after day, silent, not eating, not moving. I don't think she could. She didn't wash, cook, or clean, or sew or issue commands. My stepfather commanded, we obeyed.

"I don't really remember much else, everything was and is sort of disconnected. But my mother's face looked strange. I remember her sitting there in her bathrobe, with no change of expression. Finally, after several weeks, my stepfather started in on my half brother and my half sister and me. He was scared. It was our fault, he said. We were to blame that my mother was sick. Look what we'd done to her, we must now be extra good, did we hear him? I wanted to kill him.

"My stepfather cooked. We ate, went to school, came home. My mother sat there in her bathrobe, my invincible mother, who'd never been sick a day in her life. She began to lose weight: the robe hung on her. I hated her for something I saw growing in her eyes; she seemed to believe what he said about its being our fault. He fed her with a spoon, and you'd have thought he'd never hit her at all. He cared for her like a baby, like he cared for his mother, and she let him. I wanted to throw up."

Stanley cheered silently once more. It was painful, he knew, but it would help the woman to discharge her hidden anger. The cheering subsided when, from behind the woman's bangs, a pair of soft young eyes peeped out.

"Do you think," asked the tiny, childlike voice, "that we were bad and made the mother sick?"

"You didn't make anyone do anything. When the woman was speaking just now, she referred to the parents as 'hers.' Were they her parents?"

"No," the small voice said. "The person sending her the words thinks we should say it that way, even if they weren't our parents."

"Who was the person speaking?"

"I don't know," the child said. "We haven't sorted all of our selves out yet. But I know a secret that not everybody here knows. The woman can talk, but she can't think. Everything her structure makes her believe she's thinking is coming from one of us. She doesn't tell you each time that idea comes into her head, because it would be silly."

"Nobody's feelings are silly," Stanley said. "You think that you made the mother sick. That's a feeling and it isn't silly, because it bothers you. But you didn't cause anything. I suspect that your stepfather was treating your mother the way he wanted to treat his own. He was venting his hatred of women. All women."

During the break, Stanley shuddered to himself. After the break, he gave the Troops something positive to think about.

"Those college courses," he said. "You could take a college equivalency test and amaze yourself."

"That can't be true." The woman looked pleased but shocked. "Anyway, the book comes first."

"No reason you can't do both," Stanley told her.

She replied that is was necessary to earn a living, and again stressed her stupidity, saying that she had to work twice as hard as anyone else, to compensate for it. He told her she should slow down, that workaholic executives had heart attacks under much less pressure and strain. Ten-Four didn't buy that.

"Bull," she said. "People use ten percent of their brains. And most of them are so sedentary that they only use three percent of their physical energy. We once worked more than twelve hours a day for seven years without a vacation or a day of sick leave. The only time we took off was when we were bored silly."

"No one ever gets sick?" Stanley asked.

"I don't think so," Ten-Four told him. "Somebody, we don't know who, has allergies but when it gets bad, somebody without allergies comes out. When we went to the doctor, he'd diagnose something or other, but on the follow-up visit he couldn't believe that it wasn't there anymore. We quit going. It was a waste of money."

Stanley told whoever might be listening, that in the case of multiple personality one person might test as having some ailment while the other selves wouldn't show any symptoms at all.

"Like a cold or the hives?" Ten-Four asked.

"Sometimes even more than a cold or the hives. The headaches I hear being mentioned are quite similar to migraines, but they don't respond to medication. Multiples don't respond well to medication overall. It seems to have very little effect, almost as if multiples have other ways of dealing with those symptoms."

"The last shrink gave us tranquilizers," Ten-Four said. "I threw them away."

"I don't want to frighten you," he said, "I know that you've been trying for recall on your own and that's wonderful. But I think it might be better if you waited and let it come out in the sessions where I can help you with it. Have you got a friend you can call during the week if things get too heavy?"

"There's Sharon," the woman said, "but I hate to bother her. What's happening to me, the way things are happening to me, frightens her. It sounds too crazy. I'm not worried. I seem to be staying afloat in the business world for the time being and even in my personal life, what there is of it. Even if the others do rage inside me at times, I've got control. Don't I?"

Stanley insisted that the self-control, the iron will, had to go. No matter how proud she was of it. He told her she was blocking emotions that were valid, to which she had every right.

"Control is all I've got. Letting go means that people who see me switching from one person to the other will hate me. If I hang on tight, that won't happen. Besides, I know that somebody in here is mean as hell. I could never let her out."

"Or him." The woman had never expressed any feelings about having Mean Joe, a male, inhabiting her female body. For some multiples, Stanley knew this aspect was frightening.

"Another male?" The woman looked at him quietly. "You mean there could be another male like Mean Joe Green?"

"We're all made up of male and female. . . ."

"I know that. Androgyny, the combination of male and female characteristics. I don't see us putting Boy George out of business. But Mean Joe is so big, he's the only one who could, if he decided to, break somebody in half. Suppose I do relax and he is the mean one here? What if he does something horrible to someone who doesn't deserve it?"

"Give your people more credit," Stanley said gently. "They protected you all these years, and anger can be a good thing."

"You've lost me, Stanley," the woman said. "Norman hates my rage, everybody hates it. My mother hit me when I got angry."

The woman left the session, and Stanley watched her progress down the hallway. Even if she were not the first-born child, what must it be like, he wondered, to operate in the world, knowing that she might be doing things of which she was unaware?

It was a terrifying idea, no longer being able to blame herself for everything. Funny how clear things were becoming lately, and how that made it all the more confusing, as if everything had been turned inside out. Who was the mean one here? What really shocked her was that more often than not, Stanley looked at her idea of bad and mean and laughed.

That night, the woman sat down at the typewriter, preparing to incorporate the day's notes into manuscript pages. Ever since the white light in the session that day, it had been a recurring thought in her mind. She didn't know what it meant or if it meant anything at all, and had not discussed it with anyone, including Stanley. The woman only knew that the idea of it was comforting. After all, she could go back there anytime if she got desperate enough. It made her smile as her fingertips struck the typewriter keys.

The Front Runner frowned. She sent the message to Mean Joe, who had been waiting. He answered promptly that the sleeping cores were safe. The Front Runner sent other messages and the Outrider paused for a moment, listening carefully to each reply.

Now, the Front Runner said, and there was a cadence in the word, a sadness and something else. It came from the darkness of the Tunnel, a silent battle cry, uttered by thought alone, from one who was proud and confident of the Troops around him.

Elvira listened to his battle cry and grinned. Better pack a lunch, *she hollered.*

At the keyboard the woman's fingers stopped moving. Definitely, undeniably not alone in the gallery, she felt invaded, threatened, as if war had been declared on her. Her head began to pound and tears hit the white bond paper.

Flick. The smell of straw and manure—the milk cow standing in the old barn—its rolling, brown, saucer-eyes with the whites showing. The stepfather had his trousers off, he stood on a wooden crate at the back of the cow. His face alternately scrunched and smiled, in rhythm with the forward and back motions of his body. Why? Through a child's eyes, the woman watched and did not understand what he was doing. She understood his expression as he saw her in the barn doorway. She turned and ran but her feet wouldn't take her fast enough. Suddenly her face slammed into the dirt pathway leading to the farmhouse. The stepfather's rage as he landed on her, and something else about him that scared her even more, were twined together in words she heard like an evil cry from hell. The stepfather was not only angry, he was excited. Pain shot through her arms as he dragged her back inside the barn. He yanked her white cotton pants off and no amount of screaming could have stopped him. The cow swung to look at the two of them—its tongue, like a huge pink caterpillar, unfurling. The stepfather had her in his arms, he was holding her up to that pink caterpillar tongue, his fingers baring her flesh to it.

The woman was screaming and trying to reach the phone to call Stanley, and the voices in her head wouldn't stop. One voice, above all the others, cried out to her and sanity seemed like a very fragile thing.

23

The headache was vicious last night," she screamed. "There were voices, all talking at once, vague and far away. They showed me a wooden crate and the stepfather standing on it, at the back of the cow."

Even before the words left her mouth, Stanley knew what she was going to say. He'd suspected it for some time but it still shocked him. The woman told him the rest of it, her face red and her fingers twisting each other so hard that he could hear the knuckles cracking.

"Is it true? Could the stepfather really have done that?"

"Yes," Stanley said. "It's called bestiality." Unfortunately, he thought to himself, your stepfather was capable of so much, which is why you've got amnesia.

"Then there was only one voice, one lone, single voice, that I don't think I'll ever forget as long as I live!" The woman could not control the shaking that overtook her. "Do you know that it's sinking in, but I'm not sure how long I'll be able to grasp it before it's taken away again? Look at me! I hear people who give memory and then take it away. One minute it's as if I'm the one who had all the experiences they tell me about and the next minute I know I've always been so empty that I never experienced anything, then or now, and if you don't tell me that makes me crazy, I'll never believe another word you say!"

"You aren't crazy. Tell me about the voice."

"It kept reciting something in my head: 'Into the jaws of hell, into the valley of death, rode the six hundred.' And don't tell me it makes sense, because it doesn't.''

"That's not an exact quote from the original verse but it probably makes sense to the others. Somehow 'The Charge of the Light Brigade' must have special meaning to one of them."

"The voice talked about danger, and then it said something about 'Sister Mary Catherine.' "

"Did the voice have a name?" Stanley asked, hoping.

" 'I am the Seventh Horseman,' is what the voice said." The woman looked embarrassed. "I'm sorry," she said. "It sounds so ridiculous."

"There is one among you," Stanley said, easing his voice into the more singsong style he used just prior to putting her under the light hypnosis, "who knows everything, who remembers it all. Would that person come forward?"

No one spoke. The woman knelt on her knees, looking like a whipped dog. Stanley asked again for the one who knew everything, and the woman's face shifted.

The Seventh Horseman emerged with a quick flash of grey-green eyes in an angular face and body movements that almost hummed, as if she were possessed of hundreds of tiny, danger-sensitive antennae, all working at once. She used her hands like whips to accentuate her carefully enunciated, sandpapery words. She explained that another Troop member had paved the way for her as she herself at times paved the way for others, making the journey safe.

"I asked," Stanley said, because current documentation showed an established pattern among many multiples, "for the one who knows everything. Did you come forward because you are that person?"

"You have a long journey before you reach that Troop member."

Stanley remembered getting the same answer from someone else, in reference to the cores. The Seventh Horseman told him that she never appeared in public. Her thoughts, she said, might "spill onto the woman" or whatever Troop member happened to be "out" at the moment. But after what she called her "tour of duty" at the second farmhouse, the Seventh Horseman had either been retired or had withdrawn of her own volition. It was just as well, Stanley thought. Her topics of conversation did not lend themselves to social outings.

Stanley listened as she told him the balance of last night's recall. She said that the woman, after they'd brought her the image of the cow, had been unable to absorb more and had "thrown the flicks away."

"She just couldn't look," the Seventh Horseman said. "But the stepfather had a number of dogs over the years. When he was finished with them, they were killed and buried. With what the stepfather taught the dogs, he had to kill them or the mother would become suspicious and wonder why they sniffed at us, at the stepfather—so constantly."

"He involved you with the dogs in a sexual way?"

"Yes. One of them was a Great Dane, a magnificent animal. But not as controllable as the others. When the stepfather began his instructions—with us and with the Great Dane, he tied it up on the hedgerow that led to the back orchards and the farm beyond, where the transient workers were. The hedgerow had been an escape route, the only one available because the field next to it got muddy in the spring, like a swampland, and in the summer, the grass was tall. The stepfather was taller, he could see us running through it, trying to hide, but we could not see him. We were frightened that saying no to the stepfather would be as dangerous to Sister Mary as it had been to the others before her. Among us, certain ones had died because they said no. We've attempted, in at least three drafts of the manuscript, to convey the concept of such a death to you without disturbing anyone here."

Because he could find no other words, he asked if such a death was a permanent one. She said yes, that life was cut off. Action by the dead ones now, if there was any at all, was only a "remainder," a ghostly automation.

Stanley's mind was in a turmoil, clutching first at the memory of a severely damaged child describing how the stepfather had hung her down a well, and then at the visage he'd thought the woman herself showed occasionally—the blank, empty eyes and frozen features of someone less than alive; a visage with which he had not yet come to grips.

"We couldn't take any more chances. There was a need for me at the second farmhouse," the Seventh Horseman said, "for a person who could warn of danger. The mother was no help, she purposely tried not to see. She'd say, 'I don't want to hear any more screaming from you.' The stepfather took advantage of that. He lulled us into a false sense of security by smiling and making things look safe and then he pounced. Afterward, if

235

anyone tried to shut him out, he goaded them into reaction, into screaming or cursing or hitting him.

"Sister Mary was trapped in all of that long before she was ten years old. We couldn't tell anyone, we didn't have the words. Our memories were so fragmented among us that we'd start, but everyone wanted to speak at once and it confused people. They thought we were only ranting, exaggerating.

"I had been present for a long time before my birth, but inactive. When the Great Dane arrived at the farmhouse, I 'arrived,' too. It was my job—not to find an escape, because there wasn't one—but to warn beforehand of danger. The hedgerow leading to the orchards was Sister Mary's biggest roadblock. She was so afraid to show fear in front of the dog because he sensed it and barked louder and lunged at her. He sounded ferocious and his teeth were very long. How many times I instructed the Sister, 'Listen, fool, do not try to escape by the hedgerow. The dog will kill you. Go around,' I would scream. 'Crawl through the field!' "

Strain had begun to show on the Seventh Horseman's face and her tensely held body. He heard the occasional tones of a child leaking through the sandpaper rasp.

"After the stepfather had trained the Great Dane, it wasn't only Sister Mary who became terrified of it. Other Troop members were terrified, too. The dog was so big . . . the stepfather decided to get rid of it by starving it to death. The cruelty of that pleased him."

The tension in the Seventh Horseman's face grew. She seemed to be listening to her own words while straining to hear those being spoken in another room.

Stanley had wanted more recall and he was getting it. His fingers ached from gripping the pen and holding the clipboard propped on his knees. He didn't dare look over at Tony in the control booth. He was remembering the miniature cassette tape the woman had given him the other day. She'd simply handed it to him, saying the flicks were worse than ever. When he'd played it back later that night, the words had been garbled through the static. It had been apparent by the hysteria in her taped voice that things were escalating rapidly. He'd called her then, warning her not to push too fast.

Stanley heard a whisper of brogue in some of the words.

"Sister Mary refuses the flicks even though she recognises them, as the woman does not, because the recall is a reminder

236

of failure on her part. If she'd listened to my signals a long time ago, she wouldn't be suffering now. We all do our jobs here, and no room for miscalculation exists. Our component parts function; the machinery is finely calibrated, if you will, to an infinite degree. But if one of us slipped, we would all go down for a time. On such occasions, the Front Runner keeps us going while the Foot Soldiers carry the wounded.''

The faint brogue vanished. As she continued, it was easy for Stanley to imagine her reciting ''The Charge of the Light Brigade'' in her sandpapery and dramatic voice.

''The woman, or at least the seed of her, has been with us since the first-born child was two years old. The woman's actual birth took place much later. Her construction allowed her to operate in the world—no different before her birth than after it. She was empty then, she's empty now. We operate through her when we need to, otherwise we act on our own. Please try to understand,'' she continued, ''that except for the woman and a few of the others, the period of time from our 'inception' to actual birth is a learning time. But even with years of observation beforehand, it is no simple task, orienting ourselves after we are born, to the things going on around us.''

''I imagine a lot was going on at the second farmhouse in particular,'' Stanley said. ''It had to be painful for the Troops.''

''For most, yes.'' The Seventh Horseman stared straight ahead. ''You've met the Zombie? Her name is Grace, as in 'Grace Under Pressure,' but 'Zombie' suits her better. When the woman's strength wanes drastically, the Zombie steps in and moves for her, one foot ahead of the other. She is one of those who were immune, impervious, deadened, removed from it all.''

''But still the Zombie operates, for herself and others, in that deadened fashion?''

''Some of us are 'deadened,' not 'dead.' There is a difference. The Zombie serves her required function, she's alert enough to receive signals and respond. Sometimes, like the rest of us, she even 'listens in,' on purpose. Up until a short time ago, we couldn't listen in to each other. Now at times we do, those of us who are currently aware of each other, if we choose and are allowed.''

''How do you know,'' Stanley asked, ''when the woman is listening, as you call it?''

''We allow it or we do not,'' the Seventh Horseman said. ''This is a complicated process for you, isn't it?''

Stanley told her he was learning. He asked the meaning of her name.

"It pleases me," she said. "Just as the Collector's pleases him. Or the Recorder or the Renegade. Some of us choose names as I did; other names are given to us by each other and some names simply arrive, unbidden, as it were."

"You don't mind that I know your name?"

"I did not give it to you. I mentioned the Collector; I am inextricably bound to him for all time. The Collector will never speak to you. He saw too much on the farms and has closed his eyes against everything. He spends his time discovering and hoarding words and other precious things which he happens to find appealing. For him I am like the blind man's seeing-eye dog. I go where the Collector cannot go; I recite for him his favourite poetry and the snatches of literary wisdom which he has gathered over the years. That shores up morale within the Troop Formation, just as Elvira's relating anything unpleasant to one song or another wipes out the sadness we feel."

Stanley wanted to ask if the Seventh Horseman had been building morale for the woman last night by reciting "The Charge of the Light Brigade." Perhaps without the distraction of it, the recall of last night might have been even more terrifying for his client.

"Nothing," the Seventh Horseman was saying, "is ever passed to the woman except through another of us. It is difficult for her to make sense of some of our conversations, or even to know to whom each voice belongs, especially since she hears only shreds. Most of the time the woman thinks of it as her own voice speaking. At other times she hears nothing because she is not present. These days, Sister Mary, due to the nature of the latest recall and her part in it, is doing most of the passing. The woman heard Sister Mary speaking clearly last night and yet she cannot believe it, cannot accept it."

"Bestiality," Stanley said, "wouldn't be easy for anyone to accept, child or adult."

"Accepted or not, that's what the stepfather trained the dogs for. As to the cow, the stepfather stood on a crate so that his penis would be level with the cow's vulva. The child saw him one day, tried to run away. He decided to make her part of the activity. He wanted her to stand there fondling him while he copulated with the cow."

Tony did not know what to say at break time. Stanley told

238

him that what they'd heard today was only the tip of the iceberg. Tony then muttered something about being embarrassed to face the woman.

"Don't worry," Stanley told him. "She didn't hear a thing."

"My god," Tony said, "it's her life that's being taken apart in there."

"No. I think it's theirs. More than forty of them that I've counted so far. That's what it took to deal with it."

After the break, Stanley offered to put the woman under light hypnosis. He wanted to help her see what was behind the Seventh Horseman who had frightened her so badly. He told her to concentrate on the hedgerow and sent her under. Nothing happened. After five minutes of silence by Tony's wall clock, the sandpaper tones of the Seventh Horseman returned.

"There is something in front of me that I do not understand," the Seventh Horseman said faintly. "What is it?" Her hands went out in front of herself, like a blind man seeking landmarks. "It's tall and rusty, like an old iron pole. It's the pole the stepfather tied the dog to on the hedgerow. I don't know what it's doing here and something else is wrong!"

Stanley figured out the reason for the Seventh Horseman's confusion. He'd put the woman under light hypnosis and the Seventh Horseman had surfaced almost at the moment of her own "birth" as a full-fledged self. On the farm, she had until her own birth existed only in the background as a very "detached" observer. She was describing now her shock after birth, her unfamiliarity with things around her.

Her composure had shredded so quickly and she had become agitated, dropping whole syllables of her last sentence. She now yanked frantically at her hair and broke the yoga position. She fought to retain her balance but her tones grew faint again.

"Wait," she whispered, "there is something here; I am very old, but this is like a bud, a new green bud on an old tree."

Stanley knew she referred to a child. He felt a coldness and realised that he always did when certain young Troop members evidenced.

The Seventh Horseman's composure threatened to collapse entirely as she glanced to her right three times in quick succession, exclaiming that she was lost and that the other selves were moving in on her. Stanley, watching the face before him, saw the cheekbones resurface, the eyes slant.

The woman had somehow joined the Seventh Horseman. They

were together, sharing the same vision; the woman smiled in wonder and the Seventh Horseman charted in a far-away voice the emergence of the long-awaited third presence on their right.

The emergence was that of a child-essence, closer than anyone to the first-born, and enveloped in this moment with what amounted to awe on the part of more than one Troop member. It was that awe which swept through the woman's mind.

Still hypnotised, the woman stared at what she perceived to be a small child sitting at her elbow. The woman began to paint a verbal picture of a very tiny, silent person, with a head of pale gold curls and a brown dress.

"Sticky," the woman said. "The little one is sticky."

The Seventh Horseman's raspy voice broke in; she was viewing something with shock and abhorrence. What she saw meant danger to the woman and, unbeknownst to Stanley, she chose to exert her own powers. For this session and for weeks to come, the woman would hear the word "child," and at times, even see this particular one. Immediately, she would receive, as today, the word "doll," and a like image, being superimposed over it.

The Seventh Horseman's sandpaper voice ground in Stanley's ear, as she described not a child, but a doll, with its head pointed toward her, with a cap of golden curls and no clothes. She described the stepfather standing before her, standing at the doll's feet; how he was reaching out and pulling its legs apart. She held back and was silent as the woman cried aloud.

"But he couldn't do that, could he?"

The Seventh Horseman bore down, with all that she was, and evidenced to the woman. The woman began to scream that she saw her; she described a figure, "a long way off, leading a battalion mounted on horseback." The uniforms were grey and there was something red on the front of their hats. She said they carried long spears or poles and that it was raining. The raindrops, the woman told Stanley, hit the road on which they were traveling and shot up like geysers.

"Dear sweet jesus, Stanley," she screamed as if witnessing the parting of the red sea, "what is it?"

Stanley could only surmise that the woman might be "receiving" the Seventh Horseman's "essence" in the therapy today, just as she had received without hypnosis the essence of Mean Joe and Miss Wonderful that day in her car.

The woman sobbed, straining to see what the Seventh Horseman had supplanted. Because that particular danger had passed and because a second of vision wouldn't hurt, the Seventh Horseman relented.

"I see the child." The woman wept, rubbing her arms and shaking with a cold that Stanley felt, too. "I see her plain as day, but I don't know what her name is."

The image faded and suddenly, the woman and the Seventh Horseman were seeing jointly the image of the rusted flatbed car. It sat innocently enough to one side of the hedgerow leading up to the orchards. The panic in their two voices escalated. The voices grew in number and were joined by others, all distinctly different. The panic became full-blown. Stanley threw out post-hypnotic suggestions at what he hoped were all of them, but they came and went too quickly.

The Seventh Horseman, grasping things the woman did not, asked in her raspy voice, "How do you put the skin and the fur back on Rabbit?" The woman continued to complain that the child they were seeing again to her right was sticky with an unknown substance.

24

She had killed her stepfather, sometime during her teens. Nothing supported the suspicion, except a constant guilt that mounted daily and resisted all other explanations.

"I have to pay," she said to Stanley over the phone.

"It was twenty-five years ago," Stanley said. "Believe me, whether you did it or not, you've paid."

With little real assurance that she was not a murderess, that a policeman would not come pounding on her door some night, the woman wondered if this was the reason she avoided answering doors or telephones or opening the mail. She had to find out. She added it to the weekly list: call the stepfather. Make sure he's still alive. And all the while, of course, the hope swept over her that he was dead as a doornail and rotting in hell.

The long-handled wooden kitchen spoon with which his parents had beaten him might have terrorised the two-year old boy in Virginia had he lived long enough to become an adult. There were supposedly innocuous things that petrified the Troop members and the woman, collectively and individually: the open hood of a car (Stanley suspected that a great deal of sexual abuse might have gone on behind the hoods of the many vehicles the stepfather repaired as a hobby); wicker baskets (in which one Troop member hinted that the stepfather had collected the snakes); muddy paths (reminders of the hedgerow); animals (Stanley expected further details on that); the thought of high places; having to sit in chairs; having the bedclothes anywhere near their faces; anyone who hugged them too tightly or even put out a hand too quickly in greeting; and, of course, the sound of anyone "slobbering," as one Troop member put it, over food. From other victims and even adult offenders who had been subjected to oral sex as children, Stanley had picked up that masticating sounds held the power to disturb their subconscious minds greatly enough to cause overt eruptions of anger.

When not terrified by outside forces, the Troop members aggravated each other and terrorised the woman. The journey, as the Seventh Horseman had called it, had begun in earnest.

"I can't stand it," the woman yelled one day. "I want to know if what's happening to me is normal. Am I normal?"

"Yes," he said. "Within your own frame of reference."

Stanley suspected, as the woman did not, that a vital part of the journey to which the Seventh Horseman had alluded would include a more potent "evidencing" by Troop members who had previously been quiet or at least more restrained.

He was right.

That night in the loft bedroom, the woman found her black dress slung over a wing chair. Fear snaked inside her mind. Why wasn't the dress in the closet where it belonged? She'd worn it only once, to a funeral. The jewelry thrown casually on top of it didn't look funereal; it looked gaudy.

The off-balance sensation tightened inside her. Yanking herself upright against the doorjamb, she tried to crush the pulse that had stared to throb, and then beat, between her legs.

Click. Click, click. In the woman's mind, the sound of beads shattered the silence, as if the skylight had burst above her head.

Hell, the voice said, *you're going to hell.* Click.

Poor Sister Mary, another voice said, and Sister Mary answered: Click. Click.

The woman sensed that nobody was talking to her. She didn't touch the dress and in the morning it was gone.

Equanimity fled each time she faced another flick or click. As the hot and humid August days passed, her desperation grew and control slipped away. The tiny person whom she and the Seventh Horseman had seen under hypnosis seemed to press closer. Little else remained of that session, except for the memory of the silent, golden-haired child, to whom the woman referred, without understanding why, as a "doll."

She took the crayons Stanley and Jeannie Lawson had given

her and hid them up in a kitchen cupboard. For a nonmultiple, it might have been an irrational act.

Sorting out the voices was more difficult. They were all in her head as individual thoughts, distinctly different and belonging to individual people; but, more often than not, her confusion welded them together instead of separating them according to their owners. She decided to ask Sharon for help with the sorting process. Therapy was fine, but somebody other than Stanley had to listen, tell her it was alright. Late one afternoon, over the phone, the woman started explaining multiple personality to Sharon. Sharon took a deep breath, said she'd already explained it, and that it still sounded ridiculous. "You talk," Sharon said, "as if these people are real, as if you see and hear them!" The woman replied that they were, indeed, "real," that she could in fact "see and hear them," but that she had no memory of having told Sharon anything about MPD. The easy laughter of their thirteen-year-old friendship vanished. For the first time since the woman had known her, Sharon could not find time for coffee.

It wasn't until the next morning on her way to a business meeting that the rejection hit her. She stopped the car in a parking lot while something awful welled up and the one who brought it cried. The gap between what she perceived as herself and the outside world was unbridgeable. Since she'd never experienced loneliness, she did not understand what engulfed her at that moment.

She went into the business meeting, attempting to juggle the voices in her head, but her mind was fastened on guilt and Stanley's insistence that she was guilty of nothing. His lessons came back to her: "Children are naturally sexual creatures. Boys frequently have erections at birth and, like girls, can be sexually aroused by the touch of an adult or another child stroking any portion of their skin. No adult has the right to take advantage of that early sexuality or lead a child into areas where it is not prepared or equipped to deal."

It sounded too easy, laying the blame on the stepfather instead of herself. She viewed herself from the mother's perspective; the guilt descended. Stanley's words warred with the mother's. Suddenly the weight lifted from the woman's shoulders. The settlement check lay forgotten in her hand.

Had the mother really, as Stanley said, starved her daughter for affection and made her a prime target for the stepfather? She stood for a moment staring at nothing, searching for the child she used to be. No memory surfaced.

Feeling badly treated as a child, scared witless and angry because of it—that memory came but only from an enormous distance. As if the small bits clogging her mind right now had never touched her.

Walking back to her car in a light summer drizzle, she watched with grave concentration people thronging the street on their way to lunch, seemingly at ease and self-confident. A man looked straight at her. Remembering her mother's "You'll never be pretty, you'd better be neat," she averted her eyes, pretending concern with the carry-all purse. Did any of these people keep their houses neat to the point of sterility? Did they take two and three baths a day or devote hours of painstaking preparation for a date or an appointment or even just to sit at a typewriter? Did they fear a knock on the door, someone catching them disheveled and ugly?

Flick, snip, images of the stepfather and the odour of his warm body sweat plunged straight to the woman's brain. Furious, she ran the rest of the way to her car and slammed the door shut, wishing his head were caught in it.

Stanley explained to his class the fear some incest victims experienced.

"This woman," he said, "just prior to therapy, allowed someone she'd thought of as a friend to blackmail her for over sixty thousand dollars. She accepted blackmail rather than allow one insignificant love affair to surface in public."

"Lesbian?" a student inquired.

"Plain old heterosexual," Stanley said. "But to somebody in the Troop Formation, the sex act is filthy and should be hidden."

"But she permits these tapes to be shown around here at the university . . . ," the student began.

"In that respect, at least, she's come out of hiding. Eventually we both hope the videos will be used in training other therapists. Of course when we began, she and I, we had no idea we were dealing with multiple personality."

"Doctor Phillips," a Protective Services worker raised her hand. "Is there a test for this sort of thing? I'm working with an incest victim right now who sounds so much like this woman. I'm wondering if the reason we aren't getting anywhere with her is that we're just not seeing the right problem."

"It's possible," Stanley told her. "There's a short question-and-answer form that you could begin with: Does the client have

245

blackouts, severe headaches, dizzy spells? Does the client make numerous lists? Do people recognise the client on the street many times, but the client doesn't recognise them in return? Etc. I'll give you a copy after class.''

It sounded so easy.

If multiple personality was uncharted territory for Stanley and for the researchers working on it, it was the same to the woman experiencing it. For almost each new occurrence so far, she'd demanded to know if another multiple had encountered the same. Stanley could not confirm or deny much of anything. One day at home, she stared at her hands, the ones that didn't look familiar. She went to the bathroom mirror and stared. The eyes changed immediately, both in colour and expression. The mouth took on a fuller, more languid line and the cheekbones rose into place. These things had always happened. How did they happen?

Someone smiled at her in the mirror.

It will make sense only if you give up the fright and look at it properly. We're trying to tell you one single fact: you can't do anything unless we do it through you. Got that?

The woman got it. She'd gotten it before but this time they let her hang onto it a little longer.

Someone began to sing "Secondhand Rose," reinforcing that if she existed at all, it was secondhand, through her other selves. She stared into the mirror and while the voice sang there wasn't one thought in her own mind. The singing stopped.

The woman's mind went completely blank, devoid of what had been passed to it just a few seconds ago.

We give and we take away, the voice said.

The woman started to cry, knowing with someone else's thought that something had been snatched from her grasp before she could pin it down as her own. What they were doing to her today was worse than waking up on the highway at fifty miles an hour, wondering at unfamiliar landmarks, or sitting at the dinner table with Page, trying to hear a conversation she was not part of.

"I hate you," she cried. "I hate you for treating me like a child! There's a secret here that someone isn't telling me!" As Brat acted through her, the woman felt a child's anger. She stamped her feet on the tiled floor of the bathroom and beat her hands on the countertop; the heavy aroma of spilled perfume filled her nostrils.

There is a secret. It just isn't shared with you.
"Why am I left out?"
You are the secret.

"Goddamn them and their riddles, they can't frighten me, Stanley!" The words were vehement but the woman appeared disoriented. "Why," she asked him, "do I feel as if what I just said wasn't of my own volition? As if someone put the words in my mouth and spoke them for me?"

Stanley laid down the clipboard. "Who did that?" he asked. "Which one of you?"

"Which ones of us?" The voice was taunting and he knew by the woman's glazed expression that even though the words came out of her mouth she wasn't conscious of them or of the tears on her face either.

"You're not giving her a chance to speak," Stanley said.

"She can't."

"What do you mean, she can't? She's human, with a mind of her own, isn't she?" Stanley kept his voice noncommittal.

So they explained it to him.

"In order to understand our 'process,' as you call it, you might want to liken 'her' to an empty paper bag in a high wind. Remember that the bag itself is nothing; it is merely a thin shell with no stability of its own. It has no real experience and therefore no conscious self-thought. In order for the paper bag to withstand the high winds of life, if you will, we, one or more of us at a time, must continually leap in and 'fill' the bag. Do you understand now?"

The Troops were telling him again that the person he saw as his client didn't think. They did her thinking for her. Stanley shook his head as if to reject the idea and caught himself, but not in time.

"Gotcha," Elvira said. "We don't care if you voice your opinion or show emotion. That don't bother us at all. Do you remember Descartes' rule of thumb, 'I think, therefore I am'? The woman ain't, Stanley. She runs around all day, wondering," and Elvira began to sing off key, "Oh, god, how come you do me like you do, do, do?"

"I doubt if she says that," Stanley said, misunderstanding Elvira's humour.

"Hey. Lighten up. Y'all want us to weep and moan?"

"Days of freedom, days of grace, amen," Elvira chanted irreverently in the woman's mind. Stanley had gone off for the weekend, to a seminar on multiple personality. A whole Saturday morning with no session, no business to conduct. Fear moved aside long enough to fry bacon and two eggs. She dipped hot buttered toast into golden yolks, munching happily as someone else swallowed, although she didn't know that. She'd always believed the humming sensation along her veins to be normal for everyone. She hadn't noticed how it had increased these last minutes.

Upstairs in the loft, while she ran water for a leisurely soak, the humming sensation traveled more rapidly through her muscles. Time passed. From a great distance as she lay quietly in the water, the woman watched a tiny child taking up the bar of soap. Almost dreamily, the child lathered it between fat-fingered hands, blowing bubbles, round and rainbow-like, that plopped with small hisses against the tiles and faucets. There was no other sound in the bathroom. Again time passed. The woman felt detached and lazy.

Once out of the tub, she avoided her reflection in the mirror, suddenly aware of not having looked at herself in months. The humming inside her veins was now like a thousand tiny electrical shocks.

The Troops were moving in.

The old white cotton robe would not stay belted around her middle, no matter how tightly she tied it. As it slithered unaided to the tiled floor, the woman stood in front of the mirror, naked and frozen. There seemed to be a pair of hands moving over her body, inspecting the flesh. She could feel them, separate and apart from her own.

"No," she whispered. "It's my day." It didn't help to know that one of her other selves was about to emerge. Knowing and believing were two different things.

"Catherine," the presence said with wry amusement, as if introducing herself. She held something in her hand, which the woman could not see. "Red," Catherine murmured, "I'm terribly, terribly fond of it; you'll get used to it."

The woman looked into the mirror. Her lips were flooded with the blood-red colour of an ordinary accounting pencil she'd never seen before.

"There have got to be some changes here." Catherine's hands slid over the woman's flesh again; they plucked at her hair twisting it this way and that. "Look at yourself," Catherine prodded, "a pale blob. You need colour, lots of it."

It shocked and revolted the woman to see how pretty the red actually was on her mouth. She snatched up her clothing, hurriedly pulling nylons on, right over damp flesh. Along with the humming sensation, cold water seemed to be shooting through every vein in her body. Out of nowhere or perhaps with someone else's help (because the woman felt more than one other presence now), a strange pair of white ankle socks slid on over the nylons.

Behind the terror it was funny. At least one voice told her so. She was being told a lot of other things in an awful Southern accent. Clothing in hand, the woman stood listening to the radio belt out "Proud Mary" while two separate persons, one of them Catherine, the other still mercifully unidentified, pressed down on her, forcing her by a means she couldn't define to accept them, accept their attitudes and their very states of being.

Confused, unable to delineate their voices, the woman heard them separate and merge again. Both urged cooperation on her part, a willingness to "see our side of it." All the woman could see was a blood-red, wanton mouth in the mirror and her own body, leaping to the rhythm of "Suzie Q," the wildest version she'd ever heard.

Battle lines were drawn between herself and them, as another voice, huffy and displeased, started demanding decorum in tones that might have belonged to a duchess.

The woman ran into the bedroom. She threw on her clothes, remembering Stanley's repeated instructions to "let them out." The red would not come off her mouth, no matter how hard she scrubbed, not even when she put Ajax on her toothbrush and scoured her lips.

She faced how people would see her through these three alone: wanton, silly, raucous, pretentious. If, as Stanley said, they'd always been there, then people had already seen her this way, and probably laughed behind her back.

She stumbled toward the bed, to escape into sleep. It was the safest place left. There was something strange about the bed, some reason not to go near it; she turned as if to flee the room. A voice, softly, plaintively called her name. The woman whirled around and faced the bed. A small presence in a brown dress

249

sat there waiting all alone, with tiny, fat-fingered hands lying quietly in her lap.

Solemn-eyed, the child followed on tiny, padding feet as the woman headed away from her, down to the gallery. The woman turned on the tape recorder. She felt it in each of her movements, a haughty, easily offended attitude, exactly like one of the voices just moments ago. She pictured outsiders observing that attitude, and could barely operate the recorder buttons. She remembered the session with the Seventh Horseman and the child in the brown dress—the same child who now sat at her elbow, here in the gallery.

Doll.

Child.

The stampede in her mind grew thunderous. Whoever had emerged today would be followed by others—selves who belonged to all the quarrelling voices.

Someone screamed, "You are the secret," and it was as if someone had taken fistfuls of either side of her brain and tugged brutally in opposite directions. She had just experienced what Frank Putnam's research termed "jamming," the act of one self fighting to take away the too-dangerous thoughts of those selves closest to the sleeping cores.

She screamed aloud but the small presence at her side acted as if nothing had happened. In her quiet eyes and her miniature mouth that seemed to have been glued shut, there was a strong aura of sadness. The little one was the kindest of them all, the woman told herself, the little one didn't speak a word.

She reached out to pick her up, to hold her and say, "It's alright, I'll make it better."

She couldn't. The stickiness on the small mouth and hands prevented her.

The woman stood there, recognising Catherine's voice and seeing with Catherine's eyes other, as yet unidentified, Troop members standing directly behind her, hidden in the shadows cast by her presence.

"Get ready," Catherine said pleasantly, "their turns are coming."

25

The little one hovered in the window seat, uneasy in the gloom, and reminiscent of another little girl a long time ago who had sat wishing her father would come take her away from the farm. A stiff breeze had come up, rattling the tree limbs against the gallery walls. Shadows loomed. When it rained, as it would shortly, this room got dark before any other in the house. All day long things had moved or seemed to move, somewhere just beyond the woman's vision. She still wanted to pick the child up and hold her, but empathy vanished at the sight of her tiny hands and mouth. The woman's mind fastened on jelly beans or frosted cake, but neither produced such a residue.

The child, from her perch at the window, saw the woman's indecision, her torment, and sent a message in silent, childlike thought. Catherine stepped forward to translate: A substance more directly related to the childhood sexual abuse had caused the stickiness.

The woman accepted the idea without understanding it and began to cry someone else's tears.

Patience, someone said, *the child's job today is only a part of the overall picture and she's slow. Bear with her. Your mind and hers, like a few of the others here, are a lot alike—unformed.*

Wondering if they would ever stop, the woman saw the tears fall onto her skirt as she sat up straighter at the typewriter. Her hands shook while threading a new ribbon into the Smith-

Corona. The carbon, black and oily, stained her fingers and the keys. It didn't budge when she went on scrubbing, moistening Kleenex with spit and going back over each finger. Slowly it dawned: somehow the mind right behind hers preferred to think of the carbon as the source of the stickiness—not the child who had left the window seat, carrying a doll in one hand. She was coming across the gallery.

On tiny feet she went, her essence encapsulated in the minds of those in the Troop Formation who knew her identity. They had suffered her infant rage for her, too long. The rage burst among them. It reached her.

The first-born's child mirror-image, finally grasping her place in the Troop Formation, felt an onrush of anger. The anger, bigger than she was, filled her mind, gave her a momentary strength beyond her normal capacity for movement. She held the doll in front of herself as if it were a sword and as she advanced on the woman she sensed denial from too many other Troop members and her anger grew . . . until from the Tunnel, she heard it, as her small steps brought her closer: the cadence of old Gaelic, bittersweet in message; in words that were so ancient they disintegrated as she heard them, and all she could remember ever after were the cadence and the warmth of someone as old as the words themselves. And he spoke again.

Child, he said. *Y'r place be a fine one and as y' mature, y'll treasure it as we treasure you. Go softly, little one; carry y'r brain before ye and look beyond y'r pain. Y'r pain be the armour. Give it t'a the woman. She'll need it all an' more.*

Chilled by the cold air which seemed to come from the child, the woman felt herself taken in other hands, strong ones, which forced her into a yoga position on the red oriental rug. The woman rubbed her arms, desperate for warmth. The cold air and the nearness of the child became unendurable. So did the sticky substance on her dress and hands and around her mouth. The woman tried to fight back the tears with no idea why she cried.

For a moment, the child sat on the rug, playing with the doll. The cadence still softened her rage and she laid the doll carefully in the woman's lap. Her mind worked at a solemn pace, pointing out matter-of-factly that what the Seventh Horseman had presented in that session had actually been a small child, less than three years old, made of flesh and blood—a small, naked child, without a single pubic hair, whose legs the stepfather had taken in his hands and pulled apart.

252

In the face of every excuse denying the stepfather's purpose, the child merely stared the woman down. The child insisted that the expression the woman had read on the stepfather's face in that same session was what it seemed. Gleeful, goading, he had enjoyed the act and the pain it caused.

The pattern in the red oriental rug swam in the woman's tears. For the last few weeks she'd been trying, for no reason and to no avail, to visualise herself as a small child without pubic hair. Her people, she realised, were careful with the images they transmitted. Comforted by their concern and remembering Stanley's instructions to "go with it," the woman allowed the child to guide her further. As she did, she caught somehow not the sound, but the sense, of a tiny lisp. Together, minds joined, the child held up the flicks and the woman watched what had previously been obscured.

Flick. A child, six years old. The starving Great Dane on the hedgerow barked at the end of his chain. He lurched against it. His teeth were long and sharp and despite the lack of food, his muscles still powerful. Flick. The dog faded and so did his barking, but the hedgerow itself did not. Blue tin doll dishes were spread out on a rock underneath the hedgerow's wild cherry trees. The woman crouched beneath them, smelling their fragrance and staring down at the tiny plates and miniature silverware. From her peripheral vision, two big black shoes laced up the middle appeared in front of her and paused. The stepfather's words were not clear, but she felt his anger and saw the shoes move. They came down crushingly on the silverware and the blue tin dishes. Yanking her up by one arm, he flailed her through the air like a bundle of rags.

Flick. Someone slid it into the woman's mind: a navy plaid dress with a fragile lace collar and puffy sleeves, a golden locket on a chain. The child was very dressed up; it was her father's visiting day and he was due any minute. She was clean, too, fresh out of a bath in the old tin washtub, her hair smelling of shampoo.

All around, the fields and paths were bogged in spring mud. The woman saw the child scrambling to her feet, trying to escape the stepfather's anger.

"Don't try it, the mud will slow you down!" The Seventh Horseman, wild with anger at the stepfather, called out and the woman saw the horse above her, white and gleaming in the early morning dew. "Up," the Seventh Horseman urged from atop the dancing animal, "I'll take you!"

The Seventh Horseman's call had reached no one's ears that day because she was still dormant, lying in the incubation stage just before her birth. The woman caught a sense of that, and drew back, unfamiliar with the process and therefore disbelieving.

Flick. The stepfather had been quick and unafraid of the mud. The little one showed the woman the brutality of the sexual assault occurring then on the hedgerow. The woman could not look and started to cry and laugh hysterically. Because, regardless of the stepfather's brutality, she felt protected, wrapped in that warm blanket her people seemed so fond of.

She did not see Mean Joe, massive and flinty-eyed in the dim gallery light, a bulwark of strength from which the little one drew her own. Nor did she sense him sending his own signals to yet another of his charges who waited just out of sight. The switch from one child to the other would soon be made, for the first child's strength was waning. For now, she struggled on, with Catherine translating her thoughts into adult words.

"The stepfather," she said, "hated it when the father came to visit. He made us pay that day. It wasn't enough for him, though, he tripped us on the way back to the house and when we fell, he put his foot in the small of our back, grinding us into the mud. When we got to the house, the mother was angry over our dirty clothes."

The woman clutched her head, trying to concentrate on rage for the stepfather, at what he'd done so long ago. Putting this recall down on the pages in a way readers would accept would be a horrendous task. Would anyone ever accept the way her people brought the recall?

Stanley had laughed so quietly the other day, and he'd told her that other victims who had seen the tapes accepted it all.

The little one placed a tiny hand in the woman's and, along with the feeling of stickiness on the small fingers, came a shock of realisation. The woman fought to tear her hand away, but the child's grip was too strong.

"There was," the little one said, "a search for particularly quiet, hidden places. They changed from one location to the other, depending on the time of day, the circumstances, and the proximity of others."

The woman refused the thought.

254

"But you will believe," the child said. "All this and much more. You will feel the warmth, feel the pleasure."

Two other selves spoke to the woman and the blanket was drawn tighter. Tiny hands, more than one pair, patted hers, comforting but determined. The woman smiled at their concern but one of them urged, through Catherine, "Go on, get it out of your mouth, stop thinking about how much you hate the word 'pleasure,' or how much Sister Mary hates it. The search for hidden places was constant in the stepfather's mind. Like a game he had to win. The flatbed car on the hedgerow was part of the game. It could not be seen from the house. In the summertime, green weeds sprang up around it and in the fall and winter, the weeds turned brown and scruffy. The stepfather lay under the flatbed car on a piece of woven cloth. See it now, the burlap, in the furthest, darkest corner under the flatbed car?"

The little one, though she had been calm throughout the recall, stopped. Catherine could hold her no longer and, with a faint cry, the child's thought crumpled.

Mean Joe moved fast, his hands huge and black against the pale skin. He snatched up the waif in the dull brown dress. Her head of golden curls drooped against his shoulder. He signaled for the one who waited just out of sight.

Now, he said.

A little voice continued but it sounded different to the woman. There was something about the lisp that was the same as before but not quite. . . .

"The stepfather," Lamb Chop said as she filled the gap, unaided by Catherine, "would catch our eye and if the mother wasn't looking, that pink thing appeared. It was the signal. He'd leave the room those times and go to whatever place he'd decided on beforehand. Whenever the stepfather signaled, one of us followed him. No matter how it wound up—him putting us with a dog or himself—one of us followed."

Catherine's voice broke in over the cursing that had erupted. "Don't be distracted by Sewer Mouth," Catherine told the woman. "Sewer Mouth is an extremely angry lady. Do you blame her? You're going to be sick. Hurry up, we'll be here when you get back."

And they were. The woman left the bathroom ten minutes later, unable to understand why she could not throw up. The urge, almost unbearable, produced nothing except a watery substance. One of the children threw up but the woman wasn't there to see it.

The Zombie placed her like a block of ice down on the bedroom floor with the tape recorder. The other selves hovered. Again the small hands in the woman's larger ones. Again, a flick showing a tarpaulin under the flatbed car. The tarp looked black and smelled oily. Rain had collected in the center of it. Small bugs and larvae showed beneath one edge and the little one's mouth formed an "O" at the sight of them.

Sewer Mouth cursed at the next flick. The woman felt the tips of the child's small, grubby fingers curled inside her own clenched hand. Where had the stickiness gone?

"Say it," a raspy voice instructed.

The woman obeyed, woodenly. "I feel the warmth, the stepfather's touch, and even though it kills me to say it, I get the feeling that there is willingness."

The flashback shredded at the word "willingness," then it swung back, fully formed. From her yoga position, the woman lowered her head to the floor. The child stared, silent and waiting. The stepfather's face in the flashback showed clearly, suffused with pleasure as the pink thing, exposed in the zipper opening, moved from side to side and then curved upward. His hands gripped the small thighs which were rubber-ball firm and quite short. His hands were slipping inside the white cotton pants, the dress was being shoved up to the child's waist and steadily there came a pounding, then throbbing, warmth.

Now positioned atop him, the child felt the pink thing squeezed between her small, bare legs, the warmth of his body against hers, the heavy odour of his sweaty work clothes. The child's arousal. Confusion tore at the woman's mind. The first small recall today had shown the brutality of the sexual attack on the hedgerow. This segment showed arousal, pleasure, willingness.

The Seventh Horseman seeing the woman's confusion, spoke: "We're giving you our memories," she said. "One of us was created to deal with the arousal. It's a normal part of one's sexuality but, under the circumstances, it is also ugly. We all have our jobs, the one who dealt with the arousal didn't want hers, but life doesn't always give choices."

The Seventh Horseman reinforced with louder messages, giving the woman a portion of their joint session. Very briefly, she went into various Troop dates of actual birth. Including the woman's own.

"You lie!" the woman screamed. "I've always been here!"

The Tunnel darkness deepened.

"No," the Seventh Horseman corrected her without explaining. "And I don't lie, ever."

The Seventh Horseman waited to see if the woman had absorbed to the point of understanding and full acceptance. But the woman, aside from feeling her face scrunched with anger and flushed red, simply looked puzzled.

In the Tunnel, Twelve turned to the Gatekeeper. The one sitting behind the woman doesn't understand math. Someone will have to find another way.

No, *said the Gatekeeper.* The second skin of memory is not ready. But can you imagine such a gift in view of what we know and what the Weaver is weaving? To have it laid in your face that you were born of no parents at all?

The selves offered little escape from the recall that day. Just before dinnertime the woman called Sharon. Coffee she could not remember making perked on the stove, fragrant and welcome. But she needed more than coffee, she needed the sound of a human voice, as much to make her own self real as to find comfort.

"How much longer," she whispered into the phone, "can I hold on and cope with all of this?"

Sharon exploded. "Look, I know you! I've seen every side of you and they're only mood swings! You are not sick, you haven't got multiple personalities. Phillips is so used to seeing very sick people, people who are really insane, that he can read almost anything into what you're telling him!"

The woman vanished. In her place at the kitchen table the Zombie nodded in agreement at Sharon's voice on the other end of the line. Methodically she poured five teaspoons of sugar and liberal amounts of milk into her coffee. Sharon told her about the value of mind relaxation and encounter groups. The Zombie closed her eyes.

"You are what you think you are," Sharon insisted. "You beat the system in so many ways over the years, you can do it again if you just put this multiple business right out of your head!"

The Zombie listened and sipped her coffee with precise movements. There was no need for her to be careful in handling the cup of scalding liquid. The Zombie never got excited, never made a mistake.

While the woman heard Sharon's frantic tone of voice, it came from far away. It didn't make sense that her friend had become so outraged, so frightened. The woman hung up the phone and took a mouthful of coffee. Shocked at the sweet taste, she spit it out, emptied the cup, and rinsed it at the sink.

"Sharon," the Zombie said, "doesn't believe you. She's frightened for you and would rather we all disappeared. You've already tried most of the remedies she suggests. They didn't work. We can't just go away, it isn't possible."

The rain outside the kitchen windows had started to pound, and so had the woman's temples.

"Tell you what," the Zombie said, and for the first time, the woman noticed her speech pattern. The Zombie spoke with a definite pause between each word: "This cup of coffee is mine." She poured more coffee into another cup and added milk and sugar.

Well, the woman told herself, here we are. All my life there's been this insatiable need to be alone. Now I really am. Just me and them.

26

Sunday shoppers, carts loaded with miscellaneous bargains, elbowed through the drugstore aisles, ahead of and behind the woman. Each time the evidencing grew stronger as one self took over from another, she experienced it. Nobody gave his or her name. Right now, she felt, heard, and "saw" a child. With her toes pointed in, Lambchop was skipping down the aisles, inspecting the merchandise. Undaunted by the ninety-degree weather outside, she hummed "Deck the Halls."

Lambchop stumbled over some of the words. The woman identified another voice as one she'd heard yesterday; one which helped the child and, in the process, considerably embellished the song: " 'Tis the season," Elvira sang aloud, "to be greedy. . . . Deck the halls with boughs of money, tralalalala . . . lalala."

The child was staring at one of the displays. Squarely between two worlds and trying to acclimate herself, the woman reached out, ignoring other shoppers, and put two boxes of crayons into the shopping cart. There was a small sigh of happiness.

On a main aisle, a teddy bear sat on the highest shelf. Lambchop smiled at the stuffed animal. She looked different than she had this morning. Before the woman could pin down what the difference was, Mean Joe had blocked her vision. He snatched the bear down from the shelf. The woman shut her eyes, hoping that no one noticed him, hoping that no one in the store could see or hear or feel him—or the other selves—as she did.

At the checkout counter Lambchop held back, afraid to join the line of customers. A bored, nasty-faced clerk balked at large bills and didn't seem to know the price of anything that wasn't marked. Several people left their items on the counter and walked away, grumbling. The woman's turn was coming up. She trembled, the way she always did in public, except that the Buffer was usually there, and often the Front Runner was sitting ahead of her, so no one really noticed it.

Lambchop wasn't frightened. She smiled at Mean Joe, as an older black man gathered up the items his wife handed him. The black man walked up to the bored clerk, all six foot, seven inches of restrained determination and politeness and strength. He laid his wife's items on the counter. The clerk wasted no time ringing them up and giving him change for a very large bill. The woman took note and stopped trembling. She, after all, had Mean Joe, who was every bit as intimidating.

Lamchop watched the black man, so big and capable of commanding the clerk's attention. The woman herself, still unaware of Mean Joe's own blackness, knew that for some reason, the little one associated him with the black man at the checkout counter, and therefore felt the stranger to be safe. She could only assume the child's trust, as her own, was based on their similar tallness and strength.

The child, under Mean Joe's watchful eye, was playing a mind-game; thinking of herself as miniaturised into a tiny piece of lint. Mentally, she was gluing herself, in the form of that lint, beneath the black customer's armpit.

"I'm going to stay right here," she whispered, "and nobody can ever touch me again."

During it all, the woman, unable to control a single action, found herself propelled by the child's mind, as close to the black customer as she could get.

No one in the store, including him, seemed to notice anything out of the ordinary.

Mean Joe watched the interaction between the black customer and the woman and what she thought of as the same little one who had emerged to her in the bedroom yesterday. Mean Joe glanced from side to side, from out of his beautiful, slanty eyes, tracking the movements of everyone in the store. Lambchop, finished with her mind-game, smiled up at him. The tiny person asleep on his shoulder, disturbed by the closeness of so many people, uttered a small cry, and Mean Joe crooned softly. The cry faded away.

The woman paid her bill, felt Lambchop's hand in hers, and wondered again why her hands weren't sticky. In the parking lot, walking past other shoppers, she became desperate with the desire for invisibility, desperate that her people not be noticed, as they piled into the car.

Before she realised what had happened, a simmer began at the injustice of their place, or lack of one, in the world. Sewer Mouth was raging. Catherine couldn't step in quickly enough to siphon the anger to Black Katherine. The woman jammed the keys into the car's ignition, while the hum grew in her veins. She turned the key this way and that. The motor would not turn over.

When summoned, a mechanic from the shopping mall gas station took charge.

"Lady, there ain't nothin' in the world wrong with this car." Wiping his big oily rag, the mechanic stared into the engine block. "God damned tank truck, built for battle. Has it happened before?"

Don't tell him, Catherine warned, *don't tell him it won't start when that back-burner, dead-white rage stews too long. Because this man will say you're crazy and they'll lock you up. This time they really will.*

More than fifteen minutes had passed since the car had malfunctioned. Catherine, who knew the car would shortly start up of it own volition, put a smile on the woman's face and began to speak for her.

"As a matter of fact," Catherine said to the garage mechanic, "it's happened several times. But we just weren't turning the key properly. There's a trick to it, you see."

Back at the house, the woman glanced around the spotless kitchen, noticing how the hanging ferns flourished when she couldn't recall tending them. She watched what she regarded as "the little one" clutch her new teddy bear while foraging on the lower cupboard shelves for cocoa. The woman would have sworn that she sensed more than one small child—one who was sticky and one who was not; one who spoke words, and one who conveyed thoughts only.

Catherine demanded diet cola. The woman never bought soft

261

drinks, she hated them. Puzzled, she opened the cupboard doors. There they were, Diet Coke, Diet Pepsi.

In a burst of affection for the teddy bear, Lamb Chop planted a kiss and a gob of butter on its nose. The butter came from the toast she had to have, even though dinner was being prepared. Lamb Chop remembered afternoons at the second farmhouse, when there had been hot tea with plenty of milk and sugar and jam on the bread, or tiny slices of rich chocolate cake, from the recipe on the back of the Hershey's cocoa box.

The one whose voice sounded like a duchess reclined in a chair at the kitchen table, with no sense of humour. She watched them all, unsmiling and offended. She announced her full and proper name to be Lady Catherine Tissieu and, over roars of protest, loaded her plate with cauliflower, Brussels sprouts, and string beans.

The others refused to eat. They hated vegetables. Now the woman knew why a hatred of families struck her so often. She was too tired to consider what she might like for dinner. Over the aftertaste of something suspiciously like jelly beans, she pondered, believing her "family" to be complete.

The others heard. The silence in the kitchen was palpable. And when the woman looked into the mirror over the sink, her eyes were strange: apple-green with a thread of black around them and in the center of each, a tiny, dead-black iris.

In answer to the woman's usual question about the normalcy of the drugstore incident and dinnertime afterward, Stanley told her, "There's never a never and never an always. We're dealing with the human mind, and there aren't any charts or graphs or yardsticks to measure the normalcy of your," he searched carefully for the word, "experience."

"That's a cute word, Stanley." The woman shifted her position on the cushions. "It's not so cute when I have to consider myself a possible murderer."

She asked again about her fear that she'd done something awful in her past. She believed more firmly than ever that she might have killed her stepfather back at the second farmhouse.

Stanley knew he was walking a very fine line. His duty was to her—to make her more accepting of the other selves but without encouraging antisocial behavior simply because she or the other selves might desire it. He'd already decided which came first, however, so he concentrated on her fears about Mean Joe as regarded the stepfather.

"Any mind," he said, "has a limit to how far it can be pushed. Those two farmhouses would have blown the average mind sky high. You have recalled a lot, but I've a feeling your subconscious knows the upcoming layers will be far more frightening. Hence, partially, the extreme panic now and the need for Mean Joe when you were growing up. If Mean Joe retaliated with violence back there he'd have been dealing in what I call ultimate ways. Sometimes that's what saying the final 'no' boils down to. Ultimate ways."

Stanley hesitated as the blank expression on her face dropped away. For a moment she stared at him. Then she began to laugh out loud, and pound her knees.

"Stanley, I love those words! Ultimate ways. They sound without reservation, so beautifully bloody! I'm going to treasure those words always. I'll tuck them away in my mind and when I am lonely, I'll take them out and enjoy them again."

The woman couldn't stop laughing. Stanley shielded a smile behind his coffee cup and, in the booth, even Tony smiled.

"Mean Joe is very nice," she said. "I realise he guards the little ones and Miss Wonderful. I can feel him doing it. Sometimes I catch just a small glimpse of what their world must be like. I never get to see very much, just snatches, and I can hear tiny bits sometimes of what I know must be whole sentences as they speak."

The woman described Mean Joe as best she could. It became obvious to Stanley that she didn't know Mean Joe was, as one of the other selves had described him in admiration, "black as the ace of spades."

Stanley tried hard to convey a lot to her without bringing up the question of who she was within the Troop Formation.

"You don't remember most of your life," he told her, "because you weren't there. The others were. They have the memories. Think of Rabbit with no skin and no fur, as one of your people describes her. In Rabbit's lifetime, she's had nothing but the pain. Think of the one with no name, who lives for music with a loud beat, refusing as she does to think of anything sad."

Stanley just mentioned you, *Twelve* whispered to the Outrider. Why don't you sing him a little song? Give him a clue to your first name.

So just for the hell of it, the Outrider did.

Twelve listened with grave politeness. Maybe you should have singing lessons, *she said.* We'd all chip in.

The woman seemed to be humming under her breath, a tune Stanley recognised as the Oak Ridge Boys' "Elvira."

"Psychotic," the woman whispered, "means one afflicted by a psychosis, and psychosis means a severe mental or emotional disorder; a partial or complete withdrawal from reality. That sounds like me. But you keep telling me I'm sane."

"You are. You haven't withdrawn from everyday reality, you're simply part of another world as well." Stanley explained how he prepared his students for her videos, telling them to lay aside for a moment their own sense of reality. "I tell them," he said, "that for some incest victims, some sexually and/or physically abused children, this is reality."

She asked if the videotapes were helping anyone.

"Yes," he said. "They give my students and the people they talk to a very graphic sense of the situation. The police officers were astounded. They saw how important it is to understand and accept what child abuse actually does to the victims.

"A lot of people won't listen to you," he said, "because if they do, your pain will be too real for them. I'm afraid that, for the time being, you'll have to live with that."

"It's alright," she said. "I can't talk about some of these things to anyone, anyway. Like the sexual feelings."

Stanley laid down the clipboard. The woman looked abysmally ashamed. He handed her Kleenex as one of the selves made the sign of the cross. The woman took on the peculiar, eyes-right, eyes-left, listening attitude that he'd grown used to.

"Sexual," she said. "The disgust just sweeps over me!" The fists beat on her head and again, there was the sign of the cross. "I keep hearing beads clicking, as if someone is . . ."

"Praying?" Stanley ventured. "I imagine someone prays a lot. Sex to her," Stanley was thinking of Sister Mary, "is for one purpose only: procreation within the confines of marriage. For her, sexual pleasure is out of the question. So, she is deploring either past sexual acts with the stepfather or those acts taking place now."

"Now?" The woman looked blank. "I haven't been anywhere with anyone."

"To the best of your knowledge," Stanley said, and pretended he did not see the fingers of her left hand begin to twine a lock of hair, very slowly, while the mouth relaxed into a sensual, languid, plump line.

The woman began to tell him about her cars, three of them in the last few years, that had been traded in because of electrical problems—and how the other day her selves had brought the solution to her: when the car won't start, get away from it for a while.

"But the fuses for the overhead lights, the cigarette lighter, and the clock blow out, I don't replace them anymore. The light bulbs in the house flicker and blow out too soon. The television, the stereo, my little tape recorder, the car radio, these video-tapes we're making, everything is so full of static."

"Well," Stanley said finally, "don't you want to know if you're crazy?"

"Stanley, this is a mechanical problem. Except that agents have driven my car and it doesn't happen to them. Only when I'm in the damned thing, does everything blow."

She turned to face him, squarely. "It's got to do with energy, the energy of the mind, doesn't it?"

"Yes," he said. "it does."

The session and Stanley's calm reply to her question stayed with her all that morning, along with a hundred flicks that came in rapid succession. The woman finally felt someone's anger. Then she felt their rage. The stepfather deserved death, even without more recall. But had she killed the bastard or not? A voice in her mind told her to hurry. Before she could refuse, she was dialing the long-distance operator.

Yes, the operator singsonged. That gentleman did have a phone listed in his name. Without asking and contrary to telephone company rules, she began to put the call through.

"Hello?" the woman said.

In the classroom, a Protective Services worker raised her hand.

"The woman I mentioned to you the last time," she said, "scored an eighty percent on her test."

"She could have scored twenty-five percent and still be a multiple," Stanley told her. "The process has revealed almost no absolutes. Observation is your best tool. Watch the facial and body movements, the figures of speech, the attitudes toward established social and moral values, the habit patterns. Particularly in the case of my client, anyway, watch for someone distracted, bemused, who gets lost easily, can't follow directions. And then look for just the opposite, and all the variations thereto.''

The time was almost up. Stanley wanted to go on: Could your client have been a gifted child, perhaps one that nobody recognised, because multiples hide or fragment their creative, extreme intelligence? Does your client indicate, as most gifted children do, familiarity with the paranormal, and, quite possibly, does that disturb your professional aplomb? But those were his own questions, as yet unfolded to a complete degree, and he put them aside to pack up his equipment.

''Did you at one time live in a small town, Far Crossing, New York?'' The woman shook so hard. Even the Buffer sitting in front of her couldn't absorb all the fear.

''Yes, I did,'' he said.

Just like that. In the same tone of voice, the one he used on her as a child to let her know that no matter what, he was right, Ten-Four thought.

''Who are you? What do you want?'' he demanded to know at least three times before the woman, amazed and shaken, hung up.

The stupid bastard was still alive. The woman bit her lip until the blood dropped onto the kitchen table. He had to be in his early sixties by now. She had wanted him dead, but hadn't killed him after all. Knowing that, why didn't the guilt go away? If she hadn't killed him, what had she done?

Sewer Mouth knew. Her curses filled the air that night, in the wooden fortress the woman called her bedroom. Around her, meticulously placed, were built-in dressers, heavy with clothes and books; odd pieces of antique furniture and wall hangings and drifting ferns. Personal, yet impersonal possessions, the accumulation of many lifetimes, but certainly not hers.

''Don't worry,'' Catherine said. ''Some of it's mine, some of it's theirs. Like the worm farm in the living room.''

Children's voices sounded then, claiming whatever in the house belonged to them. The woman felt someone's tears on her face and saw a child grabbing for the teddy bear, holding it with pained, accusing eyes.

The question of what the woman was seeing, her reality, as Stanley had mentioned in the session today, his hope for her acceptance of it so that she would accept the recall, too, had until now been far away. But this child was real.

The woman went where the child led her, seeing through her eyes, everything bigger than she was, at eight years old. Hurry, down the hedgerow from the black orchards. Past the old pear tree where the crazy owl with the gemstone, hooded eyes, cried each night, swerving quickly toward the farmhouse, follow the dirt path to the side of the old garage.

Chicken wire had been nailed on the side of the grey frame building. Rambler roses in scarlet profusion climbed the wire, heady with scent. Two persons stood on the dirt path; one was the stepfather, frowning at a loud refusal. He reached out, seized the arm of the young girl in front of him. Through the child's eyes, the woman saw the cement wall that formed the base of the back porch, saw the stepfather hurling the girl who was screaming . . . and the cement wall coming up so fast to meet her face, her arms flung out in front of her face, blood gushing, spattering the wall. . . .

Click. There was an instant image of a long, dull black robe . . . something white at the throat of it, and something black covering the head.

Sister Mary Catherine had evidenced.

27

Monday morning arrived in a thick blanket of August humidity. Directly behind the woman's, there was a mind in which turmoil and agony boiled. The extreme summer heat beat on the woman and the one behind her, weighed them down, sealed them together, in sweat and confusion. As the temperature rose into the high nineties that day, so did their joint rage. The stepfather was alive.

Beyond Catherine, who was busy lacquering her fingernails in a frosty peach colour, the eyes of a small child stared at the woman, solemn and accusing.

Help me. Why can't you help me?

The woman sent back her own message: "Because I'm guilty."

Guilty of what?

"I don't know!"

Meanwhile, at the university, a student was raising her hand.

"How long before the woman realises that the guilt stems from sex acts with her stepfather, not his murder which she never committed?"

"First," Stanley said, "she'll have to believe fully that those sex acts ever took place. As of last night, she knows that he's alive. I'm not sure how she feels about that."

"How can she not believe in the abuse?" the student protested, waving her notes. "These videos, that's all the two of you talk about."

"The two of us?"

"Sorry," she said over general laughter.

"Possibly one reason for her inability to believe is that the abuse didn't happen to her; it happened to the other selves."

"How many of these 'selves' have you delineated now?"

"Roughly fifty persons to date. Which gives her a lot to deal with; she's moving so fast, partly due to the manuscript and partly because of some kind of inner drive, hers and theirs. By the way, a question has arisen, at least in my mind, as to who the 'woman' really is, inside the Troop Formation."

The student was taking rapid notes. She looked up. "I'm following you, Doctor Phillips," she said, "but the first-born child has to be there somewhere."

"Perhaps," Stanley said. "But when you look at what happened so early in its development, the state it's in may not correspond to what we think of as 'living.' "

"How do you differentiate 'persons,' as opposed to emotional behavior alone? How have you arrived at this present body count of fifty?"

"Different emotions don't give a person different handwriting, eye colours, brain waves, intelligence quotients, or memories. Catherine, for instance, never had a child and can't relate to the suggestion that she was ever married. Catherine was never part of those experiences."

"Why," the student asked, "is the Troop Formation's structure so much more complicated than an Eve, or a Sybil?"

"I've tried several times to suggest to the Troops that if measured on a scale of one to ten against many other cases presently documented, the degree of their abuse may well be a fifteen or twenty. But they don't all share the same memories, so they don't accept my suggestion."

"Are you saying the high body count represents the degree of abuse and damage?"

"No one knows, as yet. Fifty isn't a high count, but then we've barely scratched the surface of the Troops' childhood. The degree of abuse, the intelligence of the original child, the degree of secretiveness within the family—perhaps these things all come into play, and perhaps none of them, in some cases at least, applies at all. There is a very small percentage of multiples who were never abused as children."

"Those posthypnotic suggestions I hear you handing out on

the tapes," Captain Albert Johnson shuffled his own notes, like any other student. "They're a lot like brainwashing, correct?"

"Reverse brainwashing, Albert. In the woman's mind, she's so bad, so stupid and powerless, all messages implanted by a manipulative abuser and a reinforcive mother. Twenty years of positive stroking won't take all that away."

At home or in public, odours triggered recall. The shakes continued, but at least no Troop member screamed or dissolved in tears publicly. The woman knew what the time lapses meant now. She wanted to know what did go on when she wasn't 'there.'

Stanley told her to trust the others. The woman replied that she couldn't, and just would not go out or talk to anyone. Trust. He'd chosen the wrong word.

"Norman and Page," the woman said, "know things about the years I spent with them. I listen to what they say about our lives together and I nod and smile and at the same time, I'm scared. Because I don't know specifically what they're talking about, and I know they wouldn't lie."

"Neither are your people lying about the abuse," Stanley said.

"You're telling me I have to believe something I can't see or touch; I can't see what goes on when I'm not present."

"You can't see the far side of the moon, either," Stanley said, "but believe me, it's there."

He'd never worked with anyone so frightened. She had to compete in the world, but at times he wondered how. If it were not for the other selves, she couldn't. He'd noted, for instance, that the moment his client left the studio to walk back down the hall with him to the parking lot, she usually took on one of two tones: utter distraction, in which she appeared unable to locate any path through the building, to her car, or out through the university grounds to the highway; or, at other times, a casual but sharp bantering which suggested a mind capable of finding the way out of a foreign jungle unaided. He doubted that either of them was the woman.

He'd seen the distracted, befuddled one in action many times— lost in the university hallways, or on the telephone at the head of the stairs trying to nail down miscellaneous business appointments. Once he'd studied her in the 7-Eleven, as she remained intent on purchasing coffee and his diet soda while neglecting eighteen dollars in change. Finding the soda behind refrigerated glass doors and pouring the coffee into a paper cup had been no problem. But she'd become uncertain the moment they approached the checkout counter. Without even looking into her purse, she'd yanked out a bill and handed it over to the cashier. She'd hesitated then, her face red. Whereupon Stanley had heard a child's voice innocently requesting a paper sack for the coffee.

He'd failed to see the big deal over asking for a paper bag. Then he did and anger gripped him. "Help" was a word his client couldn't master. Asking for a second helping at the dinner table, pass the salt, do you have this dress in another colour, is this seat taken, can you *help* me? How many times in the sessions had he seen her avoid asking him directly for help? The well incident, when the stepfather had refused help, had terrified the Troops as children; subconsciously, it terrified them now.

That day in 7-Eleven, it had been impossible to tell who stuffed the money into the purse after Stanley had nudged her.

Stanley's calm teaching style and his casual handling of the sessions helped both his students and the woman to accept and even at times understand to some degree what was going on. More often than not, he wondered if he understood anything at all. There were pieces of the puzzle still unaccounted for and perhaps never to be fully answered. He placed a call to Marshall.

"Marshall," he said, "my client complains that nothing electrical—lights, stereo, radio, television, even her car motor, is ever entirely free of . . ."

"Interference?" Marshall laughed. "Stanley, after watching those tapes, I'd be amazed if there weren't interference. Nobody in our field, with a few exceptions, wants to talk about it publicly, but there are experiments going on. I don't know if anyone is working with a multiple in this field, but our bodies, our minds, are made up of energy. Your client is more than one. Think about it."

"She's only got one brain, Marshall."

"That brain operates independently for each one of the selves. They generate different energy levels, some of them pretty high. When more than one of them is out at a time or you get a number of them coming and going at once, the overall energy level soars. When one of them tries to repress an emotion like anger or rage, it just heightens the energy level, like built-up electricity with no outlet."

What Marshall was saying made sense. Stanley told him about the woman's dream several years ago, how she described what

271

he'd known to be that sharply receptive alpha state, between waking and full sleep, wherein she'd seen the name of a small town in another state printed on a pack of cigarettes, the same brand she smoked at the time. When she'd repeated the dream to a male friend who'd just returned from a trip, he'd looked amused and said how funny that was, because he'd just bought a house in that same small town.

"I don't want to be melodramatic, Marshall, but behind the amusement, he told her that his blood ran cold. He'd been keeping it a secret, even from his wife, for reasons I won't go into."

"Is there any way at all that she could have known?"

"No. I ran her through it many times; she just sat there looking bemused but casual, as if it were no big deal. There have been other things all along, but they're adding up lately . . . the way the Troops seem to read my mind, for instance."

"She survived those two farmhouses," Marshall said. "Extreme intelligence, the paranormal; one is usually the foundation for the other. It's hard to say which one creates the most denial in an observer. Did you know that few shrinks, for instance, want to give credence to their own enormous energy highs when working with a client like that?"

"Let me tell you," Stanley said, "about those energy highs."

"You don't have to. You get charged up in the sessions from a transference of her energy—and drained afterward. Perfectly normal. If the Troops can interfere with electrical appliances, they can interfere with the energy in your brain."

Afterwards Stanley reflected on Marshall's reinforcement of the same thing Jeannie Lawson had described to him. Some of Jeannie's biggest problems still centered on trying to hide not only a gifted mind but extrasensory perception and the same kind of electrical problems the woman evidenced. People, Jeannie had told Stanley bitterly, ran from the notion of multiplicity, but they bolted outright at the idea of anything to do with the paranormal.

The words she was about to say felt like her own and yet borrowed. She felt wonderful and relaxed and free . . . and she did not feel anything, except through the other Troop members. Through a wave of euphoria, she approached Page with what the child might consider ridiculous.

"Page," she said, "before this thing goes much further, I have to talk to you."

"OK."

The waitress brought a huge plate of chocolate chip pancakes smothered in sweet butter. Page raised her fork, looking grown-up in a beige knitted dress and three-inch heels. She flipped her strawberry-blond hair back over her shoulders and gave the bus-boy the eye. He gave it back to her. Page was fourteen. The busboy looked eighteen.

"Too old," Page informed the woman in a whisper. "Yuch."

The two of them raised their glasses of water and toasted in unison. Their booth was at the back of the International House of Pancakes and the other breakfast patrons had their heads bent over their own food. Still, there floated just out of the woman's reach a hope that all the voices inside her would be lowered this morning.

"I know what you want to tell me, mother. I asked daddy why he has a family and you don't. He started to cry. He said to me, 'I knew you were going to ask me that someday. I don't know what to tell you.' Then he said you have multiple personalities and he told me about the incest, sort of."

"Page, do you understand, I mean really understand, any of it? Do they ever mention child sexual abuse in school?"

"My friends talk about it. What I don't understand is the multiple part. I mean, I do but I don't, you know?"

The woman noticed the humming in her veins and a pulled-back feeling as if someone were reading a story aloud, through her, not as if she, herself, were saying anything at all. "Page, you have a lot of friends, right?"

Page agreed.

"Well, try to imagine that they all share your body, while each one of them is still him- or herself."

Page thought about that. She laughed.

"Hey," she said. "Anne in my body. I'd get to do everything she does, stay out late and wear all her clothes."

"No, you wouldn't. Because Anne would be staying out late, not you, and you might not like her clothes. Once you became aware that Anne shared your space, then you might stay out late, even if you didn't want to. But you wouldn't always be there to make the choice."

"It doesn't sound like fun," Page said.

"Fun? It may sound funny at times, but it's never fun, Page, no matter what," the woman gritted her teeth because her mind was empty. What had she been going to say? She waited for help and it came, through a voice she listened to, saying words she'd read in books or had heard other people say but in much softer

273

tones. The words sounded good. They raised her above herself. "You know I love you, Page. Always have and always will. My leaving your father was something I had to do. My anger toward everything had risen to such a pitch, I was so afraid it would rub off on you and be a bad example. But leaving him didn't change the fact that you're my daughter, that I'd kill for you."

Page grinned. "I know," she said. "Do you think you could make one of your persons come out for me, I mean we three could have breakfast together? Do any of them like chocolate chip pancakes?"

Nails drove Page back to her father's house, and her skin crawled the whole time. It was as if somebody had unleashed a force way beyond anybody's power to deal with it. The woman had sat at the booth, watching Page with the eyes of the one directly behind her. Those eyes had held bemusement and agony and, worse, had reflected an awful yearning to be linked more closely to Page. The one behind the woman was no more Page's mother than the woman was. The yearning would never be realised.

Nails knew why the flesh on her body crawled. She could feel the one in the Tunnel, gathering himself to correct things. She did not look forward to what was only hours away.

"I'm going to kill you." The woman said it aloud, with the taste of pancakes still in her mouth. The stepfather's phone number lay on the page of the address book, a threat, a taunt. How long had it been written there? She didn't know. Was there no way to beat him? He was still big as a mountain and she was still guilty.

I'm going to kill you. Aside from that one thought, her mind this afternoon was as empty and as silent as the house around her. Only the steady ticktock of the grandfather clock in the foyer broke the quiet.

Page was growing up overnight. There was no time to waste if she was ever going to share . . . inside the woman's mind, one of the selves screamed in protest at the threat of the closeness to another human being. Someone else lashed out at the protest and spit on the floor. The woman gave up trying to delineate voices.

Like a student in a classroom with an invisible teacher, she listened to what skipped through her head. The voice was friendly, uninvolved.

She had put up with a lot of people, the voice said, bending over backward, as Stanley often pointed out, to be perfect in their eyes. So they would accept her. And all the time she'd struggled to be perfect, silent about her own desires and needs and blaming her lack of satisfaction on those to whom she never voiced them. Then she'd tried harder to be more perfect, demand less and less so they would love her more and more. It had been a vicious cycle.

She was, the voice said pleasantly, a doormat.

Another thought from another mind: things would be different from now on, she would become a person in her own right. The woman grabbed the thought and hung onto it. A desire to have it for her own, lodged firmly as if it would never leave. Just as quickly, realising that neither thought nor desire was hers, she looked for her own. There was none.

On the night of the twelfth August moon, the Irishman moved through the Tunnel. Like silent water he went, straight into the woman's sleeping mind—until the tide lapped at the edge of wakefulness and she stirred and fought to keep the dark.

Darlin', he said, as if he offered nothing and everything beyond, 'tis time. The third one must evidence.

There would be no running. Before she could even try, the Weaver blocked the way. The Irishman leaned down and he laid her in the dead center of her own being. He held her buoyant so that she floated in the space that was her own and she received because the space was so vast and empty and therefore allowed it—the total essence of those who surrounded her like an army, and their cries were hell itself.

The woman had just evidenced.

Do y' see now, what y' are and do y' see y'r purpose?

She saw.

Existence in y'r case, and he was laughing but it was not unkind, has nothin' t' do w' y'r specific presence. Y' exist because y' d' not.

She absorbed what lay to one side of his unspoken thought. Separate from all the other Troops, the silent, far-off figure of the adult core and her mirror-image came to hover just inside the woman's mind. What stood far beyond them made her want to run, but again the Weaver blocked the way.

The woman found herself looking out of her mind and at the same time, looking into it and beyond. There was no sound except that of a faint, faraway wind that chilled her to the marrow of her bones. The Weaver seemed to have her pinned, rooted in some fashion she could not describe, and so she just stood there, hearing the wind and feeling nothing except the coldness.

The Irishman then showed her the other place, constructed of time alone. The child core and her mirror-image hung inside it, in a space that was not a space because they were contained by nothing. The first-born child and her mirror-image shared that same space and shared nothing because there was nothing left. But the silence surrounding the four small figures was like a wall, universe-deep and eternity-wide.

The second skin of memory, comprising all that had happened so far in the Troops' lifetime, as recalled by the selves who had evidenced, was folded. Nothing showed. The skin lay cradled in the Weaver's hands.

When you give that to me, *and the woman seemed to have shrunk into herself,* will I have to wear it every day?

No, darlin'. Only when the denial sweeps in.

Who denies?

All o' us. 'Tis the nature o' the thing. Too horrible, I suppose. Y' see, denial is only a balm, a false one t' be sure. In our case, we need somethin' else a good deal more. We need, without harmin' the sleepin' cores, a recognition o' all o' it.

When?

On the night o' the high feast, darlin'.

And again, she read thoughts beyond his silence.

The face o' this earth was created t' hold those who canna' see more. Tonight y've gone beyond anythin' most people know. But there's another beyond and 'tis final f'r this journey. When the time comes, I'll be takin' y' there.

And in that place of thought beyond the Irishman's silence, she joined him and saw what he saw, felt what he felt about it, and was glad for the vast emptiness of herself. Because the vision flowed and filled even her space and his, and more.

When the Weaver wove that night, he wove away only the knowledge of the Irishman's presence.

The woman slept until dawn in the curve of Mean Joe's shoulder. He held her as if she were a burn victim in whose tormented brain even thought dared not alight.

28

A succession of days went by. Eventually the woman saw that Catherine had washed her hair and fluffed it in a loose style. She was wearing old jeans and a T-shirt grimy with packing dust. Catherine was silent and quite unlike herself; she did not issue scathing statements full of projected changes for the future. In fact, no Troop member said anything. The silence went on, as if a wake were being held.

The big black letters on the kitchen calendar stared back: September. Next to the kitchen calendar hung a long list, apparently designating the contents of the packing boxes scattered across the floor. The woman was not aware of climbing the stairs to the loft bedroom each night. Sometimes she would awaken, feeling the carving knife in her hand and the stepfather's vital organs, bloodied on the bed beside her. She knew each time, as sadness welled up, that the organs weren't real. The knife was and it frightened Rabbit who tried to hide under the bedclothes.

When she surfaced at all, it was briefly, sluggishly. Almost the only sensation she experienced was the thousands of needles stinging her arms and legs. The move was made without her presence. One day she became aware that her surroundings were different. Her surroundings were nothing more than four weather-beaten walls, a floor dirty with pigeon droppings and a grey light filtering through small windows. She was in a warehouse loft, and the memory of being in it once before skittered into sight and was gone.

The wake atmosphere had lessened only slightly. Along with the headache, another Troop member moved in and evidenced. As he did, the woman "saw" an enormous trash heap: metal and paper, wire and wood, enclosed behind a tall mesh fence. On one of the stepfather's excursions, looking for spare parts for the cars he repaired, he used to stop at many junkyards. The Troop member evidencing seemed to rise slowly from the juxtaposition of texture on texture, his body bent to meld with the various objects blanketing him. "Junkman." The name lay in the woman's mind. She caught a sense of him, as being the essence of all hiding, all "removal" from the world. She smiled, accepting him and all that he was, for he asked nothing except his right to stay hidden. That right seemed to be protected in some way, by Mean Joe.

Mean Joe, with Sidney Poitier cool, had lugged something out of the car and into the freight elevator. He carried his burden gingerly into the dust-laden, run-down warehouse loft. The weight and beauty of the stark white collage had never been so apparent as when Mean Joe hefted it into place on the wall nearest the exit door. The Junkman looked happy. The woman knew then that he had created it and when she saw the children behind him, she knew for whom he'd created it.

"I have something to tell you," Elvira said.

The woman turned away. The question of time, how much time she'd spent in these seedy quarters already, scared her: "It's only a question of time. It won't be long now. Eventually, I'll get you." The words were old ones, belonging to the stepfather. Time. The knowledge sat squarely in her head: it was not that she'd squandered her time somewhere. Her time had never existed. Everybody else in the world knew where their time went, they had certain things to show for it: a college education, the yardstick measurements on a doorjamb to indicate a growing child . . . memories.

Elvira pressed closer and wouldn't go away. The woman disappeared. The others argued among themselves. This warehouse, an investment made five years ago, was probably uninhabitable.

"Screw that," Sewer Mouth said. "We've lived in worse."

Elvira sat on the unpacked suitcases, estimating the space in the third-floor loft area to be around twelve hundred square feet.

It was good space and, because there was no rent, they could buy a bed, a refrigerator, a hot plate, a few ferns to make Catherine happy, and perhaps a shovel for the bird droppings.

One hundred yards behind the warehouse, the train went down the tracks and rumbled away in the distance. The woman didn't hear it. Darkness had fallen, had she slept? Her teeth hummed. There was no sense in brushing them; the humming signaled another gum infection. It was too much effort to haul out the baking soda and peroxide. Sometime later, she considered the effort it would take to get a phone and get the number to Stanley. It would, of course, have to be unlisted and unpublished. There was no reason to change practices now. The woman laughed, feeling quite unlike herself, and heard someone ask what it would be like to be herself. That made her laugh harder. Putting both hands over her mouth did not shut the sounds off. She inspected each of her hands carefully and received a conclusion: since the ring and the bracelet were familiar, maybe the hands were hers, too. She wore no watch and there came a misty recollection of throwing one out a car window. How many watches had there been? Many. But no time at all.

She slept heavily atop the suitcases until morning.

"You can't come down from those suitcases," Elvira said, "until the floors are cleaned."

"I hate you," the woman said. "Go away."

"You're only feeling what we all do when we first evidence to ourselves," Elvira said.

For a long moment the woman sat with a blank look on her face. Then she started to laugh because Elvira was sending her laughter.

"You see?" Elvira turned on the radio and the music got loud. "Life is a joke. Learn to laugh at it. All along, you've said, most of the time, 'my mother, my stepfather, my father.' But the one to whom the parents belong is dead. None of us are related to anyone except ourselves."

Two days later, Ten-Four got ahold of the building superintendent.

"George," Ten-Four said to him, "we need the water turned on up there in the warehouse."

"I won't be responsible," George told her. "I'm not sure the pipes will hold water."

"Think of something, George."

Why, the woman wondered, did she feel as if she'd just said something rude and aggressive to somebody? She stared at the phone in her hand, wondering who she'd been trying to call. She shopped quickly, head down, and fled back to the car. Back at the warehouse, the rickety freight elevator rose shakily to the third floor. She hauled the bags out and dumped them inside the four dim, cavernous walls. Tomorrow the bed would be delivered.

"She's moved out of the house, there's been no trace of her for over a month."

Captain Albert Johnson agreed to check it out and closed his notebook.

"One thing, Albert. If anyone of your officers were to find her, I'd rather they weren't in uniform."

Albert grinned. "Too bad I'm not a black male and about twelve feet tall. Am I right?"

"You are perceptive," Stanley said.

"Ever heard of a white multiple female having a black male personality before?"

"I never heard of a lot of things," Stanley said. "That doesn't mean they're not so."

"If she harms herself, they'll lock her up. If she harms anyone else, she'll be locked up. Nothing I can do about it." Albert's face was closed, he studied the floor carefully.

"If she's alive."

"Yeah," Albert said. "That, too."

On one of the days when her mind did not sleep, the woman made a trip for cigarettes. After the gloom of the warehouse loft, bright sunlight came as a surprise. Elvira could not resist a test and when they came to an apartment complex on their left, the woman recognised the structure as one she'd lived in after leaving Norman eight years ago. With a seemingly perverse mind of its own, the car turned into the secondary driveway and moved slowly past brick buildings and a common pool. The complex to her left seemed familiar; it had to be the one. It struck her that while she had lived there and could recall the apartment layout and the decor, she could not recall entering or leaving it on any occasion.

Something she'd mentioned months ago to Stanley came back. "I can remember, sometimes," she said, "being on the school

280

bus. Sometimes I can remember getting ready for school a couple of mornings, and being briefly in a couple of classes. But nowhere in my mind is there ever a memory of getting on or off the school bus.''

"Somebody else remembers it," Stanley had told her. "You're struggling with one of the most terrifying facets of MPD. You may never understand, and neither will I, exactly where you go when somebody else comes out, or how they can operate completely free of your knowledge, but you will believe that it does happen. That belief won't arrive in a blinding flash. You'll simply encounter different pieces of evidence as you become more aware.''

The woman stared at the apartment complex. The terror she experienced at that moment was something that the Weaver would never take away as long as she lived. She began to scream and cry and grip the steering wheel with white-knuckled hands.

Once back at the warehouse but unable to stop the Mixmaster tremble, she scrambled into the bed and lay there, not daring to move. Someone specific seemed to tear along the edges of her mind, raging like a banshee.

"Goddamn you, we're losing the battle, the bastard is winning! The stepfather is still alive and we're dying here in this stupid warehouse!''

The children's voices picked up on it, but from a distance only, as if she were repellent to them. They hung back, shrinking from her. The adult voices were closer, gathering war clouds of rage—hers and theirs.

Kill him. It started as a chant and turned into a mantra. She couldn't listen anymore. Her mind rejected everything, their reality and her own. She went to sleep.

Some days, the fright started as far down as her toes. With the first glimpse of daylight it consumed her and stayed until she managed to fall asleep again. She slept a lot. She was scared a lot. But safe. There was no mail to worry about and no one knew that she now had a phone. She had no idea how long it had been since she had last called Stanley.

"Have to get in shape, look decent, be neat first," someone said.

While pondering sudden anger at the hot plate resting on makeshift bookshelves next to the sink, she realised finally that somebody wished it were a gas stove. How did you stick your head into a hot plate?

Shaking the thermometer, the woman read it again and let it drop to the floor: 103°. The thermometer's confirmation of illness wearied her. She burrowed deeper under the quilt and drifted off, with every bone and muscle aching. Later, a stranger looked back in the mirror over the porcelain sink, with a face like an overfed squirrel, eyes bloodshot, hair greasy and matted, and lips cracked dry. There did not seem to be a drop of moisture in her entire body. She drifted off again.

"He'll win if you don't get out of that bed."

"Fuck off," Sewer Mouth said.

The woman had begun to like the swearing. She slept until the next morning when only someone's need to urinate forced her, on deadened feet, back into the bathroom.

"She seems to be living in a warehouse," Albert said. "A classic-car buff stores his antiques on the first two floors. She's living on the third. County records say she owns the building and when I checked it out, there she was, in the driveway, hauling groceries. She creeps around the damn place like half a mouse."

"Does she have a phone?"

"Unlisted, unpublished. Want me to go and get her?"

"No." Stanley thought a moment. "I'll take it from here. And thank you, Albert."

The black-and-white television picture flickered. The announcer's voice punctuated the vastness of the warehouse loft. She lay on the bed with no desire to move, her body heavy with exhaustion and her mind vaguely centered on the television screen. The humanlike appendages of a gigantic, solid white turtle were moving in slow motion, producing a mesmerising effect.

After the first few moments the woman found herself unable to wrench her eyes from the turtle. Its dreamy, trancelike motions were repeated until the pale, translucent skin seemed in danger of splitting. Eventually she realised that the Smithsonian segment of "Our Reptilian Friends" was over.

She put on the flannel nightgown, shivering in the dampness of the big room. She did not know that her temperature had dropped; all she knew was that she did not ache so badly. She flicked off the bedside light, welcoming darkness and sleep. Her eyes were shut tight when it happened. As on a negative, the turtle was no longer a pale image but a darkening grey. It pumped its long, thick arms up and down, lowering and lifting itself, so slowly.

And she was sitting up in bed, the animal sounds coming from her mouth. Because it wasn't the reverse-image of the turtle above her, but the stepfather. It was his smell in her nostrils . . . it was his chest, his arms . . . lowering, lifting him above her face.

The pattern for most sexually abused multiples was to deny recall, each time other selves presented it. The woman might in the future deny or reject many other presentations but she would never forget this one.

Elvira turned on the light and waited patiently until the woman was hit with the full realisation. It was important that the room not be dark, that the music be loud. She turned the radio up and Jim Croce's song "Bad, Bad, Leroy Brown" played full blast.

The woman, with her face in the soft velveteen body of the teddy bear, didn't have strength to reject anything. Several selves moved at once, gave her images of the sex act and let them lie there. Sister Mary Catherine's revulsion came alive, screamed out loud.

The woman couldn't move. At what point had he first achieved penetration? How old had she been?

The calm exploded. The woman ran from the bed and threw herself in the corner. She crouched there, wrapping the night-gown close.

No one spoke.

"Alright," the woman screamed, filled to suffocation by the mind surfacing inside her own, "how old was the one to whom it happened?"

"Pick one," somebody said. "Pick any age."

The lace of the long flannel gown grazed her ankles; she shrieked, not wanting to be touched by anything or anyone. Through the night, she slept, awoke, crouching and freezing in the furthest corner of the enormous room, with the quilt over her head.

"We're almost there," they said.

She awoke one afternoon to find another snake in the bed, and looked at it dully, not caring whether it was real or not. The snake swam in a clear pool of water amongst fallen leaves. This time a complete, debilitating weariness precluded fright.

Sometime that same week, the sensation in her mouth finally

forced her to the mirror for a firsthand inspection. Only the sight of purple gums from which a yellow substance oozed drove her to haul out the peroxide and baking soda, which she mixed into a paste and applied gingerly with an old, soft toothbrush.

Catherine laughed at the woman's stricken face.

"To hell with the dentist," Catherine said. "See how that marvelous swelling takes away the tiny crow's-feet around your eyes?"

"You are quite disgusting," Lady Catherine Tissieu told her.

"Leave me alone," the woman said.

They wouldn't.

They made her look at the mother, dating after they'd forced the stepfather out of the house, and inviting her to go along. How appealing it had seemed until she'd heard the strange sounds in the front seat of the car, the mother, obviously doing what she'd always told her daughter was evil and wrong. The woman, a teenager at the time, frozen solid next to her own date, could not see the mother from the back seat. What she did see eventually was that the mother was pregnant. Suddenly one day it had been very apparent, along with a hideous repugnance for her that nothing overcame. So she'd left the farmhouse, carrying the guilt along with her.

"The only thing is," Twelve said, "you've dumped the guilt on us. You're blaming you and us."

The children's small voices sounded angry. They began to cry, to talk about a teapot, about scalding hot tea. They shivered and cringed and seemed to be in pain. Their pain didn't affect the woman; she couldn't understand what they were talking about. She put her head on the pillow and went back to sleep.

That night someone began to read aloud to the children.

29

"Do I know you?" Stanley was polite.

"Sure you do, Charlie." Elvira stared him in the eye for the first time since he'd entered the warehouse loft. She seldom called anyone by their correct name because doing anything according to the book scared her. Obeying rules rather than making her own gave her the feeling of being hemmed in, up against it, subject to somebody else's authority and mercy. Edgar Allan Poe had said that as a name, "Charlie" always called up the image of a good man, that when one heard it, all apprehension fell away. She didn't know if that were true or not, but she'd decided to deal with Stanley, using "Charlie" as a sort of shield belonging to herself alone.

"Do you have a name?" Stanley asked.

Late afternoon sunlight slanted through the warehouse windows. Elvira puffed on her cigarette, inhaling the smoke and blowing it out quickly. His question had triggered a deep fury. How many times as children, hiding from the stepfather, had the Troops heard the name of the first-born child being called? How many times had the mother screamed that name in rage?

"Listen," she said. "I sent you the note."

There were five places Stanley should have been over an hour ago. While the Troops had been absent, his schedule had grown tighter every week. Right now he should have been exhausted but a familiar energy surged through his blood vessels.

"To hell with this garbage," Elvira went on, transmitting for

285

other, unwilling Troop members. "We've got to get moving. The woman is fucking incapacitated."

"The woman is scared," Stanley said, knowing that while she might sound like Sewer Mouth, the body stance and speech pattern were much different. He felt like a fool after so long a time, talking about his client as if she weren't there. "Do you hear music?" Stanley had been watching her body, her hands, swaying and snapping to a silent beat.

"Sure do," Elvira said on her own behalf and then Sewer Mouth's. "I hear my own music. It drowns out the crap. Lotsa crap around these days, you know?"

"Where do you, uh, hang out when someone else emerges?" Stanley asked.

Elvira, from her peculiar place within the Troop Formation, felt the emptiness of the woman and the mirror-images of all the dead children around her.

"I have places to go, things to do." Almost as an aside, she said, "We are going to kill the stepfather, Charlie."

"Don't you think," he asked, "that the book and the training videos will be satisfaction enough?"

"Hey." Elvira took a last puff and stubbed out the cigarette. "Don't try me, Charlie. You know damn well that nothing will ever be enough, not where the stepfather is concerned, or the mother, either. We got raided, Charlie, we got stomped on."

She'd begun to grip her forearms and the knuckles were turning white. He thought it was the woman who surfaced moments later and began to cry, talking about things unrelated to the conversation he'd been having.

"Look," Stanley told her. "You've got a choice. Either accept the fact of multiple personality and therefore the upcoming recall, or hide again and face life as you've been living it. It's October. Do you know it's been two months since our last session?"

"It can't be more than two weeks!"

Someone was struggling to complete an emergence. It had thrown the woman off balance; she was shaking her head, dazed. From a distance, she was hearing spoken words, clearly.

"I hear you talking, suddenly, but I can't get in, I just can't get in. You said it's October. Where's Christmas? Did I miss Christmas?"

For the woman, all sound in the room then ceased. Too disoriented to question Stanley further, she stared at her hands. The joining began, her mind with that of the adult core's mirror-

286

image. Between the two of them, flowing from the silence and emptiness, a recognition passed. The woman from her own emptiness accepted what she could not return: a hideous feeling of empathy and a blinding bemusement.

The look went from fear to dismay, to panic-stricken shock. "Where's the time?" she screamed. "Where's the time? The farmhouses, there was never a clock, I never saw a clock! Did we have a clock, we must have, but I never saw it, where's the time?"

Stanley busied himself rewinding the second tape and inserting it into the recorder. What accounted for so big a time lapse? Had he gotten so used to thinking of the Troops as belonging to an unclassic case of multiplicity, a case wherein the changes simply melded from one to the other with no appreciable lapses between one self and another?

He studied the person in front of him more closely. Then he remembered a past session and the discovery of a self new to him, someone who surfaced far less often than the woman. Someone who mirror-imaged her in a way he could not explain. The differences then, as today, had been so slight that he'd caught but not defined them.

Marshall already knows, Stanley thought. This is what he told me I'd eventually figure out for myself.

Breaking through to this one seemed an impossibility. He tried, but nothing worked. This one felt left out, or locked out of this conversation—and perhaps an entire lifetime. Finally, she simply faded away.

The woman glared accusingly at the two white envelopes on Stanley's clipboard, recognising one of the many handwriting styles she saw almost every day in the manuscript notes.

"I got them three days ago," he said. "One had your telephone number. The other contained a tape recording. I played it. There was almost nothing but static." He busied himself with the recorder again, trying to determine the least offensive way of saying what he knew she'd hate to hear. "If I were you, I'd be scared to death going through this. The whole thing is odd, even bizarre. And no one you talk to is going to understand it enough to discuss it with you. After all, how would you feel if somebody said to you, 'Hey, there are fifty of me. I'm fifty different people. I do things I'm not aware of. There are blanks in my life for which I cannot account.''

Stanley let that sink in and went on. "Unfortunately, ignoring these people won't make them go away. We're not treating a cold here, or even cancer. The documentation on multiples is scarce. The proof that others have gone through it, the way they managed, or even how their various persons expressed themselves as they emerged . . . it would be nice if you could run down to your local newsstand or talk to other multiples and reassure yourself that what you're experiencing is normal.''

The person in front of him wasn't deaf to his voice but she gave no sign of agreement.

"It's a hard thing to face. The choice,'' he said, "is yours.''

Who heard him now? Her reality could be so alien to him. If it confused him, what did it do to her?

At the door, he stopped to wonder how many more rules of therapy he'd have to break before this was over.

"Most incest victims,'' he said quietly, "most multiples, have a support system of friends and family. You don't. I want you to understand that from now on, I'm your support system. Is that clear?''

It was the closest he'd ever dared to come with her to being parental, authoritative, and nurturing. He waited for the explosion. Instead, something suspiciously like gratitude crept into her eyes. The woman was incapable of expressing it verbally.

She nodded.

At home that night, Stanley dialed Marshall's number. He wondered if their views would coincide.

"This afternoon, after a two-month hiatus,'' Stanley said when Marshall answered, "we had a session and I saw a sort of mirror-image of the woman, someone who surfaces so briefly and seldom that I always thought they were the same. They aren't. The one who emerged this afternoon kept saying, 'I can't get in,' as if she doesn't know how. It made me think: suppose the woman was created as a façade, someone who passed in society because of what she didn't know about the abuse?''

"I didn't want to influence your conclusion, Stanley, but we're in agreement.''

Together they began to sort out what Marshall had been seeing in the manuscript pages, what little Stanley had had time to read of them, and what had come out in the sessions so far: the woman had been created to stand in the stead of the original first-born child. Her other selves referred to the woman as an inanimate object, an entity with no capability for thought—indeed for anything that her other selves did not first give her.

"The Troops,'' Marshall said, "created for themselves the perfect doppelganger; someone with no memory of the abuse beyond a far-away sense of terror . . . of the literally unknown. The woman has been able to operate in society only by virtue of what they call her 'nonexistence.' Had she known all along what the Troops do, she couldn't pass for what society considers normal.''

"Now that I believe it, or rather now that I understand it, how do I tell this woman she's not the first-born, the original child?''

"You don't,'' Marshall said. "The Troops were gone for two months. I think they already told her.''

The calendar said November. The weather had turned cold. Wind knifed through the cracks in the warehouse walls. Inside, on the loft floor, with six-pound weights on her arms and legs, the woman listened to Catherine's voice directing the exercises.

"Don't stop, darling,'' Catherine told her. "There is no such thing as an irretrievable muscle. Thirty times each leg and then thirty times each arm and then a nice jog around the loft, since you're so scared of the street.''

Many levels of awareness were working today and confusion mounted in the woman's mind. "Smoke on the Water'' blared in the background as the arm weights swung from ceiling to floor and back. It felt strange, as if she were lifting only feathers. And quickly, as if two of her people were emerging and retreating unsynchronised, a muscle in her shoulder snapped. She felt the quick jab of searing pain—and it was gone.

She'd never felt pain before.

In a shot she was up off the floor, standing resolutely by the front door. It was a heavy one, made of solid oak. She opened it with fingers that didn't seem like her own and slammed it against her head. She waited. There was no pain.

The tooth infection had finally been beaten down with massive applications of baking soda and peroxide; the lingering temperature rode daily at only 99.5°. The relief gave the woman added energy. She prowled the warehouse loft, until the need to call Stanley became unbearable.

"What about Page?'' the woman whispered. "I look at her when I dare, I think of buying her things to make up for what I can't give her. It's the way I've always expressed emotion, with things, gifts. But she needs a mother, not gifts. She'll be grown up in another two years. Stanley, there's something I should tell you, I would tell you, except it's so . . . Stanley, where's Page's mother?''

"I don't know," he said. "So many of you went through a developmental cut-off; Page's mother may be one of those who just didn't make it. She had a lot to deal with; a pregnancy that to her was the vilest thing on earth. . . . You're doing well," he said into the phone because it was the only thing he could say. "Your progress is fantastic."

"Yes, it is. Except that I shake so much and if anyone told me I had three legs I'd have to check it out before I could say they were wrong."

Her voice was too quiet, as if she had made a decision about something.

"There's a sheet of paper here in the loft," she went on, still in the too-quiet voice, "with airline information. To Rochester, New York."

"Where did it come from?"

"I don't know," she said.

"What do you want to do with it?"

"It'll have to be a joint decision. I don't know at the moment."

The personnel agent faced the woman and shook her head. "This is your résumé? You have an incredibly varied background. You've got to work on your typing, though. We gave you three tests. You scored thirty-seven, eighty-five, and one hundred and twenty-five words per minute. Can you explain that?"

"I want a job," the woman said.

"My dear." The agent shoved her chair back and got up, smoothing the wrinkles from the lap of her dress. "You're capable of almost anything in the work force, but this is a government town. You have no educational credentials for the kind of job you should have. I can't place you. We have entry-level positions, but they'd bore you to death. You wouldn't last. We'd lose our fee."

It was the third employment agency the woman had been to that morning. They all said the same things. Back out on the street the November wind cut through the woman's coat. A sailing leaf flew into her face. Ten-Four grabbed and crushed it with brutal force. After job-hunting for over a month, it had become apparent that employers wanted credentials, and without them, the going wage for a woman was seven dollars an hour.

"I can drive a truck," Ten-Four said.

"Shut up," the woman snarled. "I'm trying to think."

30

"I told you, Norman, it isn't one isolated occurrence that Stanley can pull out like a rotten tooth. It will take a while."

"So much for progress," Norman said over the phone. "Can you meet me for dinner tonight?"

"Dinner? Out? I could make dinner here in the loft."

"Still hiding? If you'd put this thing in perspective; how many times have I told you? Eight years ago that shrink was a fool and now you're burying yourself with another one!"

"Goddammit, I'll meet you for dinner!" Crash. The receiver hit the wall. Seconds later in the kitchen area, the woman felt herself removed, watching. Dish after dish crashed against the walls, a fern was torn to shreds and the dirt flung in all directions. If Norman had been there . . .

I'd have taken his throat in my hands, someone said, *and not let go.*

"Why," Stanley asked, "didn't you tell Norman how you felt?"

"Are you crazy?" she whispered. "It would hurt him."

"Do you hurt?" Stanley asked whoever was listening. Pain was usually buried under rage; until fully surfaced, both were poisonous. He decided to try an old method, designed to let a client see the amount of anger he or she normally kept well-hidden.

"Take that cushion," he said. "Go ahead, take it."

The woman didn't move. There was no sign that another self,

291

whom he only sensed, and whose name he couldn't determine, would move either. Unwilling to bend enough to evidence fully, Black Katherine's presence flickered behind the woman's own. He shoved the pillow in front of the woman's knees.

"Show me the rage," he said. "You know why it's there. I once had to treat a professional killer behind bars. Whoever you are, your eyes are exactly like his."

"A hit man? What was he like?"

"Very much like you," Stanley said. "He could kill with a smile, without an instant of remorse. He was a pro."

The voice was harsh with delight. "On the farms I wasn't evolved enough and by the time I was actually born, the stepfather lived too far away. But opportunities recur."

"Hit that." Stanley pointed to the pillow. "Go ahead, show me the rage. Pretend it's the stepfather."

Neither the woman nor Black Katherine would lift an arm, so he did it for them. He lifted and let the arm drop five times. The woman laid her head on the pillow and began to sob.

"I hate me," she wept. "I hate me."

She was saying what most incest victims said. Hatred that should have been directed toward her abuser had been directed inward.

"I don't know where your angry friend went just now, but you've got to let that kind of emotion out. It kept you alive through those two farmhouses. It's the healthiest part of yourself. If you don't let it out, one of your selves will, and you won't be there to designate recipients. People may be frightened, they may try to negate your anger, pass it off as momentary insanity. But you aren't insane and you have a right to every last ounce of anger."

"I have none," she said tiredly.

"It's there. Believe me."

While waiters glided past in the softly lit restaurant, the woman hid her damp palms against the tablecloth. Before ordering, Norman had outlined his plans for Page and how he intended to shape her into a "respectful" human being. He'd gone into religion and how he believed it a good thing, steering people down the proper paths of life, especially, he'd said, those teenagers with no sense of respect for their parents.

His placid face, his self-assured belief that he had the right to lay down laws for another person . . . a child. Be calm, too many Troop members thought; don't let it show, don't react.

The woman heard a verbal agreement to encourage Page to study more and cut out the frivolity. She gripped the wineglass hard.

"Norman, this intense desire of Page's for friendships, the fact that she can't stand to be alone for a minute, shows a feeling of rejection."

"Phillips says so, right? I've never rejected her. She needs to crack the books. Nobody's life is perfect and I won't mollycoddle her when it comes to grades."

"I rejected her, Norman, and that's my fault, but I won't get down on my knees to you about it."

"You're raising your voice, you're getting angry," he warned. "Can't you sit quietly and enjoy this meal?"

"Once upon a time, I sat in a farmhouse, quietly as you say, when I should have gotten up and smashed my stepfather's head in. You want me to be a lady now and keep my voice down. Have you any idea how that makes me want to hit you?"

She handed him a brown paper parcel and stood up.

"You've been angry all night," he said evenly. "You can't control your emotions so you're beating retreat now like a spoiled child."

"You bet we are. Much as that offends your sense of propriety."

"What offends me is the way you're throwing your life away by concentrating on hatred for your stepfather. It's crazy!"

In unison with a self whose teeth were gritted, the woman leaned down to stare into Norman's eyes.

"The manuscript is in that package," she said. "Read it and then tell us the anger is unwarranted, that it's out of proportion."

Norman would laugh at the manuscript. Twelve wished he didn't have it and the woman, feeling someone else directly behind herself, wished she could remember exactly what was in it.

His call came in well after midnight.

"Dear christ," he said. "Your stepfather deserves more than death. Your manuscript made me angry too. Not just for your loss but for my own and Page's. But you should try to make the emergence of these other selves more real in the manuscript. It isn't real the way you're writing it."

"I'm sorry," she said, because if nothing else in the pages

293

was clear or real to her, the emergence of the other selves was. "That's the way it happens, exactly as it's written."

Had Phillips ever mentioned putting her away for a while, Norman asked. The woman misunderstood and told him she was fine. Norman asked if it had been Rabbit, frothing at the mouth and howling, just before the woman had left him for good.

"We think so, yes."

"You think so? You mean you haven't catalogued these people yet?" Norman sounded horrified.

"It takes time. Some of them are very frightened. There are so many of them."

"How many?" he demanded.

"Over fifty to date." She didn't give him the new figure. Norman would never believe it.

He made a choking sound. The woman felt the anger thinning out. Norman, a layman without Stanley's background, understood, merely because he'd been shown the actuality of it by the manuscript. There was hope.

"Sorry," the man said, his arms loaded with packages.

"You've got super reflexes, mother."

Page grinned as they prowled the racks for her winter coat. The woman, however, grew quiet, filled with someone's memory of the man who had just shoved her without meaning to—and how her arm had swung back, ready to strike. Sometimes, seeing exactly how much instant rage so many were capable of . . . it wouldn't take much to deal a lethal blow. There were times when she sensed just how satisfying such a blow might be if directed at an enemy. Might Page ever be considered an enemy?

She didn't wait until they'd finished shopping. She called from a pay phone while Page window-shopped in a pet store.

"No," Stanley said over the phone. "No danger to Page, not from you and not from the others."

She took Page home and watched her race around the perimeter of the loft, her hair flying in the sunlight. When she inspected the worm farm and declared that its inhabitants had multiplied, the woman shrugged. All she hoped was that Page didn't run into any of the other things that seemed to pop up in strange corners. Some were weird, some were downright frightening. But each time she tried to remove any of them, small voices told her not to.

294

• • •

On the heels of the woman's phone call, Marshall dialed Stanley.

"Somebody's finally figured out a term for what your client's going through," he said. "It's called the 'revolving-door syndrome.' Probably the most frantic, confusing time of all for a multiple; it happens when the going gets really rough. The people come and go rapidly, yet the changes, while almost constant, are fully formed."

Page left immediately after dinner that night, to go home and study. The woman found herself at the hot plate, brewing tea. Haughty and unsmiling, with her knees primly together under the table in the loft's kitchen area, Lady Catherine sat, ready to be served. In front of her was a fragile cup the woman had seen many times but never used.

Of the group expressing themselves to the woman at that moment, no one neglected to use their name. Catherine snorted. She didn't have a title and always, snidely, referred to herself in Lady Catherine's presence as "Just Plain Catherine." Actually, Catherine did not regard herself as plain at all, but rather the best of the lot. She lifted an eyebrow and drummed her fingernails on the tablecloth.

"Why," the woman asked, "couldn't you two have had different names?"

"She's not original," said Catherine, studying her image in the glassware. "She copied me."

An argument broke out over who had emerged first. The woman tried to evade them all, but their strength today forced an examination of each one. Lady Catherine of the prim kneecaps refused a cookie but Lambchop ate two, catching the crumbs on her tongue.

"I was here first," Lady Catherine told the woman. "If it were not for me, there'd be no manners, no sense of proper behavior. And while I countenance no abuse, verbal or otherwise, you, on the other hand, let everyone rag you to death." She adjusted her skirt and breathed through narrow, fine nostrils, elevating her chin.

"Screw you, darling." Catherine opened a bottle of wine.

"None for the child!" screamed Lady Catherine, sending the glass out of Catherine's hand with a blow that spoke not of drawing rooms, but of downtown bars.

• • •

295

"Stanley," the woman said in the next session, "they're children."

"Some of them are. For others, their development was simply halted along the way."

She looked over at him, through both her own eyes and those of the Troop member right behind her. "They're shoving something into my mind right now. . . . Do you understand how somebody could go their entire life like me . . . with no act of penetration, anywhere in their head? Especially with what the others say about the farmhouses?"

"Yes, I think I do," Stanley said.

"It doesn't surprise you a bit?"

"We're trained to ask the right questions and listen carefully to the answers. Right from the first day I met you, you couldn't say the words for sex organs when they related to anything remotely connected to you. Others in the Troop Formation have had sex, but you weren't there."

"Who was?"

"They'll tell us when they're ready. My sense is, there's more than one, possibly as many as four."

"Oh god," she said, as somebody thought of Mean Joe. "Does that mean I could be a lesbian?"

Stanley smiled and shook his head. Then he laughed. "No," he said. "My senses are not leading me in that direction."

"People like Sharon and Norman are confused. They insist that to a degree, everyone has multiple personalities, that everyone has different sides, and sometimes they can't remember things either."

"In your case," Stanley said, "we're talking about a continuum. The opposite end of the spectrum. Other people remember what their different sides or personalities do. They don't have extensive memory blanks. Researchers feel that inside any one multiple group, there's someone who knows everything. I don't know if that's true in your case, or if everyone in the Troop Formation may be said to have extensive memory blanks."

"It's really hard in the manuscript to convey me, how the thoughts and feelings of the others just . . . flow through me while I'm empty. The process, as you call it—sometimes describing it makes everybody really angry. It's like we write for two days and spend six trying to make things clear. Do you, at least, understand more now? Do you understand that at this moment—as always—the others are flowing through me with their thoughts?''

"I'm afraid I do," Stanley said. Her innocent facial and verbal expression told him that she didn't understand the full implication of what she was saying. Logical progression made her situation plain—his human compassion still made an attempt to deny that situation.

Kill him. For days the chant had sounded so good. But each time the woman saw what it would take to kill the stepfather, she ran smack into the idea of having to touch him, to be in the same room with him.

Bobby Dylan's voice on the stereo blended with the chant as he ground out, beyond a wall of static, the song Black Katherine loved. Bobby Dylan seemed to know what he was talking about. As he sang about his renegade subject, the words pierced the Weaver's veil. The words exposed in the woman's mind another layer of Troop reality.

> She never stumbles, she's got no place to fall
> She's nobody's child, the law can't touch her at all
> She wears an Egyptian ring that sparkles before she
>   speaks,
> She's a hypnotist's collector, you are the one she can
>   teach

The hatred in Black Katherine's mind raced with voracious appetite, through the woman's as well. The mirror above the worm farm, alive with a light of its own in strong sunlight, cast a glow on the face reflected back. As if two wild animals had caught sight of each other in a forest glen, the stranger in the mirror gazed into the woman's eyes. Trapped in Black Katherine's world, the woman froze. The song played on:

> For Halloween buy her a trumpet
> For Christmas give her a gun.

Their eyes locked, one upon the other; and in the strange, mirrored eyes, the woman read over the words of the song, a maddened pain, a torrential outpouring of hatred. The song faded. The woman tried to break away but in the silent loft, the battle raged between them. A lifetime of anger and anguish rushed from one brain to the other. It seared the soul of both.

With a last torn look of acknowledgement, the woman forced her gaze away, and as she did, the strange eyes seemed to follow her. They were pale apple-green, with a hairline of black at the rims and in the center of each one, a tiny, dead-black iris.

That night in the Tunnel, the story being read to the children took on a particularly bloody tone.

31

"It was like looking into the jaws of hell."

"My sense is that she's been in hell." Stanley regarded his client matter-of-factly. "First of all, you ask questions because you need reassurance. There's nothing wrong with that. Second, I believe I have heard of such a phenomenon, but only once. That doesn't mean it isn't going on out there. Let me try to understand. You saw someone else in the mirror?"

"Music was playing, that Bobby Dylan song 'She Belongs to Me.' When I looked in the mirror, I saw Black Katherine. For a minute I just stood there, she wouldn't let me go, her eyes locked with mine. She seemed to be in front of me, superimposed over me but completely separate; she sent me her thoughts, they entered my mind, and I knew what rage is. I knew her."

"How did that make you feel?" Stanley asked softly.

"Not so much fright as empathy I guess her thoughts, with all that she's been through, really scared me. But that made me understand the rage. Instead of hating her for it, and wanting her to go away, I just wanted to hold her, take the pain away. But nobody can do that, can they?"

"Someday, yes."

"There's more. I've tried to walk right up to the flicks, four giant steps, but then I run away. I'm such a coward."

Stanley put down the clipboard, wanting to strike something with it. "You aren't a coward," he said. "I've told you, I stand in awe of incest victims. Somehow you manage to survive against pressures, tortures, as great as any concentration camp ever devised."

From the moment she entered the studio this afternoon, he'd sensed how she hung right on the fine line between relative order (no matter how disorderly it might seem) and complete chaos.

"Except for moments of extreme awareness," he said, "most of you are too caught up in the machinery, to feel the agony at its fullest. One day on down the road, you'll be telling me it was a bitch, a bummer, a shot in the head."

"What will happen to me then?"

"We'll all be here for you," he told her, "your people and me."

"The pain." There was a flicker of apprehension. "I don't feel pain now. I tried to feel it the other day, but the others don't let it through to me. One day soon, I know they will."

"We'll give you," he leaned forward, grinning, "only the most exquisite pain."

His manner had broken through the tension, the dread that had been circling. He'd managed to encompass both the absurd bravado of whistling in the dark—and the expression of enough confidence in her to treat the problem as joke material. She laughed, glad for the distraction before having to tell him the latest recall.

"Last night I saw myself standing there in the field, no higher than the stepfather's belt buckle, his pockets were so tempting. I couldn't figure out at first why I had to get my hands into them. The thought of warmth was in my mind; I wanted whatever was in those pockets. Suddenly we were further out in the field. The sun was buzzing hot, droning; the light lay in the field like a reflection from a giant mirror.

"He's lying down and his pants are open and I'm on top of him. I see that goddamned pink thing so clearly. He positions me so that I'm squatting above it, and the thing touches me."

The woman had been holding her head between her hands. As Sewer Mouth emerged, the head whipped upward, the teeth clenched. Stanley heard both of them speaking, one after the other.

"The feelings inside me the whole time the recall was hitting were—say it, bitch—erotic."

Sewer Mouth spit over her right shoulder. The woman's eyes were closed. Suddenly the words weren't hers or Sewer Mouth's, but Rachel's. Rachel, having evolved from Sewer Mouth over a nine-year period, had finally been born at the second farmhouse, exactly what she would always remain; a fifteen-year-old with the knowledge of a whorehouse madam. Rachel conveyed her nature today without her usual sensuous movements; an acknowledgement, perhaps, that many in the Troop Formation considered her overt sensuality an affront. The woman sat there, hearing Rachel's voice, young and very far away.

"It's over," the woman said. "The stepfather is up, closing his trousers. But just as quickly . . . whether it happened that day or another, I couldn't tell . . . but I follow him. *I seek him out, I want those pockets.* Of course I know that the pockets are not primary. The pockets represent something else." An unpleasant smile flitted over her face. "The pockets represent the pleasure. Over the fields, stumbling, running as fast as the stepfather ever ran after me, *I run after him!*"

Someone again shoved it into her mind and let it remain for a moment: the fifteen-year-old girl in the field with the stepfather was another self.

"You weren't there all the time, remember that." Stanley's posthypnotic words were spoken hurriedly. He couldn't tell who heard him or who was spitting the words out.

"I find him, as if we were surreptitious lovers. His body is warm and I rub my own against it, son of a dirty rotten, shit-faced bitch, it was so clear the other day, where does it go?"

"The others take it away momentarily, to give you a chance to recover," Stanley said.

Sewer Mouth's angry street language, and the now simultaneous laughing and crying, grew louder. The battle went on, between the woman and which of the others besides Sewer Mouth Stanley could not tell. He saw it again, the wild flurry of muscle structure and the cheekbones shifting upward, the jawline lowering. The face had become a masque.

"You sought him out, looking for warmth," Stanley's voice was soft. "Who held you as a child?"

"No one." The masquelike expression had shifted again, leaving the impression of nothingness behind.

"Did your mother ever hold you? Caress you with affection and tenderness, tell you how pretty you were?"

"No."

"You panic now because there were good times with your stepfather, when he first took you and your mother to live in that first farmhouse. There was laughter and affection from him, aside from the incest. But if there was any good in him, that makes you the bad one, doesn't it?"

"Yes." The eyes were now dead and completely empty.

Stanley believed that just behind the masque, he might ᵇ
seeing the essence of his client, for the first time.

"He's still to blame totally, for all of it. No matter how
warmth or affection he supplied when you needed it, in th
of a mother who didn't know how or wasn't willing to n ..ᵤᵣₑ
you, your stepfather manipulated, guided you, into areas too
much for any child to handle. Your stepfather was the perpetrator
of the crime and he is guilty. Not you."

You can't hold off, Stanley told himself.

"Do you remember the day your daughter was born?"

The figure before him, completely motionless, stared at the wall;
the head swung slowly towards him. Somewhere far back in the
empty eyes, a flicker of something he could not fathom crossed the
wall of the iris. The figure opened its mouth and spoke.

"What?"

Stanley sat there, looking at what the woman had never seen
because each time she had ever looked in the mirror, one of the
others had always looked back. Stanley could find no expression
of life in this face. For one awful moment he understood.

He was looking at the woman, devoid of input by the others.
He was looking at her as she was, as she had been from the day
of her "birth."

Avoiding the reflection of her body in the mirror that night, the
woman put on the nightgown and the white ankle socks, still
negating the existence of the other selves as she dressed. She
felt someone's awe at trying to fully accept any of this. Jeannie
Lawson had said that her acceptance had come during the final
moment of integration and had been almost "spiritual."

A cup of hot chocolate belonging to Me sat by the bed. Me
seldom came out. The woman sensed that the child did not find
things fun. The woman crawled under the blankets, too tired and
confused to feel the terror. Except that she knew it was there.

As she handed over the sheaf of cartoons, the woman was un-
prepared for the look of shock on the face of Ms. York, the
account executive for the advertising agency.

"They're precisely what we wanted: strange little children,
the lot of them, each one individual, easily remembered. But
this job," Ms. York protested, "is budgeted to take eleven
months. We didn't mean for you to do so many of the drawings
in six weeks."

302

Stung, the woman folded but Catherine did not.

"Really? Shall I take back the majority of them?"

Ms. York turned, distracted, muttering to Catherine that she must wait while she straightened out the timing on the project. How, she muttered, could the agency pay so much of the fee, all at once? Ms. York picked up the cartoons and marched into the back offices of the agency, slamming the door shut behind her.

With distaste, Lady Catherine observed the disarray of Ms. York's desk, how her coat hung askew on the coat rack, the mad filing system inside her open briefcase. Expressly annoying to Lady Catherine was that the briefcase was plastic, not leather, and she elevated her nose. Inefficiency everywhere, and bad taste as well. Peasants.

Ms. York returned. "Look," she said. "It's almost five. How about a drink someplace where we can throw this around quietly? I don't know what we're going to do."

"No thank you," Lady Catherine said. "We have plans."

"One moment then," Ms. York said, as if held together with steel rods. "Let me catch up with one of the department heads."

The door slammed shut behind her for the second time.

"Do that." It was plain Catherine who picked up the phone on Ms. York's desk without asking. Plain Catherine never asked anyone for anything. She took.

Page answered immediately as Catherine smiled into the phone. "Hello, darling," Catherine said. "Did your father make an appointment for you so that we can investigate learning hypnosis?"

"My father changed his mind," Page told her. "He says hypnosis screws up your brain. Mommie, does it?"

Hands shaking with rage, the woman dialed Stanley's number.

"In view of the amount of hypnosis I've had, Stanley, how screwed up does Norman think I am? He doesn't believe hypnosis will help Page so he can't possibly believe it's helped me. He does think I'm crazy!"

The woman heard the low-pitched, hissing rage in her voice. Stanley told her the anger level was good but the volume needed to be revved up a little.

"I have a job," she said. "We're cartooning a five-hundred-page manual for an ad agency."

Stanley wondered which of the Troop members was the artist for this job. He asked what kind of cartoons.

"Children," she said. "For some reason, as I draw them the flicks are wilder than ever and the smells; if I smell manure one more time, I'll scream. I'm scared. I shake all day doing the cartoons at home and then I shake while delivering them. It's hard to be sure I've done enough, well enough, but I guess we're OK. There's something else. My half brother's face is in one of the sketches. I could never draw that well, Stanley, but there he was, line for line. As soon as I saw his face, the others slid it into my mind: the stepfather did horrible things to him, Stanley, things that went beyond emotional or physical abuse."

"Sexual abuse usually goes hand in hand with the other two," Stanley said. He didn't like doing therapy on a new issue over the phone, but she sounded ready for it.

"Would the stepfather do that? The others seem to be saying that he would."

"Your stepfather was capable of anything. That's a blanket statement and I make no apologies for it. As a child, I experienced, as do most children, a very few unpleasant things. So I pulled back on those occasions. But within the Troop Formation, the first-born child pulled out completely. You, the other selves, were created to handle what she could not."

"Stanley, what can be worse than what the others keep shoving at me? They're getting stronger, they seem so active lately."

"They're going to bring further recall. In order for them to do that, you must get to know each one. You see, in view of all that went on, you still don't have enough memory. Perhaps it's not that they're stronger," Stanley forced himself to be more direct, "but that you are more aware of them."

An hour later, the woman sat with smoke in her eyes, acclimating herself to the low-lit, noisy room. There'd been no time to repair makeup, or straighten her hair after the windy street.

"I adore happy hour," Ms. York said. "Two for one."

"It gets you there faster, right?" Elvira surfaced completely. She threw back her head and laughed, snapping her fingers to the beat of the band behind them.

"You're a listener," Ms. York said, well into her fourth bourbon. "Listening is a fine art that disappeared a thousand years ago. I can't believe you're real."

"Oh, we're real. Tell me. What's your first name and what were all those little bottles on your desk this afternoon?"

"Thementa, and please don't laugh. My mother was a Southern lady who married a crabby Northern banker. She named me to let the world know he'd driven her crazy. It's a sort of take-off on 'dementia.' As for the pills, I have backaches, allergies, and an ulcer. The advertising business, you know.''

"My ass," Elvira said, now transmitting for Sewer Mouth and Ten-Four, who needed time before they could surface in a socially public place. "What do you guys do for fun?"

The woman heard only music, "Devil with a Blue Dress on."

"At the agency we expire a little more each day, the pressures, you'll never know." And Thementa related the terrors of her job as she knew them, complaining forthrightly, to the woman's horror, loudly in a public place.

"You're so cold," Thementa said, "and then you're so understanding. I don't understand you at all."

Catherine gave an enigmatic smile. "Everyone," she said, gazing around the room, "will understand us very shortly. That's why we're here."

From the far reaches of the Tunnel the brogue sounded. The Weaver listened to the weighty statements being made and halted at his task. Tonight the woman would be privy to, and would remember, large portions of the evening ahead of her.

This will be fun, *Me said.* Do we get to stay up and watch or do we have to go to bed?

Sleep is not so beneficial as instruction, *said the Irishman.* Watch if y' will.

What are you drinking? *Me asked.*

Nothin' y'd be interested in. There's not a bloody drop o' chocolate in it.

Through the smoke and the noise, the woman could not say what had passed through her mind just then. She watched Thementa head off to the ladies' room and congratulated herself. It was turning out to be a rather nice evening. She lit a cigarette, staring at the one already in the ashtray. Hadn't Thementa taken hers with her to the ladies' room?

A well-knit man of medium height, wafting the persuasive scent of Givenchy Gentleman, with hair so dark that it was almost black, and an enormous pair of blue eyes, came to ask for a dance. The woman took a last sip of scotch and went into his arms. And it began.

There was faint conversation, heard as if from another room; she "stood back" as if watching a movie not in Technicolor but

305

in black and white. She would remember it afterward, how the colour had gone out of everything. The actors and actresses, in the form of bar patrons, moved in front of her; the words she thought were coming from her mouth changed, even as she heard them, into other words—that had nothing to do with her.

Tonight was much like her whole existence; wandering about, disconnected from everything and everyone. Under her fingertips, she felt the man's suit jacket. She caressed it for a moment, attempting by the action to absorb him, make him real, to give her some bearing on who and what he was. She drifted in his arms, dancing the way he did by incorporating a borrowed observance of his dance steps into her own. She laughed when he did and tried hard to follow his conversation. It got away from her too often, and she felt herself slipping into her own mind and then beyond.

The man led her back to the table, his voice resonant and assured, as he sat down, still talking. He showed no sign of boredom or the urge to leave. Thementa had altered her black business suit and severe hairdo to a lowered neckline and loosened hair. The woman, in her beige-on-beige clothes, without even a bright scarf to relieve the tedium, felt out of place among the casually dressed dancers.

But Thementa appeared irked after a while, and the dark curling tendrils from her long, floating hair were electrified and bristling. Thementa's ire had to do with the man's job description. Since the woman couldn't catch what he was saying, she leaned closer to grab Thementa's words.

"He's in nuclear fission," Thementa hissed. "He's right here in town, he's one of those *bomb* makers." Thementa didn't care that she talked loudly enough for everyone in the room to hear her, even with the band at full blast.

The man defended himself but no remark he made struck Thementa pleasantly. The woman discovered him gesturing to her in a way that suggested dancing. She smiled as if she'd heard, and they carved a path through the dancers.

He talked as they danced. She grew more confused. He had some kind of cadence to his voice, twined in words she wasn't catching fully. It was charming but phony, she was sure. It floated in and out of her mind, and eventually she lost track of time completely.

Thementa mentioned the cadence to her when they went back to the table for another drink and the woman floated away again. Irish? The man had no accent at all that she had noticed.

306

When a male mouth, she didn't know whose, fastened itself on her cheek a while later and she felt strangely like a twelve-year-old, she simply went along with it. She had no kneecaps. Her legs, limber as hell, whirled and spun her around the floor to every beat the band played.

I don't dance, she kept screaming in her head.

But I do, Twelve said.

"My dear," Thementa slurred her words as she danced past in the arms of a balding salesman, "you seem to be having a great time! Who is Nails?"

Nails. The name was one of those things buried deep in the woman's brain that surfaced seldom and made her want to throw up. Were her people carousing here in a public place? She tried to blame it on the scotch and knew she wasn't drunk.

Want to hear a secret? Twelve asked.

The woman did not want to hear anything.

During a social evening, Twelve said, *when so many of us are out, we may get only one drink apiece. We can last all night. Our drinks do not affect you. We are all separate from one another. Of course, one of us may drink faster and consume more than the rest. That person might get soused but it's his or her problem, not yours.*

The woman faded. But one of her people yanked her right back, threw her into the gyrating dancers, and she found herself facing a black man who'd become separated from his partner. The rubber knees she possessed as if they were hers got right into the beat of the music with him, propelling her in his wake. He told her that he studied something heavy at Columbia University and wrote songs for distraction. He told her she was brilliant and a lot of other things, but the woman heard none of them.

She wondered if she were having a good time tonight. Possibly, possibly not. The black man laughed just then, and with difficulty she focused on his face. He was handsome and very young, but there was a look of pain in his eyes that caught the woman's attention. The attention became riveted. As it did, she experienced something so strong that is was like being wrested from herself and thrown bodily across the room. Another's thoughts entered her mind; and in that brief second, the woman knew what it was to despise injustice and prejudice and man's inhumanity to man.

The one who lived far back in the Tunnel had just sent the

woman all that he had ever known and objected to on the subject; he sent it en masse in one huge, lightning-quick wave. He was many things, but this thing, above all others, crowned his "essence"; it was the core of his being and the woman felt it, was inundated by it.

The black man laughed. "I'm having a great time," he said. "You know music, and you can talk about anything."

The woman felt a hand take the man's arm. There in the dim light with the smoke a grey haze over their heads, someone smiled a twelve-year-old smile and talked about subjects so deep that the woman heard them and could not be sure they existed.

Twelve, with her flying mind, had been transmitting the words of the Tunnel Troop member, and much of his brogue had been hidden behind her young voice. The conversation had indeed been deep, the kind that wraps people together in an exposure of emotion unfelt in most lifetimes.

Nails, whose duty it was, among other things, to keep the woman from such exposure, stepped in.

"Watch it," she said to the man firmly.

The woman wasn't there as Twelve took the man deeper into himself, laying out ponderous truths in a wondering fashion, some of it expressed by the thought transference of the one who lived in the Tunnel and some of it her own. Twelve marveled at the black man's mind and thought of Mean Joe who kept his own brilliance under wraps.

The woman surfaced occasionally but from a distance and knew there were tears on her face that did not belong to her. The man's eyes were misty too. What was everyone saying?

The woman never knew where the time had gone. Suddenly the Irish bomb maker, as Thementa called him, was kissing the woman's hand at the door and all the lights in the bar were going off, a signal that the evening was over.

Seated in her car in the parking lot behind the bar, the woman looked down to find the bomb maker's dark head resting in her lap and his feet hanging out the window. She shook him and he didn't move; she tried to be polite about it while shaking him harder, and he leaped up. It took a while, smiling and making excuses, to convince him she couldn't go home with him. She accepted his telephone number and saw him to his car around the corner, feeling competent and in full control, but desperate to get away from the sound of his voice although she couldn't have said what bothered her about it.

Thementa's voice trilled over the phone the next morning, "I danced all night. My feet are killing me."

"Arrrgh," the woman said, peering from gritty eyes.

"You certainly have a lot of energy. I seem to have more than my own share this morning. It's the best I've felt in a long time."

In the warehouse loft, traipsing at the woman's back like a stealthy ghost, one of the Troops had left a trail of activity behind in the form of Alka-Seltzer packets and drinking glasses frosted with a powdery white residue.

She started talking in the session that afternoon, and couldn't seem to stop.

"Stanley, the Alka-Seltzer glasses frightened me. I was tired from lack of sleep but somebody had a hangover. The evidence sat in front of me, in those glasses . . . you don't know what that's like, to see the actual traces of someone besides yourself. They're angry with me, what can I do to make them understand that I get frightened? The next day, there is guilt over having a good time, even from a removed position, the shame over things I imagine must have happened."

"You've got to realise how active and strong, how much a part of your life they always were. They protected you. All they're asking for now, is what they've always had: their own lives."

"I wish I understood that. If I created anybody, I certainly don't remember it."

"You didn't do it alone," Stanley said.

"We created ourselves?"

"You are all real parts of the first-born child." He knew he hadn't answered her question. Nobody knew how, in spite of the research going on.

"I don't know what it means," she said as the session ended, "but someone is reading aloud at night to the children. It reminds me of the farm when the mother used to read to us."

"That sounds very nice," Stanley said.

"Nice? There's something ominous about it. I can't tell whose voice is reading, or even what the subject matter is. The children seemed lulled by the voice and the story, but I'm not. I can't shake the feeling that it's a sort of prelude."

32

The next five nights in succession, the children listened to the sonorous voice and nodded between wakefulness and sleep. The woman sensed in some of them an almost terrifying quickness, a keen comprehension of the most difficult of concepts. For the voice wasn't reading only children's stories; the voice seemed to be imparting an inner knowledge born of both extreme compassion and a warlike desire for justice.

One morning, standing in a bright shaft of light reflected off the snow outside, the woman found a sheet of paper in the typewriter and when she tried to read its contents a second time, the page was gone. Her mind would not reconvey to her a single word.

Nails drove to the session that morning, enjoying the snow on the streets and the long fingers of ice on each tree branch and twig. The snow and ice reminded her of the farmhouses, the utter silence of the countryside during long winters—and of the contrasting turmoil and screaming inside the farmhouses. Nails smiled. Christmas was now just a month away.

In that identical moment, Nails' anger surged into the woman's mind. She almost smiled all by herself, the pleasure was that great.

The pleasure faded.

Having emotions, even secondhand, entails responsibility, someone said. *It means involvement, response, confrontation.*

• • •

Almost before the session began, the woman laid the sheet of paper in front of him. Stanley read it:

As many years ago as there are drops o' water in the ocean 'r grains o' sand upon the beach, a mighty warrior rode down from the hills and raised his sword on high, preparin' to slay the vast numbers o' enemy stretched before him. So too, rode a man o' mere words with no sword a'tal, only the power o' his mortal tongue.

The battle raged on for as many years as there are drops o' water in the ocean 'r grains o' sand upon the beach, the mighty warrior and the man o' mere words fightin' with supreme diligence and dedication to duty, each preserved from the other within his own beliefs and desire t' win.

And the time came then, t' count the bodies o' the fallen enemy and 'twas discovered to the great shock and dismay of the observin' crowds that the mighty warrior had indeed slain to the left and slain to the right—as far as the eye could see, and a bloody, awe inspirin' sight it was.

But behold—the enemy as attacked by the man o' mere words, stumblin' and damaged in droves, ner t'be safe ner sane again—stabbed and gutted beyond repair, diminished in mind and spirit by the tongue o' the man o' blindin', roilin' words, goin' forth t' carry the message far . . .

And so it goes—each man o' us, no matter his method o' fightin', and preserved one from the other in his own beliefs and desires t' win, each within his own fashion, must mind the deadly sabre, whether it be forged o' steele 'r flesh.

EAN FOR THE TROOPS

Ean. Stanley laid down the page. The name had an Irish ring, although he would have expected it to be spelled with an "I" as in "Ian." Did Troop members hide, even behind spelling choices?

"Whose name is this?" he asked.

"Is there a name on it?" The woman's face was blank; she stared at the page, fixedly.

It had been in front of him all along; today it finally sank in. She heard, smelled, felt, remembered—saw—only at the discretion of the others.

"Now that you've read it," she said, "what does it mean?

311

The voice was reading that to the children. The next morning the page was in the typewriter. Later I found it in my purse. I can't seem to keep track of it, it never stays in one place.''

"I think Ean, whoever he is, means several things. The most obvious, is that the pen is mightier than the sword. Beyond that, he's saying it required as much courage for the man 'o' mere words' to go into battle armed with nothing more than his tongue, as it did for the man with the sword of steel.''

"Courage," she said. "The thing I haven't got.''

"Are you telling me that it takes no courage at all to sit in a house with that manuscript in front of your face, no matter how much you do or do not grasp in it? I don't buy that. You might not have lived these experiences the first time. You may even be 'pulled-back' as you 'live' them this time, but they're getting heavier, both in content and in the way the others give them to you. I'd say that takes an extraordinary amount of courage, the kind most people haven't got.''

"No.''

"No? Would you like to know what kind of company you're in? There are two hundred cases of multiple personality, documented since the early eighteen-hundreds.'' Stanley waited for the reaction.

"In the entire United States?'' The woman's voice was a whisper.

"The entire world,'' he said. "In the next three years I expect that perhaps another two hundred will be documented. Yours will be one of them. You will have done most of the documentation yourself, through the manuscript and the training films.''

"So few cases,'' she said.

"Exactly. But it's out there and we know that it may not be as rare, relatively speaking, as once thought. Would you tell me that other multiples are not courageous, that it didn't take guts and stamina for them to survive?''

"No.''

"Then give yourself the same points. You've also had something else to contend with. My therapy methods move a client faster than usual. Sometimes too fast for safety and surely too fast for complete comfort.''

Sewer Mouth told him that the Troops were angry as hell. With all that anger motivating them, she said, the entire formation should have reached their goal of therapy completion.

"Some of you are hesitant, still feeling me out. Some of you

312

know that we're working toward the merging of everyone into one whole human being who will enjoy whatever is enjoyed now as separate people.''

The woman had surfaced again. "Merging? I'm not sure anyone here wants to do that, Stanley, I don't want to do that. It wouldn't be fair to any of us.''

"Well, it's something to think about," Stanley told her.

"There's something else here, long before we come to that. It won't go away.''

"Your fear that you've done something comparable to murder? Suppose Mean Joe, for instance, that person who in your mind is a strapping black man with the power of the gods and the will to protect the little ones, were to do something . . . ultimate? What if the little ones were really in danger and he had to act in an ultimate way to save them? What if there were no other choice?''

"You mean if someone were about to rape or kill one of us?''

"It happens all the time in society. Would you sit there without defending yourself?''

"Why can't I accept what you say and be done with it?''

"The patterns of a lifetime don't go away so easily. The progress you're making, all of you, is remarkable. You can't see it fully, just yet.''

"I know you won't call it progress when I tell you that we are going to kill the stepfather, Stanley. But we are. Regardless of anything else, courage or no courage, we are. And nobody here is dumb enough to think we'll get off scot-free. Just remember when it happens, Mean Joe had nothing to do with it.''

Stanley watched her shrugging into the raincoat and tugging on her boots. Short of locking her up, there wasn't much that could be done about the decision.

"Stanley," she said at the door, "say that to me one more time, that thing you say about the chips. Sharon says it's a trite phrase, but I don't care. Somehow, every time you say it, I feel better.''

Stanley laid down the clipboard. "Let the chips fall where they may.''

"Thank you, Stanley. For whatever reason, I find more courage in those words than any others, except maybe, 'Let the devil take the hindemost.' I love it. I really do.''

• • •

That night the woman heard a garbled conversation. Someone who sounded like a preteenager explained with grave politeness to someone else that, loosely translated, "Let the devil take the hindemost" meant "to moon the devil." The translation was not well received. Someone of a more literal nature, and not nearly so polite, cursed and said, "Be real, you twit." The woman wanted to hear more and could not. She went on applying "Worth" liberally, at throat and wrists. Smelling good was important these days; it drove the odour of manure from her nostrils. Me, with her teddy bear in her lap, sipped hot cocoa and yawned. It was past her bedtime. For one tiny moment the woman felt someone's fright and a desire to stay home. At that, "Tube Snake Boogie" began to play and Elvira screamed aloud. The music played until the woman arrived at the restaurant.

Norman smiled. "I read what you underlined in the book you gave Page. Learning hypnosis sounds good to me. I guess you were right."

The woman raised her glass to his, feeling wonderful and very much in control. That battle was won. A red carnation sat in the vase between their place settings. Its green leaves seemed pressed between the layers of her mind. Green. For no apparent reason, the colour made her smile. She gazed out of the window onto the street beyond the restaurant. She did not see the snow. She saw green land, be-hilled and rolling, misted and stretching forever. She saw the joy of battle and ultimate, triumphant victory.

The woman's fingers were twisted together in her lap. She did not feel her smile grow wider as the fingers slowly relaxed and then went limp, as if time itself were meant to slip through them. Not her own time, but someone else's; someone who touched her mind softly, transferring knowledge so tenderly that she was hardly aware of it. *Time, and the voice was a faint whisper in her mind, is not meant t' be grasped and hoarded, but rather wrung dry o' all its juices and then let go. Because there is plenty o' time and more when that is gone.*

The words held an invitation, and the one who spoke them beckoned to her, unknown and unmenacing. He also held out the idea of the white light: that place free of problems, the need for decisions she felt inadequate to make, wars she was uncertain of winning; and, most of all, the agony and consequent punishment of daring to fight at all. And she heard his laughter as he laid aside the idea of escaping into the white light, as if he knew her mind better than she did.

She'd always tried to run, rather than face anything, and if he took away the possibility of the one sure escape she needed to have ready . . . especially since there was a feeling she couldn't put aside lately, a feeling of dread, that things had reached a boiling point within the Troop Formation, within herself and the one right behind her, and everything was about to blow sky high. . . .

Eventually, she realised that she and Norman had a strange waiter. The man slapped plates down on the table with an icy stare. Norman asked if she couldn't keep her voice down.

"Our chat tonight is turning sour," he said.

Chat? The woman, unaware of any conversation, had wondered why Norman was so silent. She had not spoken a word, afraid that somehow she'd offend him. Why was he giving the other diners embarrassed glances and why were they looking away?

Time slept again for the woman until some of her people got in each other's way as they came and went, holding a conversation with Norman which she could not hear. A piece of chicken lodged in her throat as she tried to swallow, unaware that the act of eating was not her own. She was suddenly gasping for breath, fighting for air. Norman saw her face going red. His own flushed as he reached across the table.

But another Troop member flung the woman's head back and forced breath into her mouth. Dazed, she experienced being helped, even as she knew that no human hand had touched her. She swallowed again with a raw throat and tears from the effort stung her eyes.

"There's no need," Norman said, "to bring that language to a public restaurant. And where did the new one come from?"

"What language? What new one?"

Norman was motionless on his side of the table. "Have you heard any of this conversation tonight?"

"We haven't had any conversation!"

"Slow Hand" played as Nails wheeled into the parking space outside the ad agency. The woman looked at the travel alarm that had replaced her wristwatch. Clocks that sat in her purse worked, watches worn on her body did not. They were twenty minutes late but Elvira refused to budge until the song was over. Someone began to cry, afraid of being late, jeopardising the job.

315

Someone brand new to the woman's complete awareness laid a hand on her arm, then brushed away the tears. The woman felt the smile; tender . . . and uncontrollable. She felt the innocent youth and kindness that was the essence of this new person. Wrapped in all of that, yet standing above and beyond it, the woman became enmeshed in the soaring intelligence of a brilliant mind. She had just met Twelve.

The appointment went well. The woman sensed how easily people responded to Twelve's manner. She had a knack for listening, for turning problems into common meeting grounds, for cutting through to the solution without wounding anyone.

After the appointment the woman found herself out on the street with a different attitude toward the world around her. Some of the fear was gone. They passed a brick wall on the way to lunch. Twelve's hands sought the warmth each brick had absorbed from the late morning sun; she listened to the trickle of melting snow along the sidewalk. Twelve said kind things, and, thunderstruck, the woman heard them and recognised the sensation of being twelve years old out on that dance floor. This was the Troop member who had danced and looked at people, wide-eyed with enjoyment; the one who had talked so deeply with the black man.

The woman sought out her favourite hiding place—the dimestore lunch counter down the street from the ad agency. The food wasn't bad, and it enabled her to be among people without being recognised. Twelve ate a bacon, lettuce, and tomato sandwich. She dropped crumbs everywhere, wanted milk, and looked from side to side, checking out her company manners.

Grimly as it happened, the woman wrote it all down in the daily journal and gave the waitress distracted orders for whatever Twelve fancied. To test this "happening," the woman lit a cigarette after the meal, tasting the flavour of tobacco, as if she'd never smoked with these taste buds before.

Twelve did not cough, her eyes were gleaming.

You're enjoying this, the woman said silently, you've smoked before, haven't you?

Twelve did not answer. The woman was startled by the sound of her own teeth crunching down on the shred of BLT from Twelve's plate. Twelve wanted a strawberry soda; the woman wanted to throw up. She disliked strawberry.

• • •

Wanting that evening to do something without being told for once, and to show them all that she was on their side, the woman brought out milk for dinner.

"What," said Twelve, taking her place at the table, and showing what a normal twelve-year-old she could be once somebody got to know her, "no chocolate milk? I could share this with the little ones if it was chocolate."

The woman made a trip to the local carry-out, bought a carton of Yoo-Hoo, got in the car, and handed it over.

"What," said Twelve. "No straw?"

That night the woman got into bed with a bottle of Yoo-Hoo in her hand while a mad desire for scotch and a cold bottle of beer rattled her taste buds. There were cookie crumbs on her sheets. The little one whose identity she'd never been able to pin down had to be around somewhere, because even with the white socks and the heavy flannel nightgown, the woman's skin felt icy.

"Stop calling me 'the little one,' " said a small voice. "My name is Lamb Chop. It was the only thing I liked to eat on the first farm. Lamb chops with mint jelly."

I didn't wake her up, did I? *Lambchop liked this part of the evening, when everyone was getting ready for bed. It wasn't like the two old farmhouses.*

Mean Joe glanced down at the tiny, sleeping face. Nobody can wake her up. *He looked at the others, who were still sleeping.*

They want to mush us up, make us all one, *Lamb Chop said.* They'll kill us.

Not as long as I'm here.

Catherine put on the black lace nightgown. She kicked the white flannel under the bed.

"Are you listening to me?" she asked the woman.

When the woman did not answer, Catherine bore down again.

"You won't listen when Stanley talks to you about the stepfather. You won't accept fully his acts against us. But you need to know that stepping on a cockroach would be more sinful than killing him."

Before breakfast the next morning, the woman dialed Norman's number, determined to hear the worst and deal with it.

"It was a horrible meal," Norman said. "All I know was that the person speaking never made one single mistake with that cadence. The voice was a man's, lower than yours, more husky,

317

but refined. The brogue was unmistakable. He told me I had no idea what was going on out there in the world, made me feel like a dunce. Then the one with the garbage mouth came out and started swearing. Actually, I remember her when we were married."

"Norman says there's someone here with a brogue," the woman told Stanley. "I can't believe him. I've never heard it."

Later in the session, Catherine stood back and showed Stanley one of the selves who lived in the shadows behind her. The Troops had been talking about time, how little there was of it to do all the things they wanted to do in the course of a day. The person who emerged just then let him see how the Troops had made it possible to do a mind-boggling number of mundane, routine chores in a relatively short time span, thus freeing them for more esoteric pursuits. The movements were unbelievably quick as the newly emerged Troop member went through the purse, sorting out piles of loose change, makeup, money, sketches, and lists. She could not seem to sit still, he could see her mind working as fast as her hands.

"Why can't you believe it?" Catherine asked, even though he hadn't said a word.

"It just seems humanly impossible. What's her name?"

"Mable. She can clean a whole house in forty minutes, from top to bottom. She can apply a full makeup in three minutes flat. She sews, irons, cooks, organises the closets, buys the groceries, and keeps the manuscript files straight."

"Mable," Stanley muttered.

"She doesn't hire out," Catherine said wryly. "There are others behind Mable, each one with her own specialty. One of them does very fine stitching, one of them is a gourmet cook, one has the ability to endure, for more than three or four hours, a roomful of Clorox, ammonia, and Top Job. It's a very powerful cleaning mixture, dangerous if inhaled. The fumes don't bother her at all. Before you ask, I don't know their specific names, I only know that they are separate."

"The Outrider," Stanley said. "Does she live in your shadow, too?"

"The Outrider is her own person," Catherine said, "the only one of us to have two identities. Half of her duty entails creating . . . a certain atmosphere, to disguise our unhappiness and pain, and perhaps even her own, no one knows. The other half is to

318

ride herd, to acknowledge and bind our wounds without drawing attention to the blood. She is the essence of all camouflage. She taught the Junkman to survive by hiding, when he thought all was lost. Others live in her shadow, too: Twelve, until she became a Front Runner; some of the sexual ones, Sixteen and Rachel; Brat and Me and a few of the more literarily creative ones, to mention just a few. Surprises you, doesn't it?"

Catherine wouldn't tell him the Outrider's second identity, but Stanley had made a guess, based on the sessions and the manuscript pages.

"I'm glad to have this little conversation," Catherine said. "Because I have a bone to pick with you. In the last session, and I quote you verbatim, you said, 'suppose Mean Joe, for instance, that person who in your mind is a strapping black man . . .' Stanley, I know you're comfortable telling the woman that she lives in two separate worlds, ours and reality, the latter of which I assume is your reality, too. But have you ever wondered how real your world actually is? As you sit there, you perceive things in a certain way and assume all of it is real. That's only natural; it's your frame of reference. But how can you be sure that somewhere another world doesn't truly exist wherein your reality, as you perceive it, is just as ridiculous, or at least as strange, as you perceive ours to be?"

"There are times," Stanley said, "when I wonder whose world is more real, yours or mine. But I can only go by my own references."

"Just as we can only go by ours," Catherine said with the wry smile that had stamped her identity in his mind from day one. "So we are at loggerheads on this issue. There is something else. You mentioned integration. Whom would you choose among us to live beyond that integration? Whom would you kill? The whole Troop Formation is up in arms. For them, contemplating integration is like living back at the farmhouses when the daily threat of death hung over their heads. Do you think we survived the farmhouses only to have you convince us of the advisability of mass suicide?"

He said integration was up to them and tried to remember where he'd gotten the idea that eventually, all multiples in therapy accepted the idea of it. In the interest of more recall, Stanley put Rabbit under light hypnosis. Stanley watched the woman drift in and out sharing Rabbit's recall.

The selves had been active today: expressions of terror and

sadness; an amused, wry look now and then; the happy smile of someone who had to be around twelve years old. But always, interspersed among the others, there were glimpses of one specific attitude—someone who heard her own music and whose body moved in time with it.

As Rabbit moved through the recall of being beaten with a leather strap, a low, keening wail began, and escalated into a howl. The actuality of the beating that had caused Rabbit's howl suddenly reached the woman. She was fully conscious of the presence that hurried to her from somewhere with a deep, furious concern, the way that presence entered her being and took the breath from her lungs . . . the awful concentration of that presence as she and it, in unison, sucked the breath of both . . . and held it. The breath was released. The pain was gone.

After the break, Stanley made a decision.

"How would you like to meet some of the abusers?"

"You trust me that much?" The woman knew she didn't trust herself at all.

"Why not?" Stanley grinned. "I'll be there, running interference. I think that seeing you might help these men understand why their daughters need therapy."

"Amen," Sister Mary Catherine said.

In the bathroom that night, someone lettered in a childish scrawl, with a lipstick on the side of the claw-legged tub, "Two, four, six, eight, we don't wanna integrate!"

"Stanley is a mean man," Lamb Chop told the woman later. "He wants to kill us."

"That's not what integration means. . . ." The woman couldn't finish the sentence. What did integration mean for them all? They were individuals, no two alike.

"Are you going to let Stanley kill us?" Lamb Chop stood first on one foot and then the other, suspicious.

"No," the woman said.

"On the farms, the stepfather could have killed us all, he was stronger and bigger. Stanley is stronger and bigger than us. I'm scared."

"Don't be," the woman said. "We have choices now. Stanley gave them to us. Nobody here is going to die."

The words comforted Lambchop. But the woman experienced the dizzy feeling . . . someone else bearing down too hard, using hammer thoughts instead of subtlety to express their own

320

terror. The subtlety was what had always kept the woman on a relatively even keel, giving her the impression that she was just like everybody else, capable of acting on her own.

Mean Joe bought a bottle of Grey Flannel cologne, torturing her with the possibility that she might sometimes smell like a man. Each night her planned wardrobe vanished, to be replaced with whatever the others wanted to wear. Three days in a row, she found herself in the same black skirt and vest with the same smartly patterned blouse.

She looked forward to meeting the abusers as proof that she could, even if through others, face someone on an issue, any issue. But being in the same room with men who had done the same things the stepfather had done . . . no one in the Troop Formation had assurances that the meeting would not turn out to be the disaster of their century.

33

At dusk, a cold sleet needled their faces as they navigated the parking lot. The woman entered the doors of the Protective Services agency at Stanley's side. They passed through the reception area, where a number of volunteers sorted through boxes of canned goods and used clothing. The building was cold with the draft from the front doors, but the woman didn't feel it. She and Stanley continued on, down the hall to a room at the end.

"Are you sure nothing I say will harm their therapy progress?"

"No way," Stanley said. "Let the chips fall."

Pale green walls, a worn leather sofa, and a circle of chairs, some upholstered, some the plastic folding variety. The room seemed to explode with masculine, joking voices, and she stood there in the doorway, to one side of Stanley, watching the men watch her and hearing the sound of their voices stop.

She sat down next to Stanley. Wary but self-contained and anxious to finish, each man introduced himself, giving his chosen fictitious name and a description of what had brought him here. Some looked her in the eye, some did not.

"Of course she knew what she was doing," one man told her in reference to his girlfriend's eight-year-old daughter. He was new to the group. He sat back in his chair, one leg crossed at the knee. In a round, cherubic face, pale brown hair and eyes were the only colour.

"What do you mean?" the woman asked.

322

"I mean," he said, "that by her actions, the way she came at me, asking for it, she wanted what I was giving her."

Another of the abusers made a quick motion as if to object to the statement but the woman heard herself interrupt him.

"Are you telling me," she sounded almost noncommittal, "that at the age of eight, she knew what sex was all about?"

"Well," he paused.

"Didn't it occur to you that maybe someone else had gotten to her first, one of her mother's boyfriends or even, possibly, her own father?"

He looked away and admitted that could have happened.

The short man she turned to next was only forty-two. But his face was deeply lined, with dark circles under runny blue eyes. "I ain't got the vocabulary these other guys got. Only thing in my mind is that I know I done a bad thing to my daughter. When she was fourteen, it started. My life stunk and there she was, the only warm person in it. I'm gonna be sorry the rest of my damn life. I know I hurt her."

His last lengthy comment of the night was that Stanley used too many fifty-cent words.

"I just ain't up to it," he said, and faded away abruptly.

From then on, the woman kept eye contact with him, both to ensure his comfort in the face of her presence—and to make certain he knew that she was a real person. Somehow she knew that in the mind of each man here was an unseen mechanism that made their acts and their children unreal for them. That was how they avoided confronting much of anything.

How did a mechanism like that get started? Something went click in a couple of Troop minds. Their therapy, combined with the intensity of reliving it through the manuscript pages, had reached a point where a session like this one, with these men, would open doors they'd never dreamed existed. The woman heard crying in her mind and it came from more than one Troop member.

She saw the eyes of the third man. Under the yellow lamp glow, his sexuality seemed to be in them, flat out and offensive.

"I've been working with Doctor Phillips for three years," he said to no one in particular. "Ever since they let me out of jail. Finally, I'm almost ready for the 'streets.' My daughter and I have a good relationship with each other now. She knows I love her and that I'm sorry it happened."

"Is she in therapy?"

"Doesn't care to talk about it. She saw someone from Protective Services three times. She can handle it on her own." He had a toneless, mesmerising voice and the pipe in his hand let out an aromatic stream of smoke.

"But it's taken you three years to be able to handle it?" The woman looked down at her skirt.

A rawboned man of twenty-eight with strapping muscle structure, whose shaggy blond hair shaded a wide face, acknowledged his turn. His voice rumbled in the woman's right ear as he told how he and his two-year-old daughter had fondled each other, how that had escalated into oral sex. The incest had gone on with only minor interruptions caused by his daughter's tears or tantrums, and once her failing grades, until a year ago when she'd turned eight. His wife had discovered her crying in her bedroom and confronted him. The man told of turning himself in to the police, of being booked and fingerprinted. The police commissioner told him, "Buddy, your ass should be in jail. You're scum and the first time you break probation, I'll get you."

The woman recoiled at "scum," even as she knew it to be justified and at the word "fondle," which was being used here a great deal tonight. Some Troop members sent emotions indicative of a desire to stomp these men to death. Some huddled against remembered terror. Others reached out mentally to each man, with understanding. From the depths of the Tunnel, someone roared out a silent command to the Troops for patience, courage, and silence.

"By the time I got married," the abuser went on, "I needed love and affection so bad. Without trying to put any blame on my wife—she's what I'd call cold, and so was my mother—I turned to my two-year-old daughter. She was always there, I was there, and my wife couldn't seem to lay an affectionate hand on either of us to save her life. Every time my wife left the house, I'd get a hold of my daughter and just . . . sink into it. I love my child and I knew what I was doing was wrong, but I couldn't stop. The fondling meant warmth and affection to me, more than it meant sex."

"Wait a minute," the woman heard herself say to Stanley. "His daughter knew how to fondle at two years old?"

Stanley and the abuser both nodded.

"He taught her," Stanley said.

That a small child could be taught something like that was so new an idea . . . at least to the Troop member who was the adult core's mirror-image.

"What did your stepfather teach you?" Stanley was making a note on his clipboard. His watchful expression and the pressure being exerted by too many Troop members . . . the woman received their thoughts: What the men in this room had been taught to do by their parents, the Troops had been taught by the stepfather.

Stanley had some of the men recount their own physical and sexual abuse as children. There had been mothers, foster mothers, aunts, grandmothers, sisters, who had used them sexually, as small boys. Their fathers had beaten them, some had used them sexually, there had been emotional abuse and dehumanisation.

Click. There was the similarity.

"I don't understand." Twelve turned to Stanley. "We went through the same things they talk about, and more. But we never thought of Page as a sexual object. Why?"

"You've had a lot of help from each other," Stanley said softly. "Other than that, I don't have an answer for you."

The men didn't understand what Stanley meant. The blond-haired man spoke up, again. He told of his grandfather's sexual abuse of him, how his brothers and even his mother had availed themselves of his small body. "My grandfather was ten feet tall from the time I was four years old. Even now when I think of him, I shudder. Nobody ever said no to him."

Twelve wanted to punch out his relatives, as much as she wanted to kill the stepfather. Her voice was a whisper in her head.

"Are you telling me that even boys can be scared?"

He smiled. "Still am," he said. "But I've gotten up the nerve to be on the radio with voice distortion and I did an anonymous newspaper article. Maybe that still makes me a coward but my family couldn't survive if I were recognised and lost my jobs."

Jobs. Stanley had said that most of these men worked as many as three jobs to keep separate roofs over the heads of themselves and their families during the therapy process.

A fifth man, smaller than the others, sighed when Stanley signaled his turn. He gave his name, adding like an automaton, as had the others, "I'm a child abuser.

"She was ten. My wife's daughter by her first husband. I started . . . fondling her, you know, friendly-like at first . . ."

325

"Friendly?" Nails' voice was cold. "Describe it to me."

"Well, the first time, I took her to the movies. Her mother was working. It was a Walt Disney cartoon and I put my coat over the arm of the chair, between us."

"How did you start, what was your first action?"

"Under the coat, I sort of put my hand on hers, then her arm, then her thigh, and she . . . didn't object."

"She didn't move or say anything."

"No, she didn't. I moved the hand higher, to her crotch."

"She was ten years old," the woman repeated softly.

"Yeah. Ten." His eyes swung to the wall and he didn't look at her again. "Listen, lady. She never said *no*!"

"How could she?" the abuser to her right cut in. "She was what, three and a half feet tall? You have to be seven feet tall to her! I'm a big guy, but to me my grandfather is still a giant."

"There's more to it," Twelve said. "Victims feel as if they somehow invited the incest and therefore can't object. We're taught from day one to do as our parents, or as authority figures in general, tell us. We're powerless."

" 'Powerless,' " The abuser who'd been abused by his entire family leaned forward. "I still am, when somebody hits on me."

Coffee, strong and hot, was being passed around in white paper cups. The woman surfaced and wished these men would sit on the floor, so she could follow suit. In the opaque bag in the chair beside her, the teddy bear lay concealed, a comfort no one dared to take up.

"My client," Stanley nodded at her, "is, as you all know, an incest victim with a particular . . . problem, as a direct result. She's going to explain to you what she's going through, many years after the fact. And I'd like you all to remember as she speaks, that her problem is not unique, as was once thought."

She gave her name and spelled it for them, gave the name of her company, and told them she was a real estate broker. "I'm using my own name," she said, "because I've got to get used to this, because someday perhaps we'll meet on the street. Should that happen, I hope you say hello to me. I'll say hello to you."

No one looked away from her.

"It's important that each one of your sons and daughters gets therapy as early as possible, that they learn to talk about the incest freely, to understand it. Otherwise, as Doctor Phillips has told you, they're going to wind up my age, sitting in a room like

326

this one tonight. And they won't know how or why it happened; they'll just know they missed the majority of their lives. Incest victims even without my particular problem go through hell every day, whether they are fully aware of it or not.''

There were nods of agreement from all but two of the men. Stanley had explained that they would be willing to listen, if not to agree. She was very conscious just then of the erratic, sharp sound of her voice in the cramped room. Show them reason, she told herself, not what may be, to them, insane behavior. But it involved a control she wasn't sure she had. Someone inside her head laughed and told her to relax. She tried. It had been so long since she'd talked about the incest or the multiple experience to a human being outside of Stanley, that once in a while he had to break in and keep her on the track.

When it came time to say ''penis,'' and ''vagina,'' another mouth opened onto her own and pried the words out for her, one by one. She felt eyes, cold against her skull, forcing each male eyeball in turn to meet hers as the words poured out, words she couldn't hear. The stepfather's voyeurism in the outhouse, his acts of sodomy and bestiality, caused the men to look at one another.

''We're not suggesting,'' Stanley broke in, ''that any man in this room would go to such lengths. Her stepfather was a severely disturbed man. He was sick.''

The woman nodded. ''It all seemed normal to me at the time. I hated it and it scared me, when he'd stand in the barn doorway, waving his penis at me . . . but it wasn't until I got out in the world that I knew other people were different.''

''Jesus, I hope so.'' The man to her right poured coffee all around.

''There is one thing, though.'' She didn't look at Stanley, knowing he wouldn't give her signals anyway. ''Incest leaves the victim with no real connection to him- or herself or anyone else.''

There had been a flurry of facial structure and body changes for the last hour. To someone who didn't know, it might simply have been ''mood swings'' affecting the face and form of an unusually expressive person. As she looked up from the twisted hands in her lap, the voice that came out of the woman's throat had taken a deeper tone, heavier with restrained anger.

''You've all mentioned loving your children. We have a child who is fourteen. We can't honestly say we've ever felt an emotion like love. Hatred for various things, yes. Love, no. Incest

327

is a thief; it steals more from its victims than you can ever imagine. Make no mistake—by whatever pretense—incest, child abuse, stinks out loud.''

Why did the men and the Protective Services worker stare at her that way? What had happened? The woman lit a cigarette even as she knew the one in the ashtray, filter-deep with pale lip gloss, had to be hers. She told them that she was a multiple and tried to make sense of the mechanics for them. Her explanation of Mean Joe and Miss Wonderful's emergence for the first time, of the needles in her hands and their strength overriding her own, forced the abuser to her right almost to his feet.

''My god,'' he said. ''You've got to be out of your mind with fright every day.''

It was too much for Nails, who'd been fighting her way into this gathering, on and off.

''You got it,'' she said to him, smiling quick and sharp.

It struck the woman as strange that not one of her friends had ever acknowledged her fear this way; they'd discounted it.

Afterward, one of the men followed along to the front door.

''Listen,'' he said to her. ''I kinda sorta admire you, somewhat.''

Laughter roared in her throat. She gazed at him, dumbfounded. ''That's a qualifying statement if I ever heard one,'' she said.

''What I mean is, you got more than sixty of you to deal with this. We only got one each of us.''

Stanley held the door open, he gripped his clipboard. He looked ready for anything, even if the woman's mouth was wide and friendly.

''Now you listen.'' Tears of laughter spilled from eyes which were suddenly yellow-green. ''Those two new men in there, you and the others better work their asses into the ground. Next time I talk to Stanley here, I want to know they're sweating bullets. More than that, I want to know they understand why victims get multiple personalities in the first place.''

After the meeting, Stanley accompanied her home to the warehouse, anxious to process what he knew had been a difficult evening. A modest dent had been made in the barrenness of the loft. Tall palms in their wicker baskets slid thin, dark fingers over the empty walls, and a smell of old wood, rich and heavy, came up from the newly polished floors. He sat drinking tea while his client drifted in and out of her own mind, bumping into so many of her people that she lost count and so did he.

Pain ground in her head, followed by swift and raucous laughter, followed by eyes swimming with grief for a loss she could not measure. The wild, free smile of someone who was definitely feminine and sensually inclined, although the woman couldn't dwell on it long enough to "receive" a name, even had one been offered, charged over the innocent happy smile of Twelve. And still there were the fresh sad tears of yet another newcomer to the woman's awareness. Would these new additions to the Troop family never cease to surface? How could there be so many of them, unrevealed to her all these years? Their differences became magnified then, as if they were pressing their individualities home to her, imprinting themselves on her. Through a solid wall of rainlike tears, she could not speak to tell Stanley the emotional impact all of this had, or that the pain in her body was fierce. But no sooner had the pain begun than it shot off, only to be replaced by hilarity.

Elvira had emerged. She laughed aloud. "Hello, Charlie," she said, grinning at him through the individual and collective tears. "Do you like your name? We like your name."

Ah, Stanley thought, the lady with two identities. After all these months he knew her well enough, even without a name, to understand that she was both saluting him and making a joke, feeble as it was, to curtail the sadness surrounding the woman tonight. Her Southern drawl accented every word.

"You're so all-fired name-happy," she taunted him, "so desirious of handles. Well, I'll give you a name. You can call me Elvira. I've got two new forty-fives by that name. *Elvira!* Yeah, I do like that name!" Her fingers snapped to the silent beat of the Oak Ridge Boys.

"Listen, Charlie. The adult core's got to look at it through my eyes right now. I laugh a lot; it's the only way. If she looks at it through her own eyes, she'll go mad."

Someone tried to push past, and grab for the teddy bear, but Elvira's grip on the situation was grim and tight. "You can call that dissociation or anything you want, but that's the way it is. What do you want from us? Do you wanna make us one? That means only one thing, Charlie, our destruction. But we are the supreme and guiding force and have been for a long, long, time."

"I realise that," Stanley said, trying to grasp the flow of her

329

hell-fire and brimstone sarcasm. It was almost impossible, the way she ranted; tauntingly, mixing it like an expert old-time religion preacher, with the rock-and-roll beat of her speech.

Stanley peered at her, accepting the name she had given him, but knowing that she was also the "Outrider." The Southern drawl abated; the voice he heard next was cold and steady.

"We're trying to tell her that by fourteen, there was enough sexual experience among us to run a bordello."

There had been differences between the abusers and the stepfather, differences that twenty-four hours later, as the women and Twelve prepared dinner in the warehouse loft, would not go away. The stepfather would have torn down walls, broken bodies and heads before admitting his guilt. When the woman saw Twelve cutting up vegetables for a salad, with angry chopping motions, she realised that Twelve was not the only source of war cries this afternoon. Just outside the kitchen loft area where the woman and Twelve worked over their preparations, Lambchop seemed to stand guard over something. Her little face was red with rage.

"What's Lamb Chop doing?" the woman whispered to Twelve. "What's that she's got?"

"The children," Twelve said, "are getting ready for Christmas. Didn't Catherine tell you?"

"We don't have money for Christmas, we'll celebrate next year. Didn't we all agree on that?"

"We've saved up. Myself included," Twelve said. "The children have to have something."

The woman had never seen any gift that could summon up the look on Lamchop's face at that precise moment. It wasn't the kind of look one could describe.

From a corner of one eye as she put Twelve's salad on the table, she caught sight of the bright red lacquered box into which Lamb Chop peered with a grave concentration. Hesitantly, the woman approached and opened the lid. Two maggots curled up in one corner of the red box on a piece of pungently rotted meat.

"Don't touch that," said a tiny, lispy voice. "It's mine. You leave it alone." There was a huff, then silence.

The woman let the lid slam shut and pushed the box away.

"And don't slam it around like that. They're asleep. You'll disturb them. You're just like the mother, always poking around in other people's things."

330

"What do you mean, they're asleep? What are they?" The blood had drained from the woman's face.

"They're just enough to take care of those two big words." The small lispy voice faded but not before the woman heard the voices of many children behind it.

"If that's a Christmas present," the woman said, "who would it be for?"

"The two big words are revenge and retribution," Twelve said from her place at the kitchen table.

"It's a game, isn't it?" The woman's voice went dry.

"Yes," Twelve said. "A game."

Sleet lashed against the windows, a horn honked on the street below. In the cold air of the loft, "Hell Is for Children" played on the stereo. Twelve left it at that and the woman, much as she wanted to, couldn't go further. She felt Twelve's mind probing for her own, as if they were linked together tonight, almost perfectly synchronised.

"There wasn't anybody in that meeting quite like the stepfather," Twelve said. "Aren't there more like him?"

The woman didn't know. Stanley had mentioned treating only one brutal abuser, the hit man. Stanley had reminded her that brutal abusers lived, as a rule, within families scared to death of them. Nobody snitched on the brutal ones, so they didn't come to light until a child died. Violently.

"Black Katherine was waiting, you know," said Twelve. "She's part of the Big Three. They handle frustration, anger, and rage. If just one man had said that he handed out sex to his child because it was good for her, or to teach her how to enjoy it with a husband later, or because she was his possession, to do with as he pleased . . ."

"I'd have reached out and slaughtered him," someone said.

Twelve smiled. "Among us, there is a proverb. 'When Rabbit howls, can Black Katherine be far behind?' It's like, Mean Joe protects Miss Wonderful and Lamb Chop and the rest of the little ones but Black Katherine moves in on anyone who hurts Rabbit. Black Katherine gives 'em the pain they deserve; she's the strongest of the Big Three. But when you got stuck in Rabbit's pain that night in the session, Black Katherine took it away for you. Same way when the chicken got stuck in your throat in the restaurant with Norman."

Twelve stopped speaking aloud. She began to do something that had always been very simple for her. While this was not the

331

first time she had tried it out, her success with the woman to-night was almost unprecedented. She honed in, with a not-quite-smug vengeance, sending thought and picture and logic, scene after scene, in colour and clarity, leaving nothing to the woman's imagination. All was laid out in unavoidable, orderly fashion, and when Twelve was through, the woman knew Black Katherine exactly, with no room for doubt.

"She won't hurt you," Twelve said. "Black Katherine isn't here to hurt you or us. But she is the source of the rage, and it won't ever go away. Some of it will always be here."

"Norman wouldn't agree with you," the woman hissed. "Psychologists say that no victim is healthy, harbouring vicious thoughts, ideas of revenge."

"Stanley says no victim is healthy without the anger," Twelve replied casually. "The victims themselves say it never goes away." As if to prove her point, she moved aside and let the woman feel Black Katherine, full force.

An invisible knife twisted, something broke inside, and rage flooded the woman with something as old as time itself. It felt wonderful, for it was a brutal, a fine, killing rage.

Instantly, the woman knew where it should be directed.

Cheers went up all over the loft.

In battles of yore, intoned a voice with a suspicion of brogue, *we enjoyed such a passion, without remourse.*

34

By nine o'clock on the first Monday in December, a group of forty people, Stanley's students, friends, and colleagues, were gathered in his candle-lit town house. Their voices blended with the Christmas carols being played on the stereo.

Down by the makeshift bar, Captain Albert Johnson poured drinks from almost as many bottles as there were people. Jeannie, determined that this big, gruff man should have a good time, repeated jokes she'd collected at the university and waited for his reaction. There was none. With a nod of her head, she signaled across the room to Stanley, who began working his way through the crowd.

Albert had been scooping ice from a big tin tub under the bar. When he looked up at Stanley, his eyes were a flat, cold grey.

"I like your booze, Stanley. I don't like what's happening with that Troop Formation. Throwing away inappropriate guilt, as you call it, and recognising inner rage is one thing. Acting it out is another."

"Doesn't it depend on how they decide to act it out?" Stanley helped himself to eggnog, frothy in a clear plastic cup.

"My wife," Albert said, "was Irish. The Irish know one way: war."

"Aren't you forgetting a lot of other things the Irish are famous for?"

"When my wife got angry, there was only one thing she cared about. The Irishman in that damned Tunnel is up to no good and you should put a stop to it. Christmas is only a few weeks off.''

Jeannie knew what Albert meant. In Stanley's classes, she often sat with Albert, listening and watching the videos. Troop anger had reached a point she knew too well. Her own therapy was not that far behind her. She'd come awfully close while in that therapy to doing exactly what the Troops were planning— and still, on occasion, wished that she had.

The documents today were only a formality, a clearing away of prior settlement details. Ten-Four was, for all intents and purposes, no longer in the real estate business. The purchaser reached over and lit her cigarette and the flame exposed every crevice in his mature face. Would she ever be able to look at a man without first searching for some sign of the stepfather?

The stepfather had created a legacy of emptiness, bounded on all sides by fear and daily apprehension. *Legacies are handed down,* someone said in the woman's mind, *but one does not have to accept them.*

I'm scared, the woman cried.

Unfinished business, the voice replied. *We can't go further until it's finished.*

During the business meeting, boredom set in for the little ones. Afterward, they hit the street, running. Twelve demanded a movie; Nails said no, there was too much work to do, but Elvira insisted. They fought the entire way to the carry-out store, where Lambchop stamped her foot on the pavement.

"Someday," Lamb Chop warned them, holding Rabbit's hand in hers, "I'll be all grown up. Then you'll be sorry."

"Do you have to be all grown up to win?" Rabbit's voice carried on the frosty winter air.

The Troops brought a bottle of wine to the next session.

"Drink up, Stanley," Nails said. "If it weren't for you, there wouldn't be any good news. We've almost finished the manuscript. We cooperated long enough, all of us, to bring the whole thing together without killing each other. Can you imagine that? The only thing is, if *Rabbit* is ever published, how do you verify our reality? Some of us may never be able to look at the manuscript as a whole picture, but for those of us who can—we realise how strange we sound."

"There's nothing to verify," Stanley said. "What's in the

pages is reality for you. Someday, through books like yours, the public will understand that reality.''

Behind the woman's eyes, as she surfaced, happiness threatened to explode. Her head sunk to her chest.

"Oh, god." Her voice was a whispered wail. Someone else, with a rounder, more relaxed face, had to experience what she could not.

"Oh, Stanley," Miss Wonderful said. "Isn't it truly a miracle?"

Right then, Stanley considered going into primal scream therapy. Hellish therapy and recall and thousands of draft pages . . . a miracle, Miss Wonderful had called it.

And then he laughed out loud.

Maybe Miss Wonderful was right.

"You'd better keep venting that anger," Stanley said.

"I'm trying," the woman sounded tired. "But around the children, I need control or I'd swat them. I'm finding evidence, traces of the way their minds work. I don't like it!"

"What frightens you?"

"Spying on them makes me feel like the mother, and I hate that. But the things they bring to the loft are bizarre."

"They didn't grow up on the Muppets and *Star Wars*. They grew up," Stanley said, "playing a very real game. By adult rules."

"You keep telling me that I need more recall and you're right. I can't face that bastard without a mountain of proof at my back. It seems as if the most recall comes to me when I'm dead tired. How can I get more tired than I already am?"

"Look. You've just finished conducting real estate transactions in a rotten economy; you're finishing the manuscript, illustrating and doing the camera copy for a five-hundred-page booklet, seeing your daughter, and having six hours of therapy a week. It's all a strain and ninety percent of it involves a very draining creativity."

"You're saying normal people don't go at this pace."

"I'm saying you're speeding. And you're too hard on yourself. Tell me, is it possible that the reality of the book will satisfy those who desire revenge?"

The cold expression just then belonged to Black Katherine's mirror-image.

"We're all rational. It's enough, I suppose, that through the book and the training films, others will have choices we never

335

had. Just don't ask us to recant and extend him compassion, or a kind word. Ever."

His death would not be enough, anyway. As the thought entered her mind, the woman received an instant flick of memory: the stepfather's face, his eyes with the angry yellow lights, glinting as he watched her. He was amused, holding down a child, her small legs kicking, her mouth open and screaming obscenities at him.

"Try it," he was saying. "Go ahead, try it. I'll grind your face into that cement wall. Then you won't be so smart."

Flick. He was staring at her while she ate, his sloppy grin turning into a laugh, then a leer as the mother left the table to get something. "Go ahead, tell your mother. You're so smart, tell her. You do, and I'll break your ass, whore."

She recognised a larger message as well: I'm bigger than you, I can humiliate, torment, torture, and dehumanise you, and there isn't a thing you can do about it, or anyone who'd dare believe you, if you told. I'm the winner, *you lose*!

In the woman's mind, the children were crying. They began to stamp their feet in anger, and their voices grew fainter as they drew close around one another.

Stanley couldn't peer into the woman's mind; he didn't know what was going on. All he saw was her empty expression and the huddled way she sat on the floor cushions.

At five the next morning, she got up and worked steadily on the manuscript, with breaks only for tea or to stretch cramped leg muscles. At midnight, she was still at it, still wide awake. So she jogged around the loft, to the tune of "Elvira," and "Tube Snake Boogie," with energy to spare. The fury of the children had not gone away.

"When do we get our turn?" Lamb Chop cried.

"The book will do a lot of good." The woman poured hot chocolate and kept her tones even.

"Baloney," Twelve said. "The book is for adults. We've got to have something for us."

"What are you saying?" the woman demanded, because she truly did not understand.

"I'm saying that adults look at things one way, children look at them another."

"You may be too smart for your own good."

"That's what the stepfather used to say to us."

The woman started to cry because she knew it was true. Many little feet, belonging to sullen and angry owners, stomped through the kitchen area.

"We didn't deserve it." Lambchop threw the paper from her straw on the floor and refused to pick it up. "That strap hurt, and being told you were crazy every time you cried wasn't nice, either."

"Why were we punished so much?" Rabbit lifted red-rimmed eyes to the cup of hot chocolate sitting on the table.

"The mother knew he was a monster," Lamb Chop said. "She just wouldn't say so. I used to watch her face. After a while, it got all closed looking when he did bad things right in front of her."

"So how come she said we were the bad ones?" Twelve turned to the woman, frowning. "It doesn't make sense to me."

The woman went on with snack preparations, trying to shut them out, diminish their humiliation and anger; to tell herself that she knew what was best for them.

As the mother had done, years ago?

"Not fair." Lamb Chop yanked a cookie out of the bag on the counter. "Do you think it was fair that he beat us that way, with that silly smirk of his? Like we were so dumb he could get away with anything?"

Silence. The small Troops, some of them still unrevealed to the woman, were sharing memories.

Mean Joe crooned softly, but even the small sleeping face on his shoulder began to stir.

"What about the day with the teapot? All that hot, scalding tea." Twelve wanted to run from her own words.

Rabbit, who had been crouched on the floor silent, was silent no longer. Her howls rent the air.

The woman stood stock still. "What teapot?"

Two or more of the small selves told her then that when Stanley called them out in the sessions, their bellies still burned with its liquid. Rabbit continued to howl and hold her head in her hands, her tears a river on her sweater.

Snacks forgotten, the woman headed in the direction of the bed and didn't quite make it. She lay where she'd dropped and grabbed for the teddy bear. It was very important, for some reason, that it be with her.

Flick. She could see the mother seated across from her at the kitchen table. The mother's eyes were wild and emerald green

337

under the piles of rich, red hair. She held the teapot with a hot pad in her left hand; she reached with the right for her six-year-old daughter . . . and tilted the pot. It was a pretty piece of china, white with pink flower designs. Steam hissed from the spout. Tea, boiling hot, flowed in a steady stream.

Rabbit uttered a banshee scream as the water coursed down and shriveled the white cotton blouse she wore. It sogged, instantly, the crust-trimmed tuna sandwiches on the plate in front of her. Rabbit moaned and held herself, but not too tightly, for the pain was fierce.

The recall, encapsulated in one of the widest flicks the woman had ever encountered, wearied her terribly before it faded. She found herself making a nest of the floor cushions and tucking her head into the curve of one shoulder. In a foggy, floating haze, flashbacks clear as winter ice continued. Smells of flowers, tuna fish, and a hot summer rain. The flashbacks halted. A sensation of nothing more than movement gripped her.

The little ones waited.

Alright, Lamb Chop said. *Now.*

I'm scared.

Don't you dare be scared. It will only take a second and don't you make a sound. Not one.

They might have been counseling over a game of hide-and-seek, in the dusk of another time. Movement. Forward and back, steady at first, then jerky. The woman's mind began to accept what it was being given. Like a motor running unsteadily, the sensation cut on and off. The woman refused it. Lamb Chop summoned up all the strength she had, and bore down harder. The flicks went on, showing an enormous white square of cloth. The square grew larger on all sides, it stretched in the woman's mind, sparkling white.

Now, Lamb Chop told Rabbit. *Now.*

The words *kitchen table* circled in the tortured mind of the woman while she battled to identify the white square. Lamb Chop wasn't giving up. She pressed harder. The woman saw it then, the tiny child who'd seemed to accompany the Seventh Horseman, whose hands had been so sticky . . . the woman saw her head of golden curls and the little scrunchy eyes . . . dressed this time in navy blue corduroy trousers and a knitted top of faded mauve. Jerky, forward-and-backward motions, a child's crying as it struggled, choking for breath. The child sat in the middle of the wrinkled sea of white cloth.

338

A sheet. She sat on a sheet, there in the second farmhouse kitchen. The mother always covered the kitchen table with a white sheet during the canning season. The woman didn't know how old the little girl was, except that she was too young to climb down from the kitchen table by herself.

The image of the child receded to permit a glimpse of the stepfather. His huge, muscular arms reached out and grabbed the child around the waist and wrenched its stomach in a choking motion. As one would do to someone who'd swallowed food the wrong way. There was the pink thing, a balloon deflating back into the stepfather's zipper opening. Then the woman saw the pale, gooey, white stuff, spurting from the child's mouth, dripping from her nostrils.

She slept.

Catherine had been waiting. She followed the woman into the bathroom. Presently, water filled the claw-legged tub. The dazed woman lowered herself into it.

"Well, darling, just no rest for the wicked, is there? Do me a favour. Don't turn away recall again, just because you don't recognise an object as being familiar. The stepfather put the child on the table occasionally, and for a change of pace, ejaculated into her mouth. One day it backfired on him. She nearly choked to death."

Why didn't the recall sink in? The woman pushed herself further under the water and watched it lap against the sides of the tub. Her mind drifted, looking for escape from Catherine's words, as if there had been something awful in them, aside from the recall. A second later she was down on her knees by the toilet, feeling harsh splinters of wood in her kneecaps. She held her head in her hands while Rabbit's moan rose to an inhuman pitch.

Still, none of it applied to her.

"Get up," Catherine said. "We just showed you the mother's idea of punishment and the kind of act that precipitated it over the years. Things like hot tea always came after the mother's discovery of one of the stepfather's games. When she couldn't get through to him with her rage, she turned on us."

Rabbit sobbed with her hands over her ears, unable to stop. Catherine issued a command and Rabbit pulled herself to a standing position at the bathroom sink.

Catherine's voice softened. "Good," she said to Rabbit, including the woman in her remarks. "I knew you could do it.

339

There's more but we'll take it slowly." Rabbit scuttled away, back to the furthermost reaches of her own private hell.

The child still sat in the middle of the sheet with a peculiar expression on her face. Catherine waited a moment, but the woman did not react as the meaning in the child's expression, and the thoughts she sent, became clear.

"This is me you're looking at," the child was saying, "me, not you. Help me."

The woman realised that the child's thought was being expressed through Catherine's adult mind. Catherine wouldn't shut up.

"Are you listening?" she asked.

"Down and dirty," Elvira said, and in her voice there was a hint of sadness.

The silent child waited.

"She's the sleeping child core's mirror-image," Catherine said. "One of the dead. I just transmitted for her—thought and longing that's dead and gone. Makes your own position more palatable, doesn't it? And now as you try to answer me and can't—you feel the other one who says 'I can't get in,' the adult core's mirror-image—all that blankness, just minutely saved by the bemusement as she stares at the shreds and pieces of our lives."

"Catherine is a bitch," Elvira said to the woman, "but she's a truthful bitch."

Elvira turned up the music and Joe Cocker began to lament in his croaking style. The woman couldn't speak or move. She sat there with her blank face and a loose look about her mouth, as if she were made of wet paper.

It didn't stop Catherine. She said that when the first-born died at two years old, she split into two cores: one potential child, the other potential adult. She explained how both cores slept and that mirror-images had been created for them, to absorb what happened to the other selves. The cores themselves, she said, absorbed none of the abuse.

"The cores," the woman said, "sleep on Mean Joe's shoulder. I know, I can feel him protecting them. I just didn't know what they were."

"Mean Joe is their safety," Catherine said. "The cores may have the same kind of memory you do. Nothing more than a far-off sense of the abuse, and a daily apprehension."

"Go away." The woman did not cry. She didn't know how.

"You are only a replacement for the first-born; you started

340

evolving at the moment she became two cores who would sleep in safety. You acted through us, long before you were actually born. Someone had to present a facade, someone who would not know what killed the first-born, or what happened afterward, to us as individuals. The few glimpses we've had of the child core—she is so undeveloped that she can't voice her own words. Lamb Chop transmits her mirror-image's essence to you. As to the adult core, did you know that she saw her elbow for the first time the other day, while I was taking a shower? I never understood before, how separate, how protected, she is . . . that her own elbow could be such an amazement to herself."

"I'm not sure I want to know," the woman said. "But then I guess wanting to know everything was the basis for the therapy in the first place. I feel very empty."

"No offense, dear, but you are empty. That is your essence. It's hard for all of us when we discover that we are not the original child, the first-born."

"I can't believe it."

"Do you know what it's like for us to hear constant denial? I hated you for that until I understood where it was coming from: from all of us, in the backs of our minds, a sort of protective mechanism that we all share, I guess. Even if we know it's useless. And you—standing outside the abuse, feeling only a way-off terror—I understand that for you, the terror is as bad as our actuality."

"But there is a purpose for me, isn't there?"

"Oh, yes," Catherine said. "There's a purpose."

The woman didn't know what that meant and nobody explained. They were all getting ready for bed.

"Is it hard for you," Lamchop asked the woman, "knowing that you don't think on your own—that all you are is us?"

The woman didn't reply because nobody gave her an answer for Lambchop. Twelve had been about to tell Lambchop to shut up.

"Maybe," Twelve said, cautiously, "you could say that the woman is very important among us. If it weren't for the woman, the adult core's mirror-image probably couldn't pass her thoughts to anyone. She'd be totally locked out of the Troop Formation."

"We think and talk a lot, don't we?" Lamb Chop was getting sleepy. "I hope we get to hear another story tonight. The one in the Tunnel talks more than anybody."

341

35

A storm had hit Cashell, Maryland, in howling gales of wet white snow, but the Troops didn't care. They stood at the windows of the warehouse loft that night, pointing out Christmas tree lights, winking blue and green and red, in the distant houses.

"Pretty soon, Christmas," Lamb Chop said. "Those men were right. The stepfather did always seem to be twelve feet tall. What do you think, Twelve? Think he's maybe only ten feet now?"

Lamb Chop had captured a seat in the old rocking chair first, and allowed Rabbit to join her. The red lacquered box sat in the darkest corner of the warehouse loft.

"Maybe only nine," Twelve said: "But then he isn't sitting right in his room, either."

Lamb Chop whispered to Rabbit with momentary doubt in her eyes but the bravado of childish innocence won out and she giggled.

"I just want to win," Rabbit said.

"We'll win." Suddenly Lambchop didn't look so innocent. "It won't be long now."

"That's what he used to say." Elvira tossed her head to the low-down, snake-level beat of the music.

Captain Albert Johnson had a Christmas tree in his precinct office, but he hadn't paid much attention to it, except to wonder when the needles would begin to drop.

342

"Stanley, how can I wrap these damn presents when I'm wondering what's going on?" Albert sat with the phone to his ear, drumming his fingers on his desk.

"Albert, they've decided not to kill him after all."

"You sure about that?"

"I'm never sure of anything." Stanley hung up the phone.

The woman had gotten used to waiting for Stanley in the university hallway outside his office. She always brought whatever part of the manuscript was currently being worked on. The number of pages turned out in those half hours never ceased to amaze her. It all seemed so effortless.

"For you, it is," Catherine said.

A number of students walked by and said hello. The woman had gotten used to that, too. At 9:00 A.M., Stanley's door opened and someone came out. She was tiny, with fragile bones. Pretty and feminine in a white lace blouse and designer jeans; around twenty-two years old and so fresh-faced that she called to mind an apple tree in full bloom.

She walked slowly from Stanley's office but on seeing the woman waiting on the bench outside, her pace quickened.

Stanley was quicker. "Lisa," he called. "There's someone I want you to meet!"

She came back. Sorrowful blue eyes under a fringe of black lashes scanned only the space between the woman and Stanley.

Silence.

Unsure of herself, the woman folded. Sister Mary Catherine reached out and gently tapped the girls' white knuckles with a black, felt-tipped pen.

"It gets better," she said, passing along Jeannie Lawson's message to the Troops, months ago.

As if to question the statement, Lisa looked quickly at Stanley. Tears lay along the edges of her eyes. Without a word to either of them, she turned and walked away.

"I don't know," Stanley said, distracted, "if that was appropriate of me or not. She's reached a tough spot in her therapy, she's clinging by her thumbs to what she considers her last gasp of sanity. Lisa is a sister under the skin."

"Victim and multiple," the woman said, trying to believe it.

"All the signs are there," Stanley said. "I've tested her. I'm trying to tell her as painlessly as possible."

"Well," Twelve said, "when she's ready, we'll give her cray-

343

ons and a teddy bear. Do you think that will help? Does she have a lot of little ones? Is she very scared?''

Stanley said a teddy bear would be nice and that yes, Lisa was very scared. In going from what he called "one heavy session to the other," his fumbling motions with the tape recorder, usually so unobtrusive, caught the attention of the other Troop members. That and the drawn, worried look in his eyes caused them to announce silently to one another that Stanley was human, something they'd known but not fully believed.

"Guess we can tell him anything," Twelve muttered.

In the control booth, Tony nursed his dials.

Stanley watched from the corner of one eye, his head bent over the clipboard. Thoughts marshalled themselves inside the woman's head. There were too many; she felt light-headed, out of control. The room seemed to sway.

Stanley was about to become privy to one of the strangest mechanisms of multiple personality.

"What was I saying?" Pain began at the back of the woman's neck, then it rapped smartly on her skull, as if demanding her full attention. "Oh, wow." She heard the words, there was a giggle, and her mouth felt slack. "Time just goes away."

For the woman, momentarily, it had. Twelve sat on the cushions, experiencing the same light-headedness. Twelve wasn't laughing as another Troop member shoved her aside, speaking over her words. Stanley was told how the Troops had explained to Norman the latest recall about the white sheet when the stepfather had practiced oral sex with almost fatal results.

The lone, unknown voice faded and the woman surfaced again, but she'd picked up the threads of the recall, sobbing.

"When I'd finished telling Norman in what I knew had been clear, concise English," she said, "he repeated the conversation back to me. He said I told it using an allegory, as if it were a white sheet coming out of the child's mouth . . . a white sheet, instead of the semen I had described. I sat there on the floor in front of him that night, feeling rotten because not only had I failed again, but I hadn't heard myself correctly."

Stanley had never been able to put it into words, the process that now crystallised for him.

Norman had heard the incident reported to him by means of an allegory, which the woman had not used. Stanley concluded, from this and what he'd learned in past sessions, that information considered too harmful to be spoken within earshot of certain

Troop members could be disguised by one of the Troop members. An entire concept might be passed to the listener as a parable, and in the case of certain words or phrases, allegories were used. Stanley wasn't sure which Troop member employed the subterfuge, but obviously someone in the Troop Formation was able at chosen times to "override" the voice of whomever sat out front. Which meant that words actually heard could be different from what the woman or even some of the other Troops heard. It was entirely at the discretion of the overriding Troop member.

He believed that in this case, the allegory had been used not to protect the woman, but perhaps another damaged Troop member—or the cores themselves.

"I started to argue with Norman," the woman said, "because I just couldn't believe him. Then he asked me, 'Why are you doing that with your hair?' At first I didn't know what he was talking about. Then I could see a black shape above the front of my forehead. It moved. I didn't get scared, Stanley; it was happening at a distance, too far away from me in my mind. Later I made sense of it. Because of the distanced, removed feeling, and since looking at Norman through my bangs caused a distortion of vision anyway, the black shape may have seemed to belong to someone else . . . except that it wasn't my hand that was moving. How do I explain this to you? At that moment, I didn't seem to have appendages of my own: no feet, no hands, just my mind!"

Abruptly, the woman's face relaxed and took on a smoother line. Her eyes brightened. Stanley heard a child's voice.

"Norman got angry," the young voice said. "We gave him our teddy bear and we said, 'Isn't the bear cute?' "

It was the voice of a child and yet it was not. Stanley didn't think he'd heard it before.

"We told Norman that it was our bear. He didn't know what to do. He just sat there and held it and said, 'Oh, jesus christ,' over and over. And we sat back down on the floor and giggled and the look on Norman's face was so silly. We told him how the little bear's tummy was stuffed with ground nut shells instead of cotton and that we liked the bear a lot. We couldn't stop giggling, no matter how angry Norman looked. We told him Page had taken the bear to sleep with her the other night. Norman just said, 'Whose bear is it? Who am I talking to now?' "

"Charlie," Elvira's more mature voice broke in, "nobody here is going to tell Norman their name. He'd laugh."

At Elvira's words, there were different voices and, interwoven with them, there was the cadence, heavy with sadness and then umbrage. Some of the voices were testy and argumentative, dealing with immediate problems. Others were weighted with remembered pain. As things grew more confused for Stanley, the woman still sat there, empty-eyed and seemingly oblivious.

Stanley felt energy surging through the studio. It didn't surprise him, with the number of Troop members appearing and reappearing. Again, a child spoke.

"Norman put his head in his hands then, and his eyes looked funny, as if he would cry. We felt very bad about that, we don't want to make anyone cry. Norman sat pinned to the sofa, unable to look away from us all, not even knowing what he was looking at. Will he ever? Will people always think we are one?"

"Does everyone want to remain separate?" Stanley asked.

"Would you want to be mushed up with your next-door neighbor or your own brother?" Twelve's voice was faint and then the woman surfaced, shredding Kleenex in her lap. "The bear," she said, "was in my hands, that's all I know. Norman seemed anxious to change the subject, steer it away from the bear. He went into something about mind relaxation. He thinks we need it. He said that some people are so good at it that they are able to see a white light. I told Norman I'd already been there. I never told you, Stanley, but in one of the sessions, I went up into the white light. It was blinding, fierce, like the center core of my being. All of a sudden I wasn't here, but truly, in the center of my own brain. It was as if I wandered around up there, content and laughing to myself. I knew that I didn't have to come back."

Stanley stared at the woman, who was explaining how she'd attained, alone, what religious scholars and others down through the ages had yearned for. Most of them had failed.

"Tell me," he said, "more of what it seemed like."

She shrugged. "First of all, there wasn't any 'seemed to' about it. It was quite real, it was happening to me. Or rather I was a part of it. A space, without beginning or end. So vast, so empty . . . so bright. White. I was completely alone up there, inside the essence of myself. Under the circumstances, I should ask you if I'm crazy."

"Do you know what that white light you encountered in the

346

session is associated with? Do you know what many people believe it means?''

"Norman told me what he thinks it is. I have another view. Norman says it's 'spiritual.' " The woman spit the word out. "Putting yourself in touch with the almighty."

"Or," Stanley prompted, wanting to hear her view.

"It's got nothing to do with god, but the power of my own mind. I have to save me, no one else can do it for me."

"People have experienced what you've just described. Do you know what was done to some of them?"

"They were burned as witches," she said.

"The church, religious leaders in past centuries, were afraid of those who could reach such a state. But they weren't all burned. There were those who, having finally achieved it, the white light you speak of . . . do you know what happened to those people?''

"They became fanatics? Religious fanatics?"

"No," he said, "those who weren't burned were later canonized as saints."

"You couldn't pay me to be a saint."

"Do you," he asked, "know what a medium is?"

"Yes. Someone who communes with spirits."

"Aside from that, a medium is someone who does consciously what you do subconsciously."

"I don't understand."

The voice suddenly was alert with a child's innocence. Stanley and Marshall had discussed the phenomenon of the quick and fully developed changes. They'd agreed that aside from that, one or more specific adult Troop members of undetermined identity could at times speak through certain other Troop members.

"The yoga positions," Stanley said, ignoring this change as he had the others, "your ability to withdraw so totally from the world around you. Your powers of concentration, of complete focus; they're all a part of the same general abilities. Some might even call them gifts."

"You're saying I do subconsciously, what mediums and yoga practitioners do consciously. I do all those things without being aware of it?''

"That's exactly what I'm saying. Some researchers feel that such a gift may be the basis for multiplicity."

He didn't add that he'd begun to suspect that Twelve, not the woman, was the source of the "gift." Such an identification

347

could drive Twelve into deeper cover, and he needed her, up front and verbal. If his powers of detection were working, Twelve had been very verbal tonight.

He called for a break and went down the hall to the lavatory, thinking of Lisa and Jeannie and the Troops. Similarities and differences. Jeannie had had three selves. Lisa would probably finish therapy with nineteen. After tonight, with the unknown voices and the newest manuscript pages, the Troops were probably around ninety in number. All three subjects were super-achievers with either superior or superintelligence. Jeannie had wanted, sought, integration. He didn't know what Lisa would decide. The Troops, steel backbones and iron minds to the fore, would never agree to it. Jeannie, Lisa, and the Troops all had the same problems with electrical energy. Lisa's friends claimed she was a "hands-off" TV repairman, that she could "command" perfect picture and sound, or static and blur. All three subjects evidenced precognitive "gifts," but tonight's "white light" had come as a shock.

Intelligence aside, was there one, indisputable commonality among the three women? His mind fastened immediately on a single element: immense rage.

Stanley put cold water on his face, unbuttoned his shirt-sleeves and held his wrists under the faucet for a long time.

Back in the studio, the woman was seated on the floor cushions, her face blank, and the small sound just then was not quite a giggle. But right away, Twelve's slightly older laughter echoed, over a pleased, unfrightened smile.

"Oooh," Twelve said. "My head, my head." She turned her head to the left and pointed to her nose. "My head is filled up to here, Stanley. I feel so light, so floaty. Drunk. I feel drunk."

Twelve had often tried in the past to describe the feeling of imbalance the woman complained about. Stanley recognised Twelve's voice now, even if she wouldn't give him her name.

"There are so many of you here tonight, it's no wonder you feel that way," Stanley said.

"Yes." Twelve smiled and swayed on the pillow, trying to acclimate herself.

Stanley caught brief glimpses of the woman, confused and obviously frustrated, as she heard Twelve's voice.

"Stanley," Twelve whispered. "The barn. I sit behind it, facing the fields, the apple orchard. Against my back there are splinters and the heat of the barn's old wood planks. It's August,

348

a very hot day. There's sunlight on my knees, I see it, my knee-caps look polished, tanned. The weeds next to me, we used to call them elephant ears, their leaves are huge and green. I want to hide under them, where the earth is thick and black. I've been out here a long time, the stepfather is calling again. I don't want to go.''

Twelve's voice was replaced by another, just as young but less feminine in tone and more ''reportive'' than ''experiencing.''

''We gotta go, when he calls you gotta go, there's a narrow, worn flight of steps inside the barn at the back. It's a long way up those stairs to the loft. There's hay up there, the smell of it, dust floating in the sunlight that comes in from a big opening in the wall. The stepfather has the grey cat by the scruff of the neck, the kid under his arm. He walks up the staircase, his shirt smells sweaty like he hasn't washed in a couple of days.''

''Harness,'' Twelve whimpered, ''I see the harness hanging on the wall up here, harness.''

For several moments, there was nothing but the sound of Twelve's weeping.

''My tummy hurts,'' Twelve said, ''the way he yanks me up. The cat is mad, it's yowling. I hate the cat. He'll start doing things to it.''

''What will he do to the cat?''

''It's hard for me,'' Twelve said. ''The words aren't here.''

Stanley looked closely at her, recognising her voice and features, yet wondering why she seemed so different. Then he knew. Twelve was speaking as the six-year-old she'd been at the second farmhouse.

''He's got the harness ready but he hurts the cat first,'' Twelve said. ''It's a boy cat. When we say no, he sits on us so we can't move, then he puts the cat on our chest. He makes the cat's little red finger come out and then he pinches it. The cat scratches me. I'm bloody all over myself.''

''Dumb game,'' Lamb Chop broke in. ''I don't like being buried in the hay up there in the loft, it frightens me when it gets up over my head and pokes my eyes! Oh,'' she wept, ''he's got his foot in my back, he won't let me up.''

''The floorboards are weak,'' Twelve muttered, ''and it's a long way down. No one is supposed to go up here.''

''It's really dumb,'' Lamb Chop sobbed. ''Sometimes when he's got his foot in my back, he walks that way. Dumb!''

"What?" Stanley looked perplexed and Lamb Chop's small face wrinkled in an effort to convey meaning.

"Like if you had a skate on one foot and none on the other," she said. "The harness hangs on a hook on the wall. And there's an old wooden chair."

The sight of the chair made Lamb Chop cry and shake her head. "Hook," she said. "There's a hook in one of the timbers, way far up in the ceiling, over the center of the barn." She was crying harder and Stanley knew that the terrified moans and softer voice were coming from Rabbit.

"The stepfather puts us in the harness. He stands on the chair, hooks the harness to the pulley. The pulley moves us, high up, swinging out over the barn floor. I hate him. It's a long way down. Are all games like this?"

"That's all," Lamb Chop said firmly, but Stanley hadn't spent over nine months with this client for nothing.

"Who comes out now?" he asked.

With a flurry of cheekbones, Elvira emerged. She opened her mouth wide. The words were those of the small child she had been, back at the second farmhouse.

"I donwanna, I donwanna, I donwanna," she screeched.

"What does he want you to do?"

"The pink thing," Elvira said more calmly. "I won't touch it. I won't touch the cat's, either. The stepfather gets mad. When he goes in to lunch, I decide right then, 'Goodbye, cat.' I drowned it. The stepfather was too big to kill. I thought about doing it a lot, with the gun or the knife, but he was too big. So I drowned the cat."

It was a child's logic. Stanley accepted it. "And the one whom the stepfather forced to have sex?"

"She was here," Elvira said, "but Catherine sent her away. Sixteen has been driving Sister Mary to the edge for weeks. It was too much. Sister Mary can't stand anyone who says right out that they're fond of sex." Snap, snap, went Elvira's fingers to an unheard beat.

"Sixteen can't stay?" Stanley asked.

"No," Elvira said. "Sixteen is scared. Sister Mary threatened to have Nails break her arms. What Sister Mary doesn't know is that Sixteen is only camouflage for Rachel, who is more sexual than Sixteen ever thought of being. Rachel has disappeared, too. She knows that if Sister Mary won't accept Sixteen, she'll never accept her."

350

Elvira's features shifted and Twelve looked up at Stanley with a fuller face and younger eyes.

"We're growing up, you know, some of us. Not Rabbit." Twelve made a motion, belt-buckle high. "Rabbit will never be any taller than that. Her nose will always be pressed . . . right there." Twelve made another motion, at crotch level.

Suddenly Twelve burst out crying. "The swallows. They nest in the barn. Beautiful, free-wheeling things they are, with long tails. What happens to them if there's a fire?"

Again, the flurry of cheekbones and Elvira's older eyes. "I did it," she said. "I got out of my bed one night and I set fire to the damn barn. Just like that. Goodbye, barn." She waited for Stanley's comment, but he waited for her to continue.

"I wanted," she said, "to drive the stepfather out into the open. The barn was too convenient a cover for the bastard. Sister Mary Catherine just stood there that night, watching the flames. The mother told her to go into the house, bring out anything she wanted to save. They were afraid the house would burn, too."

"Where was the woman, my client, all that time?"

"When the first-born died at two years old," Elvira said, "the woman started evolving. But it wasn't until the night of the fire that she was actually born—Mean Joe's shoulder is her birthplace."

After the session, they started out through the snowy parking lot where their respective cars sat covered in ice.

"There's something I've wondered about for a long time," Stanley said. "A number of you seem, at times, to read my mind. How do you do that?"

"It isn't very nice, is it?" Twelve smiled. "At least that's what Sister Mary Catherine says. When one of us starts to do that, she says, 'Get out of there.' Because we don't read minds, Stanley. We get right into them. We've been in yours."

36

Christmas Eve. The night had come.

"Isn't the snow lovely?" Lamb Chop stuck out her tongue to catch the flakes falling past the open warehouse window.

"Hurry up," said Rabbit. "I've got to wrap my last package. Twelve is going to help me."

"Close the damn window!" Sewer Mouth yelled from behind them.

"Do yours wiggle?" Lambchop struggled with the window sash. "Mine wiggle and I'm worried the trip will hurt their brains."

"Twelve says they don't have brains, any of them."

"Good," Lambchop said. "Then the stepfather won't feel lonesome."

Brown wrapping paper and cord littered the loft as the small ones hurried to fetch their treasures from all the hidden corners. They were reminded of the old silver thimble the mother used to hide in so many places and the hours they'd spent looking for it.

"I was good at that game," Elvira said.

"All games are not so simple." Lamb Chop snipped the cord on a small package.

There were over ninety persons gathered in the warehouse loft. They did not all know each other. Milk meant for the little ones bubbled on the hot plate, fragrant and steaming. A bottle of scotch had been opened by one of the adults and the smell of it was potent in the air. Along the woman's veins, something just as potent sang and hummed, alerting her to the change in the overall Troop attitude. Sister Mary was the most obvious part of that change. She sat on the floor, knees bent, working away on the last manuscript revisions. The beads were nowhere in sight.

Everywhere the woman looked, she saw concerted effort, heard the murmur of voices, everyone bent to a task she could not define. The warehouse occupants had divided themselves into two groups: adults and children. The woman struggled to catch what was being said, but what she heard was silence.

"Nails, what do you think of all this?" Catherine asked. "Such excitement. I can feel the ones who haven't yet emerged. It's like a stampede again, in the woman's head."

"You got it," Nails said and flicked her ashes. She missed the ashtray.

Lady Catherine Tissieu, busy numbering pages, looked up, ready to object, and thought better of it.

Far back in the cavernous, dim loft, a weight shifted. Time was broken almost violently and then suspended for them all. In the far corner, where shadows cloaked him in a mighty darkness, one of the adults smiled and he raised his glass to the words. For they were his own.

"Do y' know me now?"

Sister Mary Catherine's hand paused over the manuscript pages. She tilted her head and listened. So did the woman. But while Sister Mary remained on the floor, wrapped in her black habit, the woman became intellectually galvanised. Slowly, she got up and moved through the loft, paying attention to none but the voice in her head.

The thought of dinner with Norman that night, the icy waiter, the dregs of a peculiar cadence in her ears, the fright brought on by what she'd known even then, had been a new one, more powerful than all the rest—that someone telling her how time was not meant to be hoarded but wrung dry of all its juices, because when it was gone there was plenty more . . . and it came to her how she had been unable to hear the brogue in the Irish bomb maker's voice that night she'd joined Thementa for drinks.

The woman began to tremble, even as Sister Mary did, and they were conscious of soft, wailing sobs. Down on the floor with the manuscript pages, Sister Mary went click, click with the beads. Ten-Four poured scotch all around, and her face was grim.

The lisping sobs grew louder and beat on their ears.

"Hush, child," the voice said. "Our finest hour be upon us; a bit o'balm to pave the way—for the journey yet t' come."

The voice spoke to the thrashing, keening thing that Mean Joe clasped against his shoulder. But no one saw Mean Joe or his burden, and the woman thought the voice spoke to her.

"I'm leaving you now," she said. "I'll not pay attention."

"Y' cannot leave me this time," said the voice. "Already m' cadence has become your own. The times ahead will not be easy."

The woman felt the gentleness and the power—she could not deny what he pressed upon her.

"I thought the idea of killing the stepfather had been given up," she said slowly, "only the children aren't satisfied. They want revenge."

"They shall have it. 'Tis nothin' more than their due."

The woman stood in front of him and for the first time she saw his face. She saw a thousand opposing things in his eyes and all of them were true.

"I ha' many sides, and man may win by more than one method. It seems t' me that the wisest choice would leave us all free t' fight on many fronts and for many days, instead o' only one. True, 'twould be a grand occasion, that one day, but o' what value i' we all go down w' the enemy?"

The woman wasn't sure she agreed with him. In that moment she held the stepfather's bloodied intestines in her hands, watched him die for a longer moment.

"Tell that to the children," she said.

" 'Tis exactly what we're goin' t' do," he said.

"You're the one who's been reading to them lately. Why didn't I hear your brogue before?"

"Y' were not ready," he told her. "But now y' are. Ready for y'r job. You alone, o' all the others, feel nothin'. The children will believe your strength, your invincibility even in the face o' him."

"You said we weren't going to kill him."

"I said we'd do it in a way that would leave us free t' fight on many fronts and for many days." He laid the balance of the manuscript pages in her hand. "The ending has n' changed; it always belonged to the children, it always will."

The Irishman gave the signal.

The second skin of memory lay in the Weaver's arms. The skin comprised all that his nimble fingers had ever taken away. The woman knelt as always, knees beneath her, head lowered. The Irishman seized the skin; he held it shoulder-high and let it drop. The memory of more than ninety selves began to fill her. There was no stopping for breath; the second skin for one brief moment in time flowed and encased the woman like her own. She was the others, they were her, of one mind, a million memories.

Mean Joe could not move to hold her; he was inside her and his memory was hers. A soughing began in the cavernous warehouse loft, as if each blade in a thousand fields of tall grass cried against a storm that would never end.

The Irishman lifted the skin. He let the woman go.

She felt the scalding of an awful question. "If I am nothing but an empty shell, a facade, is anything mine in all of this?"

"More than y' ever hoped for," he said. "More than y' ever dreamed." And he took her to him with his mind and all that he was and forever would be, and he showed her the balance of the Troops, waiting their turn to emerge. He showed her the dead children on Mean Joe's shoulder. The woman stood in awe before them, her mind seething with outrage at their pain. Her desire for revenge was overwhelming.

The brogue grew softer as he bent her one more time, exposing her to other, much different emotions, in dizzying, kaleidoscopic profusion.

Shaken, the woman took in a breath of the sweetest air she had ever breathed. "I can have that? All on my own, just for me? Exactly as other people do?"

He knew the answer: for as long as she lived, she would experience only through the others, never precisely on her own. As long as she lived, the others would always be there. But since they were learning to absorb more of life's pleasures and some of the suspicion and hatred were draining away, there would be much for them to give her.

And so he lied.

"Aye," he said. "All that and more."

He operated on a grand scale, so for him it was not, relatively speaking, a gigantic lie, only a small white one.

But in the Tunnel that night, because he was a kind soul and had never been able to contain or hide his feelings, the sound of

355

thunderous crying would be heard and the walls themselves would tremble with his rage.

For now, he merely gave the final signal and the children began to gather at his knees. The loft was barren of a Christmas tree and there were no gaily wrapped presents, just a collection of tiny parcels done up in brown paper and tied with cord, clutched in their hands, held tightly in their laps.

Catherine laid her fingers over her lips.

"Ssssh," she said. "Let the children celebrate."

The voice began to read in a heavy but gentle brogue:

THE CHILDREN'S HOUR

Between the dark and the daylight,
    When the night is beginning to lower,
Comes a pause in the day's occupations,
    That is known as the Children's Hour.

I hear in the chamber above me
    The patter of little feet,
The sound of a door that is opened,
    And voices soft and sweet.

From my study I see in the lamplight,
    Descending the broad hall stair,
Grave Alice, and laughing Allegra,
    And Edith with golden hair.

A whisper, and then a silence:
    Yet I know by their merry eyes
They are plotting and planning together
    To take me by surprise.

The children's eyes were gleaming. With no further preamble, Henry Wadsworth Longfellow was laid on the arm of the rocking chair and the one who was reading in such a fine brogue, resonant and clear, so that no word might be missed, picked up the last pages of the manuscript and he continued: ". . . Who will go with me, into the jaws of hell, into the valley of death?"

Stanley's town house was very quiet. A platter of French bread, clove-baked ham, diablo mustard, and scallion-butter sat on the coffee table. With the woodsy scent of pine cones burning in the grate, Stanley took up a bottle of Irish whiskey, and two glasses of Waterford crystal that pinged sharply as the bottle clinked the rim.

"Present to me from the Troops," Stanley said to Albert. "They asked that I invite you here tonight and share this. Because you've been so concerned and because they've written you into the manuscript and into this final chapter."

"Why me?" Captain Albert Johnson looked pleased but skeptical.

"They've always feared authority figures," Stanley said. "I guess someone like you doesn't frighten them anymore. The other chapters were literal, right down to Lambchop's childish inability to spell her name. Through it all, the Irishman tried his damnedest to hold back. Now he extends a warm fire, good food, fine drink—and his gift to the children. Have you ever noticed, Albert, that adults give children the kind of presents they really want for themselves? Things that please them, not the child? In this case, Albert, I suspect that the Irishman still holds back, giving the children not what he wants, but something truly to their liking."

"So," Albert said, "You're going to read me a Christmas story?"

"Yes," Stanley said. "In honor of the high feast tomorrow, I am."

He picked up the last chapter and began to read:

The woman felt so calm within the protective placenta the Zombie had placed around her this morning. Just before the end of the session yesterday, Stanley had warned that the scary part wouldn't go away entirely, ever. It would simply diminish as time went by. The feeling of living in a pressure cooker, he'd said, would abate as the steam was allowed to escape slowly, through the surfacing memories.

The Seventh Horseman waited by the door of the warehouse loft, impatient for them to be off. But the coat must be admired first. The Troops had a new one, unlike anything the woman had ever owned.

Miss Wonderful loved the redness of it; Rabbit said it looked like blood. But it was warm, that was Mean Joe's opinion, warm enough for the Arctic. Ten-Four took one look and expressed disgust that anyone would buy such a heavy coat when the winters in Cashell, Maryland, didn't call for it. Lamb Chop and Twelve hung by its hem, brushing the cloth over their faces.

In the pocket of the coat was a round-trip airline ticket. Holding the ticket in her hand comforted the woman as she stood at the loft window, watching for the taxi. Sister Mary Catherine stood with her—neither one wanting to acknowledge the reason for the ticket.

"Listen," Black Katherine said. "Did you think that for every action there would not be a reaction?"

Sister Mary pretended she was too busy stuffing Tylenol into the woman's mouth to answer, and pulled the coat tighter around her. She fastened the shiny, blood-red buttons at the woman's throat, ministering as if to a sick child. But the woman wasn't sick and, while she trembled, it wasn't with fear.

Catherine could not resist a last purr of satisfaction over the beauty of the coat she'd chosen, as she wished the woman and Mean Joe and the children luck for the trip. Catherine's purr was muffled by the deadly heft of the woman's purse as it bumped against her thigh, a purse filled with the small, paper-wrapped parcels of the little ones.

The Seventh Horseman opened the door.

And the woman was walking out of the warehouse loft, headed to the freight elevator, placing one foot ahead of the other, the way the Zombie had taught her.

She entered the taxi from a snowy, wind-swept street, telling the driver, "Dulles Airport, please."

Albert described her to the attendant at the ticket counter as best he could. All signs above the attendant's American Airlines cap pointed out the flights to New York City, from where, Stanley had said, the woman would have to transfer over to Rochester.

The attendant was way ahead of him, as if she had a fixed picture in her mind, of his precise quarry. She pointed with a gloved finger and Albert saw a white fur hat bobbing above the crowd, over the prettiest coat he'd encountered since giving his mother one last Christmas.

From the back, the style of it accented her broad shoulders, flowed down, elegant and blood red, to suck at a dainty waist and flow further, to the tops of beige suede boots. What caused him to recognise her, even hidden under the hat and facing away from him, was her walk—innocent, unconstrained, and proud. A child in a new outfit, heading off to visit for the holidays.

What was it Stanley had kept babbling, less than an hour ago, while Albert stood in his town house, demanding that Stanley intervene, stop her, stop them, from what would surely happen if they were allowed anywhere near her stepfather?

"I won't do it, Albert. I can't." Stanley had tossed the newly delivered mail, like a man-made snowstorm, down on his dining room table. "Trust is a two-way street between therapist and client. No matter what anyone says, the Troops are sane. I trust them, Albert. I trust them to do what's right—for them."

"And what if her stepfather harms her?" Albert was unwilling to leave it alone.

"Albert. That woman and her people were trained in deadlier arts than you or I can imagine—by a man who has never been caught at his game. By the very man whose legal rights men like you are sworn to protect. Except, of course, that he's out of your jurisdiction. Just offhand, I'd say he should run for his life this time, not the other way around."

"Goddammit, Stanley." Albert hurled his last protest. "She's only a *woman!*"

"But some of her people aren't."

The red-coated figure had gone through the gates and was about to be swallowed up by the yawning mouth of the loading gallery. Albert lit a cigarette and shoved his hands into the pockets of his ski parka. The cigarette sat rigid between his lips as he strode to the airport bar.

Outside the airplane window, there was nothing but blue sky and shredded grey clouds. A tip of the carefully folded, blood-red coat jutted from the overhead storage rack and the woman fastened her mind on its brightness, willing herself to stop swallowing and dry-washing her hands in her lap.

The stewardess came around, and Mean Joe ordered scotch on the rocks for him and a beer and two glasses of

359

chocolate milk. With straws. There was just enough liquid to go around. He kept his right shoulder carefully hunched.

"He's a pretty big guy as I remember him," Mean Joe said. "I hope nobody thinks this is going to be easy."

"I don't care how big he is anymore," the woman said. "I hope he's big as a mountain. Big enough to warrant all this sweat under our armpits." The woman leaned back in the seat and the teddy bear peered with one beady eye from beneath her elbow. Having been wide awake all last night, she drifted in and out of sleep now, until Mean Joe stirred and stretched his long legs.

The meal they were served was elaborate, but not enough for him. Mean Joe got empty, often. He was glad for the fast-food bag the woman handed him an hour later, and he shared its contents: hamburgers and potato chips and jelly beans. The stewardess, bewildered with the amount of milk the woman was consuming, made a comment and was ignored.

For the passengers across the aisle, there were occasional, deadly, sideways glances and the husky drawl from Mean Joe, along with a filling-out of the woman's facial structure, as an occasional little one forgot, and stirred. Since the children startled people more than any of the adults did, they'd promised for the plane ride itself to speak only when spoken to by one of their own. For the most part, it went swimmingly.

The stewardess announced their arrival in Rochester, and warned them that the weather was ugly. Lamb Chop giggled and handed Mean Joe a huge pair of leather gloves. She counted out the small, paper-wrapped parcels and smiled—a scrunch-eyed, round-faced, happy smile.

Mean Joe could not help it. He looked down at Lamb Chop in the silly, too-adult, white fur hat.

"Are you having a good time?"

"Oooooh," she said, and shivered with delight.

Back in his town house, Stanley slit open the mail at his dining room table. His client, or rather her crew, had sent him not one Christmas card, but two. The first was a commercial number, a pen-and-ink, single-line drawing of a musician, with a part of the face undrawn, unconnected. That card was signed, "Your unfinished symphony."

The second card, handmade, bore a title, "A Genuine Old Gaelic Blessing," and the words went thus:

When the night wind blows sharp as a rapier from the frozen dark reaches o' the North; when waters become ice beneath y'r feet and in y'r veins; when the passage is barred to ye and no man comes with the key nor even a soft word t' mend the mind, then on the darkest o' nights when no moon shows, may the moor be lit for y' always, with the light o' a finer source. And further, lest we forget the most important thing o' all, may no bottle y' ever encounter, be empty o' the finest brew.

Stanley was puzzled by the signature because it was looped and scrawled as if written by a scholar at least a thousand years old, but finally he deciphered it: "Ean, for the Troops."

The taxi left them off at the corner of a very nice street, with neat little houses and Christmas wreaths dotting the windows. The stewardess had been right. It was bitter cold, as cold as thirty years ago. A dusting of what looked like the same snow brushed their faces as they left the more protected corner and headed down the street. The woman took off her mitten and shoved a small hand in Mean Joe's larger one.

"I'm glad you're here," she said.

Age had done nothing to the man who answered the door, except to pull his features closer together and etch a curious path of tiny roads across his face. His hair was no longer black, but iron grey. The woman greeted him with a twelve-year-old smile that under the white hat was forty and deadly.

"Do you remember me?"

"No." But a question sprouted in his yellowish eyes under the grey brows, and then there were a hundred questions. He didn't believe anything his mind was telling him, so he tried to tell her "No" again.

"You're as rude as you ever were," the woman said over the beating of her heart. "It's cold out here."

361

He was still a very big man, stepping back into a moderate-sized living room crowded with over-stuffed furniture, a television that played softly, and a large German shepherd that ran in nervous circles around his legs.

"Git," Mean Joe said to the dog.

The dog turned tail and went.

"Still like animals?" The woman's gaze went around the room, took note of the stacks of detective magazines, the scarlet-and-white packets of Red Man chewing tobacco, the mantel with all the faded pictures of his family. His mother's picture hung square in the middle of them all, showing her henna sausage curls, and a pouting, lipsticked mouth.

The stepfather shoved his hands into the pockets of the same kind of dark green work pants he'd always worn on the farm.

"Are you who I think you are?" His voice was gritty and old.

"I'm a lot of people." The woman eyed the stepfather with no expression at all. Her people were being kind today; they were giving her no emotions. Just the Zombie's one-foot-ahead-of-the-other actions.

"You always were the strange one." The stepfather turned to lean against the mantel.

"Crazy, right?" The woman shrugged out of the blood-red coat. She remembered the sneer on his face. It hadn't changed.

"Right. You always were. Not a brain in your head." The sneer grew larger. He'd moved from the mantel now and began to circle her, as the dog had circled him earlier.

"It's going to be a long night," Mean Joe said to him. "Sit."

The stepfather did not want to sit down in the overstuffed chair Mean Joe maneuvered him into. But Mean Joe, after all, was big and burly and muscled. And his slanted, hazel eyes blazed.

The woman was reading from a stack of white pages. Some of the passages caught the stepfather's attention. He wanted to fight back. Mean Joe had him in a very tight grip. The woman stopped reading. She broke open the first of some small brown parcels. She looked so strange as she did it, so childlike and innocent, sitting there, explaining the game.

The capsules with the quick-melting gelatin, she said in a tiny, clear voice, held delightful surprises. Just for him. He couldn't move when she tore open the other packages and laid out their contents, one by one, on the coffee table.

"None of it will kill you, man." Mean Joe smiled. "You'll just wish it had."

Rabbit wanted to go first. But Lamb Chop insisted that she was first, or the game would be spoiled. She outlined the plan, like a tiny gnome-biologist. The capsules containing the tiny maggot larvae which she'd been growing so long, so carefully, in the piece of rotted meat, were ready to hatch. She must, she said, insert those larvae capsules into the nostrils, placing them just so, and quickly, before the gelatin melted.

Twelve, she said, had read it to her from a book. A big one. Twelve was busy, already fishing in the brown paper bag for her own specialty, which would find a warm, moist home inside both the stepfather's ears.

He objected violently and often. Then he didn't object to anything. He just sat there, because Mean Joe leaned over with his right shoulder carefully tucked and said something in the ear that Twelve wasn't working on. Adrenaline pumped through Mean Joe's body, a surging, rushing stream of strength that had, in his lifetime, allowed him to lift and move incredibly heavy objects, to the consternation of a lot of people. Without that adrenaline, the stepfather might have gotten up and broken everyone into very small pieces. It seemed such a long time until the woman handed Rabbit the nicest capsules of all. Rabbit got to lay them on the stepfather's tongue and administer a tiny sip of water.

"There you go," Rabbit told him, daring to reach out and pat his hand. "Tapeworm babies. It won't be long now. Isn't that what you used to tell me?"

The stepfather trembled quite violently, for he really was quite old. The children ignored his whines. They looked to Mean Joe when the man seemed determined to get out of the chair and defend himself, but the adrenaline only pumped harder. Mean Joe showed no fear, even when the stepfather sneered. The woman stepped forward with Mean Joe, and their hands were clenched. They looked as if they'd like the stepfather to get up and make a move. Too bad, the children thought, that they had never been able to com-

363

mand the respect the stepfather was handing out tonight, to these two enormous adults.

The woman wasn't finished reading the story, so the old man sat there and listened to the rest of it. Bit by bit, his mind began to break away from him. Because at some parts in the manuscript, Rabbit howled and her sounds grew fearsome.

Mean Joe's shoulder, tucked through it all, remained tucked, but this time his hands cupped the ears of the tiny thing nestled with its face against his throat.

Twelve looked down at the stepfather and smiled.

"You seem displeased and uncomfortable," she said. "Have you forgotten that it's just a game?"

"Is he as crazy now as he made us feel all these years?"

Lambchop looked as though she really wanted, had to have an answer. The woman gave her a smile—the collective effort of ninety-two selves.

Lamb Chop cried with relief, holding onto Twelve's hand. Mean Joe and the woman gathered up the manuscript pages and the wrappings from the parcels. They didn't say goodbye. There wasn't anybody there who could hear them, even if they had.

The snow was still falling, in gentle, crystal flakes. The street was empty for it was very late. And the little ones scampered out into the night at the side of the tall black man.

"Mean Joe," Lambchop said, "thank you for the Christmas story."

"Thank the Irishman," Mean Joe told her.

"You made him understand that we should have it." Lambchop was working her way around a giant Hershey's candy kiss.

"Candy rots your teeth. Brush and bed, OK?"

"M'throat," the Irishman complained when all the children had been tucked in. The night lay around himself and Mean Joe like a soft, dark blanket. "M' throat is sore from readin'." He peered into the depths of an empty bottle.

"Here." Mean Joe set down a full one. "Something to get us through our own night." He took out a tray of ice cubes and his hands on the scotch bottle as he poured were huge and steady.

"M' heart is sore."

"We can't have everything, can we, now." Mean Joe had started to grin.

"Ah, but what I would n'a give f'r real blood, a sword in m' hand. A hearse.''

Mean Joe knew he meant a horse. He also knew something else. "Days o' yore?" Mean Joe laid the words out, one by one. He was still grinning. "You going to talk to Stanley about that?"

"M' condition has no place in the manuscript," the Irishman said.

"Hypocrite." Mean Joe took a long swallow and waited until the warmth flooded him. "You're the one who preaches individuality and the expression of self. What about your own?"

"M' own." The Irishman's face lit up. "Well, 'tis minutes only 'til Christmas day is over. I suppose . . .''

"C'mon." Mean Joe took a second swallow as the ice clinked in the Irishman's glass. "You can't hold her back, any more than you can hold the rest of us. Try and tell me you didn't hear that."

In the darkness of the night as it enveloped the warehouse, there had come the sound of hooves from a long way off . . . then nearer.

"Listen," Mean Joe said.

The Irishman smiled. His eyes got brighter. "I d' na hafta," he said. "She comes from a distance as great as m'self—m'lady, m' companion.''

And she did. The Irishman moved aside to let Mean Joe see: a lady with raven hair and a body as slender as a single stalk of cornflower—who shook out her skirts as she stepped down from the waiting carriage.

Mean Joe was looking into a forest glen as dark as this midnight hour, with only the moon for light. In the glen, the carriage and eight horses had halted, on a road with no beginning, no end. Mean Joe heard the horses snorting, their hooves pawing the earth with restless urgency.

"The horses," Mean Joe said with a note of astonishment in his voice. "They're not like the horses of today. They're built for . . .''

"F'r speed, Mean Joe. The hearses 'r' built f'r speed.''

And the Irishman was moving now, in a line straight as an arrow, toward the lady with raven hair.

Mean Joe's voice followed him.

"You can go," Mean Joe called, "but you can't stay. Ean, there's barely a minute until this day is over!"

The Irishman did not stop. He merely looked back with the expression of a thousand warriors down through time.

"Who," he asked, "d'y' think elongates the time when the Outrider plays her music? Barely a minute will do. I'll be wringin' it dry, Mean Joe."

Epilogue

The story of the unfolding of the Troops in therapy has now been told. For the first time in print, multiple persons have allowed us inside a most amazing awareness and process. In an important way the Troops differ from other multiples who have been described in the professional and popular literature.

They offer a new option for resolution. After I became aware of the multiple persons I fully expected that the goal of psychotherapy would be to find the central person and to integrate the others into the process of that one. However, I discovered that the "core" was dead, and that the process of healing would most likely result in a number of persons who spoke through the "shell" of a woman. The task became cooperation of many, rather than the integration into one. This book has been the result of that cooperation and demonstrates the efficacy of this means of resolution. Increasingly, therapists who work with multiple personalities report more than one type of resolution.

In the case of the Troops the first-born is dead and the decision is to maintain multiplicity. The developing resolution for the Troops has meant increasing awareness of each other and a sharing of those important and traumatic experiences that resulted in the development of multiple persons. Communication among the Troop members has been enhanced, and there is evidence of an increased ability to cooperate and work together. This book became both the catalyst and the vehicle for encouraging healthier working relationships among Troop members.

The final chapter of this book has probably raised many questions for the reader. Was this the story of an actual trip to wreak revenge on the stepfather? A careful reading of those pages indicates that this passage is in fact the story that Ean reads to the children. The rage of the children cried out for revenge for the brutality many of them experienced. In effect the ending helped the children release their pent-up rage at the stepfather without putting themselves in legal jeopardy. Therefore Ean's Christmas gift to the children is the story of revenge—their revenge.

The most mysterious part of the book is the final passage. Its meaning remains to be fully plumbed, and at this time might only be resolved by a trip with Ean to an Irish pub in order to help loosen his tongue w' a taste o' mead. We see the figure of a man with a brogue—a man surrounded by the aura of mystery. Who is Ean, really? He seems to be part of the Troops—yet also is separate from them. It is said that Ean sits "above." He works powerfully behind the scenes to choreograph the comings and goings of the Troops, and he emanates great energy. It is also said of him that he is not only of this time but also timeless. The power of Ean appears to be beyond this time and place, but what does that mean? Are we seeing into the realm of what modern persons call psychic phenomena, or are we viewing the vestiges of past lives? Perhaps we are peering into a world of which we cannot conceive, and are privileged to go beyond our senses into the world of the spiritual.

The appearance of the lady with the raven hair in a carriage pulled by powerful horses suggests another world, a world long past, but also a world that knows no time. There is more than a hint that Ean has an awareness and a life beyond the Troops—a life that calls him, if only for a moment that has to be stretched. Yet who he is and where he is from remain a mystery yet to unfold.

The reader may wonder where the Troops are now in their process of finding health. In October 1986 I spoke to the Troops in order to help them to assess themselves. They sent me a written response which speaks for itself. They write:

Where are we now? Until the publicity for this book begins, we are working for a well-known corporation in a position of somewhat autonomous nature, and we are very much in the public eye. No one knows, as they pass our desk each day, that we hate and fear the rules and regulations others take for granted as part of their lives, or how scared we are that within society's system, our mistakes will someday get us killed.

Trust? Some of us keep daring to, and then run in the face of it. Relationships bump along under our fear, suspicion, and the old anticipation of pain. Victims usually expect pain, are too willing to accept it, and never learn to like it. They either make the wrong choices in a bonding partner (where some pain is only natural), or they choose their partner wisely and well and then destroy what they are fearful of losing.

More often now we raise our heads, look around in shock that everything is going so well. It feels wonderful.

Our Mean Joe can't protect us from everything; there are times when we try to protect him. The children are trying to grow up, some of them against all odds. The Irishman cries at night for what he refers to as the "old sod," and perhaps we shall go there for a visit. Perhaps through whatever happiness the Irishman seeks under his long-ago sky, the rest of us shall find the key to our own.

For the most part, Ean is still a mystery to us, but in writing this book we were forced to acknowledge his power. After that final wrestle which every writer must face as the work draws to a close, we sighed with absolute relief but were then shocked to find ourselves once more at the typewriter, a fresh page in front of us—and the keys were clattering, describing something from one of the therapy sessions—except that Ean seemed determined to take things where only he can go. So the last two pages of this book, as they materialised that day, not only exposed Ean's deep relationship with Mean Joe, but showed us why the Tunnel walls reverberate each night with an awful wailing. As Ean wrote, it became ever more plain. He stood there in that silent, moonlit glen that was not of this time, and he stared at the waiting carriage and the eight horses and at his lady— and in his mind he was taking her to him and his cry made us want to scream with his emotional pain.

"A'garoon a'fain," he bellowed. "M'darlin', a garoon a'fain!"

Somewhere, some old scholar of Old Gaelic will understand what he meant. We do not; we aren't even sure of the spelling, only the sound of the rolling *r*'s and the torment behind the words. It was not until the manuscript had been delivered to our literary agent that we began to wonder: was our Irishman in his final scene going off to steal a long-delayed tryst with the woman who has obviously been his down through time—or was he going with her at his side to do further battle? What further battle was there? Somehow as we write this now, we feel Ean saying that beyond one war there's always another . . . and that's why the road has no beginning . . . no end.

This reprise of the current state of the Troops gives me an excellent indication of the progress that has been made since I first saw them in September 1980 in the woman who I was told was Truddi Chase. There is evidence of increased functioning since that time and a greater acceptance of who they are and how their multiplicity works for them. Their decision to write in order to enhance their therapy is the prime example of their gravitation toward health. Fears are still present, and at times the experience is almost overwhelming, but when the resources of the Troops are called into play, they are able to overcome those fears and go on. The energy that has led them toward life and empowered them to survive, and then begin to thrive, will be a major asset in their decision to confront life and explore relationships. Trust will remain an issue for the Troops, but for good reasons. A positive note is that they are no longer as often paralyzed by their fears of others.

Although the Troops are in another metropolitan area and I remain in Washington, D.C., and Chevy Chase, Maryland, we maintain regular contact both informally and therapeutically by phone and occasional plane trips. The prognosis is good for further growth and exploration, and distance will not hinder our therapeutic alliance. For as with Ean, our communication has gone beyond words, and time, and space.

ROBERT A. PHILLIPS, JR., PH.D.